DATE DUE

DEMCO 38-296

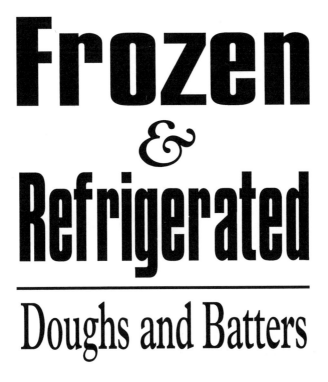

Frozen & Refrigerated
Doughs and Batters

Edited by

Karel Kulp
Klaus Lorenz
Juergen Brümmer

Published by the
American Association of Cereal Chemists, Inc.
St. Paul, Minnesota, USA

Library of Congress Catalog Card Number: 95-79821
International Standard Book Number: 0-913250-88-0

Printed in the United States of America on acid-free paper

American Association of Cereal Chemists
3340 Pilot Knob Road
St. Paul, Minnesota 55121-2097, USA

Contributors

Daniel Best, Best Vantage Inc., Northbrook, IL 60062

G. Brack, Federal Center for Cereal, Potato and Lipid Research, D-32703 Detmold, Germany

J.-M. Brümmer, Federal Center for Cereal, Potato and Lipid Research, D-W-4930 Detmold, Germany

Gregory P. Casey, Red Star Yeast & Products, Universal Foods Corporation, Milwaukee, WI 53218

V. A. De Stefanis, Elf Atochem North America Fine Chemicals, Buffalo, NY 14240

James J. Foy, Red Star Yeast & Products, Universal Foods Corporation, Milwaukee, WI 53218

Daniel Y. C. Fung, Department of Animal Sciences and Industry, Kansas State University, Manhattan, KS 66502

U. Hanneforth, Federal Center for Cereal, Potato and Lipid Research, D-32703 Detmold, Germany

Karel Kulp, Consultant, 2330 Grandview Terrace, Manhattan, KS 66502

Klaus Lorenz, Department of Food Science and Human Nutrition, Colorado State University, Fort Collins, CO 80523

R. Paul Singh, Department of Biological and Agricultural Engineering, University of California, Davis,. CA 95616

G. Spicher, Federal Center for Cereal, Potato and Lipid Research, D-32703 Detmold, Germany

E. Varriano-Marston, E. V. Marston & Associates, Windham, NH 03087

Jim M. Venetucci, Liquid Carbonic Industries Corporation, Chicago, IL 60629

Ronald L. Wirtz, American Institute of Baking, Manhattan, KS 66502

Preface

Freezing as a means of preserving the freshness of bakery products has undergone several modifications in technology.

In the first stage, fully baked products were frozen and distributed to customers and users in either the frozen or defrosted state. This approach is still widely practiced industrially for many bakery products. It is also commonly applied at the household level. An emerging modification of this technology is the production of partially baked (par-baked) products, which can either be fully baked before distribution or offered to customers for completion of baking in households or institutions.

In the second stage, doughs were frozen and distributed through retail channels for baking at household or institutional locations.

The third and most widely used method today is the topic of the present book. It involves the preparation of frozen doughs and batters for various bakery foods in commercial bakeries or plants dedicated to production of these types of products, which are then supplied for bake-off to distribution centers such as supermarkets or bakeries in institutional settings. This method of distribution has a distinct advantage since it offers customers freshly baked products with all the desirable attributes of fresh bakery goods, including organoleptic and textural properties.

The feasibility, extent, and technological modifications of frozen dough technology are determined by economical, distribution, and manufacturing factors as well as by the requirements for product quality, which vary in different world markets. In the United States, this technology is influenced by the market size, by the requirement for a relatively extended shelf life, and by long-distance distribution pathways. Thus, achieving quality stability of doughs and batters in frozen storage is more demanding in the United States than in other countries, where this technology is applied to shorter-term storage only.

In addition to yeast-leavened doughs, chemically leavened doughs, generally referred to as batters by the industry, are frozen in an unbaked state. They are used in the production of cakes, muffins, cookies, etc. The market for these products is much smaller than that for yeast-leavened doughs. Two chapters of this book are specifically devoted to these products; however, many of the general principles of physics and engineering discussed here are applicable to both yeast- and chemically leavened bakery foods.

The present book was designed to cover the basic problems encountered in application of frozen dough technology. In the 14 chapters, economical, technological, biochemical, rheological, microbiological, and engineering considerations, as well as principles of ingredient selection, are discussed. One chapter is devoted to the physics of freezing, and the concluding chapter lists recent patents in this field.

The authors of the individual chapters, selected for their expertise in their respective areas, are from universities, research institutes, and the industry. They provide readers with a basic overview of and practical insight into the problems in this field and also give guidelines for future research and development. In addition to U.S. authors, we were fortunate to have the cooperation of our German colleagues as authors of several chapters. We believe that this cooperation broadens the scope of the book, making it more useful to an international audience; it also contributes to a valuable international exchange of ideas.

A multiauthored book is always as good as the individual authors. In that respect, we believe we were lucky in finding not only outstanding but also patient authors, who were willing to undertake various revisions of their chapters. We express our sincere gratitude for their efforts.

We also acknowledge James Dexter for a thorough review of the book and the professional staff of the American Association of Cereal Chemists for their assistance during the publishing process.

Karel Kulp
Klaus Lorenz
Juergen Brümmer

Contents

CHAPTER 1

1 Economic Potential of Frozen and Refrigerated Doughs and Batters. *Daniel Best*

Frozen-Dough Manufacturers • In-Store Bakeries: A Growth Industry • Foodservice • Conclusion

CHAPTER 2

19 Yeast Performance in Frozen Doughs and Strategies for Improvement. *Gregory P. Casey and James J. Foy*

Effects of Freezing and Thawing on Cells • Strategies to Improve Yeast Performance in Frozen Doughs • Future Approaches to Developing Improved Frozen-Dough Yeast • Concluding Remarks

CHAPTER 3

53 Preparation of Stable Sourdoughs and Sourdough Starters by Drying and Freeze-Drying. *G. Spicher*

Definition of Sourdough • Role of Sourdoughs • Procedures to Extend the Keeping Quality of Sourdoughs • Evaluation of Sourdough Stability • Utilization of Stable Sourdough Starters • Dry Sourdough As Sourdough-Starters • Discussion

CHAPTER 4

63 Biochemical and Biophysical Principles of Freezing. *Karel Kulp*

Frozen Doughs • Retarded Doughs

CHAPTER 5

91 Functional Role of Microingredients in Frozen Doughs. *V. A. De Stefanis*

Frozen Dough Quality • Oxidation in Frozen Dough • Conclusions

CHAPTER 6

119 Microbiological Considerations in Freezing and Refrigeration of Bakery Foods. *Daniel Y. C. Fung*

Origin of Microorganisms in Bakery Products • Spoilage Potential of Bakery Products • Effects of Refrigeration on Microbes • Effects of Freezing on Microbes • Specific Considerations Concerning Bakery Products • Conclusion

CHAPTER 7

135 Freezing of Doughs for the Production of Breads and Rolls in the United States. *K. Lorenz and K. Kulp*

Effects of Ingredients on Frozen Dough Quality • Mixing • Fermentation • Dough Makeup • Freezing • Packaging • Distribution • Thawing, Proofing, and Baking

CHAPTER 8

155 Bread and Rolls from Frozen Dough in Europe.
J.-M. Brümmer

The Frozen Dough Process in Europe • Principal Requirements for Freezing • Quality of Raw Materials and Formulations • Mixing • Dough Handling • Proofing • Freezing Process • Storage and Transport • Thawing and Baking

CHAPTER 9

167 Freezing and Refrigeration of Cake and Muffin Batters in the United States. *K. Lorenz*

Formulation • Packaging • Freezing and Frozen Storage • Thawing and Baking • General Guidelines for Freezing of Cake Batters

CHAPTER 10

177 Freezing of Confectionery Dough Units in Germany.
G. Brack and U. Hanneforth

Unyeasted Frozen Confectioneries • Yeasted Frozen Confectioneries • Summary

CHAPTER 11

193 Principles of Heat Transfer. *R. Paul Singh*

Thermal Properties • Steady-State Heat Transfer • Steady-State Heat Transfer • Unsteady-State Heat Transfer • Heat Transfer During Freezing of Foods

CHAPTER 12

219 Cryogenic and Mechanical Food-Freezing Equipment for the Baking Industry. *Jim M. Venetucci*

Cryogenic Freezing Equipment • Advantages of Cryogenic Freezing • Mechanical Freezing • Standard Mechanical Freezing Equipment • Comparison of Freezing Systems

CHAPTER 13

245 Packaging Materials for Frozen and Refrigerated Doughs.
E. Varriano-Marston

What Are the Requirements? • Material Selection Affects Product Quality • Packaging Costs and Product Quality • Frozen-Dough Packaging • Refrigerated Doughs

CHAPTER 14

255 Selected Patents for Frozen Dough, 1983–1993. *Ronald L. Wirtz*

Yeast Technology in Improvement of Frozen Doughs • Use of Additives in Improvement of Frozen Dough • Special Processes and Equipment for Frozen Dough Products • Summary

275 Index

CHAPTER 1

Economic Potential of Frozen and Refrigerated Doughs and Batters

Daniel Best
Best Vantage, Inc.
Northbrook, Illinois 60062

The single biggest contradiction posed by the success of frozen and refrigerated baked goods is their defiance of a traditional economic precept— frozen and refrigerated doughs both cost more than and generally lack the quality and "authenticity" of the "scratch" and "mix" products they presume to replace. That point alone underscores that a more fundamental economic premise lies at the foundation of what has become one of the bakery industry's greatest structural transformations: the gradual centralization of bakery goods manufacturing into hubs defined by frozen distribution channels.

In part, the success of frozen baked goods reflects the costs of convenience. Their success is symptomatic of a highly competitive industry aggressively pursuing cost efficiencies in the face of society's evolving demographic and economic constraints. This trend reflects the centralization of retail distribution, as well as the recognition that bakery goods manufacturing does not lend itself well to retail supermarket economics, at least in purely financial terms. Finally, the success of frozen baked goods underscores that two of the baking industry's leading challenges remain the need to compete on the economics of scale and the need to confront a declining labor pool.

Definitions are in order. The general term "frozen baked goods" encompasses several product categories. Bread products, for example, can be sold in three forms: as refrigerated or frozen doughs that must be thawed, proofed, and baked ("bake-off"); fully baked products that are frozen, thawed, and either slightly reheated or sold ready-to-eat ("thaw-and-sell"); and partially baked, frozen, thawed, and baked ("par-baked").

In many references, "par-baked" goods are included as a subset of "bake-off" products. Other products, primarily in retail channels, are sold frozen or refrigerated, such as bread loaves, cookie doughs, cheese cakes, sweet goods, and decorated cakes. Bagels and decorated cakes are often sold to in-store bakeries or food-service outlets in thaw-and-serve formats, while more and more breads and rolls are sold in par-baked formats. Frozen-yet-spoonable cookie doughs, meanwhile, have presented brand-label marketers with phenomenal growth opportunities in recent years.

The term "frozen baked goods," in its broadest form, may refer to breads and rolls, croissants, pies, cakes, cookies, Danish rolls and similar sweet goods, and doughnuts. The term's limitations become evident, however, when one begins to include breakfast breads (such as frozen waffles) and savory products, such as frozen/prepared pizzas, croissant sandwiches, puff pastry dishes, egg rolls, and others, all of which have frozen dough components that fall outside of traditional definitions of bakery goods. Nonetheless, such products represent significant outlets for the baking industry and for the centralized frozen bakery goods manufacturers that supply these niches.

Some baked goods are prepared from "scratch" ingredients, while others are sold to retail outlets as mixes, leaving it to the operators to execute the final mixing and baking steps.

There are also multiple market segments to consider. "Retail" refers to sales made directly to the consuming public in a non-consuming environment. Retail sales may occur via independent bakeries, supermarkets, convenience stores, or vending machines, each of which is defined by its own unique economic parameters. Two retail outlet categories that have been the subject of particular interest are wholesale clubs, like Sam's or WalMart, and high-value specialty boutiques, both of which have posted significant growth in sales in recent years at the expense of traditional supermarkets (Dietrich, 1992).

There are two primary types of retail bakery outlets: "Retail" refers to either direct sales outlets, such as local neighborhood bakeries, or to in-store bakeries that represent profit centers within larger retail operations. "Foodservice" refers to any location where foods are prepared "ready-to- eat" and typically refers to sit-down restaurants, institutions (such as the military, hospitals, prisons, or universities), and fast-food outlets.

Although these definitions are used as such during the rest of this chapter, it is granted that the distinctions often blur. For example, more and more products are sold preprepared and ready-to-eat through supermarket establishments, while many foodservice outlets sell their products "retail" through mail-order services or adjacent to their cash registers.

For simplicity, the primary focus of this chapter is on frozen baked goods that are retailed through in-store bakeries. The principles that drive this growth category are shared by other categories in which frozen baked goods have prospered.

The rapid rise in popularity of frozen baked goods has been driven in large part by the economic attraction of centralized manufacturing and distribution. Economically, it makes more sense for a single bakery to service a chain of fast-food outlets or in-store bakeries than it does for each of the outlets to maintain its own bakery. In terms of raw product costs, defined as wholesale costs or "costs of goods sold" (to use accounting terminology), frozen baked goods cost the retailer more than do mixes or scratch ingredients. Consequently, the higher costs of frozen baked goods must be offset either by higher prices charged to the consumer or by additional cost-savings captured by the retailer as a consequence of using these products. Given that the general consensus on many frozen baked goods is that they lag the marketplace in organoleptic quality (though not in the consistency of their quality), it follows that their use must entail the accrual of one or more economic benefits to the retailers of such products. This point is driven home even more by the observation that, by some ·measures, in-store bakeries are money-losing operations. This puts even greater pressure on retailers to bring their in-store bakery division costs under control (Progressive Grocer, 1992).

Frozen-Dough Manufacturers

The attractiveness of frozen baked goods has engendered a fragmented industry posting sales in the range of $4.5 billion to $6.5 billion at the wholesale level, depending on the source. A partial 1992 listing of frozen baked goods manufacturers provided by the American Institute of Baking listed 192 manufacturers (R. Wertz, American Institute of Baking, Manhattan, KS, *personal communication*).

A proper assessment of this industrial category also requires proper definition: At one end of the spectrum is the entry, via acquisition, of highly diversified multinational giants such as H.J. Heinz, Pillsbury (Grand Metropolitan), and Van den Bergh Foods (Unilever) into frozen bakery goods manufacturing. At the other end, supermarket chains such as Giant Foods (Giant Foods, 1990), and restaurant chains such as Subway Sandwiches or the Boston-based Au Bon Pain (Au Bon Pain, *personal communication*) supply their outlets and those of other restaurant chains through their own in-house facilities for the manufacture of frozen bakery goods.

One survey of the leading-100 in-store bakery operators (Krumrei, 1992) found that 22.5% of the operators surveyed were supplied by centralized bakeries operated by their respective companies. Meanwhile, retail cookie manufacturers such as W. Frookie (Adweek/Marketing Week, 1991) and Otis Spunkmeyer (Frozen Food Age, 1990) have marketed their brand-labeled cookie doughs to in-store bakeries in frozen form, often with added service features. To help promote product acceptance, Otis Spunkmeyer Inc. offered its customers the option of leasing portable convection ovens preset to bake the company's cookies "to perfection" (Spunkmeyer, 1992); Dunkin Donuts (Allied Lyons) markets frozen bagel doughs to in-store bakeries (Milling & Baking News, 1990). A 1992 in-store bakery survey by a leading trade magazine suggested that a number of large consumer-brand food companies were poised to introduce branded products through in-store bakery outlets (Krumrei, 1993a). Economies of scale as well as the inherent advantages of centralized production and consistent quality would argue in favor of frozen preparation, distribution, and handling formats for such products.

According to Minneapolis-based Wessels, Arnold & Henderson, an investment banking and securities firm, the 1992 market leader in frozen dough products was Rich's Products (based in Buffalo, NY), which was expected to post an estimated $360 million in sales for 1993 (Davis, 1993). According to Wessels, Arnold and Henderson, this represented only a 3.3% market share of the frozen dough market. Rich's Products was followed by Country Home (Bridgeport, CT), Pillsbury/Grand Metropolitan (Minneapolis, parent of McGlynn Bakeries), Hazelwood Farms (Hazelwood, MO), and H.J. Heinz (Pittsburgh) as the leading purveyors of frozen baked goods (Table 1).

Given the highly fragmented nature of this industry, the continued trends toward centralized manufacturing in the bakery industry, the economies of scale to be gained by consolidation, and the size and growth rate of this industry segment, it is likely that the process of consolidation by acquisition will continue for some time.

H.J. Heinz, for example, publicly announced its intention (Milling & Baking News, 1991) to increase its frozen dough sales into a $500 million (sales) business by 1996, primarily via acquisition. Companies acquired by H.J. Heinz since 1990 include Tasty Frozen Products, Pro Bakers Ltd. (Canada), Pro Pastries Inc., W.P. Foods, Pestritto Foods, and Chef Francisco.

Factors working against rapid consolidation of this industry include lagging product quality; the need for retail outlets to differentiate their products from those of their competitors, including scratch and mix products; and economic limitations on frozen sales, storage, and distribution channels.

Size and Growth Projections

Estimates of frozen baked goods sales vary widely, a fact that reflects both problems of definition and the highly fragmented nature of the industry.

A 1990 annual report from Wetterau (now Hazelwood Farms) estimated

Table 1
Estimated Sales of Frozen Baked Goods[a]

Company	Calendar 1993 Sales ($ millions)	Market Share (%)
Rich's	360	3.3
Country Home	160	1.4
Pillsbury/McGlynn's	155	1.3
Hazelwood	130	1.2
Flowers	102	1.0
H.J. Heinz	100	1.0
Maplehurst	75	0.7
All others	9,850	90.1
Total	10,900	100.0

[a] Source: Davis (1993); used by permission.

1990 frozen dough sales to be $6.5 billion (Wetterau, 1990). The 1993 Wessels, Arnold & Henderson report on Flowers Industries claimed that frozen baked goods generate $10.9 billion in annual industry-wide sales (Davis, 1993). On the other hand, data provided by Chicago-based Technomics, an industry research service, estimated total 1992 sales of all frozen baked goods (excluding pizza dough sales to in-store supermarket delis) to be only $4.5 billion at the manufacturers' level (R. Rush, Technomics, *personal communication,* 1992) (Table 2).

Fifty percent of the sales cited in the Technomics study were posted to in-store bakeries, with the remainder generated through foodservice accounts (including pizza manufacturers). While these numbers fall below the stated estimates of other studies cited later in this chapter, the values cited in subsequently referenced studies refer to retail values rather than to manufacturers' wholesale values. Given the relatively large gross retail margins (40–60%; Litwak and Maline, 1993) of baked goods in general, these numbers are not inconsistent. The patterns discerned in this study also appear to be fully consistent with those outlined in other studies.

Frozen doughs were the product of choice for in-store bakeries, representing 69% of all frozen baked goods sales to these accounts, while thaw-and-sell products were preferred 56 to 44% over frozen dough products by foodservice accounts (R. Rush, 1992, *personal communication*). This likely reflects the need of foodservice operations to prepare large product volumes within relatively short time frames (fast-food being the clearest case of this), as well as the constraints of incorporating specialized equipment such as proofing ovens into nonbakery enterprises. In-store bakeries, structured as they are for much lower volume sales and product turnovers, are amenable to a higher level of product preparation at the retail level.

In-store bakeries presented the greatest growth opportunity for frozen baked goods, according to Technomics' research, which projected a 7.4% growth rate in 1992 (primarily as frozen doughs) against a 3.8% projected growth rate for frozen baked goods sales through foodservice accounts.

Table 2
1992 Estimated Frozen Baked Goods Market[a]

	Foodservice		In-Store Bakeries	
	Manufacturer Shipments ($ millions)	Growth Since 1991 (%)	Manufacturer Shipments ($ millions)	Growth Since 1991 (%)
Frozen dough	860	5.0	1,770	8.0
Frozen thaw/serve	1,080	3.0	795	6.0
Total frozen[b]	1,940	3.8	2,565	7.4

[a] Source: R. Rush, Technomics, *personal communication* (1992).

[b] Includes bread and rolls; cakes, cookies, Danish, muffins, doughnuts, and other sweet goods; puff pastry; savory products; and pizza dough. Does not include pizza dough sold to supermarket store delis.

According to FIND/SVP Inc., a New York-based research firm, retail sales of frozen baked goods (that is, goods retailed through frozen display cases) reached $1.3 billion on volume sales of $745 million pounds in 1990 (FIND/SVP, 1991). The study indicated that sales grew at an annual compounded rate of 4.3% between 1983 and 1990.

Such estimates often include frozen products not traditionally characterized as "baked goods," however. Frozen "breakfast breads" (such as waffles) alone were estimated to represent a $1 billion (in annual sales) industry in 1989, with a projected annual growth rate of 9–11% through 1994 (R. Bregenzer, Information Resources, *personal communication*). The market is dominated by food industry giants such as Kellogg's (Eggo's, NutriGrain, and Common Sense), Quaker Oats (Aunt Jemima), and Campbell Soup Co. (Swanson's Great Starts).

In-Store Bakeries: A Growth Industry

A 1992 survey of the in-store bakery market (Litwak and Maline, 1993) placed 1992's total sales volume at $8.9 billion, a 12.6% increase over the previous year's sales. Average weekly sales per in-store bakery unit increased 7.4% from $7,117 in 1991 to $7,643 in 1992, according to the survey.

The *Supermarket Business* study (Litwak and Maline, 1993) indicated that 82% of the in-store bakeries surveyed had increased their sales by an average of 6.9% during 1992. None of the respondents reported sales drops during that year.

According to *Bakery Production and Marketing*'s annual survey of the in-store baking industry, (Krumrei, 1992), the United States had 23,725 in-store bakery units in supermarkets and warehouse clubs, 45% of which were controlled by the "Top-100" companies: The Top-100 companies generated approximately $4.5 billion in sales alone, with average weekly sales of $8,011 per store. By 1993, the total number of in-store bakery units was projected to increase to 24,212, with warehouse club stores presenting particularly good growth opportunities (Krumrei, 1993a). A separate study (Litwak and Maline, 1993) claimed in-store bakery penetration of the 30,800 supermarkets in the United States to be 69.5% in 1991, up from 67.3% the previous year. By 1992, penetration had increased to 73.1%.

The leading products sold through in-store bakeries in 1991, as defined by their contribution to total in-store bakery sales, were white and variety breads and rolls (30.0%), followed by decorated cakes (16.6%), cake and yeast-raised doughnuts (14.5%), sweet goods (8.2%), cookies (7.7%), bagels/croissants/muffins (7.5%), layered cakes (6.3%), and pies (6.8%) (Litwak and Maline, 1993). All these products lend themselves to frozen preparation, handling, and distribution.

According to a 1992 survey of in-store bakeries conducted by *Progressive Grocer* magazine, 45% of the respondents included muffins and cakes as being among their fastest-growing categories, followed by bagels (43%), cookies (35%), and doughnuts (31%). Breads were listed as the fast-growing category for 29% of the respondents (Progressive Grocer, 1993a). They are also the most likely products to be prepared from frozen doughs; 76% of operators surveyed used this method according to one study (Lee, 1992). Only 2% of the operators reported using thaw-and-sell bread and roll products.

Frozen baked goods were used as the primary method of production by 43% of all in-store bakeries, according to the 1992 *Supermarket Business* survey (Litwak and Maline, 1993). Of that 43%, only 4% used thaw-and-sell preparation, while 39% used bake-off preparation. Another 37% of all stores used a combination of methods (including bake-off), while 20% used scratch or mix baking as their primary production format. This distribution appears to hold relatively constant across a number of surveys (Krumrei, 1992; Lee, 1992).

Frozen doughs were preferred by in-store operators for preparing cookies (67%) and Danish-type products (71%), while thaw-and-serve products were most likely for muffins (19%), cake doughnuts (16%), and cakes (14%) (Lee, 1992). A separate in-store baking industry study indicated that bake-off preparation was also preferred for breads and rolls (73%), yeast-raised doughnuts (61%), sweet goods (66%), pies (80%), croissants (89%), and bagels (90%) (Litwak and Maline, 1993).

In-store bakeries, in sum, represent growth vehicles for supermarkets. Total in-store bakery sales between 1988 and 1992 alone averaged 9.9% annual growth in dollar-sales (Litwak and Maline, 1993), and frozen baked goods have played a major part in sustaining that growth rate by maximizing the dollar returns on such sales.

But Is It Profitable?

At first glance, bakery products should be one of the most profitable segments in supermarket retailing. According to the 1992 *Supermarket Business* survey, the average gross margin of all in-store bakery products was 56.7%, with 39% of all retail outlets reporting gross-margins of 60% or more (Litwak and Maline, 1992).

A separate report, the highly detailed 1992 *Progressive Grocer* "Marsh Supermarket" study (Progressive Grocer, 1992) of an Indianapolis-based supermarket chain chosen for its "typical" demographics and business environment, provides another base for comparison.

For this particular supermarket chain, in-store bakeries represented the highest gross-profit contributor of any edible grocery product category, posting an average gross margin of 44.46%. This was well above the average gross margins for other categories, such as dairy products (27.6%), frozen goods (33.5%), meat and seafood products (25.0%), and "middle-aisle" edible groceries (20.6%). The total composite gross margin for the entire supermarket chain, including nonfood items, was 26.3%.

Gross margin (or gross profit) refers to the difference between a product's retail price and the wholesale cost of the product to the retailer—i.e., what it costs the retailer to buy the merchandise that is placed on the retail shelf. The cost of these products to the retailer is generally termed the "cost of goods sold." Thus, "gross margin" represents a product's contribution to a supermarket's income pool, against which the supermarket's operating, administrative, depreciation (or amortization), and all other expenses are charged. Whatever is left represents the supermarket's "net income before taxes."

At first glance, supermarkets should want to favor products with higher gross margins. As the following section shows, however, this assumption does not necessarily hold true.

Concepts of Direct Profitability

While classical accounting concepts such as "cost of goods sold" and "gross margins" accurately reflect the invoice costs of products received at the point of sale, they do not reflect all other attendant costs of such products. Different products require different levels of labor, utility, storage, and other inputs. Scratch bakery mixes require more intensive labor inputs for handling and preparation by supermarkets than do cans of carbonated beverages, for example. Utility costs for freezer displays are higher than they are for dry-good displays located in the middle aisles of supermarkets. Also, product losses (shrinkage) are higher for perishables than they are for nonperishable products.

One cost accounting technique that some supermarkets have used to better allocate such peripheral costs to specific products has been termed "direct product profitability" (DPP). Whether formally adopted as an accounting method or not, many of the precepts of DPP are at least instinctively recognized by supermarket operators.

DPP recognizes that different products require different investments of resources to maintain them in inventory. It provides a model by which all costs directly associated with specific products are properly allocated to those products. A DPP profile would include items such as labor dollars per product unit, warehousing and transportation costs, display costs, inventory costs, utility costs, product shrinkage, and paperwork costs.

For example, products that are shipped in three 12-unit cases per shipment have a higher invoice handling cost per unit than products shipped in 50 24-unit-per-case deliveries. These costs can be significant. The Marsh Supermarket study (Progressive Grocer, 1992) cites the example of two warehouse invoices, for a single 735-case shipment and for an 11-case in-store delivery. The first invoice cost $0.0074 per case to process; the second cost $0.0527 per case. A DPP analysis can vary in its degree of sophistication to the point of even considering the labor involved in bagging a specific product at the checkout counter.

Costs that would not be included in a DPP model include general and administrative costs associated with the operation of the company (or supermarket) as a whole, such as book-keeping expenses, general utility costs, or general office expenses.

A DPP analysis begins with a product's gross margin and tacks on additional direct revenues specifically allocatable to that product, such as prompt-payment discounts, trade allowances, net "forward buy" revenues, etc., which reduce the product's *de facto* cost to the retailer, This calculation yields an "adjusted gross margin" (Fig. 1).

From this adjusted gross margin are deducted the peripheral costs that are directly allocatable to the product, termed direct product costs. The resulting DPP value provides a strong indicator of an individual product's (or product category's) actual contribution to store profitability (Deloitte Touche & Tohmatsu International, 1986).

DPP can be measured in several ways, depending upon a store's specific analytical needs. For example:

- DPP measured as a percent of store sales. This value includes the actual cost to the store of providing the display space for a product. This performance measure is particularly applicable for new retail outlets, where the cost of shelf space must be amortized, or for retail situations where shelf space carries specified slotting allowances.

- Short-term DPP. This value reflects DPP per week per square foot of facing. This value is not reduced by the cost to the store of providing the shelf space. The cost of shelf space, by this measure, is deemed a long-term cost. So measured, short-term DPP provides an opportunity value for the shelf space.

- DPP as a percent of gross margin. This value reflects a product's or

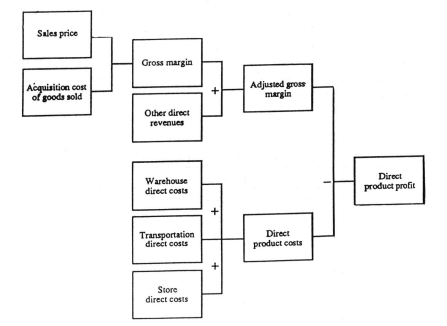

Fig. 1. Direct product profitability (DPP) provides highly detailed allocations of costs associated with retailing specific food product categories. (Reprinted, with permission, from the Food Marketing Institute, 1989)

category's direct contribution to a store's margin of profitability once direct costs have been factored in.

It would be unfair to focus upon DPP cost analysis without pointing out that DPP has come under considerable criticism from several quarters as an accounting technique. In general, criticism of DPP analysis has centered upon its limited focus on direct cost/revenue relationships to the exclusion of broader issues such as the service- or loss-leader value of product categories that may not otherwise pass muster on the basis of their DPP value. These issues beg the point: DPP analysis is not meant to provide a benchmark of a product's value to the retailer. However limited in scope, DPP analysis *does* provide valuable insights into a product category's contribution to retail profitability and serves as a valuable decision-making tool for enhancing the efficiencies of retail operations.

Bakery's In-Store Profitability

Contrast the various inputs that go into ordering, storing, measuring, mixing, and proofing the many perishable and nonperishable ingredients that are required for scratch baking with the simplicity of thaw-and-serve and one begins to understand the inherent attractiveness of frozen baked goods to retail operations. Thaw-bake-and-serve products may not yield the quality of fresh-baked products, but they can still generate the aroma and perception thereof—without the cost associated with fresh-baked goods.

Retailers operate on thin margins that dictate an adherence to strict standards of cost accountability. A DPP cost-accounting system does not allocate labor costs to ill-defined overhead accounts but instead allocates them to actual labor contributions associated with handling individual items in the store, including the receiving, storing, moving, stocking, stickering (price marking), check-out, and bagging of the items (Table 3). When held to such strict cost accountabil-

Table 3
In-Store Bakery Direct Product Costs[a] (DPCs)

Warehouse DPCs	Store DPCs
Receiving products	*Preparation*[b]
Put away products	*Bakery processing*
Replenish products	*Marketing*
Select products	*Customer service*
Load products	*Checkout*
Occupancy	Occupancy
Inventory	Inventory
	Shrink/acquisition loss
	Shrink/direct labor loss on throwaway
	Shrink/markdown loss

[a] Source: Food Marketing Institute (1989); used by permission.
[b] Italics indicate labor-intensive categories.

ity, the labor intensity of scratch or mix preparation can appear cost-prohibitive.

Competitive pressures have forced many retailers to at least consider DPP factors in their inventory planning. Although DPP management can be horrendously complicated, the development of DPP computer models by organizations such as the Washington, DC-based Food Marketing Institute (FMI) have helped to lower the barriers to its adoption by retailers (Food Marketing Institute, 1989). The FMI bakery DPP model includes such variables as customer service, cake decorating, and display maintenance, as well as product-related marketing activities, inventory turnover, case-packaging designs, shrink data, package cost, preparation (recipe) requirements, and many others for 11 so-called "product family" groups (cookies, pastries, pies, cakes, etc.).

A DPP analysis of supermarket bakery operations undertaken as part of *Progressive Grocer*'s Marsh Supermarket study (Progressive Grocer, 1992) shows a very different picture of in-store bakery profitability than conventional accounting would indicate (Table 4). When compared on the basis of its contribution to gross margin, the bakery department was the greatest unit-contributor to store profitability as a percent of sales, with a 44.46% gross margin. When compared on a DPP basis, however, bakery sales represented the *least profitable* segment for Marsh Superstores: the percent DPP margin for baked goods was a *negative* 27.25%.

According to the Marsh Superstore analysis, bakery operations represent a net loss to the retailer. This indicates considerable pressure upon retailers to streamline their bakery operations and to maximize the efficiencies designed into the operations. A purely DPP focus upon bakery operations would argue in favor of increased use of frozen baked goods.

There are two very important caveats to this, however. Superficially, at least, frozen baked goods are more expensive. Costs of frozen ingredients represent 41.9% of in-store retail sales, on average, compared to 33.9% of sales for mix

Table 4
Marsh Supermarkets In-Store Bakery Profitability[a]

Product Category	Gross Margin (%)	Direct Product Profitability Margin (%)
Total edible groceries	20.6	12.2
Perishables	32.3	16.4
Dairy	27.6	15.6
Deli/bakery	38.2	9.5
Bakery (alone)	*44.5*	*-27.3*
Frozen foods	33.5	24.2
Meat/seafood	25.0	16.8
Produce	38.7	18.5
Total nonedible groceries	18.0	10.4

[a] Adapted from Progressive Grocer (1992).

ingredients, according to one survey (Lee, 1992). Presumably, raw ingredient costs for scratch recipes are even lower.

According to another study (Krumrei, 1992), in-store bakeries relying primarily on bake-off production formats appear to generate lower weekly sales ($6,577 per week) than stores relying on scratch/mix formats ($9,209 per week).

The important observation, however, is that the proportion of stores emphasizing both scratch/mix and frozen preparation formats is holding steady. The 43% of in-store bakeries that relied primarily on frozen preparation formats, cited in the *Supermarket Business* 1992 "In-Store Bakery" survey (Litwak and Maline, 1993), compares well to the 45% cited in the "bake-off" and "thaw and sell" categories in 1990s survey (Litwak and Torres-Cepeda, 1991). Meanwhile, the number of respondents relying upon combination formats increased from 28 to 37% between 1990 and 1991 and held steady at 37% into 1992 (Litwak and Torres-Cepeda, 1991; Litwak and Maline, 1992, 1993).

While nominally more expensive, the continued importance of scratch/mix preparation reflects a perceived "value-addition" associated with "fresh"-baked products. According to one industry survey, "combination formats" attracted 29.4% of store customers on average—7% more than did pure bake-off formats—and generated increased spending per customer over other formats (Krumrei, 1992). This last point underscores one of the pitfalls of relying upon DPP analysis alone. While in-store bakeries may prove to be poor profit centers when subjected to DPP accounting discipline, DPP analysis fails to quantify intangible values, such as product quality, retail cultures, customer satisfaction, and the results of marketing and promoting the freshness and "authenticity" provided by scratch-prepared products in an in-store bakery. To that end, in-store bakeries may contribute their greatest value to retail gross margins as loss-leaders.

According to one leading analyst (D. Krumrei, *personal communication*), most stores like a combination of formats in order to emphasize more costly, labor-intensive products for high-visibility displays (cake decorating, for example) that enhance the store's images. Trade journal articles on successful bakery operations often emphasize the trade-offs between the quality appeal of scratch baking and the convenience and efficiency of frozen products (Progressive Grocer, 1993b). These trade-offs will likely continue even as the quality of bake-off products improves with time. Fundamentally, high-quality in-store scratch bakery operations offer retailers a vehicle to differentiate themselves from their competitors in a highly competitive industry even as they try to control costs with bake-off product lines.

The Labor Factor

"Where have all the clean-up kids gone?" lamented the title of a 1991 article in *Bakery Production and Marketing* (Krumrei, 1991). The article highlighted the lack of entry positions for unskilled labor in the baking industry. The fact is that the baking industry, like other industries, has been under tremendous pressure to cut costs and improve productivity in the face of a declining labor pool of young, unskilled workers.

Retail baking is highly labor intensive, and, like other labor-intensive industries, retail bakers are forced to adjust to the confluence of two very significant trends: a broadening demand for skilled bakers as more and more retailers incorporate in-store bakeries into their units, and declining availability of young, low-skilled workers who can be trained to service those stores.

The number of 16- to 24-year-olds in the U.S. labor market is projected to decline from 38.5 million in 1980 to 32.7 million by the turn of the millennium, according to U.S. Census Bureau estimates (Statistical Abstract of the United States, 1991; Fig. 2). Conversely, according to estimates from the Retail Bakers of America, the number of retail bakery units is projected to almost triple, going from 23,500 to 65,000 over the same period. A confluent trend is the projected availability of retail jobs that draw heavily upon the same supply of 16- to 24-year-olds as in-store bakeries need. Retail jobs are projected to increase from 14.9 million to 23 million between 1979 and 2000, according to Peter Houstle, Executive Vice President of the Retail Bakers of America.

Given the classic economic principle that increased demand for services begets increased costs of such services, it should follow that the costs of skilled and unskilled in-store bakery labor should be on a sustained upward curve. The only caveat to this scenario is if widespread adoption of labor-saving technolo-

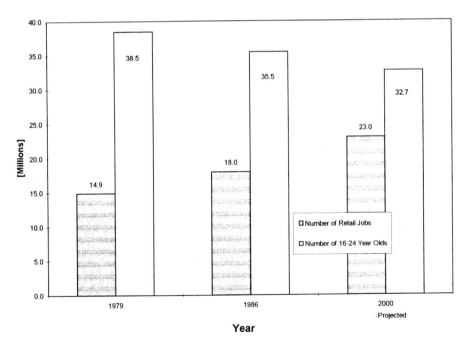

Fig. 2. Labor supply and demand projections. (Sources: Statistical Abstract of the United States, 1991; P. Houstle, Retail Bakers of America, *personal communication*)

gies across the retail industry dampens projected demands for unskilled labor over time. And, given the cost constraints upon retail bakery operations (especially the fact that they appear to be money-losing operations when subjected to the discipline of DPP analysis), there exist strong incentives for increasing both the labor pool and the labor efficiencies of retail baking.

Whereas the number of full-time employee equivalents for in-store bakeries remained virtually unchanged between 1990 and 1992, according to *Supermarket Business*'s annual in-store bakery survey (Litwak and Maline, 1993), there have been dramatic changes in the allocation and efficiencies of in-store bakery labor inputs.

Decrease in Service Percent

In 1990, an estimated 59% of total labor inputs were devoted to preparation and other production functions, while 41% were devoted to customer service. In 1992, customer service consumed an estimated 32% of total labor hours, while production and manufacturing activities accounted for 68%. The bad news is that any trade-off between a retailer's quality and level of customer service and his or her production outputs may come at a stiff price if it undercuts the in-store bakery's role as a high-quality loss-leader for other, more-profitable supermarket segments.

Increased Labor Costs

Meanwhile, total labor costs rose proportionately with increased in-store bakery sales: Labor costs accounted for 31.4% of sales in 1990 (Litwak and Torres-Cepeda, 1991) and 31.2% of sales in 1992 (Litwak and Maline, 1993). Labor costs include not only direct salaries but also direct and indirect benefits and training expenses. Training costs can be particularly high in industries drawing largely unskilled workers and plagued with high worker turnover rates.

Increase in Sales Activities

Average weekly sales per full-time employee equivalent have been rising steadily since 1988—from $742 in 1988 to $1,032 in 1992 (Litwak and Maline, 1993; Fig. 3).

In sum, the nominal cost of labor has increased even as more labor efficiencies are designed into in-store bakery operations. In-store bakery employees have become more proficient at selling products and proportionately more costly at the same time.

The highly competitive nature of supermarket retailing places added burdens upon retailers' labor costs. A 1992 survey of 2,500 retailers placed the cost and quality of labor among the top five concerns of chain managers, chain executives, independents, and wholesalers (Sansolo and Garry, 1993). These fears stemmed, in part, from the retailers' expectations of incurring increased employee health benefit costs under the Clinton Administration's proposed health care reform legislation.

There are essentially two ways to address expanding labor costs: 1) expand the labor pool to drive down the cost of labor and 2) incorporate production efficiencies to drive up the production per labor equivalent. Retailers and foodservice operators are addressing the first opportunity by increasing their reliance upon immigrant labor or, in come cases, by actively recruiting elderly workers. The second opportunity is being addressed, in part, by increased reliance on product lines that require fewer labor inputs to handle and prepare, such as self-service counters and increased reliance upon freeze-thaw-and-bake products. Incorporation of frozen products into bakery production lines not only reduces reliance on unskilled labor by minimizing the steps necessary to bring the products to customers, but it also minimizes the risk of quality defects arising from human error.

Foodservice

A similar situation exists in the foodservice industry: It may be more profitable to rely upon freeze-thaw products, but being able to offer "fresh-baked" bakery products to customers, as a number of fast-food restaurant chains have done, increases their perceived image value.

According to one study, an estimated 199,000 on-premise foodservice bakeries in the United States generate $8.7 billion in annual sales (Krumrei, 1993b). As mentioned earlier, the economics of in-store bakeries offer a good model of comparison for the foodservice industry as well. Although no DPP models exist for foodservice operations, many of the same cost and profitability constraints

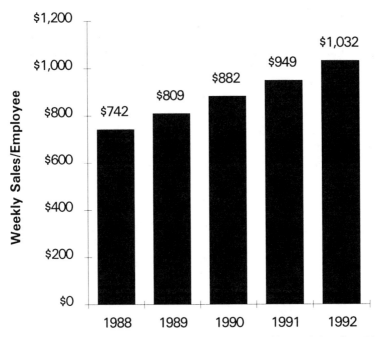

Fig. 3. Weekly sales per in-store bakery employee. (Reprinted, with permission, from Litwak and Maline, 1993)

apply. As with in-store bakeries, foodservice operations can be broken down into microoperations, each with its own allocatable costs.

In addition, foodservice operations must deal with high levels of product turnover during very narrow time frames (as in fast-food outlets during rush hour), high levels of employee turnover, and declining employee skill levels. Each of these points generates additional pressures to develop production efficiencies. As with in-store bakeries, labor and ingredient costs represent major cost factors in foodservice operations. Food costs defined as a percent of sales vary inversely with labor costs (National Restaurant Association, 1992; Table 5). For example, labor costs range from 32.8% of sales on average for full-menu/table-service restaurants down to 26.9% of sales for limited menu/no table-service restaurants (a category that includes fast-food restaurants). As with in-store bakeries, foodservice operators are cost-constrained by demographics—that is, by their access to a low-wage, skilled or semiskilled labor supply.

Conclusion

As the numerous examples of frozen in-store bakery goods demonstrate, businesses can appear to be nominally profitable while proving to be highly unprofitable when subjected to microaccounting disciplines. In-store bakeries appeared to be highly profitable in the Marsh Supermarkets study but proved to be net profit-loss centers when subjected to DPP analysis.

The fact that in-store bakeries continue to be added to supermarkets suggests that DPP analysis fails to provide a complete measure of bakery's economic value to retail operations, however. Lagging in a DPP analysis are measures of the intangible values that in-store bakeries provide, such as providing loss-leader draws for clientele. Nonetheless, the disparity between the gross margin profitability and the DPP profitability of in-store bakeries underscores the pressure that retail outlets are under to bring their in-store bakery costs in line. This provides a strong incentive for using frozen baked goods, which require fewer labor and storage inputs than scratch or mix bakery products. On the other hand, the consumer attraction of in-store bakeries provides a countervailing pressure for providing "authenticity" in the form of visible scratch- and mix-preparation activities. In all likelihood, in-store bakeries will increasingly settle for combination formats.

Table 5
The Restaurant Industry Dollar[a] (percent)

	Type of Restaurant		
	Full-Menu, Table Service	**Limited-Menu, Table Service**	**Limited-Menu, No Table Service**
Cost of food and beverages sold	32.7	33.8	32.3
Payroll and employee benefits	32.8	28.2	26.9
All other expenses	30.1	30.6	33.0
Net income before tax	4.4	7.4	7.9

[a] Adapted from National Restaurant Association (1992).

The greatest opportunity for growth in the frozen baked goods industry may be in foodservice, because foodservice units are under greater pressure to control labor costs and maintain high volumes of product turnovers, and they have less opportunity to offer the intangible consumer benefits provided by a functioning "fresh" bakery operation.

The success of the frozen baked goods industry remains first and foremost economically driven. The shared economic and demographic evolution of the foodservice and in-store baking industries will provide an ample foundation for growth of the frozen baked goods industry in the years to come. Whether marketed through foodservice or food retailing outlets, frozen baked goods provide an important venue for achieving cost efficiencies in the face of increased competition, fragmenting markets, and increasing labor costs. With time, product quality will improve as the industry climbs the technological learning curve. Also, new outlets await discovery and penetration in the wake of a changing retail marketplace.

For example, the rapid emergence of warehouse club outlets, which rely upon economies of scale to undercut traditional retail outlets, would appear to provide a perfect fit with the production advantages offered by frozen baked goods. According to a 1992 Food Marketing Institute survey presented at the Institute for International Research's "Warehouse Club Revolution" symposium, 20% of all households surveyed shopped for groceries at warehouse clubs. Separately, a Nielsen Household Services survey presented at the conference listed bread and baked goods among the top-selling items at warehouse clubs (Marketing Institute, 1993).

Quality enhancements will continue to drive growth in the frozen baked goods segment. This will particularly be the case for foodservice operations where food preparation is "invisible" to the clientele. In-store bakeries, meanwhile, will continue to balance all formats of preparation just as they balance the attraction of in-store bakery service with their need to address cost-of-labor requirements and the tangible drain on profitability these bakeries represent, at least in DPP terms.

The future growth of the frozen baked goods industry will ultimately be defined by the economies of scale to which it owes its birth. For the $4.5–11.0 billion frozen baked goods industry, however defined, the following years should bring sustained growth as both the quality of, and the economic benefits provided by, frozen baked goods establish new operating standards for retail and foodservice outlets. For now, the industry faces highly attractive growth opportunities by penetrating new markets. As the industry matures, however, it is not unreasonable to assume that economics will dictate a heightened degree of industry consolidation. This is already occurring with the entry-by-acquisition of corporate giants such as Pillsbury/Grand Metropolitan, Heinz, and Unilever into the industry. This trend should eventually pressure small independent manufacturers, regional supermarket, and restaurant chains to consolidate their operations in order to remain competitive.

Acknowledgments

The author gratefully acknowledges the contributions of all the following individuals who, in their own special ways, made this chapter possible. Grateful "thank-yous" are extended to Richard M. Davis, Jr., a food analyst formerly with Wessels, Arnold & Henderson of Minneapolis; Peter Houstle, Executive Vice President of the Retail Bakers of America; Jennifer Voskuil, of the American Frozen Food Institute; Sherri Rosenblatt, of the Food Marketing Institute; Ralph Rush, of Technomics Inc.; Ronald Wirtz, library director with the American Institute of Baking; Richard Kuberski, of Van den Bergh Foods, for his invaluable overview of the frozen baked goods industry; Wendy Webster, of the National Restaurant Association; Frank Dell, of Delmark Associates; John R. Phipps (San Francisco) and Sally Robins (New York) of Deloitte Touche Tohmatsu International for their crucial insights into DPP analysis; Ray Lahvic, Editor Emeritus of *Bakery Production and Marketing* magazine, for his cheerful support and guidance; Marykate Ginter, of the Dairy Research Foundation, for her editorial support; and finally, Karel Kulp of the American Institute of Baking for his unwavering support, patience, and faith in the author.

Literature Cited

Adweek/Marketing Week. 1991. New products. Jan. 14, p. 8.

Davis, R. 1993. Flowers Industries Report. Wessels, Arnold, & Henderson, Minneapolis, MN. Oct. 8, p. 3.

Deloitt, Touche & Tohmatsu International. 1986. Direct Product Profit: Supermarket Frozen Food Research Study. Deloitt, Touche & Tohmatsu International, San Francisco.

Dietrich, R. 1992. Today's specialty food consumer: Who, what where, when, how much? National Association for the Specialty Foods Trade. March/April.

FIND/SVP, Inc. 1991. The market for frozen prepared foods. FIND/SVP, Inc., New York.

Food Marketing Institute. 1989. The unified DPP method. In: Bakery DPP Manual. The Institute, Washington, DC. Chap. 6, p. 39.

Frozen Food Age. 1990. New products. June, p. 58.

Giant Foods. 1990. Annual Report. Giant Foods, Carlisle, PA.

Krumrei, D. 1991. Where have all the clean-up kids gone? Bakery Prod. Mark. Aug., p. 91.

Krumrei, D. 1992. The story is in the numbers. Bakery Prod. Mark. Aug. pp. 42-54.

Krumrei, D. 1993a. Becoming brand conscious. Bakery Prod. Mark. June, pp. 96-98.

Krumrei, D. 1993b. New forms of carryout. Bakery Prod. Mark. June, pp. 104-105.

Lee, E. 1992. The booming in-store bakery market. Mod. Baking June, p. 43.

Litwak, D., and Maline, N. 1992. Tenth annual instore bakery review. Supermark. Bus. April, pp. 45-60.

Litwak, D., and Maline, N. 1993. Bakery: Results for 1992 anything but half-baked. Supermark. Bus. April, pp. 34-48.

Litwak, D., and Torres-Cepeda, J. 1991. Ninth annual instore bakery review. Supermark. Bus. April, pp. 49-62.

Marketing Institute. 1993. Proc. Symp. Warehouse Club Revolution. The Institute, Div. of Institute for International Research, New York.

Milling & Baking News. 1990. Management and marketing news. May 22, p. 1

Milling & Baking News. 1991. Frozen dough as new niche for Heinz. March 12, p. 15.

Otis Spunkmeyer Inc. 1992. Press release: Otis Spunkmeyer cookies perfect for foodservice business. Otis Spunkmeyer Inc., San Leandro, CA.

Progressive Grocer. 1992. The Marsh supermarket study. March, p. 110.

Progressive Grocer. 1993a. Still going strong—Bakery update 1993. March, pp. 90-106.

Progressive Grocer. 1993b. The best of both worlds. March, p. 109.

Sansolo, M., and Garry, M. 1993. 60th annual report of the grocery industry. Prog. Grocer. April, p. 43.

Statistical Abstract of the United States. 1991. U.S. Dept. of Commerce, Washington, DC. p. 13, 16.

Wetterau, Inc. 1990. Annual Report. Wetterau, Inc., Hazelwood, MO.

CHAPTER 2

Yeast Performance in Frozen Doughs and Strategies for Improvement

Gregory P. Casey
James J. Foy
Red Star Yeast & Products
Universal Foods Corporation
Milwaukee, WI 53218

Frozen doughs are an increasing portion of bakery sales and production, and much has been written on the quality parameters that affect frozen doughs. Some of the areas studied include the effect of various ingredients and their interactions, the temperature of storage, the rates of freezing and thawing, and the stability or shelf life of frozen products. The answers have not come easily, as most of the critical parameters in frozen dough are interrelated.

The single most studied ingredient used in the production of frozen doughs has been yeast. Formulation concentration, stability, strain type, rates of freezing, and rates of degradation have all been, and continue to be, investigated. The interest in yeast is because of the fact that yeast is the ingredient necessary to provide proper gas production for dough leavening and character and flavor of the finished bread product.

The choice of the right strain of yeast and of optimized processing conditions is critical for the production of frozen doughs with acceptable shelf life. All bakers know that frozen doughs slacken and deteriorate during prolonged storage, resulting in products with longer proof times, decreased bake volumes, and poorer grain and texture properties (Dubois and Blockcolsky, 1986). Throughout the 1960s and 1970s, it was largely assumed that these difficulties were direct consequences of losses in yeast viability after freezing and thawing. Research over the past decade, however, has shown that these are clearly a combination of two factors: decreased yeast viability and activity (measured by gassing power tests) and diminished gas-holding properties associated with frozen doughs (determined with an extensigraph).

Effects of Freezing and Thawing on Cells

Events During the Freezing Process

To understand the effects that freezing and thawing have on yeast viability and activity, it is necessary to review the ways in which biological systems respond to subzero temperatures and to the solidification of liquid water.

While the freezing point of a cell's cytoplasm is about -1°C, cells generally remain unfrozen, and therefore supercooled, to -10 or -15°C, even when ice is present in the external medium (Mazur, 1965). This indicates that the cell membrane presents an effective barrier against the growth of external ice into the supercooled cell interior and also that cells neither are nor contain effective nucleators of supercooled water (Mazur, 1970). However, the undercooled water in the cytoplasm has a higher vapor pressure than the surrounding ice, and cells begin to equilibrate this pressure difference by losing water across the cell membrane. The resulting dehydration concentrates solutes (i.e., salts) in the cell's interior, thus lowering the intracellular aqueous vapor pressure (Mazur, 1970). An equilibrium is therefore established between the cell interior and its surroundings. Only if the temperature is further reduced below about -15°C can ice crystal formation begin in the cytoplasmic space. The described equilibrium is observed only in the temperature interval of -1 to -15°C. The amount of water removed from the cell is largely dependent on the time that the cell is in that temperature interval. Subsequent events during cooling, therefore, are dependent on cooling velocity and on permeability of the cell to water.

The water content of a cell cooled infinitely slowly would be lowered by that amount necessary to continuously maintain a vapor pressure equilibrium with the external ice (Mazur, 1970). Cells cooled at finite rates will contain more than the equilibrium amount of water at certain temperatures and will be supercooled. Extreme supercooling cannot occur, for cell membranes apparently lose their ability to block the passage of ice crystals below about -10 to -15°C (Mazur, 1970). As a result, cells that are cooled fast enough to contain supercooled water below these temperatures complete their equilibration by freezing intracellularly.

The critical cooling rate that produces internal ice depends on the ratio of the volume of the cell to its surface area and on its permeability to water. The critical rate should be lower for larger, spherical cells and for those less permeable to water than for smaller or more permeable cells. Mathematical models indicate that at -15°C, yeast cells contain supercooled water when cooled faster than 10°C/min (Mazur, 1970). Since cell water cannot usually remain unfrozen at -15°C, yeast cells undergo intracellular freezing when cooled faster than 10°C/min.

Regardless of whether cells equilibrate by water loss or by intracellular freezing, they are subjected to a second class of physicochemical events. As the temperature decreases, the amount of cell water decreases, extra- and intracellular solutes concentrate, pH changes occur because solutes precipitate as their solubilities are exceeded, and all solutes precipitate below the eutectic point (lowest possible temperature of solidification) of the system. Mazur (1970) has referred to these events as "solution effects." A cell undergoing slow cooling is thus exposed to these solution effects for a longer period of time.

One might expect that cells cooled below their eutectic point would no longer be subjected to further stress, but this is not necessarily the case. Reactions can and do occur in the solid state. One of these is ice recrystallization. Small convex ice crystals have higher surface energies than large flat crystals and tend to reduce their surface energies by growing or fusing with other small crystals (Mazur, 1970). The rate at which this recrystallization occurs is dependent on both the size of crystals formed during cooling and the subsequent temperature to which they are exposed. Since rapid cooling produces small ice crystals, the crystals that form within rapidly cooled cells will not only be small, but will also tend to recrystallize during warming, particularly if warming is slow (Mazur, 1970).

In review, cells subjected to subzero temperatures initially supercool. The manner in which they equilibrate depends primarily on the rate at which they are cooled and on their permeability to water. If they are cooled slowly or if their permeability to water is high, they will equilibrate by dehydration. If they are cooled rapidly or if their permeability to water is low, they will equilibrate, at least in part, by intracellular freezing. Rapid cooling produces small intracellular ice crystals that are likely to enlarge during warming because of the high free energies on their surfaces. Regardless of whether cells equilibrate by dehydration or intracellular freezing, subzero temperatures expose cells to loss of liquid water and to increases in the concentration of intra- and extracellular solutes. Figure 1 contains a pictorial representation of the events that may occur when a cell is exposed to freezing temperatures.

Physicochemical Basis of Cell Damage

Mazur (1970) suggests that solution effects are responsible for cell injury when cooling is slower than optimal, and intracellular freezing is responsible for injury when cooling is faster than optimal. The optimum cooling rate would then be a rate that is slow enough to prevent intracellular ice formation but rapid enough to minimize the length of time cells are exposed to solution effects.

Evidence that supports this hypothesis has been presented for sea urchin eggs (Mazur, 1970), bacteria (Gehrke et al, 1992), yeast (Mazur, 1967; Mazur and Schmidt, 1968), and red blood cells (Mazur, 1970). A cooling velocity of 7°C/min was found to produce maximum survival of yeast cells; higher rates resulted in abrupt killing (Mazur, 1970). The optimum cooling velocity is mainly determined by the rate of water transport from the cells. The surface to volume ratio of yeast cells having a diameter of 5–8 mm is smaller than for bacteria having a diameter of 1–2 mm. Yeast cells would, therefore, need more time for water transport from the cell interior and consequently would have a lower cooling rate than bacteria. This supposition is supported by work in which an optimum cooling rate of around 4°C/min was found for yeast cells while a higher rate of around 37°C/min was found for the bacteria *Escherichia coli* (Gehrke et al, 1992).

Intracellular Ice Formation

As mentioned previously, ice formed in cells as a result of rapid cooling is likely to grow by recrystallization during warming, especially if warming is slow. This sequence of events is believed to be the explanation for yeast cells that exhibit lower survival after slow warming than after rapid warming (Mazur and Schmidt, 1968). Research suggests that the lethal event in rapidly cooled yeast cells is the growth of intracellular ice crystals rather than their initial formation and that the damage observed during warming can occur very rapidly. In one study, Mazur and Schmidt (1968) reported that the survival of yeast cells decreased 40-fold when the time taken to warm them from -70°C to 0°C increased from 0.001 min to 0.06 min.

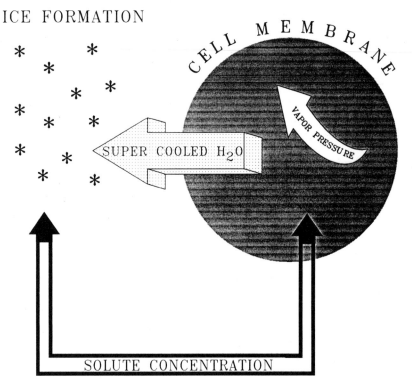

Fig. 1. Pictorial representation of the events that occur when a cell is exposed to freezing temperatures.

However, the understanding of the basis of injury from the formation and recrystallization of intracellular ice is uncertain. Mazur (1966, 1967) speculates that injury occurs because recrystallizing ice crystals exert sufficient force to rupture plasma membranes or the membranes of cellular organelles such as mitochondria. Recrystallizing ice crystals have been shown to disrupt protein gels, and cells killed by intracellular damage have been shown to suffer membrane damage and become leaky (Mazur, 1961, 1965).

Solution Effects

One problem in understanding solution effects arises from the fact that they include at least four discrete events during freezing. These events are 1) water is removed as ice, 2) solutes concentrate, 3) cell volume decreases, and 4) solutes precipitate. Each of these events has been the basis of hypotheses of injury, but all of them, except for precipitation of solutes, occur simultaneously during freezing (Mazur, 1970). This makes it difficult to assign injury to a specific solution effect.

Several mechanisms of injury, however, have been proposed. Lovelock (1954) has suggested that high concentrations of electrolyte, produced by freezing, affect membrane lipids, making the cells leaky. As a result, cells become engorged with cations and undergo osmotic shock because of the inflow of water during thawing. Meryman (1968) has proposed that damage in red blood cells results not from concentrated electrolytes, but from the inability of cells to shrink below approximately 50% of their normal volume. Meryman suggests that this establishes a transient pressure gradient across the membrane and causes it to become leaky. Levitt (1966) has suggested that freezing damage in higher plants is primarily due to the formation of disulfide bonds as a result of compaction of macromolecules produced by dehydration during freezing. Clegg et al (1982) and Franks et al (1983) have suggested that high intracellular salt concentrations cause damage to cell membranes and simultaneously cause denaturation of proteins as a result of intracellular pH shifts.

In conclusion, the majority of evidence implicates membranes as the chief targets of freezing damage. This damage is manifested by loss of the cells' ability to carry out the membrane-mediated processes of oxidative phosphorylation rather than by loss of function of soluble enzymes (Mazur, 1970).

Effects on Gas-Retention Properties of Dough

Research over the past decade has now indicated that a combination of two factors is involved in the production of frozen doughs with acceptable shelf life. The first is the retention of yeast viability and activity through frozen-dough processing. The events that occur during freezing of yeast cells and two mechanisms (concentration or solution effects and recrystallization effects) that may account for cell injury and inactivation have been reviewed in previous sections. The second factor involved is the diminished gas-holding properties associated with frozen doughs. It is not the scope of this chapter to detail potential changes in the rheological properties of frozen doughs, as this subject is covered in other chapters. However, it is important to this discussion to recognize that the physicochemical changes associated with exposure to subzero temperatures can also affect other dough ingredients, particularly flour proteins. In addition, injury to yeast membranes, caused by the freezing and thawing process, may lead to the release of certain chemical components of cells, particularly reducing compounds, that may have deleterious effects on dough structure.

Gas-retention problems can result from ice-crystallization-induced damage of the three-dimensional gluten protein network responsible for gas retention in dough, as well as glutathione reduction of the gluten network (Hsu et al, 1979b; Varriano-Marston et al, 1980). The former phenomenon was recently studied by Berglund et al (1991), by exploiting new developments in low-temperature electron scanning microscopy to examine the structure of frozen, fully hydrated doughs (all previous electron scanning microscopy studies required that water be removed from the sample before analysis). These results visualized and confirmed the breakdown of the reticular pattern of gluten structure with prolonged frozen storage and/or freeze-thaw cycles. Starch granules, originally firmly embedded in the gluten network in freshly frozen dough, were observed to become more separated. Less free water was associated with either the gluten or starch fractions, concentrating instead into large patches of ice crystals. Gluten strands were also observed to become thinner with time. Collectively these observations, showing changes in the ultrastructure, help explain the extended proof times and reduced loaf volumes of frozen bread dough. However, as the authors did not conduct control studies using unyeasted doughs, it is unclear as to what portion of the observed changes was contributed by yeast glutathione.

Inoue and Bushuk (1991), in extensigraph experiments, did compare yeasted and nonyeasted frozen doughs and found that the gluten structure of yeasted doughs was more vulnerable to the detrimental effects of freezing than that of nonyeasted doughs (i.e., dough slackening and extended proof times of frozen doughs result from a combination of yeast-related issues and physical damage to the structure of the gluten network). However, Autio and Sinda (1992) reported that the addition of dead yeast cells to dough did not affect the rheological properties, indicating that the structural changes in frozen and thawed doughs are not associated with the release of reducing substances from yeast cells. From viscoelastic measurements they concluded that there was a loss of polymer cross-linking in frozen and thawed doughs and that a decrease in relaxation half-life indicated a weakening of the gluten network.

Kline and Sugihara (1968) postulated that the chemical reduction of gluten disulfide groups, by reducing substances released from dead yeast cells (such as the tripeptide glutathione), is what contributes to the increased weakening observed in yeasted dough (i.e., shorter mixing times, increased extensibility, decreased loaf volume, and greater requirements for oxidization improvers).

However, Wolt and D'Appolonia (1984a) showed that the sulfhydryl content of frozen dough does not change appreciably during storage, and Bruinsma and Giesenschlag (1984) reported that frozen-dough weakening can occur independently of any detectable loss in yeast activity during storage. While leached glutathione is certainly involved, the precise manner by which yeast contributes to increased slackening remains the subject of debate.

Strategies to Improve Yeast Performance in Frozen Doughs

The previous sections examined the physicochemical events that occur during the freezing process and how they affect yeast viability. While yeast viability is certainly a critical issue, no discussion of strategies aimed at improving yeast performance in frozen doughs can focus solely on this subject. As depicted in Figures 2 and 3, the development of superior frozen-dough products is a much more complicated task than just the selection of a yeast strain with inherently high resistance to freezing. Numerous practices related to the manufacture of baker's yeast can ultimately affect yeast frozen-dough performance, as can issues involving bakery-related procedures (dough, even without the

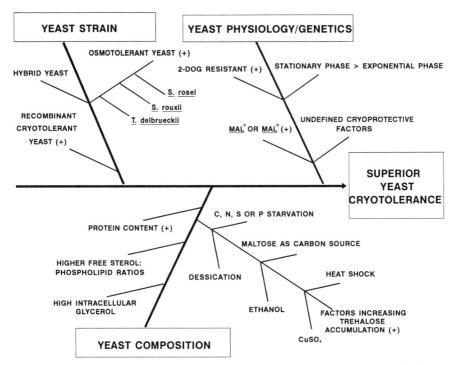

Fig. 2. This fishbone diagram depicts biological criteria that may be important in selecting a yeast strain with high resistance to freezing. Plus signs indicate criteria associated with a positive effect on yeast cryotolerance.

complicating effects of freezing and thawing, is a complex rheological matrix that remains an intensely studied material in cereal chemistry). Indeed the interactive effects of yeast-, manufacturing-, and bakery-related variables forces us to simultaneously consider all of these parameters in the development of strategies aimed at improving yeast frozen-dough performance. Therefore, while the remaining sections examine each of these three areas separately, it should always be kept in mind that the coordinated efforts of the scientist, manufacturer, and baker will be required to produce superior frozen-dough products.

Customized Yeast Strains

Before examining various strategies used in the development of frozen-dough yeast strains, it is necessary to define what constitutes a superior frozen-dough yeast strain. While at first glance this may seem to be intuitively obvious (i.e., a strain that survives freezing with 100% viability), production- and customer-related considerations demand a longer list of requirements. As the following sections will demonstrate, many yeast strains have one or more of these properties (Table 1), but very few are able to fit all criteria.

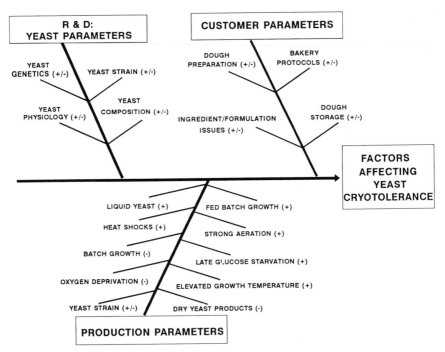

Fig. 3. This fishbone diagram depicts the interactive effects of yeast-, manufacturing-, and bakery-related variables and shows why these parameters must be simultaneously considered in the development of strategies for improving performance of yeast in frozen doughs. Plus and minus signs = factors that may have positive and negative effects, respectively, on yeast cryotolerance.

Nontraditional Yeast Strains

The current edition of *The Yeasts: Characteristics and Identification* (Barnett et al, 1983) lists 500 species of yeast distributed over 60 different genera. The vast majority of baker's yeast strains in use today belong to only one of these 500 species, *Saccharomyces cerevisiae* (Nagodawithana and Trivedi, 1991). It is therefore not unreasonable to assume that, with such a potentially diverse gene pool, there must be strains of yeast better suited than S. *cerevisiae* for surviving the deleterious effects of freezing and thawing. However, given our limited understanding of the genetic composition required for freeze tolerance, improved strains can be found only by screening isolates for their freeze tolerance and baking attributes. Despite intensive time and labor requirements, numerous claims of frozen-dough yeast strains isolated in this manner can be found in patents and published literature. In general, it appears that the genetic constitution required for high osmotolerance or stress resistance may also impart, to some degree, the ability to withstand freeze-thaw conditions. The connection between osmotolerance and freeze tolerance is not unexpected in that both phenomena involve the response of yeast cells to the stressful effects of lowered intracellular water activity levels. Osmotolerant yeasts, including *Saccharomyces rouxii, S. rosei* (taxonomically these yeasts are named S. *cerevisiae* and *Torulaspora delbrueckii*, respectively [Barnett et al, 1983]), S. *fructuum, Debaryomyces hansenii, Zygosaccharomyces rouxii*, and *Hansenula anomala*, are known to accumulate protective glycerol concentration ratios (intracellular/extracellular) greater than 1000-fold in response to growth at decreased water activity values (Van Zyl et al, 1990). Presumably, this unique ability to accumulate glycerol is involved in the strong freeze tolerance that is also observed in these yeast strains. Likewise, yeast species resistant to other forms of stresses, like the heat-resistant *Kluyveromyces thermotolerans*, have evolved protective mechanisms that also impart resistance to damage from freezing (Hino et al, 1992).

Most studies with osmotolerant strains of *Saccharomyces* yeast (i.e., S. *rosei, S. rouxii*, and S. *fructuum*) reveal several shortcomings limiting their utility in baking, including: 1) slow rates of maltose utilization compared to

Table 1
Properties of Superior Frozen-Dough Yeast Strains

1. High natural resistance to the short-term and long-term effects of freezing and thawing under both laboratory and commercial-scale conditions.

2. Superior performance in lean, regular, and sweet dough systems.

3. Ability to be manufactured economically using existing plant procedures and substrates.

4. Economically affordable (from the baker's perspective).

5. "User-friendly," i.e., have the ability to be utilized and stored in bakeries without requiring significant capital investment or protocol modifications.

6. Patentable.

traditional strains of baker's yeast, 2) particularly poor performance in lean dough systems (although sweet dough performance is usually outstanding), and 3) smaller cell diameters compared to traditional yeast strains, resulting in longer processing times to separate, wash, and press production yeast samples (Nakatomi et al, 1985; Uno et al, 1986; Hahn and Kawai, 1990; Takano et al, 1990; Baguena et al, 1991). To overcome the last of these shortcomings, researchers in Japan created a diploid yeast from a haploid strain of *T. delbrueckii* SANK 50268 (*S. rosei*) by treating regenerating protoplasts with dimethyl sulfoxide (Sasaki and Ohshima, 1987). The average cell volume of these diploids was three times that of the starting haploid parent, resulting in improved collection and pressing properties following commercial-scale fermentations (Ohshima et al, 1987). The diploid cells (*T. delbrueckii* YL3 and F31) exhibited the same superior resistance to freezing as the haploid strain, and one such diploid was stated to have replaced the SANK 50268 strain in the Japanese baker's yeast market (Ohshima et al, 1987). Presumably, these diploids still exhibit slow rates of maltose utilization, especially in lean dough formulations (doughs containing no added sugar).

The use of a *S. fructuum*:*S. cerevisiae* coculture has been proposed as one way to ameliorate the shortcomings of the osmotolerant yeast in regard to their slow rates of maltose fermentation (Baguena et al, 1991). Sankyo Co. Ltd. (Japan), for example, currently markets a commercial freeze-tolerant yeast consisting of a mixture of *S. cerevisiae* and *S. rosei* (Hino et al, 1987).

In addition to osmotolerance, freeze tolerance in yeast has also been found to be closely associated with ethanol tolerance. Hence, ethanol-tolerant strains of *S. cerevisiae* and *S. chevalieri* have been patented for use in frozen-dough systems (Kawai and Kazuo, 1983). While other properties limit the widespread use of these ethanol-tolerant strains, it is becoming increasingly clear that yeast strains better able to withstand any form of environmental stress (i.e., osmotic pressure, high temperature, or ethanol) are generally more freeze-tolerant. There is a large volume of literature pertaining to the physiological mechanism behind these tolerances, as well as information concerning structural and regulatory genes. However, considerable basic research will be required before any understanding of these phenomena can be applied in strain selection programs. This process, however, has been started in studies with the freeze-tolerant yeast *K. thermotolerans* FRI 501 (Hino et al, 1992). These researchers have developed a genetic transformation system for this yeast that will now make it feasible to begin cloning genes from a *K. thermotolerans* genomic library. These genes restore freeze tolerance to non-freeze-tolerant mutants of *K. thermotolerans*. Once isolated, these genes would be available to modify production strains of *S. cerevisiae* and improve many of the defects currently limiting the widespread use of non-*Saccharomyces* yeast in baking (i.e., increased rates of maltose uptake). These developments will, however, require an estimated 5–10 years of continued research. In light of this, it is perhaps not surprising that only strains of *S. cerevisiae* are marketed as baker's yeast in North America and Europe despite the large number of strains that are claimed to be superior frozen-dough yeasts (summarized in Table 2).

Freeze-Tolerant Strains Produced by Hybridization

In attempts to improve either the poor baking properties of freeze-tolerant osmophilic yeasts or the freeze-tolerance of non-osmophilic strains of baker's yeast, hybridization experiments have been reported involving these two types of yeasts. This approach suffers from the fact that all of the traits of interest in these crosses (i.e., osmotolerance, freeze-tolerance, and good baking characteristics) are undoubtedly polygenic and unlinked (the result of more than one genetic determinant spread over several chromosomes), making the likelihood of finding an offspring with all of the desired attributes very remote. The lack of knowledge about the genetics of these properties prevents the use of cloned markers to accelerate screening of hybrid offspring. As a result, all hybrids must be laboriously screened in growth and baking experiments to select for progeny with improved characteristics.

A recent example of creating a new frozen-dough yeast strain via hybridization is the research of Oda and Ouchi (1990). As depicted in Figure 4, they crossed a freeze-tolerant sweet-dough production strain of *S. cerevisiae* (with

Table 2
Strains of Baker's Yeast Specifically Developed for Frozen Dough Applications

Yeast Culture	Method of Isolation	Reference
S. cerevisiae FR1 802	Screening and selection	Hino et al, 1987
S. cerevisiae FR1 413	Screening and selection	Hino et al, 1987
S. cerevisiae KYF 110	Screening and selection	Uno et al, 1986
S. cerevisiae IAM 4274	Screening and selection	Takano et al, 1990
S. cerevisiae FRI 869	Screening and selection	Oda et al, 1986
S. cerevisiae MA 233	Screening and selection	Oda et al, 1986
S. cerevisiae FTY-3	Hybridization	Takano et al, 1990
S. cerevisiae 612	Hybridization	Nakatomi et al, 1985
S. cerevisiae YDY 671	Hybridization	Oda and Ouchi, 1990
S. cerevisiae FTM-1 & 2	Mutation	Matsutani et al, 1990
S. cerevisiae 3-2-6 D	Protoplast fusion	Takano et al, 1990
S. rosei	Screening	Takano et al, 1990
S. cerevisiae/S. rosei	Coculture	Hino et al, 1987
S. chevalieri	Screening and selection	Kawai and Kazuo, 1983
S. fructuum P-7	Screening and selection	Baguena et al, 1991
T. delbrueckii SANK 50268[a]	Screening and selection	Sasaki and Ohshima, 1987
T. delbrueckii YL3[a]	Protoplast fusion	Ohshima et al, 1987
T. delbrueckii F-31[a]	Protoplast fusion	Ohshima et al, 1987
K. thermotolerans FR1 501	Screening and selection	Hino et al, 1987, 1990, 1992
Candida boidinii	Screening and selection	Baguena et al, 1991

[a] All strains, except for these three, originate from Japanese sources.

poor lean-dough traits) with a maltose-constitutive, but freeze-sensitive, haploid strain of *S. cerevisiae.* Pulse field electrophoresis experiments clearly demonstrated that the resulting hybrid, YOY671, was a result of nuclear fusion, not cytoduction, as it possessed chromosome bands unique to both parents. The lean and regular dough leavening properties of the hybrid were improved over those of the freeze-tolerant parent, while freeze tolerance was intermediate to those of the two parents. However, as even the "freeze tolerant" parent strain of yeast lost 50% of its gassing power in 5% sugar doughs after two weeks of storage at -20°C, it remains doubtful whether any of the strains in this study can adequately serve the frozen-dough market. Hybrids have also been constructed in similar crosses involving strains of *S. cerevisiae, S. uvarum, S. rosei,* and/or *S. rouxii* (Windisch et al, 1976; Nakatomi et al, 1985; Takano et al, 1990). At this time it is not known whether any baker's yeast company is marketing a frozen-dough yeast strain produced by hybridization. The absence of a clearly superior frozen-dough yeast strain in the marketplace, at least in North America and Europe, would tend to suggest that there is not.

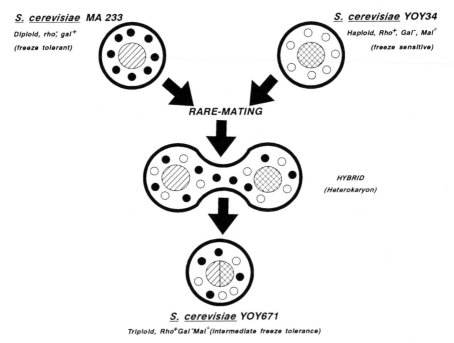

S. cerevisiae MA 233
Diploid, rho⁻, gal⁺
(freeze tolerant)

S. cerevisiae YOY34
Haploid, Rho⁺, Gal⁻, Mal^c
(freeze sensitive)

RARE-MATING

HYBRID
(Heterokaryon)

S. cerevisiae YOY671
Triploid, Rho⁺Gal⁻Mal^c(Intermediate freeze tolerance)

Fig. 4. This figure depicts the development of a novel frozen-dough yeast strain by hybridization. In this experiment (Oda and Ouchi, 1990), a freeze-tolerant, sweet-dough production strain of *S. cerevisiae* (MA233) was crossed with a freeze-sensitive, maltose-constitutive laboratory strain of *S. cerevisiae* (YOY34). The resulting hybrid, *S. cerevisiae* YOY671, was found to have lean and regular dough leavening properties improved from those of the freeze-tolerant parent and freeze tolerance intermediate to those of the two parents.

Freeze-Tolerant Strains Produced by Protoplast Fusion

Protoplast fusion, first described in yeast by Van Solingen and Van der Plaat (1977), is conceptually similar to hybridization in that it can be used to cross two yeast strains to produce novel hybrids. However, by eliminating the requirement for mating abilities in the parent strains, this technique can also be used to conduct interspecific crosses, thereby greatly increasing the potential genetic pool available for strain development purposes. In spite of this advantage, fusion, like hybridization, is never a predictable procedure, and fusion products are often very different from either parent. Therefore, it is once again very difficult to selectively introduce a single trait (i.e., freeze tolerance) into a baker's yeast without simultaneously disrupting many of the desirable baker's yeast properties in that strain. For this reason, the literature indicates that efforts to produce freeze-tolerant strains of baker's yeast by protoplast fusion have been very rare. In Japan, patented fusant strain *S. cerevisiae* 3-2-6D was prepared by fusing an osmotolerant-strain of *Saccharomyces* with a production baker's yeast strain (Takano et al, 1990). Again, it is unclear whether this strain is actually produced commercially.

The probability of isolating fusants that are essentially the same as the original strain of baker's yeast, but which have acquired one or several desirable attributes from the other strain, can be increased by using a petite mutant of the baker's yeast strain. A petite mutant is a cell that has a mutation in the mitochondrial genome and as a consequence is respiratory deficient. It has been shown that mitochondria from osmotolerant yeast species like *S. rosei* (*T. delbrueckii*) can complement a petite mutation in a baker's yeast strain. In these fusions, acquisition of parts of the nuclear genome of the nonbaker's yeast parent takes place by single-chromosome transfer, rather than by a fusion of the two genomes (Spencer et al, 1989). Therefore, the likelihood of finding baker's yeast hybrids that selectively added only limited genetic material from the osmotolerant strain is greatly increased over crosses of hybrids isolated by complementation of nuclear markers, where the complete genome of one parent eventually becomes dominant (Groves and Oliver, 1984). As our understanding of the physiology and genetics of osmotolerance/freeze tolerance increases in the future, protoplast fusion may yet eventually be a more selective and direct approach with which to develop frozen-dough yeast strains.

Freeze-Tolerant Strains Produced by Mutation and Selection

Owing to their polyploid genetic composition, induced or natural mutations are generally of little practical value with baker's yeast strains. For example, karyotype analyses of seven strains of Spanish baker's yeasts revealed them to be tetraploids for chromosome I (Rank et al, 1991). Similar results have also been observed for European and North American strains of compressed yeast, active dry yeast, and instant active dry yeast strains (Casey et al, 1990). Therefore, while recessive mutations, whether spontaneous or induced, no doubt occur with the same frequencies in polyploid baker's yeast as they do in haploid yeasts, they do not reveal themselves due to the presence of nonmutated alleles. However, this "backup" genetic safety cushion is desirable from the perspective that it results in production strains that are inherently stable against the expression and buildup of potentially undesirable gene mutations.

Despite these limitations, mutation and selection has been attempted as a method to develop freeze-tolerant strains of baker's yeast. In one report (Matsutani et al, 1990), a baker's yeast strain was mutagenized by exposure to UV light. After numerous cycles of freeze-thaw selection pressure, mutant strains *S. cerevisiae* FTM-1 and *S. cerevisiae* FTM-2 were eventually isolated. These strains, while still exhibiting losses in viability, were found to be significantly more tolerant to the adverse effects of repeated freeze-thaw cycles, although the basis behind this increased resistance was not determined. It remains to be determined whether continued mutation and selection experiments could eventually yield mutants with commercially required levels of freeze tolerance. Assuming that there is no single dominant mutation that leads to freeze tolerance in *S. cerevisiae*, it is unlikely that this strategy will soon lead to the development of frozen-dough yeast strains.

Trehalose-Enriched Yeast

Trehalose and glycogen have generally been regarded as the two main reserve carbohydrates in yeast. However, over the past 10 years, it has become increasingly apparent that trehalose's primary physiological role is not to act as a reserve carbohydrate, but rather as an efficient protecting agent to maintain membrane and intracellular structural integrity under a wide range of physiological and environmental stresses (Van Laere, 1989; Wiemken, 1990). Evidence for this role comes from the observations that: 1) anhydrobiotic organisms capable of surviving complete dehydration accumulate up to 35% of their dry weight as trehalose (Leopold, 1986, and references therein), 2) trehalose exerts strong protective effects on membranes and enzymes subjected to desiccation or freezing (Crowe et al, 1984), and 3) extracellular trehalose acts as a cryoprotectant during freezing and thawing of yeast cells (Coutinho et al, 1988). In addition, trehalose behaves in a manner contrary to what one would expect of a typical reserve carbohydrate. It accumulates in *S. cerevisiae* only after glucose is exhausted during batch growth, not while exogenous levels of glucose are abundant and could be stored to serve later as endogenous substrates during periods of starvation (Lillie and Pringle, 1980). During the last phase of sporulation in yeast, an energetically costly transformation of most of the glycogen to trehalose occurs (Kane and Roth, 1974), yet trehalose is not mobilized during ascospore germination if the nonfermentable carbon source acetate is available (Donnini et al, 1988). Compared to glycogen, trehalose yields less energy upon mobilization yet requires more energy for biosynthesis per unit of glucose stored (Van Laere, 1989). Trehalose utilization occurs only after the depletion of glycogen in stationary-phase yeast cells, followed rapidly by decreases in yeast viability (Lillie and Pringle, 1980).

How, then, does trehalose act as a stress protectant in the cells' cytoplasm? Up to one gram of trehalose per gram of protein can be accumulated by yeast cells in response to starvation, heat shock, desiccation, freeze drying, or other adverse conditions. This is an enormous quantity, which undoubtedly influences cytoplasmic water activity values (Wiemken, 1990). During baker's yeast production, trehalose levels reach up to 20% of cell dry weight within 2 hr after glucose feeding has stopped during the maturation process (Grba et al, 1975; Panek and Panek, 1990). At these levels, it is not inconceivable that trehalose would slow down cellular metabolism and promote the transition to a resting state of cells (i.e., to help guide the yeast through "bad times"). This role is consistent with the observed accumulation of trehalose shortly before or at the start of the stationary phase, its stubborn retention during the stationary phase, and its rapid utilization upon the resumption of cell growth.

In addition to slowing down cellular metabolism, trehalose may also enhance cell viability during freezing by preventing or minimizing damage to yeast cell membranes via the "water replacement hypothesis" (Clegg, 1986). This model proposes that hydroxyl groups of trehalose replace the hydrogen bonds between the phosphate group of membrane phospholipids and water, as intracellular water is drawn out of cells during the freezing process. Without such a transition, irreversible destructive changes are likely occur to the membrane, with the extent of the damage depending on the degree of intracellular dehydration. This protective role of trehalose during dehydration has been further extended to include prevention of irreversible damage to cytoplasmic proteins, where hydrogen-bonded water molecules not only help maintain the precise conformation required for a functional protein, but also act to prevent aggregation and precipitation of proteins (Wiemken, 1990).

Considerable direct evidence exists supporting the role of trehalose as a cryoprotective agent in baker's yeast. In a survey of 12 yeast strains from various genera, a direct correlation was found between intracellular trehalose concentration and cell viability after 4, 8, and 12 weeks of storage at -20°C (D'Amore et al, 1991). The osmotolerant yeasts *T. delbrueckii* and *Z. rouxii* possessed the greatest levels of intracellular trehalose and freeze resistance, while brewer's and baker's strains had the lowest levels of intracellular trehalose and freeze resistance. In a survey of over 300 yeast strains from the genus *Saccharomyces* in the culture collection of Kyowa Hakko Co., Ltd. (Tokyo, Japan), only 11 were found to have high levels of freeze tolerance. Intracellular levels of trehalose of these 11 strains were the highest seen in the 300 strains surveyed, ranging from 27 to 43 mg/g of cell dry weight (Oda et al, 1986). These levels were threefold higher than those found in commercial strains of compressed yeast with low levels of freeze tolerance (all strains were grown at the 2-L scale, with molasses used as the substrate). The authors noted, however, that there appeared to be no direct correlation between absolute levels of trehalose and freeze tolerance. They drew this conclusion because independent commercial samples of compressed yeast possessed 100–200 mg/g dry weight of trehalose yet were still as sensitive to freezing injury as the same yeast cultured at the 2-L scale (Oda et al, 1986). In similar experiments, Hino et al (1987) agreed that the correlation between trehalose concentration and survival ratio from freezing was not direct. Instead, they determined that the most critical predictor of cell resistance to freezing was the ability of a culture to maintain consistent basal levels of intracellular trehalose with or without a prefermentation period before freezing. In this survey, cultures of *S. cerevisiae* FRI 413, 802, 868, and 869 (reported commercial strains of Japanese frozen-dough yeast) and *K. thermotolerans* FRI 501 were assayed for their resistance to freezing with or without a prefermentation period. *K. thermotolerans* FRI 501 was found to be the most freeze-tolerant strain of yeast even though its prefermentation level of trehalose (approximately 20 mg/g of cell dry weight) was considerably less than the 80–160 mg/g values seen with the *S. cerevisiae* strains. Of particular interest was the observation that fermentation before freezing made the *S. cerevisiae* strains much less freeze tolerant while the *K. thermotolerans* strain remained unchanged, even after 3 hr. However, as the absolute values of intracellular trehalose, even after prefermentation, were still higher in several of the *S. cerevisiae* strains than in *K. thermotolerans*, the ability to exhibit high freeze tolerance is not simply dependent on specific values of intracellular levels of trehalose.

The above results suggest that one strategy for obtaining superior frozen-dough yeast strains is to select for cultures with alterations in their trehalose metabolic pathway that lead to higher basal levels of trehalose or slowed rates of trehalose catabolism. One such potential class of mutants is 2-deoxy-D-glucose-resistant strains of *S. cerevisiae*. Novak et al (1991) isolated such mutants from a haploid strain of *S. cerevisiae* and found that they were derepressed for maltose uptake and contained stationary-phase values of intracellular trehalose that were nearly double those of the starting parent (11 vs. 6 mg/g of cell dry weight). No attempt was made, however, to see whether these results could be extended to include polyploid (industrial) strains of baker's yeast. Additional studies have demonstrated a close linkage between maltose utilization and trehalose accumulation, as *S. cerevisiae* accumulates trehalose when grown with maltose as the carbon source (Panek et al, 1979). However, only maltose-constitutive strains are able to accumulate trehalose throughout growth on glucose. Maltose-inducible or maltose-nonfermenting strains of yeast do not begin to accumulate trehalose until glucose has been depleted from the medium (Panek et al, 1979).

While most strains of baker's yeast are inducible for maltose utilization, and hence do not accumulate high levels of trehalose, many of the "quick rising" strains of instant active dry yeast introduced to the market over the past 10 years have the ability to rapidly adapt to maltose because their levels of maltase activity are much higher than normal under repressed or nonrepressed conditions for maltose uptake. Such strains have been developed and patented by Clement and Hennette (1982), as well as by Jacobson and Trivedi (1987). The ability to accumulate high levels of trehalose appears to be important as a stress protectant to the drying process required to produce instant dry yeast. There are, unfortunately, no published results involving tests of these yeasts, in compressed form, to assess whether the elevated levels of trehalose also extend an improved tolerance to freezing in frozen-dough applications.

Modified Yeast Production Parameters

Nutrient Starvation

In 1974, Oura et al demonstrated that stopping the sugar feed toward the final phase of a commercial baker's yeast propagation, while still aerating, resulted in a yeast product of greater stability and improved baking characteristics. Numerous studies have indicated that it is the accumulation of trehalose during this period (up to 20% of cell dry weight, i.e., 0.1M) that imparts increased resistance to the adverse effects of processing and storage of commercial baker's yeasts (Thevelein, 1984; Panek and Panek, 1990). Similar trehalose accumulation can also be induced via starvation for nitrogen, phosphorus, or sulfur (Thevelein, 1984). In addition, fed-batch yeast cultures grown at significantly reduced growth rates (specific growth rate = 0.088/ hr compared to 0.117/hr) have been found to show greater trehalose synthesis and improved frozen-dough stability (Gelinas et al, 1989). In light of the evidence implicating intracellular trehalose levels with freeze tolerance, it can be assumed that any of these starvation treatments can only enhance the ability of a yeast to function as a frozen-dough yeast strain.

Heat Shock

An astonishing property of trehalose metabolism is the speed with which yeast cultures can make adjustments in intracellular levels of trehalose in response to external stimuli. One such stimulus is that of heat shock. In haploid strains of S. cerevisiae, it has been shown that 20- to 50-fold increases in trehalose can result from suddenly shifting the incubation temperature from 23 to 36°C and that these cultures are subsequently more thermotolerant than cultures previously held only at 23°C (Panek and Panek, 1990; Wiemken, 1990). The feasibility of using such heat shocks to increase yeast trehalose levels in commercial-scale propagations (and thereby improve freeze tolerance) remains to be determined. However, any increases may only be transient, as trehalose levels rapidly degrade when cultures are shifted back to normal growth temperatures (Panek and Panek, 1990). Procedures to rapidly process and cool yeast before low-temperature storage would have to be implemented to derive any potential benefit from heat shock treatments. It has also been reported that fed-batch yeasts grown at 30°C have increased cryoresistance and trehalose content compared to yeasts grown at 20°C (Gelinas et al, 1989).

Aeration

Researchers have reported that baker's yeast cryotolerance in frozen doughs is enhanced by the use of strong aeration during fed-batch growth (Gelinas et al, 1989, 1991a, 1991b; Gelinas and Goulet, 1991). Trehalose levels in strongly aerated cultures were found to be twice those in cultures grown with only partial aerobiosis (12 vs. 6% cell dry weight). This suggests a protective effect by trehalose. Even a momentary lack of excess dissolved oxygen during growth was significant, as losses in cell viability from freezing correlated with the duration of dissolved oxygen deficits (Gelinas et al, 1989). The authors did, however, caution against extrapolating yeast cryoresistance simply on the basis of absolute values of intracellular trehalose. This resulted from the demonstration that batch-grown cultures, containing up to 20% dry weight trehalose, were dramatically more sensitive to freezing than any of the fed-batch-grown cultures, which averaged 10% trehalose. While undoubtedly an influencing factor, trehalose is clearly not the sole determinant of a yeast culture's degree of cryoresistance (see Fig. 2). Other, as yet undetermined, aspects of yeast physiology have a role to play, aspects that may interconnect with trehalose biosynthesis.

Added Protectants

In conventional cryopreservation protocols, cell viability is normally ensured by the addition of specific cryoprotectants. Most of these are relatively small molecules that are easily permeable across cellular membranes (Mathias, 1991). While glycerol is most commonly used for this purpose, other cryoprotectants useful for the frozen storage of cell lines include dimethyl sulfoxide, sucrose, trehalose, glucose, methanol, proline, glycine, betaine, fructose, galactose, and lactose (Grout et al, 1990; Mathias, 1991). In a patent granted to Alko Ltd. (Helsinki, Finland), the claim was made that addition of 1–20% (w/w) glycerol to yeast (27–29% solids) made the yeast completely resistant to the adverse effects of repeated cycles of freezing and thawing, thereby greatly enhancing its shelf life (Suoranta, 1991). The patent also stated that similar protection was granted by the use of a wide range of other polyhydroxy compounds. Another patent claim was that the addition of glycerol eliminated sedimentation problems that are traditionally characteristic of liquid yeast preparations. At this time, it is not known whether any European yeast manufacturer uses glycerol in liquid yeast formulations to enhance yeast cryoresistance.

Yeast Protein Content

Several publications have claimed that yeast freeze tolerance is directly related to cell protein levels, with 57% protein being recommended to obtain good performances after freezing (Tanaka et al, 1976; Hsu et al, 1979a; Oda et al, 1986). Counter to this are claims that such high-protein yeasts exhibit higher rates of activity and fermentation before freezing, which is ultimately detrimental to yeast performance (Neyreneuf and Van der Plaat, 1991). One survey of compressed yeasts ranging from 46 to 55% protein could find no consistent correlation between yeast protein content and freeze tolerance in French frozen-dough bread (Neyreneuf and Van der Plaat, 1991). As discussed throughout this review, freeze tolerance is the result of many factors, making it difficult to generalize on the basis of any single trait.

Customized Yeast Application and Baking Procedures

The factor considered to be the most important in frozen-dough stability is the inverse relationship between the time of active fermentation before freezing and yeast stability in frozen doughs (Merritt, 1960; Kline and Sugihara, 1968; Tanaka et al, 1976; Hsu et al, 1979a; Hino et al, 1987, 1990; Holmes and Hoseney, 1987). Metabolic by-products formed during prefermentation, especially ethanol, are believed to make yeast cells less cryoresistant, resulting in increased amounts of yeast cell death upon freezing (Hsu et al, 1979a). In addition, yeast cells begin depleting intracellular levels of cryoprotective trehalose almost immediately upon contact with dough (Van der Plaat, 1988). Even under optimal conditions, this depletion occurs within 30 min of yeast addition (Neyreneuf and Van der Plaat, 1991), necessitating the baker's acute awareness of the impact of yeast activation on yeast freeze tolerance. Any practice, by either the yeast manufacturer or the baker, that helps minimize the amount of prefermentation before freezing will ultimately lead to improved yeast performance in frozen dough. Figure 5 gives a summary of such practices, with the following sections outlining these practices in greater detail.

Bulk Liquid Yeast

Bakeries have the option of using compressed, dry, or liquid yeast in the production of frozen doughs. Currently, compressed yeast is widely used for products with storage times of two to four weeks. To compensate for the adverse effects of freezing a compressed yeast, yeast addition is normally increased by 50–100% over standard levels (Bruinsma and Giesenschlag, 1984). Bulk liquid cream yeast systems, however, should offer advantages for frozen-dough applications. This form of yeast is more easily dispersed in doughs than compressed or dry yeast, ultimately resulting in decreased prefermentation times and minimizing the impact of ethanol on yeast cryoresistance. In addition, it is more evenly and uniformly held at reduced temperatures than other forms of yeast (generally 4°C). This slows yeast metabolic activity during the period between yeast manufacture and end-use and should result in improved cryoresistance. Potential advantages of liquid yeast for frozen-dough applications rely, of course, upon the baker appreciating the rationale behind its use and the strict adherence to customized bakery protocols designed to exploit these advantages.

Dry Yeast

In early studies with frozen doughs, it was believed that dry yeast was as efficient as compressed yeast and that dry yeast products at a high conversion ratio performed better (Zaehringer et al, 1951; Merritt, 1960; Lorenz and Bechtel, 1964; Reed, 1966; Marston, 1978). Theoretically, at least, the longer lag period with dry yeast should minimize fermentation before freezing and therefore result in a more stable frozen dough. However, it is now generally accepted that drying affects the structure and functional integrity of the cyto-

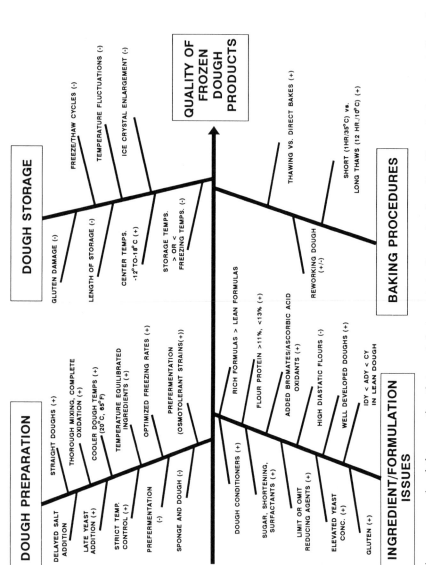

Fig. 5. This fishbone diagram summarizes bakery practices that may help to maximize frozen dough quality. Plus and minus signs indicate factors that may have positive and negative effects, respectively, on frozen dough quality.

plasmic membrane in a manner that increases the sensitivity of dry yeasts to freezing (Kline and Sugihara, 1968; Javes, 1971; Bruinsma and Giesenschlag, 1984; Wolt and D'Appolonia, 1984b; Van Dam, 1986). Wolt and D'Appolonia (1984b) found that initial proof times of active dry yeast and instant active dry yeast were shorter than those of compressed yeast in "no-time" dough formulations, but that as storage continued over 20 weeks, the proof times of dry yeast exceeded those of compressed yeast. Besides yeast performance itself, the differences in proof-time stability of frozen doughs was also possibly related to glutathione-induced damage of the gluten network. The compressed yeast, active dry yeast, and instant dry yeasts used in this study leached 0.0, 2.6, and 4.1 mg of glutathione/g of yeast (on a dry weight basis), respectively.

Recently, a form of dry yeast designed specifically for use in frozen doughs has been introduced to the marketplace (Spooner, 1990). Unlike typical dry yeasts, which have moisture levels of 5–6%, this frozen-dough dry yeast has a moisture content of approximately 25%. Prepared via a fluid bed process, only the unbound water is removed, causing lower levels of membrane damage and cell death than that typically seen in active dry yeast and instant dry yeast products. The free-flowing granular yeast is then frozen without the use of vacuum packs and can be stored up to one year at -18°C. Ice crystal formation and cell rupturing is reduced in severity due to the lack of external water. Certainly the cost of this product is higher than for compressed yeast, and it remains to be determined whether the added costs are justified in terms of improved product shelf life (claimed to be six months). At least in the North American marketplace it appears not to be so, as the manufacturer ceased the sale of this product in 1991. Performance may also be an issue, as other researchers have recently reported that a dry form of their compressed yeast produced via fluidized bed drying technology was significantly less effective in a French bread frozen-dough application than the compressed form of the same yeast (Neyreneuf and Van der Plaat, 1991). Compressed yeast therefore continues to be the most preferred form of yeast in the frozen-dough industry.

However, if a baker is considering the use of a dry yeast product, the instant form of yeast should be used to limit cell metabolism and prefermentation before freezing. While instant yeast can be added directly and uniformly to doughs without any rehydration, active dry yeast must first be rehydrated in 110–115°F (43–46°C) water for 5–15 min before being added to the doughs (Bruinsma and Giesenschlag, 1984). Active dry yeast will therefore produce a greater amount of ethanol and other volatile compounds in the time before freezing, lowering their ability to resist the deleterious effects of freezing on cell viability. An additional benefit can be derived from avoiding the use of room temperature yeasts and storing the yeast at refrigerated temperatures.

Customized Dough Processing Procedures

Timing of yeast addition. As mentioned previously, the more "activated" yeast is before freezing, the more likely it is to be adversely affected by freezing. Therefore, anything the baker can do to limit yeast activity before freezing will only improve yeast frozen-dough performance. Prefermentation can therefore be limited by adding the yeast to the mixer immediately before the start of mix. The yeast should be 33–38°F, not warmer, and compressed yeast should not be slurried to reduce friction-generated heat. Additional benefits can be derived from delaying yeast addition until after the start of mixing (Dubois and Blockcolsky, 1986; Evenson, 1987; Neyreneuf and Van der Plaat, 1991). For example, Neyreneuf and Van der Plaat (1991) recorded a 10–15% increase in frozen-dough baguette loaf volumes by delaying yeast addition until 15 min after the start of a 20 min mix cycle.

Straight doughs. Virtually all producers of frozen dough use a straight dough system (Spooner, 1990). While early studies indicated that it was feasible to prepare frozen doughs using a sponge and dough process (Javes, 1971; Hsu et al, 1979a), the fermentation that occurs during the sponge stage is now known to greatly contribute to quality deterioration. French bread prepared as no-time dough can be up to 30% larger in volume than loaves prepared using a 1-hr sponge, with the greater levels of yeast used in the sponge actually lowering loaf volumes through storage (Neyreneuf and Van der Plaat, 1991). No-time doughs can be further improved by using high-speed mixers to reduce mixing times. If a sponge system is used to develop flavor, no more than a third of the yeast should be used at this stage (Spooner, 1990).

Dough temperature. Frozen doughs are generally prepared at temperatures lower than those used for standard doughs (i.e., 20 vs. 24°C). Once again, the intent is to lower yeast activity during dough preparation. In one study (Neyreneuf and Van der Plaat, 1991), French bread loaf volumes, after 90 days of frozen storage, were 10–15% larger when the dough was prepared at 20°C rather than at 24°C. However, dough temperatures below 20°C actually diminish frozen-dough performance by not allowing for sufficient conditioning of the gluten in standard mixing times. The use of overly cooled flours should also be avoided, as these are slow to hydrate, creating an increase in hydration- and friction-generated forms of heat (detrimental if the yeast is added prematurely).

Formulation Issues

Yeast level. While many procedures can help minimize yeast sensitivity to freezing, it is important to remember that, even under ideal processing conditions, there will always be some loss in yeast viability as a result of freezing. The simplest way to compensate for this is to increase yeast levels in the formulation. The common industry practice is to double standard levels for frozen-dough formulations (Bruinsma and Giesenschlag, 1984). Fifty percent increases in yeast levels are feasible for products that are baked within two weeks of freezing (Neyreneuf and Van der Plaat, 1991). Bakers, through trial and error, should determine what additional levels of yeast are required to ensure acceptable product quality for their particular line of frozen-dough products.

Flour specifications. As with every type of baked product, flour provides the principal structural ingredient in frozen doughs. However, in light of the physical stresses that freezing and defrosting cycles place on gluten structure and dough integrity, frozen doughs should be prepared using high-quality flour only. One study conducted by Inoue and Bushuk (1992) concluded that flour from an overly strong wheat variety performed better in frozen doughs than flours with dough strength considered optimal for conventional baking. The superior performance of the overly strong flours was reported to be due to their ability to maintain higher oven-spring during baking, even after losing some of their intrinsic strength during freezing and frozen storage. This study suggested that protein content may be less important than protein quality. Extensigraph experiments comparing yeasted and nonyeasted doughs also show that the gluten structure of yeasted doughs is more vulnerable to damage from ice crystallization than that of nonyeasted doughs (Inoue and Bushuk, 1991). Presumably ruptured yeast cells release intracellular glutathione into the dough (glutathione is a strong reducing agent), which sensitizes the dough gluten network to damage from ice crystals. Combined together, the end result is slackened doughs and prolonged proof times. Generally, flours with a protein level in the range of 12.5–13.5% should be used, and it is not uncommon for frozen-dough manufacturers to supplement native protein with vital wheat gluten (Spooner, 1990; Neyreneuf and Van der Plaat, 1991).

Use of additives. Numerous studies have suggested that modifications to product formulations may help to correct defects that result from the freezing of dough. While many of these address only those defects that result from physical effects of freezing on dough structure, and not yeast viability, some do affect both. For example, products with rich formulas are well known to be more tolerant to the effects of freezing than those with lean formulas. The higher levels of sugar and shortening in the former type of product result in increased stabilization of the product's free water content (Hsu et al, 1979a). This minimizes ice crystallization in the frozen product (of benefit to dough structure and yeast viability) and reduces the amount of water drawn from yeast during freezing, enhancing cell viability. Frozen doughs are routinely supplemented with elevated levels of oxidants to chemically compensate for the damaging effects of freezing on dough gluten structure. While potassium bromate, azodicarbonamide, and ascorbic acid are commonly used for this purpose, at least one study cautions that potassium bromate can interfere with yeast activity in frozen-dough systems (Hsu et al, 1979b). Dough conditioner additives, such as sodium stearoyl lactylate and diacetyl tartaric acid esters of monoglycerides, are especially critical in frozen doughs to provide a dough-strengthening or conditioning effect to minimize losses in dough volume. However, they provide little, if any, measurable impact on yeast freeze tolerance (Davis, 1981; Wolt and D'Appolonia, 1984b).

Rates of freezing and thawing. The determination of the optimal condition for freezing dough is a trade-off between optimizing yeast cell viability and minimizing damage to dough structure. For example, it has been shown that slow dough freezing at -20°C is better for yeast viability than freezing at -40°C (Hsu et al, 1979b; Lehman and Dreese, 1981). However, slower freezes are known to increase problems with dough slackening and extended proof times (Varriano-Marston et al, 1980).

Experience has shown that more rapid freezing generally results in an acceptable retention of yeast viability with minimized damage to dough structure. Hsu et al (1979b), in a survey with freezing temperatures ranging from -10 to -78°C, followed by storage at -18°C, found that slower freezing rates, regardless of the temperature, resulted in increased yeast cell death. Furthermore, proof times and loaf volumes were most adversely affected by the coldest freezing temperatures. Transferring already frozen doughs to lower storage temperatures, rather than starting at the freezing temperature, was also found to increase proof times and decrease loaf volumes (although transferring to a warmer storage temperature had no deleterious effect). These results are considerably different than those seen when yeast is frozen in aqueous-based systems for long-term preservation, where colder temperatures generally enhance viability.

Recently, Trivedi et al (1989) recommend freezing quickly in blast freezers followed by storage at temperatures around -20°C (-5°F). The shell freezing technique is ideal for this application in that it allows for fast freezing within short periods. Only a 3- to 4-mm exterior layer of the dough is actually firmly solidified (to allow for shape retention), with core temperatures generally reading -7 to 0°C (20–32°F) (Spooner, 1990). The time required to reach these conditions will, of course, depend on the temperature of freezing, dough dimensions, and other factors addressed in other chapters of this book. Regardless of the method used, frozen doughs should be held as close as possible to the storage temperature until the time of thawing for baking. Ideally, there should be no opportunity for freeze-thaw cycles that would further decrease yeast viability and dough strength (Hsu et al, 1979a). It is worthwhile to note that doughs without gas are more dense, making them more heat-conductive than expanded, leavened doughs. These, therefore, freeze to the desired temperature more quickly, highlighting the advantage of minimizing yeast activation in frozen-dough products.

With regard to thawing conditions, Holmes and Hoseney (1987) examined the effects of thawing no-time doughs frozen for one week by one of four methods: in a 30°C proof cabinet for 1 hr; at 25°C for 1 hr; or in a 10°C refrigerator for 12 or 24 hr. The highest loaf volume and shortest proof times were obtained with the 1 hr thaw at 30°C. For example, thawing at 25°C nearly doubled the 30°C proof times (83 vs. 143 min), while thawing at refrigerated temperatures increased proof time from 83 to 110–120 min. Continued studies showed that proof times and loaf volumes could be further optimized by thawing at 38°C for 1 hr and then proofing to a constant height at 32°C. The enhanced yeast viability obtained by thawing at warmer temperatures was stated to be the reason behind the shorter proof times of the baked products, much in the same way that rehydrating dry yeast at warmer temperatures decreases yeast damage. However what effect, if any, thawing at the different temperatures had on the extent of ice-crystal-induced damage to the gluten network, and gas retention ability, was not considered in this study.

Future Approaches to Developing Improved Frozen-Dough Yeast

Recombinant DNA Technology

Even in a world in which change is commonplace, it is still almost hard to believe that the genetic engineering of yeasts via recombinant DNA technology has been possible only since 1978. That year, Hinnen et al (1978) demonstrated the complementation of a *leu2* (leucine) mutation in a haploid laboratory strain of yeast by transformation with a yeast *LEU2* gene. Since then, refinements in cloning procedures, vector construction, transformation procedures, addition of unique DNA sequences to conduct recombinant DNA research in a polyploid background (reviewed by Casey, 1991), and easy availability of reagents have all combined to make genetic engineering virtually routine in academic and industrial strains of *S. cerevisiae*.

On the surface, this technology should allow for the selective modification of the genetic composition of a baker's yeast without disrupting the countless desirable traits associated with good production yeast strains. Genes to be introduced to improve freeze tolerance could, in theory, be drawn from any source in nature (e.g., *S. rouxii* or *S. rosei*) and selectively introduced into baker's yeast strains. The reason this has not yet been accomplished is due to a lack of basic knowledge concerning the biochemistry, physiology, and genetics of freeze tolerance. In addition, freeze tolerance is undoubtedly a polygenic trait (more than one gene is involved), further complicating the application of recombinant DNA technology. A precise understanding of genes related to freeze tolerance, and their control mechanisms, is, therefore, a prerequisite before the industry can benefit from the successful application of recombinant DNA technology. However, one aspect of yeast metabolism that has potential involvement in yeast freeze tolerance and that has been elucidated on both the biochemical and genetic levels, is trehalose metabolism. As the following section describes, the first generation of recombinant frozen-dough baker's yeast may arise from constructs with altered trehalose metabolism.

Modified Trehalose Metabolism

Researchers have long known that trehalose levels are positively correlated with the gassing power of dry yeast (Pollock and Holmstrom, 1951), osmotolerant yeast (Mackenzie et al, 1988), and, as discussed previously, freeze-tolerant yeast. In yeast manufacturing, the lower growth rates imposed on yeast by lowered molasses feed at the end of fermentation result in elevated trehalose levels at the time of harvesting. As already discussed, however, this potentially cryoprotective substance is rapidly depleted in yeast with the onset of metabolic activity during dough preparation. A yeast that is genetically altered to be incapable of hydrolyzing intracellular trehalose would potentially be a superior strain of frozen-dough yeast. Such a yeast may soon be produced, as described in a patent application of Driessen et al (1994).

Before discussing the specifics of this patent, it is necessary to describe the pathways of trehalose anabolism (synthesis) and catabolism (breakdown) in yeast. As shown in Figure 6, two enzymes are involved in the biosynthesis of trehalose: trehalose-6-phosphate synthase and trehalose-6-phosphate phosphatase. Trehalose catabolism, however, is performed by a single cytoplasmic enzyme: phosphorylated trehalase. This latter enzyme increases six- to eightfold in activity upon the activation of yeast cells in dough and is responsible for the depletion of intracellular trehalose during prefermentation. In the late 1980s, in an excellent example of cooperation between industry and academia, Gist-Brocades N.V. (Delft, Netherlands) began funding long-term projects in Dutch universities designed to better elucidate the physiology and genetics of trehalose metabolism. A 1994 patent is presumably one of a stream of publications/patents that will flow from the findings of this program. In it, the cloning of an internal segment of the gene coding for cytosolic trehalase, from a lambda-based library of the *S. cerevisiae* genome, is described. Using this fragment in gene disruption experiments with diploid strains of *S. cerevisiae*, the patent describes the effects of inactivating at least one of the two endogenous genes encoding trehalase. Intracellular trehalase activity was diminished by at least 50% in these constructs, and in one strain trehalose levels were 25 times higher in the modified strain compared to levels in the untransformed parent (7.5 hr after transferring stationary-phase cells to a glucose-based medium). This clearly indicates the potential of this approach to alter yeast trehalose levels.

The patent claims that trehalase-inactivated yeast is superior frozen-dough yeast due to the inherently high levels of trehalose. Unfortunately, no data is presented to support this claim; however, it is highly probable that in the next few years patents will describe such experiments using industrial production strains in which all copies of the trehalase gene are inactivated. Given that these constructs do not involve the use of "foreign" DNA sequences, it seems likely that government regulatory agencies will grant approval for their use, leaving only public opinion to decide whether such yeasts have a place in the baker's yeast market. Given the growth rate of the frozen-dough industry and the need all companies have to introduce new products, if the constructs perform well in frozen-dough systems, it can only be assumed that such strains would be aggressively marketed.

However, there have already been attempts to market examples of genetically engineered baker's yeast. Produced using gene replacement and cotransformation procedures, one strain of baker's yeast has had the naturally inducile promoter sequences for maltose permease and maltase genes replaced with the strong constitutive yeast promoter for alcohol dehydrogenase (*ADH1*), result-ing in an 18–28% gassing improvement in lean dough systems (Osinga et al, 1989). Lacking any foreign DNA sequences, this yeast was approved for

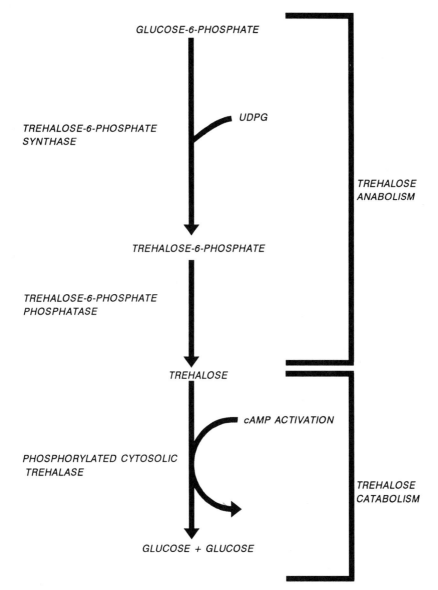

Fig. 6. Schematic representation of the pathways of trehalose metabolism in yeast. Two en-zymes, trehalose-6-phosphate synthase and trehalose-6-phosphate phosphatase, are involved in the biosynthesis of trehalose. The enzyme trehalase is responsible for the catabolism of trehalose in yeast.

manufacture in the United Kingdom by the Ministry of Agriculture, Fisheries and Foods in 1990 without requiring any labels on breads indicating the use of a genetically modified yeast strain (Aldhous, 1990). However, following considerable public furor over this matter, new laws were recently passed dealing with the issue of labeling products containing such organisms (Dixon, 1991). Presumably these recent experiences, combined with public acceptance or rejection of genetically modified yeast, will factor heavily in decisions regarding the introduction of yeast strains modified using recombinant DNA technology.

Cryoprotectant Proteins

It is well known that many life forms on this planet can survive and flourish in extremely cold environments. Research has shown that many of these organisms possess antifreeze proteins that considerably lower the temperatures at which cytosolic freezing will occur. At DNA Plant Technology Corporation (Oakland, CA), scientists have synthesized a gene that codes for an antifreeze protein similar to the one that keeps the winter flounder from freezing in polar seas (Anonymous, 1991). Studies with greenhouse tomatoes transformed with this antifreeze protein show that such tomatoes are more resistant to the deleterious effects of freeze-thaw cycles on flavor and texture. As an additive to ice cream and ice milk, the protein has been reported to reduce ice crystal size, eliminating the grainy texture often associated with these products. With yeast, the protein has been shown to result in a two- to fourfold increase in cell count after freezing and thawing (Anonymous, 1991). Whether such yeasts could result in superior frozen-dough yeast strains remains to be determined. Given that the gene involved does not originate from a yeast source, it can only be assumed that any production strain constructed in this manner would require several years to satisfy technical, government, and public concerns.

Novel Processing Developments

Undercooling

Undercooling is a technology that allows for the benefits of low-temperature storage without the disadvantages associated with freezing. In bulk water, freezing occurs because insoluble particulate matter catalyzes ice nucleation at temperatures below 0°C. In undercooling, this nucleation of ice is largely prevented by dispersing the water as small droplets throughout an inert nonaqueous carrier phase that does not catalyze ice nucleation (Mathias, 1991). While those droplets containing dust or pyrogen particles will freeze, the majority of the water remains liquid, as the ice cannot propagate through the carrier. In this manner, red blood cells have been cooled to -38°C and microbial cell suspensions to -25°C before freezing begins (Franks et al, 1983). While currently being used to stabilize enzymes and other biologically active substances in the biotechnology industry, this technology may offer a way to manufacture yeast for the frozen-dough industry. In addition to reducing yeast metabolic activity and prolonging yeast lag time during mixing, such yeasts would have considerably enhanced shelf life and consistency in performance.

Concluding Remarks

The development of superior frozen-dough products requires more than the selection of a yeast strain with inherent resistance to freezing. Processes related to the manufacture of baker's yeast and practices involved in the production of frozen bakery products can affect yeast frozen-dough performance. The interactive effects of yeast-, manufacturing-, and bakery-related variables must be considered in the development of strategies aimed at improving the performance of yeast in frozen dough. Progress being made in our understanding of yeast biochemistry, and the underlying genetic elements responsible for freeze-tolerance traits, may soon offer opportunities to exploit the tools of biotechnology to create improved strains of yeast for frozen dough. Ultimately, it will be the coordinated efforts of the scientist, manufacturer, and baker that will produce superior frozen-dough products.

Literature Cited

Aldhous, P. 1990. Modified yeast fine for food. Nature 344:186.

Anonymous. 1991. DNAP synthesizes gene for fish "antifreeze". Biotechnol. News 11:4-5.

Autio, K., and Sinda, E. 1992. Frozen doughs: Rheological changes and yeast viability. Cereal Chem. 69:409-413.

Baguena, R., Soriano, M. D., Martinez-Anaya, M. A., and De Barber, C. B. 1991. Viability and performance of pure yeast strains in frozen wheat dough. J. Food Sci. 56:1690-1698.

Barnett, J. A., Payne, R. W., and Yarrow, D. 1983. Yeasts: Characteristics and Identification, 1st ed. Cambridge University Press, Cambridge, UK.

Berglund, P. T., Shelton, D. R., and Freeman, T. P. 1991. Frozen bread dough ultrastructure as affected by duration of frozen storage and freeze-thaw cycles. Cereal Chem. 68:105-107.

Bruinsma, B. L., and Giesenschlag, J. 1984. Frozen dough performance. Compressed yeast—Instant dry yeast. Baker's Dig. 58(6):6-7, 11.

Casey, G. P. 1991. Yeast selection in brewing. Pages 65-111 in: Yeast Strain Selection. C. J. Panchal, ed. Marcel Dekker, New York.

Casey, G. P., Pringle, A. T., and Erdmann, P. A. 1990. Evaluation of recent techniques used to identify individual strains of *Saccharomyces* yeasts. J. Am. Soc. Brew. Chem. 48:100-106.

Clegg, J. S. 1986. The physical properties and metabolic status of *Artemia* cysts at low water contents: The "water replacement hypothesis." Pages 169-187 in: Membranes, Metabolism and Dry Organisms. A. C. Leopold, ed. Cornell University Press, Ithaca, NY.

Clegg, J. S., Seitz, P., and Hazelwood, C. F. 1982. Cellular responses to extreme water loss. Cryobiology 19:306-316.

Clement, P., and Hennette, A. L. 1982. Strains of yeast for bread making and novel strains of yeast thus prepared. U.S. patent no. 4,318,930.

Coutinho, C., Bernardes, E., Felix, D., and Panek, A. D. 1988. Trehalose as cryoprotectant for preservation of yeast strains. J. Biotechnol. 7:23-32.

Crowe, J. H., Crowe, L. M., and Chapman, D. 1984. Preservation of membranes in anhydrobiotic organisms: The role of trehalose. Science 223:701-703.

D'Amore, T., Crumplen, R., and Stewart, G. G. 1991. The involvement of trehalose in yeast stress tolerance. J. Ind. Microbiol. 7:191-196.

Davis, E. W. 1981. Shelf-life studies on frozen doughs. Baker's Dig. 55(3):12, 13, 16.

Dixon, B. 1991. U.K. targets some gene modified foods. Bio/Technology 9:227.

Donnini, C., Paglisi, P. P., Vecli, A., and Marmiroli, N. 1988. Germination of *Saccharomyces cerevisiae* ascospores without trehalose mobilization as revealed by *in vivo* ^{13}C NMR spectroscopy. J. Bacteriol. 170:3789-3791.

Driessen, M., Osinga, K. A., and Herweijer, M. A. 1994. Recombinant DNA encoding neutral trehalase. U.S. patent no. 5,312,909.

Dubois, D. K., and Blockcolsky, D. 1986. Frozen bread dough. Effect of dough mixing and thawing methods. AIB Tech. Bull. Vol. VIII, No. 6. American Institute of Baking, Manhattan, KS.

Evenson, M. 1987. New developments in frozen dough technology. Pages 85-89 in: Proc. 63rd Annual Meeting of the American Society of Baking Engineers. The Society, Chicago, IL.

Franks, F., Mathias, S., Galfre, P., and Brown, D. 1983. Ice nucleation and freezing in undercooled cells. Cryobiology 20:298-309.

Gehrke, H. H., Pralle, K., and Deckwer, W. D. 1992. Freeze drying of microorganisms. Influence of cooling rate on survival. Food Biotechnol. 6:35-49.

Gelinas, P., and Goulet, J. 1991. Morphology of bakers' yeast and dissolved oxygen saturation during fed-batch growth. Letters Appl. Microbiol. 12:164-170.

Gelinas, P., Fiset, G., LeDuy, A., and Goulet, J. 1989. Effect of growth conditions and trehalose content on cryotolerance of bakers' yeast in frozen doughs. Appl. Environ. Microbiol. 55:2453-2459.

Gelinas, P., Toupin, C. J., and Goulet, J. 1991a. Cell water permeability and cryotolerance of *Saccharomyces cerevisiae*. Lett. Appl. Microbiol. 12:236-240.

Gelinas, P., Fiset, G., Willemot, C., and Goulet, J. 1991b. Lipid content and cryotolerance of bakers' yeast in frozen doughs. Appl. Environ. Microbiol. 57:463-468.

Grba, S., Oura, E., and Suomalainen, H. 1975. On the formation of glycogen and trehalose in baker's yeast. Eur. J. Appl. Microbiol. 2:29-37.

Grout, B., Morris, J., and McLellan, M. 1990. Cryopreservation and the maintenance of cell lines. Trends Biotechnol. 8:293-297.

Groves, D. P., and Oliver, S. G. 1984. Formation of intergenic hybrids of yeast by protoplast fusion of *Yarrowia* and *Kluyveromyces* species. Curr. Genet. 8:49-55.

Hahn, Y. S., and Kawai, H. 1990. Isolation and characterization of freeze-tolerant yeasts from nature available for the frozen-dough method. Agric. Biol. Chem. 54:829-831.

Hinnen, A., Hicks, J. B., and Fink, G. R. 1978. Transformation of yeast. Proc. Natl. Acad. Sci. USA 75:1929-1933.

Hino, A., Takano, H., and Tanaka, Y. 1987. New freeze-tolerant yeast for frozen dough preparations. Cereal Chem. 64:269-275.

Hino, A., Mihara, K., Nakashima, K., and Takano, H. 1990. Trehalose levels and survival ratio of freeze-tolerant versus freeze-sensitive yeasts. Appl. Environ. Microbiol. 56:1386-1391.

Hino, A., Wongkhalaung, C., Kawai, S., Murao, S., Yano, K., Takano, H., and Takagi, M. 1992. Construction of a genetic transformation system for a freeze-tolerant yeast *Kluyveromyces thermotolerans*. Biosci. Biotech. Biochem. 56:228-232.

Holmes, J. T., and Hoseney, R. C. 1987. Frozen doughs: Freezing and thawing rates and the potential of using a combination of yeast and chemical leavening. Cereal Chem. 64:348-351.

Hsu, K. H., Hoseney, R. C., and Seib, P. A. 1979a. Frozen dough. I. Factors affecting stability of yeasted doughs. Cereal Chem. 56:419-424.

Hsu, K. H., Hoseney, R. C., and Seib, P. A. 1979b. Frozen dough. II. Effects of freezing and storing conditions on the stability of yeasted doughs. Cereal Chem. 56:424-426.

Inoue, Y., and Bushuk, W. 1991. Studies on frozen doughs. I. Effects of frozen storage and freeze-thaw cycles on baking and rheological properties. Cereal Chem. 68:627-631.

Inoue, Y., and Bushuk, W. 1992. Studies on frozen doughs. II. Flour quality requirements for bread production from frozen dough. Cereal Chem. 69:423-428.

Jacobson, G. K., and Trivedi, N. 1987. Yeast strains, method of production and use in baking. U.S. patent no. 4,643,901.

Javes, R. 1971. The ingredients and the processes. Effect on shelf life of frozen, unbaked yeast-leavened dough. Baker's Dig. 45(2):56-59.

Kane, S. M., and Roth, R. 1974. Carbohydrate metabolism during ascospore development in yeast. J. Bacteriol. 118:8-14.

Kawai, M., and Kazuo, U. 1983. Doughs comprising alcohol resistant yeasts. European patent no. 78182.

Kline, L., and Sugihara, T. F. 1968. Factors affecting the stability of frozen bread doughs. I. Prepared by the straight dough method. Baker's Dig. 42(5):44-54, 69.

Lehmann, T. A., and Dreese, P. 1981. Stability of frozen bread doughs. Effects of freezing temperature. AIB Tech. Bull. Vol. III, No. 7. American Institute of Baking, Manhattan, KS.

Leopold, A. C., ed. 1986. Membranes, Metabolism and Dry Organisms. Cornell University Press, Ithaca, NY.

Levitt, J. 1966. Winter hardiness in plants. Pages 495-563 in: Cryobiology. H. T. Meryman, ed. Academic Press, New York.

Lillie, S. H., and Pringle, J. R. 1980. Reserve carbohydrate metabolism in Saccharomyces cerevisiae: Responses to nutrient limitation. J. Bacteriol. 143:1384-1394.

Lorenz, K., and Bechtel, W. G. 1964. Frozen bread dough. Baker's Dig. 38(6):59-63.

Lovelock, J. E. 1954. Physical instability and thermal shock in red cells. Nature 173:659-661.

Mackenzie, K. F., Singh, K. K., and Brown, A. D. 1988. Water stress plating hypersensitivity of yeasts: Protective role of trehalose in Saccharomyces cerevisiae. J. Gen. Microbiol. 134:1661-1666.

Marston, P. E. 1978. Frozen dough for breadmaking. Baker's Dig. 52(5):18-20,37.

Mathias, S. F. 1991. Undercooling–Low temperature without freezing. Trends Biotechnol. 9:370-372.

Matsutani, K., Fukuda, Y., Murata, K., Kimura, A., Nakamura, I., and Yajima, N. 1990. Physical and biochemical properties of freeze-tolerant mutants of a yeast Saccharomyces cerevisiae. J. Ferment. Bioeng. 70:275-276.

Mazur, P. 1961. Manifestations of injury in yeast cells exposed to subzero temperatures. II. Changes in specific gravity and in the concentration and quantity of cell solids. J. Bacteriol. 82:673-684.

Mazur, P. 1965. The role of cell membranes in the freezing of yeast and other single cells. Ann. N.Y. Acad. Sci. 125:658-676.

Mazur, P. 1966. Physical and chemical basis of injury in single-celled micro-organisms subjected to freezing and thawing. Pages 214-315 in: Cryobiology. H. T. Meryman, ed. Academic Press, New York.

Mazur, P. 1967. Physical-chemical basis of injury from intracellular freezing in yeast. Pages 171-189 in: Cellular Injury and Resistance in Freezing Organisms. E. Asahina, ed. Proc. International Conference on Low Temperature Science. 1966. Vol. 2. Institute of Low Temperature Science, Hokkaido University, Sapporo, Japan.

Mazur, P. 1970. Cryobiology: The freezing of biological systems. Science 168:939-949.

Mazur, P., and Schmidt, J. 1968. Interactions of cooling velocity, temperature, and warming velocity on the survival of frozen and thawed yeast. Cryobiology 5:1-17.

Merritt, P. P. 1960. The effect of preparation on the stability and performance of frozen, un-baked yeast leavened doughs. Baker's Dig. 34(4):57-61.

Meryman, H. T. 1968. Modified model for the mechanism of freezing injury in erythrocytes. Nature 218:333-336.

Nagodawithana, T., and Trivedi, N. B. 1991. Yeast selection for baking. Pages 139-184 in: Yeast Strain Selection. C. J. Pandchal, ed. Marcel Dekker, New York.

Nakatomi, Y., Saito, H., Nagashima, A., and Umeda, F. 1985. Saccharomyces species FD 612 and the utilization thereof in bread production. U.S. patent no. 4,547,374.

Neyreneuf, O., and Van der Plaat, J. B. 1991. Preparation of frozen French bread dough with improved stability. Cereal Chem. 68:60-66.

Novak, S., D'Amore, T., Russell, I., and Stewart, G. G. 1991. Sugar uptake in a 2-deoxy-D-glucose resistant mutant of *Saccharomyces cerevisiae*. J. Ind. Microbiol. 7:35-40.

Oda, Y., and Ouchi, K. 1990. Hybridization of bakers' yeast by the rare-mating method to improve leavening ability in dough. Enzyme Microb. Technol. 12:989-993.

Oda, Y., Uno, K., and Ohta, S. 1986. Selection of yeasts for breadmaking by the frozen-dough method. Appl. Environ. Microbiol. 52:941-943.

Ohshima, Y., Sugaura, T., Horita, M., and Sasaki, T. 1987. Industrial application of artificially induced diploid strains of *Torulaspora delbrueckii*. Appl. Environ. Microbiol. 53:1512-1514.

Osinga, K. A., Renniers, A. C. H. M., Welbergen, J. W., Roobol, R. H., and van der Wilden, W. 1989. Maltose fermentation in *Saccharomyces cerevisiae*. Yeast 5(special issue):S207-S212.

Oura, E., Suomalainen, H., and Parkkinen, E. 1974. Changes in commercial baker's yeast during its ripening period. Proc. Intl. Symp. on Yeast, 4th. B25:125-126.

Panek, A. D., and Panek, A. C. 1990. Metabolism and thermotolerance function of trehalose in *Saccharomyces*: A current perspective. J. Biotechnol. 14:229-238.

Panek, A. D., Sampaio, A L., Braz, G. C., Baker, S. J., and Mattoon, J. R. 1979. Genetic and metabolic control of trehalose and glycogen synthesis. New relationships between energy reserves, catabolite repression and maltose utilization. Cell. Molec. Biol. 25:345-354.

Pollock, G. E., and Holmstrom, C. D. 1951. The trehalose content and the quality of active dry yeast. Cereal Chem. 28:498-505.

Rank, G. H., Casey, G. P., Xiao, W., and Pringle, A. T. 1991. Polymorphism within the nuclear and 2μm genomes of *Saccharomyces cerevisiae*. Curr. Genet. 20:189-194.

Reed, G. 1966. Yeast, what it does and how. Pages 126-133 in: Proc.. 42nd Annual Meeting of the American Society of Bakery Engineers. The Society, Chicago.

Sasaki, T., and Ohshima, Y. 1987. Induction and characterization of artificial diploids from the haploid yeast *Torulaspora delbrueckii*. Appl. Environ. Microbiol. 53:1504-1511.

Spencer, J. F. T., Spencer, D. M., and Bruce, I. J. 1989. Protoplast formation and fusion. Pages 64-69 in: Yeast Genetics. A Manual of Methods. Springer-Verlag, New York.

Spooner, T. F. 1990. Hot prospects from frozen doughs. Baking Snack Systems 12(11):18-22.

Suoranta, K. 1991. A novel high density yeast preparation, a method for producing the same, and the use thereof. International patent application no. WO 91/12315.

Takano, H., Hino, A., Endo, H., Nakagawa, N., and Sato, A. 1990. Novel bakers' yeast. European patent application no. 90400634.3.

Tanaka, Y., Kawaguchi, M., and Miyatake, M. 1976. Studies on the injury of yeast in frozen dough. II. Effect of ethanol on the frozen storage of baker's yeast. J. Food Sci. Technol. 23(9):419.

Thevelein, J. M. 1984. Regulation of trehalose mobilization in fungi. Microbiol. Rev. 48:42-59.

Trivedi, N., Hauser, J., Nagodawithana, T., and Reed, G. 1989. Update on baker's yeast. AIB Tech. Bull. Vol. XI, No. 2. American Institute of Baking, Manhattan, KS.

Uno, K., Oda, Y., and Shigenori, O. 1986. Freeze resistant dough and novel microorganisms for use therein. European patent application no. 86302275.2.

Van Dam, H. 1986. The biotechnology of baker's yeast: Old or new business? Pages 117-131 in: Chemistry and Physics of Baking. J. M. Blanshard, P. J. Frazier, and T. Galliard, eds. Royal Society of Chemistry, London, England.

Van der Plaat, J. B. 1988. Baker's yeast in frozen dough. State of the art. Pages 110-129 in: Cereal Science and Technology in Sweden. N. G. Asp, ed. University of Lund, Lund, Sweden.

Van Laere, A. 1989. Trehalose, reserve and/or stress metabolite? FEMS Microbiol. Rev. 63:201-210.

Van Solingen, P., and Van der Plaat, J. B. 1977. Fusion of yeast spheroplasts. J. Bacteriol. 130:946-947.

Van Zyl, P. J., Kilian, S. G., and Prior, B. A. 1990. The role of an active transport mechanism in glycerol accumulation during osmoregulation by *Zygosaccharomyces rouxii*. Appl. Microbiol. Biotechnol. 34:231-235.

Varriano-Marston, E., Hsu, K. H., and Mahdi, J. 1980. Rheological and structural changes in frozen dough. Baker's Dig. 54(1):32-34, 41.

Wiemken, A. 1990. Trehalose in yeast, stress protectant rather than reserve carbohydrate. Antonie van Leeuwenhoek 58:209-217.

Windisch, S., Kowalski, S., and Zander, I. 1976. Dough raising tests with hybrid yeasts. Eur. J. Appl. Microbiol. 3:213-221.

Wolt, M. J., and D'Appolonia, B. L. 1984a. Factors involved in the stability of frozen dough. I. The influence of yeast reducing compounds on frozen-dough stability. Cereal Chem. 61:209-212.

Wolt, M. J., and D'Appolonia, B. L. 1984b. Factors involved in the stability of frozen dough. II. The effects of yeast type, flour type, and dough additives on frozen-dough stability. Cereal Chem. 61:213-221.

Zaehringer, M. V., Mayfield, H. L., and Odland, L. M. 1951. The effect of certain variations in fat, yeast and liquid on the frozen storage of yeast doughs. Food Res. 16:353-357.

Preparation of Stable Sourdoughs and Sourdough Starters by Drying and Freeze-Drying

G. Spicher
Federal Center for Cereal, Potato and Lipid Research
Detmold, Germany

Sourdoughs are predominantly used in production of breads containing rye. The question of how much acid the rye products require for proper acidification can be answered by the behavior of the dough properties after addition of all dough liquids.

In wheat flour doughs, the stability and gas-retaining capacity are provided by gluten-forming proteins. Water binding is also an important property, since the water is bound by gluten during dough formation and serves during baking as a source of water for starch gelatinization.

The proteins of rye flours lack gluten-forming properties. Their swelling capacity is favored by an acidic environment, which also diminishes the activity of flour enzymes. Doughs produced from rye flours containing proper levels of hydrophilic rye flour components (rye gums such as pentosans or proteins), in the absence of excessive enzyme activities and when optimally acidified, typically yield good quality breads with an elastic and chewy crumb.

Sourdoughs are also used in the production of various wheat-based bakery products. In this application, they function partly as leaveners (e.g., for panettone, special breads, small bakery products) and partly but most importantly as flavor and taste improvers. The keeping quality, e.g., rope-prevention, of these products is also enhanced by higher acidity.

Definition of Sourdough

In Germany, various authors (Bode and Seibel, 1982; Seibel, 1986; Bruemmer and Huber, 1987) defined sourdoughs and related products as follows:

Sourdough is an ingredient containing cereal components (often also other formula ingredients), liquids, and active microorganisms (e.g., lactobacilli and yeasts). When employed, sourdoughs generate acidity continuously without a complete interruption of microbial activity at any time. Indigenous flour microorganisms can also be activated during this process. In addition to microbial and enzymatic reactions, changes in physical dough properties take place.

The multiplication and metabolism of the microflora can be enhanced by suitable selection of normal baking temperatures, dough resting times, and dough consistencies. Sourdoughs can be used for inoculation of new sourdough preparations. Their activity can be maintained by periodically supplying cereal products and water. The maximum degree of acidity is 40 units (a unit is expressed as milliliters of $0.1N$ sodium hydroxide necessary to titrate 10.0 g of sourdough in 100 ml of water to pH 8.5).

Role of Sourdoughs

Wheat or rye sourdoughs today perform various functions, which can be summarized as follows: 1) They improve by acidification the technological quality of doughs containing rye flour. 2) They generate flavor and aroma compounds, such as lactic acid, acetic acid, alcohols, carbonyls, and protein decomposition products, which act as flavor precursors. 3) They protect the panary fermentation from alien fermentations. 4) They provide certain synergistic effects on yeast. 5) They show antagonistic action toward fungi and protect against rope-forming microorganisms.

As a rule, doughs containing more than 20% rye flour (based on total flour) require acidification. When using rye flours of normal quality at levels of 35–45% of total flour, the bread doughs should be acidified to assure best-quality breads. The pH values of these doughs should be kept within 4.2–4.7; higher pH is advisable for doughs with lower rye flour content and lower enzyme activity.

The degree of acidity of rye bakery products is dependent on the quality of sourdough used. Sourdough quality is related to the extraction rate of the rye flour used as well as to the method of sourdough preparation. These effects are shown in Table 1.

A series of bread faults may result from inadequate or inappropriate acidification. In particular, the crumb elasticity is positively correlated with pH values. When an optimal degree of acidification has been exceeded, the crumb structure becomes coarse, with somewhat dense grain cells; the texture in that case is soft and cohesive (Spicher and Stephan, 1993).

Procedures to Extend the Keeping Quality of Sourdoughs

The objective of extending the keeping quality of sourdoughs is to keep the sourdoughs in a biologically active state, ready for addition to doughs in uniform doses. Sourdoughs should have long-term stability and should be suitable as starters for new sourdoughs as well as for acidification of production doughs.

According to the specifications, sourdough preparations are required to possess, after water addition, sufficient activity to allow further propagation and to permit bakery production to be carried out within normal schedules (Bruemmer and Huber, 1987).

Freezing of mature sourdoughs has not been commercialized as yet.

Formation of High Acidity

This method is the subject of a patent (Menge, 1980). A cereal mash is inoculated with about 10% (total grain basis of the mash) of a culture consisting of pure and mixed strains of heterofermentative lactobacilli (e.g., *Lactobacillus brevis* or *L. fermentum*) and fermented at 27°C for 48 hr. The over-acidification at completion of this fermentation inhibits further microbial activity (self-preservation).

The liquid sourdoughs are hermetically packaged (in acid-resistant wrappers, e.g., polyethylene bags or glass bottles). The stability of these products for home applications is generally six months. The liquid sourdoughs can be further subjected to various methods of drying, e.g., spray-, roller-, foam-, or freeze-drying (Menge, 1980).

Partial Moisture Removal

Partially dehydrated sourdoughs are marketed in Germany under the name Boecker Reinzucht Sauerteig (Boecker Pure-Culture Sourdough, A.G.). These products are not sterile and should be used within months. Their microbial composition is not defined. Their total cell count is about 10^9 per gram of sourdough, with the predominant part of the microflora consisting of *L. brevis* ssp. *lindneri* and *L. sanfrancisco*. Yeast cell plate count in this starter amounts to 5×10^5 to 10×10^6 per gram. The yeast present is mainly *Candida milleri* (Boecker et al, 1990).

Table 1
pH Values and Acidity of German Commercial Rye Breads

Bread Type	Recommended Levels	
	pH Value	Acidity (degrees)[a]
Rye bread	4.2–4.3	8.0–10.0
Rye-mix bread (50–89% rye)	4.3–4.6	7.0–9.0
Wheat-mix bread (50–89% wheat)	4.6–5.2	5.0–8.0
Cracked rye/whole kernel	4.4–4.7	8.0–14.0
Cracked rye-wheat/whole kernel	4.5–4.8	7.0–12.0
Cracked wheat-rye/whole kernel	4.8–5.4	6.0–10.0

[a] Degree = milliliters of $0.1N$ NaOH necessary to titrate 10 g of bread in 100 ml of water to pH 8.5.

Drying

Various authors recommend kneading of sourdough into flour as the best method for drying of sourdoughs. This method can be recommended (if at all) only for small-scale drying, as in households.

For production of a starter suitable for storage, addition of onions and spices to a fully matured sour is recommended. These should be chopped onions (one to two, corresponding to 1.6–2.0% [weight basis]) and a 0.05–0.5%, preferably 0.12% (weight basis), mixture of spices, consisting of two parts caraway seeds, one part anise, and one part fennel. One part by weight of sour is blended with two parts rye flour, and the blend is then air-dried for several hours. When packaged in granulated form, the air-dried starter keeps for several months under normal storage conditions. The activity of the microflora does not deteriorate appreciably (Kretzchmar, 1986; Wolff, 1986) during this storage period. This procedure is also suitable for preparation of spray-dried sourdoughs in conjunction with a vibrating belt granulator.

For conversion of bacterial cell masses (mainly of *L. brevis* DSM 2647) into granular or fluidized-bed dried forms, the cell suspension is first sprayed onto a fluidized bed and onto powder or granule-forming carriers.

The moisture of the dispersed mass and the carrier is reduced to about 9.0% (91% solids) by drying with hot gases (90–120°C) for approximately 30 min. The temperature of the product at that point reaches 20–40°C. The dried product is packaged under oxygen-free protective gas. The dried storage-stable sourdough, in powder form or as a granular preparation, generally contains 60–95% solids and, upon rehydration, at least 10^9–10^{11} viable cells per gram. The spray-dried product, kept under inert gas protection, can be stored for several months at room temperature (Hill, 1985).

In the preparation of granular, biologically active dry sourdough, which can be reactivated by whipping in water, a starter prepared as described above (with yields of 230–350 parts water per 100 parts flour) or a blend of pure cultures of several lactobacilli is sprayed onto a cereal flour product imbedded in a fluid-bed granulator. The drying step proceeds until the product temperature reaches 20–36°C (the pH of the product is 3.3–4.8, optimally 3.6).

The special advantage of the process is that the sourdoughs with dough yields in excess of 230 (100 parts flour and 130 parts water) can be directly utilized without further processing. The dry sour can be prepared according to varied production parameters, e.g., by a suitable selection of dough yield. The flour portion in the dry sourdough can be adjusted so that, during the reactivation, the refreshening treatment step with flour can be deleted. Upon drying, the granular product reaches 5–15% moisture and has good stability even when not refrigerated (Koehler et al, 1985).

Cooling

Kline and Sugihara (1971) describe the preparation of liquid starter for production of U.S. San Francisco french sourdough bread. This starter consists of water (150–300 parts), and flour (l00 parts), salt (one to three parts per l00 parts flour), and viable cells of *Torulopsis holmii* (asporogenic strain of *Saccharomyces exiguus*) and *L. sanfrancisco*. The culture is incubated at 12–27°C. The inoculation level varies from 1 to 5×10^6 yeast cells per gram, with the bacterial cell count 30–100 times higher than that of the yeast. The product can be cooled to 10–13°C and kept for future use at that temperature.

Freeze-Drying

The last important sourdough preservation procedure by water is freeze-drying (Klinga, 1983). There are various methods to accomplish it.

One method adds a heterofermentative lactobacillus culture as a starter to a conventionally prepared dough. The matured sourdough is dried, after addition of a protective colloid, to a product moisture level of 6–12% (preferably 7–9%). This preparation can be readily reactivated (Belohlawek and Laue, 1985).

According to another procedure, a pure-culture sour is added to sourdough and incubated. After fermentation (final pH, 3.8–4.0), the sourdough is frozen to a center temperature of -10 to -30°C and dried under high vacuum. During the actual drying step, sufficient heat is gradually supplied for vapor formation, which is simultaneously removed by vacuum. The absolute vapor pressure must be kept under that of ice, to prevent melting of the material that is being freeze-dried. After freeze-drying, the sourdough is milled to the desired particle size.

Evaluation of Sourdough Stability

New knowledge of the microbiology of sourdoughs and recognition of the significance of the action of lactobacillus species in various baking technology applications has lead to the development of stable sourdough preparations.

These fermentation starters are commercially distributed, along with instructions for sourdough preparation. Only in one case (Spicher and Stephan, 1993), are microbial composition data and a guaranteed level of viable cells given.

The development of stable sourdoughs and starters requires their control and quality assessment. This evaluation can be achieved by experimental baking tests (Bruemmer and Stephan, 1986). In these tests, the variable effects of flour quality and its microflora become especially significant in long-term fermentations. Information about microbial activity and acidification characteristics is gained when the tests are made under well-defined experimental conditions, especially in regard to the substrate composition and the proposed incubation temperatures. Generally, use of three temperatures is proposed for testing:

- 15°C, a general temperature for growth of streptobacteria. At this temperature, the lactobacilli of the *Thermobacterium* group fail to grow.
- 45°C, a temperature that permits growth of thermobacteria but not of streptobacteria.
- 30°C, a temperature that is tolerated by all lactobacilli and supports their optimal multiplication.

In description and evaluation of the behavior of the microflora, the parameters to be considered depend on the definition of the reactive sourdough. These include: microbial cell count, composition of the microflora, and the acidity-forming activity or acidifying characteristics of the sourdough. In this evaluation, considerations are given to microbial growth and acidification temperature ranges, end pH values, and the progress and extent of acid formation under optimum temperature conditions.

Sourdoughs as Dry Preparations

The content of lactobacilli in commercial products varies within the range of 40 to 2.4×10^6/g of sourdough (Table 2). The yeast cell count per gram is generally below 10^1. The pH values range from 4.5 to 3.3, and the degree of acidity from 33.5 to as high as 95.7 units. The high values indicate that the sourdoughs were also partly acidified by addition of acids (values higher than 50 units are due to acid addition).

After transfer of stable sourdoughs to growth medium and incubation at optimal temperature, the cell count reaches a level, generally within 24 hr, that corresponds to that originally used for inoculation of the sourdough before drying (approximate counts: 1.0×10^{10} lactobacilli per gram and 1.0×10^7 yeast per gram).

The acidification characteristics demonstrate that the microflora at optimal temperature (30°C) cause pH reductions partly after 9 hr and partly after 30 hr.

Breads produced using dry sourdoughs are not fully comparable in flavor to sourdough breads from formulations with high levels of rye flours. These products are recommended for wheat breads and breads produced with relatively low rye flour levels, since the predominant factor in these types of breads is not acidification but the taste effect of the formed acids (Bruemmer and Stephan, 1986).

Sourdough Starter

The starters contain cell counts of 3.0×10^4 to 6.0×10^9 per gram of viable lactic acid bacteria (Table 3). Besides lactobacilli, starters contain either no yeast cells or a low count (1.0×10^3 to 2.0×10^5 yeast cells per gram). There are also differences between original pH and acid values of starters. The pH values

Table 2
Indices of German Commercial Dry Sourdoughs

| Product | Microbial Cell Count per Gram | | pH | Acidity (degrees) |
	Lctobacilli	Yeast		
B-1	70,000	<10	4.5	36.3
B-2	250,000	<10	3.8	35.5
B-5	40	300	3.3	95.7
B-6	2.4×10^6	140	3.9	37.5
B-7	460	<19	3.7	81.3

range from 7.0 to 3.6, and the acidity units are within the range of 0.25–37.8 (Table 3). Sourdough starters further differ in composition, containing different levels of homofermenting and heterofermenting lactobacilli.

As a rule, it is necessary to determine the multiplication of lactobacilli at the optimum temperature for the time range of 24 hr. There are characteristic differences in growth rate between 15 and 45°C in this respect. Certain starters show a maximum cell multiplication at 30°C, while others multiply more rapidly at 45°C. Part of the microflora is characterized by initially having a broad range of optimum temperature for growth (30–45°C), which levels off at 30°C after 24 hr. Lactobacilli in a few sourdough starters do not multiply further at 15°C (Spicher and Stephan, 1993).

Utilization of Stable Sourdough Starters

Sourdoughs prepared from dry or freeze-dried starters do not require further preparation or activation when used in bread production. No problems in bread production are encountered that are attributable to differences in sourdough processing. Also, remarkable fermentation losses are not observed. Dry sourdoughs are available for use at any time of the day and week.

Dry Sourdough As Sourdough-Starters

Bruemmer and Stephan (1986) proposed to use dry sourdoughs mainly for practical baking as starters. In this application, one must consider whether the specified requirements for microbiological and acidification behaviors of the microflora should be different from those of conventional sourdoughs. These reservations apply less to the use of dry sourdough as a starter than to the required processing conditions (amount of starter, temperature, pH value, acidity degree, fermentation time) and to the parameters applied to their quality evaluation.

Discussion

According to German specifications, stable sourdoughs require the stabilization of doughs for acidification and propagation without appreciable damage

Table 3
Indices of German Commercial Sourdough Starters

| Product | Cell Count per Gram | | pH | Acidity (degrees) |
	Lctobacilli ($\times 10^6$)	Yeast		
A-1	2,900	>100,000	5.4	37.80
A-2	4,900	1,000	5.9	18.60
A-3	5,600	...	7.0	0.25
A-4	75	<10	6.1	1.4
A-5	800	170,000	4.0	28.4
A-6	0.028	12,000	3.6	36.6

to the microflora. The product is also required to regain its activity after hydration (Bode and Seibel, 1982). It was demonstrated, however, that freezing (-196°C in 10% skim milk) causes the survival of only 34.4–78.6% of sourdough cells, depending on the species of the acid-forming microorganisms (*L. brevis, L. plantarum, L. cellobiosus*, or *Streptococcus faecium*). When frozen cultures are used as starters for wheat-flour sourdoughs, there is no difference in the degree of acidification (end pH value and acidity units) during 4- to 24-hr sourdough fermentation periods. The levels of acetic and lactic acid, however, were found to differ significantly, depending on the species used. Frozen cell mass of *L. brevis* generated 43% less of L-(+) and D-(-) lactic acid, while *L. plantarum* produced more of lactic and acetic acids than the corresponding unfrozen preparations. These differences have no effect on the quality (pH value, acidity degree, flavor, and taste) of wheat breads. The storage of frozen cells at -30°C for 30 days was without effect on acidification characteristics of the acid-forming microorganisms (Torner et al, 1989).

The stable starters differ from an acidifying dough improver not only in the activity of the microflora but also in the fact that the acidification is a result of continuously progressing fermentation. This process can be followed by testing the levels of maleate and citrate.

Lactic bacteria in sourdoughs are able to metabolize maleate. Consequently, the maleate level in dry sourdoughs is appreciably lower than in flour or whole meal. Levels also differ, but theoretical and practical expectations are not always in good agreement (Spicher et al, 1990).

Further, during stabilization of sourdoughs, losses of ethanol and acetic acid take place. To compensate for these expected losses, it is advisable to direct the fermentation in favor of higher acetic acid yields. This can be achieved by addition of organic hydrogen acceptors, e.g., 10–15% invert sugar. Laboratory experiments confirm this approach to be advisable (Roecken et al, 1992).

Literature Cited

Belohlawek, L., and Laue, J. 1985. Verfahren zur Herstellung eines gebrauchsfertigen, getrockneten Backkonzentrates und dessen Verwendung. German patent declaration, A 21 d, 81 04 OS 3335.

Bode, J., and Seibel, W. 1982. Saeuerungen und Fuehrungen—Begriffsbestimmungen. Getreide Mehl Brot 36:11-12.

Boecker, G., Vogel, R. F., and Hammes, W. P. 1990. *Lactobacillus sanfrancisko* als stabiles Element in einem Reinzucht-Sauerteig-Praeparat. Getreide Mehl Brot 44:269-274.

Bruemmer, J.-M., and Huber, H. 1987. Begriffsbestimmungen fuer Vorstufen (Sauerteige, Vorteige, Quellstufen) und Weizensauerteige. Getreide Mehl Brot 41:110-112.

Bruemmer, J.-M., and Stephan, H. 1986. Einsatz getrockneter Sauerteige und Sauerteig-Starter bei der Herstellung von Brot und Kleingebaeck. Getreide Mehl Brot 39:51-58.

Hill, F. F. 1985. Verfahren und Herstellung eines trockenen lagerstabilen Bakterienpraeparates. European patent declaration 0131 1 14.

Kline, L. R., and Sugihara, R. F. 1971. Fluessiges Stammprodukt eines Saueteigbrotes und Verfahren zur Herstellung eines Stammproduktes. German patent disclosure document 228 119.

Klinga, J. 1983. Sauerteig in Trockenform—Ein wichtiger Rohstoff fuer die Brotherstellung. Brot Backwaren 31:21-24.

Koehler, E. G., Troeger, O., Puls, H., Ulrich, W., and Woelk, P. 1985. Verfahren zur Herstellung eines granulierten Trockensauerteiges. German patent DD 226 475 Al.

Kretzschmar, G. J. 1986. Verfahren zur Herstellung eines lagerfaehigen, gebrauchsfertigen Sauerteig-Mehl-Mischung. German patent declaration: A 21 d, 10/10. OS 3 504 686.

Menge, W. 1980. Verfahren zur Herstellung von Sauerteigen. German (BRD) patent 2 611 916.

Roecken, W., Rick, M., Mack, H., and Bruemmer, J.-M. 1992. Versuche zur Kompensierung der Essigsaeureverluste beim Trocknen von Sauerteigen. Getreide Mehl Brot 46:139-145.

Seibel, W. 1986. Sauerteig lebensmittelrechtlich betrachtet. Getreide Mehl Brot 40:28.

Spicher, G., and Stephan, H. 1993. Handbuch Sauerteig—Biochemie, Technologie, 4th ed. Verlag, BBV Wirtschaftsinformation, Hamburg.

Spicher, G., Roecken, W., and Bruemmer, J.-M. 1990. Zur frage der Feststellung der Revitalisierbarkeit der Mikroflora haltbarer Sauerteige. Getreide Mehl Brot 44:274-279.

Torner, M. J., Bainotti, A., Martinez-Anaya, M. A., and de Barber, C. B. 1989. Microflora of the sour dough and functional properties in wheat flour doughs microbial mass from lactic acid bacteria. Z. Unters. Forschg. 189:554-558.

Wolff, H. 1986. Verfahren zur Herstellung von lagerfaehigen granulierten Anstellgut fuer Sauerteig und nach diesem Verfahren hergestellten Sauerteiggranulat. German patent DE 35 10 317 A 1.

CHAPTER 4

Biochemical and Biophysical Principles of Freezing

Karel Kulp
Manhattan, Kansas 66502

Extension of dough or batter functionality by retardation and freezing is effected by lowering of storage temperatures. Retardation is used for short-time preservation and freezing for extended-term preservation. The obvious requirement for these frozen or retarded intermediate products is to maintain functional properties at levels comparable to those of freshly mixed doughs or batters. Essentially, successfully frozen or retarded doughs or batters are expected to produce end products with qualities similar to those of products prepared by unfrozen procedures. The target storage periods of frozen doughs/batters are generally several weeks and those of retarded preparations several days only. Stauffer (1993) reported that the industry will warrant good performance of frozen doughs up to 16 weeks and indicated that some experimental studies have shown good dough stability for 24 weeks in storage, a stability not yet seen in routine production.

Frozen Doughs

Bread and Yeasted Dough Systems

Bread doughs are typical products that are used in frozen conditions. They are manufactured essentially in a similar way as conventional bread. The formulas contain flour, shortening, salt, dough improvers, yeast food, and water. The simplest and most commonly used dough preparation method, the straight-dough process, is a one-step procedure that involves mixing of all ingredients in a single step. The fully mixed bread dough has distinct rheological properties: it is pliable and extensible and its consistency can be adjusted for the subsequent mechanical handling. Dough structure and strength depend predominantly on hydrated wheat flour proteins, generally referred to as gluten. The unique viscoelastic properties of gluten are developed by interactions of flour proteins during mixing. In frozen dough preparation, the mixing stage, along with subsequent mechanical makeup operations (dividing, rounding, sheeting, and forming), is especially important, probably more so than in conventional bread processes, because only during these steps does gluten formation and modification take place. In contrast to conventional baking, there is no further opportunity in the frozen dough process to correct any defects in the dough rheology by subsequent mechanical reworking after the dough pieces have been frozen. Briefly, the dough pieces produced for freezing must possess optimal rheological properties such as dough strength and extensibility and must have fully developed gluten. These factors will be reflected in the proofing time of doughs and in end-product quality characteristics—mainly specific volume, crumb grain structure, crumb texture, and external loaf appearance. In these respects, bread doughs, more than other types of bakery doughs, are very demanding. They are required to ferment rapidly, as indicated by the relatively short proof times, and to produce end products, breads, of high specific volumes.

The flour strength depends not only on the level but also on the quality of flour proteins. These factors are governed by the variety and growing environment of the wheat from which the flour has been milled, the milling process, and the flour grade (refinement). Yeast-leavened frozen doughs require high-quality bread flours, milled from hard wheat varieties, high in protein (12–13% [$N \times 5.7$], ash 0.4–0.5%, at 14% moisture level) and low in damaged starch and enzyme activities. No special differences between flour specifications for conventional processes and for those applying the retardation step are required. In these cases, normal flour protein levels, average starch damage levels, and conventional enzymatic activities of flours are acceptable. The retardation step does not require flours of different mixing and stability characteristics than those normally used in conventional production.

On the other hand, dough mixing times for frozen doughs should not be excessively long, because long mixing generates heat and enhances fermentation, which should be minimized in the preparation of doughs for freezing applications. The more fermentation that occurs at the dough stage, the more the yeast becomes susceptible to freezing damage, as detailed in Chapter 2. It is true that high-protein flours selected from good wheat varieties are strong and produce dough of good frozen stability (Inoue and Bushuk, 1992). However, these types of flours may not be ideal in commercial production because they may require excessively long mixing times, which, as indicated above, cause higher fermentation activities. These conditions are not as critical in small-scale laboratory baking experiments as in large-scale production operations, where the temperature control of doughs is much more difficult.

In selecting flours, the protein quality is generally cited as an important factor. Unfortunately, in spite of extensive research efforts by various investigators and research groups around the world, this factor has eluded a definition and full understanding.

The major protein components of gluten are gliadin and glutenin, which are very complex and heterogeneous (Bietz, 1987; Wrigley and Bietz, 1988). Gliadin consists of at least three subclasses, coded by complex loci on six chromosomes. Tightly linked duplicate genes at these loci code more than 100 proteins. Glutenin is even more complex than gliadin. Its components, coded by six complex loci, interact to form large polymers. The composition of gliadin and glutenin components within a given wheat variety is constant, which permits detection and identification of various varieties by analytical methods (e.g., gel electrophoretic, high-pressure liquid chromatographic procedures, and their combinations), resulting in unique descriptions of their patterns. This process is called "fingerprinting" (Bietz 1992). The presence of protein subunits in varieties with undesirable functional properties can be detected by these methods. Unfortunately, the fingerprinting approach does not offer means of predicting the technological performance of flours in various baking applications as desired by the technologists.

Although fingerprinting is applicable in detection of individual varieties in wheat blends, thus discouraging their incorporation into quality wheats for milling and baking, this procedure is still unreliable for routine baking flour quality prediction for U.S. wheat varieties. On the other hand, correlation between the presence of certain high molecular weight (HMW) subunits (detected by gel electrophoresis) of glutenin and indices of breadbaking quality have been observed in the studies of Payne and his group (Payne et al, 1979, 1981). The different HMW subunits have been ranked in order of their influence on baking quality (Payne et al, 1984). These results appear to be useful for English wheats and flours but are unreliable for U.S. and Australian wheat varieties.

It appears that, in addition to the wheat protein subunit profiles, other factors, e.g., protein conformation, molecular sizes of the aggregates, and location of sulfhydryl groups in the protein molecules, need to be considered in the definition of wheat protein quality.

This lack of knowledge inhibits the selection of proper wheat varieties in breeding programs for specific technological and baking applications, including those for production of frozen doughs. The current research evidence indicates that the key factor in protein quality definition is the distribution, composition, and presence of certain protein subunits forming the gluten complex. Although no comprehensive quality prediction approach is available at this point, there are certain results that favor this line of research. Thus, it would be beneficial to understand gluten film stability in frozen doughs and to identify which protein subunits could enhance this property. With this knowledge, improved wheats for this application could be developed by breeding and/or genetic engineering methods.

Gluten Formation and Stability

In dough formation, it is necessary to transform small gluten particles into a large cohesive system that exhibits viscous, elastic, and cohesive properties. In the first step of mixing, the proteins are hydrated, and then during subsequent mixing they interact with each other. In addition to protein interaction, other flour components—lipids, salts, nonstarch polysaccharides, and starch—also participate in the formation of the gluten matrix.

The viscoelastic properties of doughs are primarily the result of a continuous protein phase that, in a fully developed dough, surrounds the starch granules (Wrigley and Bietz, 1988). The rheological behavior of the gluten phase depends on the molecular properties of the interacting components and the type of bonds involved in the polymeric gluten matrix. According to Bushuk and MacRitchie (1987), the strength of the polymeric network is attributed to the concentration and strength of cross-links, the molecular weight of intercross-link regions, and the average molecular weight and molecular weight distribution of the constituent polymers. From recent publications of Inoue and Bushuk (1992) and Inoue et al (1994), it can be postulated that a high level of HMW glutenin subunits increases the flour strength.

The importance of the flour type and gluten quality is evident from the molecular characteristics of flours. The chemical bonds that stabilize the fully developed gluten proteins in bread doughs are secondary and covalent bonds. The covalent bonds involved are disulfide bonds, which form inter- and intramolecular cross-bonds in the proteins during dough formation by the sulfide-disulfide interchange (Wrigley and Bietz, 1988). The secondary bonds involved are hydrogen, hydrophilic, hydrophobic, and ionic bonds and polar interactions (Zawistowska et al, 1984, 1985; Bushuk, 1985a,b). Although the secondary linkages are rather weak, their importance cannot be neglected because they are numerous and thus produce a strong association. As a matter of fact, some investigators have postulated that the secondary bonds are more important than the cross-bonding by disulfide linkages.

The nonprotein associations that may affect gluten rheology and stability are poorly defined. They include noncovalent protein-lipid complexations; covalent bonds with flour hemicelluloses, possibly oligosaccharides; and secondary-type bonds with the surface of starch granules (Chung et al, 1979; McMaster and Bushuk, 1983). Bushuk et al (1980) and Chen et al (1992) reported an association between a carbohydrate and some HMW glutenin subunits.

One should consider the possibility of disruption and reformation of both covalent and secondary bonds as factors involved in frozen dough stability. The physical and chemical reactions that take place during freezing and frozen storage are the results of ice formation and yeast-dough interactions. The ice formation is generally responsible for physical disruption of secondary bonding in the dough and yeast. Loss of the secondary bonding is likely to alter the conformational order of the protein molecules and thus adversely affect their functional properties. The chemical agents that cleave the covalent bonds (e.g., disulfides by the reducing action of glutathione) are attributed to the interaction between leached-out compounds from yeast and the surrounding dough protein matrix. In the production of frozen doughs, these changes are minimized technologically by proper production measures and chemical additives. The optimized production is designed to preserve the dough structure to permit maximum rehydration and restoration of dough structure during thawing. It involves using surfactants that complex with gluten proteins to stabilize the gluten structure, and reformation of the protein disulfides in gluten by the action of added oxidants (for details, see Chapter 5). In addition to bromate involvement in the sulfide-disulfide interchange, a recent study of Panazzo et al (1994) demonstrated that bromate changes the apparent molecular weight distribution and lipid extractability of gluten (or glutenin) proteins. Bromate increased the proportion of glutenin aggregate, P_l. This reaction, however, was not a major contributor to bromate's ability to improve loaf volume. Another reaction, resulting from noncovalent aggregation of low molecular weight proteins, in parallel with decreased lipid extractability of gluten (or glutenin) proteins, was associated with positive bromate loaf volume response.

Although the physical reactions are not completely reversible, it appears from the actual baking results that, under optimal conditions, most of the dough functionality is preserved by freezing and regained after defrosting.

Measurements of Frozen Dough Properties

The dough stability of conventional doughs is determined by farinography, which indicates the dough stability during mixing; extensigraphy, which reflects extensibility and resistance to extension; and mixography, which describes the dough characteristics in the mixing operation. When evaluating frozen doughs, these methods may be used with suitable modifications to produce meaningful results. The information that we are seeking in evaluating frozen doughs is their stability and the effects of various dough improvers in the frozen state. Therefore, we cannot defrost and remix the tested dough to obtain meaningful information. The most suitable procedure for frozen-dough evaluation appears to be the extensigraph method as modified by Varriano-Marston et al (1980), which was also used by Wolt and D'Appolonia (1984a,b). A newer method, using stress relaxation and a small-deformation oscillatory technique, was recently applied by Autio and Sinda (1992) to the study of rheological changes in doughs subjected to freezing and thawing.

Rheological Studies of Frozen Bread Doughs

It is well established that frozen doughs in storage undergo a gradual loss of quality that is attributable to the loss of gas retention power. This change is generally explained by the release of reducing compounds (mainly glutathione) from yeast cells, which causes a weakening of the gluten network by cleaving disulfide cross-bonds in the protein polymer (Kline and Sugihara, 1968; Hsu et al, 1979a). An alternative hypothesis (Varriano-Marston et al, 1980; Wolt and D'Appolonia, 1984a; Autio and Sinda, 1992) suggests that the gluten network itself deteriorates due to the freezing process. The cause of this direct change in gluten is explained by disruption of certain gluten bonds by the mechanical action of ice crystals.

Effect of Reducing Compounds on Frozen Doughs

Kline and Sugihara (1968) postulated that there is a relationship between dying yeast cells during frozen storage and deterioration of dough gas retention during dough proofing. The effect was attributed to the action of reducing agents released by yeast on the gluten structure. The tripeptide glutathione, isolated from active dry yeast (Ponte and al, 1960), was also associated with marked effects on rheological properties of doughs. These effects of glutathione on doughs are caused by the reaction of the glutathione sulfhydryl group with the gluten disulfides, which cross-bond the gluten structure. The net rheological effects on dough then include a reduction of mixing time and an increase in dough extensibility. This reaction, using another thiol compound (L-cysteine), is often used in no-time bread processes, where the reducing reaction can be controlled and balanced by the use of proper levels and type of oxidation additives.

In frozen doughs, the situation is less favorable for the correction of the glutathione reducing action. The glutathione, leached out from the yeast cells during frozen storage, remains mainly dissolved in the liquid phase around the yeast cells. The liquid phase in frozen dough systems is limited, causing localized high concentrations of the reductant in the liquid areas adjacent to the yeast cells. Opportunity for the reactant to diffuse throughout the entire dough during defrosting is also restricted. Remixing or reworking of the frozen or defrosted dough would evenly distribute glutathione and also produce a certain degree of dough oxidation by incorporation of air. Although this step would improve the frozen dough performance, this approach is not practical. Since uniform distribution of the leached-out reductant is prevented in frozen doughs, it is likely that this reaction affects gluten structure in localized regions.

Effect of Proteolytic Enzymes

Dough weakening can be also caused by the action of proteases that cleave peptide bonds of proteins. This reaction weakens the gluten structure, with consequent reduction of the gas retention power in doughs and unacceptable extensions of dough proofing times. In flours milled from sound wheats, the level of these enzymes is probably insufficient to be a factor in frozen dough stability. They can adversely affect the storage stability only when sprouted flours, which may contain elevated levels of this activity, are used (Bhatt et al, 1981). Also, when enzymatic supplements (fungal, bacterial, or cereal enzymes) are part of the bread formulas, their effect may become noticeable. Thus, the use of these ingredients in the production of doughs for extended frozen storage is unadvisable.

Effect of Yeast Fermentation Metabolites

It is generally agreed that fermentation of dough before freezing lowers the frozen dough stability and produces low-quality breads. The effect is generally attributed to damage from freezing of yeast and the release of glutathione and possibly other reducing compounds from yeast cells.

Hsu et al (1979a) studied the effects of products of yeast fermentation. A liquid ferment system was employed (Ling and Hoseney, 1977). A yeast slurry combined with buffered liquid nutrients including sugar was incubated for 3 hr at 30°C (86°F). At the end of fermentation, the yeast (called here "activated yeast") was removed by centrifugation. The centrifugate contained all water-soluble fermentation metabolites, which were fractionated into volatile and nonvolatile fractions. The activated yeast was slightly more susceptible to freezing damage, as indicated by lower gassing power compared to that of the nonactivated yeast.

When the centrifugate, containing total fermentation products, was added to yeast and frozen, it had a damaging effect on yeast. Of the fractionated components, the volatile components were more damaging than the nonvolatile fractions. Reconstitution studies demonstrated, however, that the addition of the combined fractions was less damaging, suggesting that some highly volatile damaging compounds might have been lost during the separation process. These results indicated that yeast in frozen dough may suffer partial loss of fermentation capacity by 1) the physiological effect on yeast cells, which is enhanced by fermentation before freezing, and/or 2) the effect of certain fermentation metabolites. Although the metabolites were not investigated in this study, it has been shown that the major product, ethanol, caused a significant loss of yeast gassing power when added at a level of 2.5% (estimated formation level during a 3-hr fermentation). It is possible that the authors underestimated the effect of ethanol in frozen doughs by not taking into account the increased concentration in the residual unfrozen liquid in frozen doughs. This effect, however, is hard to predict because of the low temperature conditions of the environment at which ethanol would be functional. Nevertheless, it is quite possible that yeast metabolites may be an important factor in frozen yeast stability, with concomitant effects on dough properties (e.g., they may promote a higher degree of leaching from yeast cells).

Effect of Ice Formation on Dough Structure

Varriano-Marston et al (1980) utilized electron microscopy to observe changes in the gluten network of doughs subjected to freezing and thawing. On the basis of these studies, they concluded that changes in the gluten network are partly due to ice recrystallization, which results in an increase in the size of the ice crystals. The recrystallization process is known to cause a separation of water molecules from the macromolecules to which they are normally attached. Microscopic changes in the dough structure are evident from the scanning electron micrographs in Figure 1.

The microscopic evidence was supplemented by these authors with rheological studies to describe dough properties and their changes during frozen storage. The modified extensigraph procedure of Hsu et al (1979a,b) was used. Accordingly, cylinder-shaped dough pieces were prepared by a short procedure of Hsu et al (1979a), fermented for 40 min, molded in an extensigraph, wrapped in aluminum foil, frozen at -18°C (-0.4°F), and then stored at that temperature for two months. Before testing, frozen doughs were defrosted (while still wrapped) in a constant-temperature cabinet at 30°C (86°F) and 90% rh. After the dough reached 28 ± 1.5°C (82°F), it was tested for extensibility and resistance to extension (at 5 cm) by means of a Brabender Extensigraph. The extensigrams of nonyeasted (Fig. 2a) and yeasted (Fig. 2b) doughs show the effects of frozen storage and three freeze-thaw cycles on both types of dough. Comparison of Figures 2a and 2b

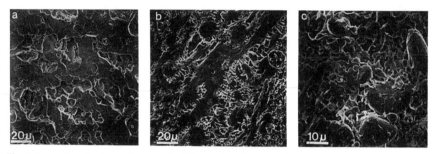

Fig. 1. Scanning electron micrograph of frozen doughs: a, no thawing, b, thawed once, c, frozen and thawed. (Reprinted, with permission, from Varriano-Marston et al, 1980)

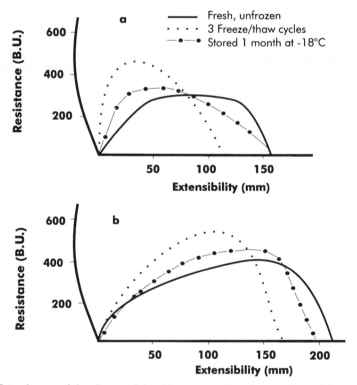

Fig. 2. Extensigrams of doughs containing 20 ppm potassium bromate (a) and the nonyeasted counterpart after various treatments (b). (Reprinted, with permission, from Varriano-Marston et al, 1980)

shows the effect of yeast, which obviously is an important factor affecting the dough properties. The presence of yeast produced doughs with lower resistance to extension and higher extensibility values than those of doughs without yeast.

On the other hand, a dough strengthening effect was observed in frozen doughs and in doughs after refreezing/thawing. This rheological change was most likely due to the oxidizing action of the potassium bromate used in the test formulas. Although detected both in unyeasted and yeasted doughs, it was less pronounced in the latter, suggesting that the action of the oxidant was partially negated by the reducing agents released from yeast.

Wolt and D'Appolonia (1984b) evaluated the effect of low molecular weight sulfhydryl compounds leached from freeze-damaged yeast cells on dough stability and the effect of physical ice damage on dough structure. Using a modified extensigraphic procedure similar to that used by Varriano-Marston et al (1980), these investigators reported the data given in Table 1. As is evident from these results, both yeasted and nonyeasted doughs increased in proportional number (resistance/extensibility) with storage, indicating a strengthening effect of doughs during frozen storage, which again was most likely due to the oxidizing action of the potassium bromate used in their formulation. These findings were in good agreement with those reported previously by Varriano-Marston et al (1980).

The observation that dough strengthens in frozen storage, reported in the two preceding studies, appears to contradict the conclusion that the weakening of gluten structure in frozen doughs is caused by physical damage from ice crystals. A plausible explanation of this conflict is that weakening results from oxidative reactions in the dough, induced either by added potassium bromate or some naturally present oxidants.

Additional data of Wolt and D'Appolonia (1984b) on the effects of reducing compounds leached out from freeze-damaged yeast showed that reducing compounds were less important than the mechanical ice damage in affecting

Table 1
Influence of Frozen Storage on the Extensigraph Properties of
Yeasted and Unyeasted Doughs[a]

Storage Time	Proportional Number[b]	
	Yeasted	Nonyeasted
Fresh	0.278	0.212
1 day	0.280	0.181
2 weeks	0.283	0.210
4 weeks	0.290	0.239
6 weeks	0.305	0.283
8 weeks	0.311	0.312
10 weeks	0.376	0.429

[a] Source: Wolt and D'Appolonia (1984a); used with permission.
[b] Proportional number = resistance/extensibility after thawing to $25°$ C.

rheological dough properties and causing undue extension of proof times. It is possible that the authors underestimated the concentration of the reducing compounds in the vicinity of yeast cells in frozen doughs, which may be active during extended frozen storage, defrosting, and proofing.

Inoue and Bushuk (1991) and Inoue et al (1994) reexamined the extensigraphic patterns of frozen doughs of previous investigators (Varriano-Marston et al [1980] and Wolt and D'Appolonia [1984a]) and confirmed the weakening of doughs containing yeast observed by Varriano-Marston et al (1980) during frozen storage and successive freeze-thaw cycles. According to them, the dough weakening could result from the effect of reducing substances leached out from yeast cells on the gluten matrix, the redistribution of water caused by a change in water-binding capacity of flour constituents, or the combination of both these factors. The extensigraphic studies of both Varriano-Marston et al (1980) and Wolt and D'Appolonia (1984a) indicated that both yeasted and unyeasted doughs become stronger during frozen storage (Fig. 2). This effect contradicted the Inoue et al (1994) study, as is evident from Table 2. In contrast to Varriano-Marston and Wolt and D'Appolonia, they observed dough weakening in frozen storage instead of dough strengthening. This difference may be due to the different action of oxidants: Inoue and Bushuk used ascorbic acid instead of the potassium bromate used by previous investigators.

In the same study, Inoue et al (1994) showed that the mechanism of dough weakening during frozen storage and due to repeated freeze-thaw cycles appears to be different. Changes during freezing storage were found to be related to yeast activity, with concomitant effects on dough extensibility (Table 2). On the other hand, the dough weakening effect caused by repeated freezing and

Table 2
Extensigraphic Properties and Gassing Power of Nonfrozen
and Thawed Frozen Doughs[a,b]

Frozen	Properties			
Storage Time	Maximum Resistance[c]	Extensibility[c]	Gassing Power[d]	
(days)	(BU)	(mm)	(mmHg)	(%)
0 (control)	627 ± 6 a	121 ± 3 a	459 ± 6 a	100
1	530 ± 10 b	122 ± 3 a	447 ± 7 a	97
7	523 ± 12 b	123 ± 4 a	451 ± 16 a	98
7[e]	407 ± 6 c	121 ± 4 a	378 ± 9 b	82
70	360 ± 20 d	136 ± 4 b	254 ± 10 c	55

[a] Source: Inoue et al (1994); used with permission.

[b] Values are means ± standard deviations (SD). Means with different letters within a column are significantly different $(P < 0.05)$.

[c] Means ± SD of three replicates.

[d] Means ± SD of two replicates.

[e] Subjected to three thaw-freeze cycles.

thawing was related to protein solubility and attributed to another mechanism such as ice crystallization, release of carbon dioxide, or some other unknown factors. Loss of some glutenin oligomers in dough proteins by freezing was also observed. Further evidence pointing to potassium bromate as the causative agent for the dough strengthening effect is provided by data of Sutton et al (1994), given in Figure 3. The extensigraphic measurements were obtained with a frozen pizza dough produced without addition of any oxidant. In this case, it was observed that the unoxidated yeasted frozen dough became weaker in frozen storage, suggesting partial deterioration of structural gluten and indicating that the strengthening effect reported previously was most likely due to the action of potassium bromate. Minimal changes in extensigraphic indices of

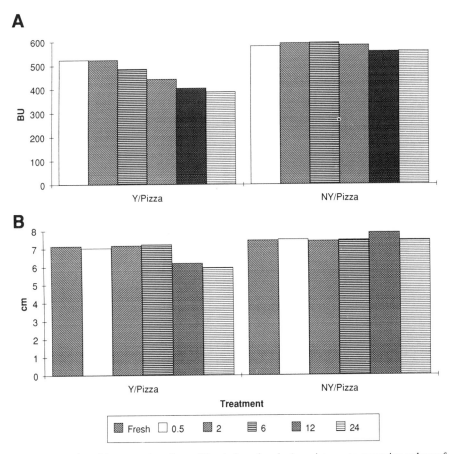

Fig. 3. Extensigraphic properties of unoxidized pizza dough. A, resistance to extension values of unyeasted and yeasted doughs; B, extensibility values of the same doughs. Treatment is the variation of the holding period (ranging from 0.5 to 24 hr at 4°C [40°F]) of four-week frozen doughs (stored at -25°C [-13°F]), and defrosted for 16 hr at 4°C. (Reprinted, with permission, from Sutton et al, 1994)

unyeasted doughs were observed. Further, more extensive studies are needed in this area to confirm this observation and to clarify the action of other oxidants.

Effects of Dough Freezing on Flour Starch

Wolt and D'Appolonia (1984b) also investigated changes of starch in breads baked from frozen doughs and compared them with those of control breads from unfrozen doughs. According to their observation, starch characteristics of bread crumbs produced from frozen-dough breads showed changes due to frozen storage. These changes were similar to those that accompany conventional bread staling. Highly significant positive correlations were found between amylose-amylopectin ratios, proof times, and loaf volumes. Amylose-amylopectin ratios were negatively correlated with frozen storage time. These data are given in Table 3. It is uncertain whether this relationship reveals any fundamental functional effect or whether it simply reflects a higher

Table 3
Effect of Dough Additives on Soluble Starch, Amylose, and Amylopectin Extracted from Crumb of Frozen Dough Bread[a]

Dough Additive	Storage Time			
	1 Day	4 Weeks	8 Weeks	12 Weeks
Control				
Soluble starch, %	2.73	2.18	2.10	2.24
Amylose, %	0.49	0.37	0.32	0.32
Amylopectin, %	2.24	1.81	1.78	1.92
Ratio amylose/amylopectin	0.21	0.20	0.18	0.16
SSL[b]				
Soluble starch, %	2.13	2.23	1.77	1.64
Amylose, %	0.31	0.38	0.18	0.15
Amylopectin, %	1.82	1.85	1.59	1.49
Ratio amylose/amylopectin	0.17	0.20	0.11	0.10
DATA[c]				
Soluble starch, %	2.00	2.17	1.96	1.95
Amylose, %	0.32	0.37	0.27	0.19
Amylopectin, %	1.68	1.80	1.69	1.76
Ratio amylose/amylopectin	0.19	0.20	0.16	0.11
CMC[d]				
Soluble starch, %	2.53	1.72	2.24	2.44
Amylose, %	0.43	0.37	0.43	0.46
Amylopectin, %	2.10	1.35	1.81	1.98
Ratio amylose/amylopectin	0.20	0.27	0.24	0.23

[a] Source: Wolt and D'Appolonia (1984b); used with permission.
[b] Sodium stearoyl lactylate.
[c] Diacetyl tartaric acid.
[d] Carboxymethyl cellulose.

degree of retrogradation of the soluble starch polymers in frozen doughs.

Based on viscoelastic measurements, Autio and Sinda (1992) observed certain rheological changes induced by freezing and thawing. First, a decrease in storage modulus G' and an increase in tan δ in frozen and thawed doughs suggested a loss of polymer cross-bonding. Second, both the relaxation modulus and relaxation half-life decreased in frozen doughs. The decrease of relaxation half-life was attributed to a weakening of the gluten network. And finally, the addition of dead yeast cells failed to affect rheological properties, indicating that release of reducing compounds from yeast was not responsible for dough weakening. Their data tend to support the conclusions of Wolt and D'Appolonia (1984b).

Autio and Sinda (1992) observed (Table 4) that freezing and thawing at 4°C increase the onset temperature of starch gelatinization. Extension of the duration of dough storage at 4°C further increases the onset temperature. They explained this as follows: in native starches, the gelatinization temperature, measured by differential scanning calorimetry (DSC), depends on the extent and type of order of starch granules, the moisture content, and the moisture distribution (Levine and Slade, 1990). The growth of ice crystals during frozen storage indicates that water in the dough is separated into large pools (Berglund et al, 1991). The increase of the onset of starch gelatinization temperature in frozen doughs may thus be attributed to the delay in the rate of diffusion of water into the starch granules or the increased crystallinity of the granules.

The reported involvement of starch in frozen dough quality seems to be minor, but it indicates that movement of moisture among the flour and ingredient components takes place. This observation suggests a disruption of the association of gluten with starch, which thus may be a part of the dough deterioration process.

The Freezing Process

Preparation of Doughs for Freezing

Freezing of various plant tissues often requires special pretreatments. For example, in many plant tissues, freezing causes detrimental, enzyme-mediated de-

Table 4
Effect of Freezing and Thawing on the Onset Temperatures of Starch Gelatinization[a]

Dough Treatment	Treatment Conditions	Onset Temperature (°C)
Nonfrozen	...	62.5 ± 0.5
Frozen	30°C for 2.5 hr	63.5 ± 0.5
Thawed	4°C for 17 hr	63.5 ± 0.5
	4°C for 19.5 hr	63.5 ± 0.5
	4°C for 23 hr	63.6 ± 0.5
	4°C for 41 hr	64.1 ± 0.5

[a] Source: Autio and Sinda (1992); used with permission

fects. To prevent these undesirable reactions, enzymes are generally inactivated by heating (blanching), before freezing. Fortunately, in frozen doughs these problems are absent since no adverse enzyme activity is present. Enzymes that may adversely affect doughs, e.g., proteases and amylases, may be avoided by selection of flours low in these activities and omission of enzyme improvers in the formulas. In the production of frozen doughs, we are concerned with maintenance of full fermentative activity of yeast and its physiological integrity. This objective is largely achieved by proper dough preparation methods and by freezing and thawing conditions.

Temperature Lowering and Freezing

Dough retardation requires temperature reduction to refrigeration temperature (4°C [39 °F]) only. On the other hand, freezing requires the product temperature to be lowered to a level where some ice formation takes place. In both cases, the preservation of the food system is accomplished by the reduction of reaction rates of physical and chemical changes that would otherwise occur at room temperature.

A number of changes occur within the freezing zone (Reid, 1990, 1983). First, there is a phase change of water into ice. This happens even in pure water. In food systems, the freezing change is more complex than in freezing of pure water; it involves many more changes that are consequential to this phase transition. Reid (1983) pointed out that, in the freezing of various tissue systems, one must consider the nature and state of the material to be frozen and the type of pretreatment, e.g., blanching, which damages the cell walls. In intact (unblanched) tissues, where the cell walls are intact, osmotic exchange of water is possible; the freezing rates affect the water translocation in intact tissues. If the freezing rate is not too fast, significant quantities of water may translocate from within the cells to the extracellular medium. The low temperatures and the formation of ice are frequently detrimental to cell membranes, as becomes apparent after defrosting, when the osmotic integrity and turgor pressure are lost. In rapid freezing, ice formation within the cells may also cause damage to cell structure and produce enzymatically induced reactions that may result in development of off-flavor and off-odors.

This general food technology experience can be interpolated and applied to bread dough systems. It is essential in dough freezing to maintain the integrity of yeast cell walls in order to preserve the osmotic transfer mechanism. When this condition is preserved, the water interchange between the yeast cells and the dough structure during the freezing (dehydration due to ice formation) and thawing (rehydration) steps is achieved, and normal rates of fermentation during the dough proofing stage are maintained. The remaining portion of the doughs does not contain native tissues that need to be preserved in native order. However, the gluten matrix, which is a highly functional component of doughs, must retain its rheological properties. In that respect, its physicochemical properties should remain intact so that the frozen gluten can be restored to its original fresh prefrozen dough state. This obviously requires rehydration from the frozen state during defrosting and minimum damage by chemical reactions and physical ice damage during processing and frozen storage.

Reid (1983) noted that if food systems could be kept at very low temperatures in a supercooled condition without ice formation, their quality could be well preserved. However, ice starts forming, which affects the physical properties of doughs and complicates the freezing process. Although water is a main component of doughs and many other food systems, it does not necessarily freeze at its normal freezing point, since the solute components depress the freezing point. Also a sharp phase transition of water into ice does not occur in these systems because ice formation in the water phase gradually produces higher concentrations of soluble materials. The effect of this concentration process is a gradual depression of the freezing point.

An additional complication of dough freezing is the state of the water in the system; besides free water, a significant portion of water is bound, associated with proteins, carbohydrates, and pentosans (Bushuk, 1966).

Freezing Curves

Typical freezing curves, shown in Figure 4 (Hsu et al, 1979b), describe the temperature changes during dough freezing. The tested dough formula contained 3% sugar, 1.5% sodium chloride (flour basis), and other minor ingredients. As evident from the first inflection in the freezing curve, initial freezing started at about -4°C (25°F). The freezing curves show two eutectic points, the temperature at which complete ice formation in the system takes place. These are indicated in the figure by arrows, one at about -12°C (10°F) in the -20°C (-4°F) curve and the other at about -35°C (-31°F) in the -40°C (-40°F) curve. Freezing at -10°C (-14°F) never reached the eutectic point, and at -40°C, the eutectic point was only slightly evident, due to the quick process of freezing. No eutectic point was detectable when freezing was at -78°C (-108°F).

The freezing curve for a yeast slurry given in Figure 5 shows that the yeast cell slurry did not have a distinct initial freezing point, but its slope suggests that most water froze at around -8°C (18°F). The freezing process did not appear to have been completed until the temperature fell below -35°C. These data (compare the curve at -78°C in Fig. 4 with the curves at -40C and at -78°C in Fig. 3) also show that the freezing characteristics of the nonyeasted dough and the yeast slurry differ.

Thermal Changes During Dough Freezing

The freezing process of dough proceeds in three phases: cooling above the freezing zone of the product, cooling in the freezing zone, and subfreezing cooling. As evident from the freezing curves (Fig. 4), the cooling proceeds rapidly, then slows down during the freezing interval. As the amount of formed ice increases, the speed of cooling becomes more rapid. These changes take place provided the available freezing capacity is sufficient to remove heat from the product. The factor that affects the cooling rate (above freezing) is the dough thermal conductivity. Because of the thermal conductivity characteristics, which are influenced by the composition, structure, and size of the material, the product exterior will be at a lower temperature than the interior. Additionally, the rate of heat extraction depends on the temperature differential of the product and the freezing medium. During cooling, only specific heat can be removed. An important consequence of cooling is the increase of viscosity of the liquid phase and the concomitant rate reduction of various reactions. This effect is beneficial, especially in dough preservation by retardation.

When the product reaches the freezing zone, in addition to the removal of specific heat, removal of latent heat necessary for the phase transition is also required. This change increases the freezer energy requirement and generally slows down the cooling rate to form a plateau around the freezing point. The length of the plateau is shortened when the differential between product temperature and

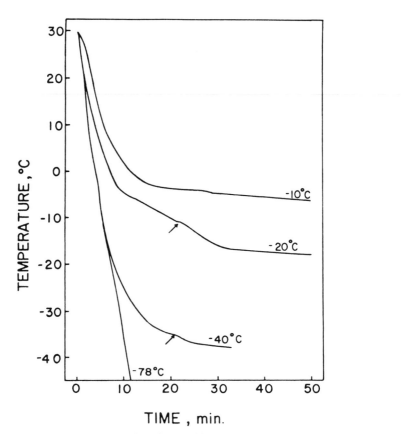

Fig. 4. Freezing curves of bread doughs submerged in a temperature-controlled bath at indicated temperatures. Arrows indicate eutectic points at about -12°C and -35°C. (Reprinted, with permission, from Hsu et al, 1979b)

freezer temperature is increased by application of lower freezer temperatures, which result in faster cooling and possibly a lower degree of ice propagation (see paragraph below). This effect is also evident in Figure 4.

Ice Formation

Freezing is the crystallization of liquid water into the solid form of water, ice. This phase change takes place when water temperature is reduced below 0°C (32°F) or, in food systems, when the temperature drops below the freezing temperature of the liquid phase. At that point, supercooling may occur without ice formation. The uncertainty in the initiation of ice formation is due to the "nucleation" problem. According to various investigators (e.g., Langham and Mason, 1958; Bigg, 1963), freezing without the effect of nucleation may not occur until around -40°C (-40°F). At that temperature, spontaneously formed nuclei are generated to produce ice. This type of nucleation is called homogeneous. In the liquid phase of food systems, various particles initiate nucleation at a temperature much higher than -40°C. This transition is called heterogeneous nucleation.

Once nucleation takes place, ice crystals may grow. While nucleation requires several degrees of supercooling, ice crystal growth may proceed with minimal supercooling. The rate of crystallization depends on the rate of heat removal. The

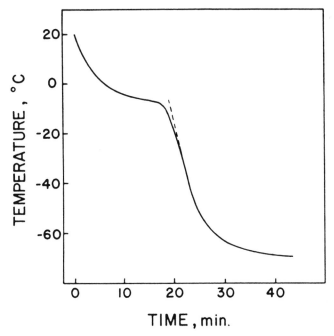

Fig. 5. Freezing curve of yeast slurry (100 g of compressed yeast and 27 g of water, placed in a glass jar an submerged in a temperature-controlled bath at -78°C. (Reprinted, with permission, from Hsu et al, 1979b)

morphology of the crystals is controlled by the rate of heat removal as well as by the direction of heat flow during its removal.

The crystal shape is also affected by supercooling of the medium (Reid, 1983). Ice propagation, a complex process in pure water, is even more complicated in the presence of various solutes in the liquid phase. This is illustrated in Table 5 (Reid, 1983), where the effects of ethanol, glycerol, sucrose, and glucose on the velocity of ice formation are given (Lucena, 1955; *unpublished data* of M. Goddard, D. S. Reid, and N. Thomas, 1979 [cited in Reid, 1983]). Another group of compounds inhibiting ice formation, called antifreeze agents, occur in natural products as protein/glycoprotein (Feeney, 1982). In many instances they affect the freeze stability of various seeds, and it is possible that they are also somewhat operative in some cereal grains and flours.

The interaction of nucleation and ice crystal growth affects the shape and size of the crystals formed in doughs. This relationship is possibly the underlying cause of the effect of freezing rates on ice characteristics. When the product is frozen at a slow rate, the nucleation is also slow and causes, at least initially, formation of large ice crystals. The opposite is true when the freezing is at high rates—these rates favor rapid nucleation and consequently the formation of small ice crystals.

Consequence of Ice Formation

Ice improves the heat conductivity of the system, which enhances heat removal from the frozen dough. At 15°C (59°F), the specific heat of water is 1 g-cal/g and that of ice [solid at -10°C (14°F)] is 0.48 g-cal only. Latent heat of about 80 g-cal must be withdrawn from each gram of water to create ice and supplied for each gram of ice to be melted.

In rapid freezing, ice is formed within cells (Reid, 1983) and may damage the cell structure. In the case of frozen doughs, intracellular ice crystals may reduce

Table 5
Velocity of Advance of Ice (R)[a] in Uncooked Aqueous Solutions in a U-Tube[b,c]

Solute	Concentration Range c (wt fraction)	Degrees of Under- cooling	a	b
Ethanol	0.125–0.20	10	7.0	−0.36
Glycerol	0.10–0.35	10	5.3	0.14
	0.05–0.40	5	6.0	0.02
Sucrose	0.10–0.30	10	3.8	−0.07
	0.10–0.40	5	4.6	−0.32
Glucose	0.10–0.30	10	4.3	0.01

[a] Expressed, over the specified concentration range c, as $\log [R/(\text{cm·sec}^{-1})] = ac + b$.
[b] Data from Lusena (1955) and *unpublished data* of M. Goddard, D. S. Reid, and N. Thomas, 1979 (cited in Reid, 1983).
[c] Source: Reid (1983); used with permission.

the fermentation potential of yeast and affect the cell wall structure. They may also disturb the order of the gluten matrix. However, simple slow freezing may not be acceptable in commercial production for economic reasons; it is time-consuming and production ineffective. Therefore, combinations of quick- and fast-rate freezing procedures, with carefully controlled temperature, are considered to be optimal. This method was illustrated by Dubois and Dreese (1984). Freezing in their study was conducted in a carbon dioxide blast freezer controlled at -35°C (-30°F) until the internal dough temperature reached -17°C (+2°F). Then the doughs were individually packaged in polyethylene bags and transferred into a storage freezer kept at -25°C (-12°F).

Other Changes in Frozen Doughs

When dough is frozen and stored, some reactions continue at highly diminished rates. These changes include physical, chemical, and enzymatic reactions.

The liquid phase diminishes when ice is formed; some compounds crystallize out; dissolved substances increase in concentration; and its viscosity increases. All these changes reduce the reaction rates.

Eutectic Point of Frozen Doughs

In Figure 4, eutectic points of a dough frozen at different temperatures were indicated. Although theoretically at these points the liquid phase should have been completely solidified, in many foods, including frozen doughs, complete solidification is prevented by the presence of certain solutes. Salts, e.g., table salt, at eutectic points are crystalline and thus do not interfere with the liquid phase solidification. On the other hand, sugars resist crystallization and remain as syrups. According to Chandrasekaran and King (1971), if equilibrium prevails for both sugar and water, sucrose-water solutions should solidify completely at a eutectic temperature of -13°C (9°F), and any solution of sucrose, fructose, and glucose should solidify completely at a eutectic temperature of -25°C (-13°F). In practice, however, one finds that solutions of these sugars form no crystallized sugar and thus do not solidify completely, even when the temperature is reduced to -40°C (-40°F) (King, 1975). Since the liquid phase of frozen yeasted doughs contains glucose and fructose, these conclusions certainly apply to the liquid phases of frozen dough and batter systems. Consequently, the eutectic system in doughs is a mixture of ice, crystalline solutes, and residual liquid phase containing uncrystallized solutes.

Dehydration and Moisture Migration in Frozen Dough

Once a product enters frozen storage, changes do not cease. Reaction rates of both physical and chemical reactions are generally reduced from those at ambient temperature. According to Fennema (1975), however, some reactions are accelerated at temperatures close to but below the freezing points. This phenomenon is often attributed to the initially rapid increase in concentration of the unfrozen matrix between ice crystals as the temperature is reduced. Although this condition is present in frozen doughs, no such effects have been studied or reported thus far. Failure to consider the concentration effects might have led to underestimation of the interaction of glutathione and yeast metabolites in some studies (e.g., Wolt and D'Appolonia, 1984b). Concentration of fermentation acids and crystallization of salts may also lower the pH values (van den Berg, 1968). It is likely that these changes occur in localized dough areas and thus affect dough stability. The solid ice phase also changes: the small ice crystals grow to form large crystals.

The presence of temperature gradients in the frozen dough systems, formed by unavoidable temperature fluctuations during frozen storage, induces water migration along the temperature gradients.

From the described changes it is evident that the components of the liquid phase in frozen dough are in metastable equilibria, which may be changing along with the exact composition of this phase during storage. Changes in the water transfer may lead to moisture loss in some dough components. For example, if the yeast cell membranes are either intact or resist the passage of ice, there is a consequent driving force toward dehydration of the cells by osmotic pressure.

Depending on the rate of cooling and the cell membrane permeability to water, the cell contents may become supercooled. With sufficiently rapid cooling, the cells may freeze internally. With slow cooling, extracellular ice only is formed and the cell dehydrates. If salt precipitates, a complex series of pH changes takes place (van den Berg, 1968). Undoubtedly disruption of certain bonds in dough systems is caused by dehydration and may affect the functionality of doughs. Judging from the practical performance of frozen doughs, however, it appears that most of these changes are reversible.

Defrosting

Frozen doughs must be thawed before proofing. This process can be conducted under various time-temperature conditions. In a study to define optimal conditions, Dubois and Blockcolsky (1986) compared four thawing procedures: 16 hr at 5°C (41°F), 24 hr at 5°C, 1 hr at 22°C (71°F), and proofing at 32°C (90°F) directly from the freezer. As expected, the warmer the dough is when placed into the proof box, the shorter is the proof time (to a given dough height). In these experiments, after 16 hr of storage at 23°C (73°F), doughs proofed by the four thawing procedures were fully proofed after 101, 61, 147, and 182 min, respectively. These data indicate that thawing is necessary for best performance of the dough. They also show that this step should be conducted at a slow rate at optimal time and temperature conditions. The functional effect of thawing involves rehydration of the system, mainly of the gluten matrix and yeast cells. It should be conducted at the refrigeration temperature (retardation conditions) to minimize various chemical, fermentation, and physical reactions. Based on the operational considerations and overall bread quality, this study recommended thawing at 5°C for 16 hr.

The higher thermal conductivity of frozen products is important in defrosting. From a thermodynamic point of view, defrosting is *not* a simple reversion of freezing. In a warmer medium, during defrosting, the product warms up quickly and the internal temperature gradients are much less than in freezing. An insulating liquid layer that forms on the surface retards refreezing and contributes to product deterioration. Thus, fluctuations of temperature above the freezing zones of products reduce their stability and quality. This condition should be avoided in shipping, handling, and storage of frozen doughs.

Proofing Considerations for Frozen Doughs

The proof times of frozen doughs after defrosting are necessarily longer than those of conventional doughs. This is due two factors: lower dough temperature at which the defrosted dough pieces reach the proof box, and a certain loss of dough gas retention power and yeast activity due to the freezing process. To compensate for these factors, proofing is conducted at higher temperature (32°C [90°F] for breads, up to 42°C [108° F] for smaller doughs [e.g., Danish pastry at a relative humidity of 75%]). The large temperature gradient in bread doughs may produce an uneven fermentation, with overproofing of the outer dough layers and underproofing of the center. Higher (85–90%) than normal (75%) relative humidities cause blisters and light blotches on the crust during baking (Stauffer, 1993).

Application of Polymer Science Concepts to Freezing

In the 1980s, Levine and Slade applied the principles of polymer science to structure problems of food technology. Of the numerous publications resulting from their research, the review in *Water Science Reviews 3* (1988) is probably the most comprehensive. Food polymer science, a term coined by Levine and Slade, had developed an approach to unify structured aspects of food materials, with the functional aspects described by the principles of water dynamics and glass dynamics. The important feature of their concept relative to frozen foods was a new insight into the factors contributing to frozen food stability.

This concept, as far as freezing is concerned, focuses on the unfrozen liquid matrix present between the ice crystals to explain the stability behavior of dough in term of the physical properties of this liquid phase. Concentration and temperature are the main factors involved here.

As discussed before, in the conventional treatment of freezing, both concentration and viscosity of the liquid phase increase with falling temperature. At some point of decreasing temperature, the liquid becomes so viscous that the motion of molecules becomes kinetically so restricted that the rate of reactions reaches a minimum. Water molecules at this condition also cannot migrate to form ice crystals.

The temperature at which this condition occurs is called the "glass transition" temperature (T_g), since slightly below this temperature the liquid system is transformed into a "glass" phase.

The T_g is an important index of the properties of the system. The higher the T_g, the faster the transition of the system into the glass phase. In subfreezing regions, the properties of the matrix are better described as rubbery and the kinetics follow the Williams-Landel-Ferry equation (WLF) rather than the Arrhenius equation. In the subfreezing zone, slower reactions are predicted by WLF kinetics than by those of Arrhenius.

What is the consequence of this concept on product stability? The T_g values locate the temperature of maximum stability of frozen systems in storage. They can be measured by means of DSC, which detects the heat capacity change accompanying the transformation from the liquid to the glass phase. At this point of our knowledge, we still depend on actual storage studies to establish stabilities of various products. However, the T_g concept may give us a clue in predicting the stability properties. The system stability, at least for aqueous systems, should depend on the location of this temperature: when the system is frozen and stored above the T_g temperature, the stability of the product is expected to be less than when frozen and stored below it. Consequently, the higher the T_g, the more stable the product would be in frozen storage and vice versa. Since the T_g is composition-dependent, this relationship offers us two potential benefits: it identifies the most stable formulations for freezing, and the T_g location can be raised by reformulation for improved frozen stabilities. Where this is not possible, ingredients can be added or replaced to produce higher T_g values. As an example, T_g values of some sugars and oligosaccharides are given in Table 6 (Kerr et al, 1993).

Although no study designed to evaluate the validity of T_g in frozen doughs has been made thus far, it is interesting to interpret the data of Dubois and Dreese (1984) in terms of this hypothesis. The effect of sugars on proof times of frozen bread dough is shown in Figure 6. Of the sugars tested, only the 62 dextrose equivalent (DE) corn syrup in the bread formula of frozen dough improved the dough stability in frozen storage as judged by the proof times. This saccharide, as expected, increased the T_g of the system and the frozen dough

Table 6
Glass Transition Temperatures (T_g') for Maximally
Concentrated Solutions as Determined by DSC[a]

	In Water	In Buffer
Glucose	−43.5	−42.5
Fructose	−42.0	−42.1
Maltose	−31.6	−30.5
Sucrose	−33.5	−33.0
Sorbitol	−44.0	−38.0
Polydextrose	−27.4	−29.0
M365	−22.1	−23.5
M250	−18.5	−19.0
M200	−15.3	−17.5
M150	−13.0	−15.0

[a] Source: Kerr et al (1993); used with permission.

stability. This relationship supports the hypothesis of Levine and Slade (1988).

An interesting prevention of enzymatic activity was demonstrated experimentally by Levine and Slade (1986) by variation of T_g. A model system consisting of glucose oxidase, methyl red, and a bulk solution of sucrose, Mores1910 (10 DE maltodextrin), and their mixture, which provided a range of T_g' values was used. (T_g' indicates the transition point on the DSC thermogram at which the freezing of "freezable water" is completed [Levine and Slade, 1988].) The enzymatic oxidation of glucose produces an acid that turns the color of the reacting mixture from yellow to pink. Samples with T_g' ranging from -9.5° (15°F) to -32°C (-26°F) were stored at various temperatures: 25, 3, -15, and -23°C (77, 37, -5, and -10°F). Samples were fluid at 25°C and 3°C; at -15°C and -23°C, the samples were solid and looked like colored ice. However, only samples with T_g' values above the storage temperature turned pink, indicating the production of acid by the enzyme. Even after a two-month storage period at -23°C, the samples containing maltodextrin, with $T_g' > -23°C$, were still yellow (no reaction). On the other hand, only samples for which the storage temperature was above the T_g' values turned pink. The frozen samples, even at -23°C, contained a concentrated enzyme-rich liquid phase surrounding

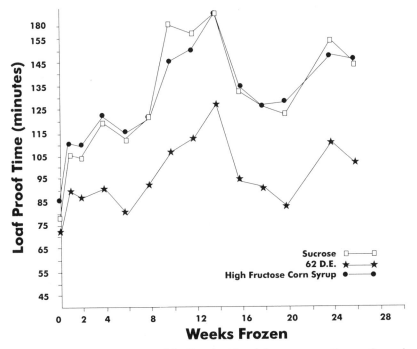

Fig. 6. Effect of sugar type (10% solids, flour basis) and frozen storage time on frozen bread dough stability, as indicated by length of respective proof times. (Reprinted, with permission, from Dubois and Dreese, 1984)

the ice crystals, while in those that remained yellow, the non-ice matrix was a glassy solid. Significantly, the activity of the enzyme was prevented by a storage temperature below T_g', but the enzyme itself was not inactivated. When the yellow samples were thawed, the enzyme quickly reacted, as indicated by the color change to pink.

This experimental design may be useful in studying the enzyme activities in frozen doughs (using nonyeasted doughs) and changes of acidity due to fermentation (yeasted dough). In general, the use of T_g as a reference point of the structural phase in food systems is an attractive concept. However, in applying it to frozen yeasted doughs, it is important to remember that the dough system contains, in addition to water, at least two components, flour and yeast, that each affect the T_g. Each of them may have a different T_g', which may have to be adjusted differently. The interaction of these components is also likely to complicate a unified description. It appears that the application of the concept is much cleaner for single-phase systems, e.g., cake batters, cookie doughs, and similar products. Briefly, the theoretical basis of the concept needs to be evaluated experimentally.

Retarded Doughs

In the United States, dough retardation is rarely applied to bread production at the wholesale level. Its use in wholesale bakeries is limited to the manufacturing of hearth crust bakery products (French, Italian types of bread, and hard rolls). On the other hand, dough retardation is a common production step in wholesale preparations of sweet doughs, Danish pastry, bagel, pizza, and croissant doughs.

Retail bakers also find this procedure advantageous and employ it in production of many bakery products, including standard breads. European bakers, who are retail-oriented, prefer dough retardation to dough freezing as a method of dough preservation (see details in Chapter 8).

Most retarded doughs retain their full functionality for 48 hr at the retarding temperature of 4–7°C (40–45°F) and relative humidity of about 85%.

Bread formulas and ingredient specifications do not require any special adjustments for retardation. The production method used is generally a straight-dough process. Dough mixing is conducted to full development, with the final temperature at 21°C (70°F). The dough then receives the conventional make-up, followed by panning of dough pieces and placing them in a retarder. After the retardation period, they are transferred from the retarder, allowed to warm up at room temperature, and proofed in a proofing cabinet. Sometimes retardation of bulk doughs may be necessary. In those cases, it is advisable to divide the bulk into 2.3- to 4.5-kg (5- to 10-lb) sections to facilitate the cooling. When, for some operational reasons, dough fermentation may not be sufficiently retarded, the yeast level in the formula should be somewhat reduced to correct for the excessive fermentation. A pale product crust may indicate that too much sugar was fermented. To improve this condition, a higher sugar level in the formula may be advisable.

The variables that should be adjusted for the retardation of Danish pastries are: less low mixing than normal, shorter or no proof times before retarding, and baking temperature at 210°C (410°F). Danish pastry may be retarded in 2.3- to 4.5-kg (5- to 10-lb) sections or preferably in made-up units.

Retardation of sweet doughs does not present serious problems. The factors that may be considered to need adjustment are the sugar and yeast levels. The higher the sugar level in the dough, the higher the yeast level required to support an adequate fermentation. In mixing, the dough temperature should be kept cooler than for nonretarded doughs, and their fermentation before retardation should be minimal. The conventional dough consistency is generally acceptable for retarded doughs.

Pizza doughs are easily retarded and become more pliable by this operation. Bagel doughs are generally retarded to produce surface blisters in finished products, a characteristic desirable for bagels.

It is claimed that croissants produced from retarded doughs have a superior flavor and are flakier and more tender than otherwise.

(The information on retarded dough is a compilation of Mares [1981] and *personal communication* from Kirk O'Donnell, R. Rodriguez, and R. Zelch of the American Institute of Baking, Manhattan, KS 66502.)

Literature Cited

Autio, K., and Sinda, E. 1992. Frozen doughs: Rheological changes and yeast viability. Cereal Chem. 69:409-413.

Bhatt, G. M., Paulsen, G. M., Kulp, K., and Heyne, E. G. 1981. Preharvest sprouting in hard winter wheats: Assessment of methods to detect genotypic and nitrogen effects and interactions. Cereal Chem. 58:300-302.

Berglund, P. T., Shelton, D. R., and Freeman, T. P. 1991. Frozen bread dough ultrastructure as affected by duration of frozen storage and freeze-thaw cycles. Cereal Chem. 68:105-107.

Bigg, E. K. 1963. The supercooling of water. Proc. Phys. Soc. B66:688.

Bietz, J. A. 1987. Genetic and biochemical studies of nonenzymatic endosperm proteins. Pages 215-241 in: Wheat and Wheat Improvement, 2nd ed. E. G. Heyne, ed. American Society of Agronomy, Madison, WI.

Bietz, J. A. 1992. How knowledge of proteins is improving cereal quality and utilization. Pages 5-15 in: Cereal Chemistry and Technology: A Long and Bright Future (9th Int. Cereal and Bread Congr., Paris, June 1992). P. Feillet, ed. Institut de Recherches Technologiques Agroalimentaires des Cereales (IRTAC), Montpellier, France.

Bushuk, W. 1966. Distribution of water in dough and bread. Baker's Dig. 40:36-40.

Bushuk, W. 1985a. Flour proteins: Structure and functionality in dough and bread. Cereal Foods World 30:447-451.

Bushuk, W. 1985b. Protein-lipid and protein-carbohydrate interactions in flour-water mixtures. Pages 147-154 in: Chemistry and Physics of Baking. J. M. W. Blanshard, P. J. Frazier, and T. Galliard, eds. R. Soc. Chem, London.

Bushuk, W., and MacRitchie, F. 1987. Wheat proteins: Aspects of structure that are related to breadmaking quality. Pages 357-361 in: Protein Quality and Effects of Processing. R. D. Phillips and J. W. Finley, eds. Marcel Dekker, New York.

Bushuk, W., Khan, K., and McMaster, G. 1980. Functional glutenin. A complex of covalently and non-covalently linked components. Ann. Technol. Agric. 29:279-294.

Chandrasekaran, S. K., and King, C. J. 1971. Solid-liquid phase in multicomponent aqueous sugar solutions. J. Food Sci. 36:699-704.

Chen, J., Khan, K., Shelton, D. R., and D'Appolonia, B. L. 1992. Isolation and fractionation of carbohydrate-containing proteins from wheat gluten. Cereal Chem. 69:475-480.

Chung, O. K., Pomeranz, Y., Hwang, E. C., and Dikeman, E. 1979. Defatted and reconstituted wheat flours. IV. Effects of flour lipids on protein extractability from flours that vary in bread-making quality. Cereal Chem. 56:220-226.

Dubois, D. K., and Blockcolsky, D. 1986. Frozen bread dough—Effect of dough mixing and thawing methods. Res. Dept. Tech. Bull. 8(6):1-7, American Institute of Baking, Manhattan, KS.

Dubois, D. K., and Dreese, P. 1984. Frozen white bread dough—Effects of sweetener type and level. Res. Dept. Tech. Bull. 6(7):1-7, American Institute of Baking, Manhattan, KS.

Feeney, R. E. 1982. Penguin egg white and polar fish blood serum proteins. Int. J. Peptide Protein Res. 19:215.

Fennema, O. 1975. Reaction kinetics in partially frozen aqueous systems. Pages 539-556 in: Water Relations of Food. R. B. Duckworth, ed. Academic Press, London.

Hsu, K. H., Hoseney, R. C., and Seib, P. A. 1979a. Frozen dough. I. Factors affecting stability of yeasted doughs. Cereal Chem. 56:419-424.

Hsu, K. H., Hoseney, R. C., and Seib, P. A. 1979b. Frozen dough. II. Effects of freezing and storing conditions on the stability of yeasted doughs. Cereal Chem. 56:424-426.

Inoue, Y., and Bushuk, W. 1991. Studies on frozen doughs. I. Effects of frozen storage and freeze-thaw cycles on baking and rheological properties. Cereal Chem. 68:627-631.

Inoue, Y., and Bushuk, W. 1992. Studies on frozen doughs. II. Flour quality requirements for bread production from frozen dough. Cereal Chem. 69:423-428.

Inoue, Y., Sapirstein, H. D., Takayanagi, S., and Bushuk, W. 1994. Studies on frozen doughs. III. Some factors involved in dough weakening during frozen storage and thaw-freeze cycles. Cereal Chem. 71:118-121.

Kerr, W. L., Lim, M. H., Reid, D. S., and Chen, H. 1993. Chemical reaction kinetics in relation to glass transition temperatures in frozen food polymer solutions. J. Sci. Food Agric. 60:51-56.

King, C. J. 1975. Application of freeze-drying to food products. Pages 333-349 in: Freeze-Drying and Advanced Food Technology. S. A. Goldblith, L. Rey, and W. W. Rohmayr, eds. Academic Press, New York.

Kline, L., and Sugihara, T. F. 1968. Factors affecting the stability of frozen bread doughs. I. Prepared by straight dough method. Baker's Dig. 42(5):44-50.

Langham, E. J., and Mason, B. C. 1958. The heterogeneous and homogeneous nucleation of supercooled water. Proc. R. Soc. A247:493.

Levine H., and Slade, L. 1986. A polymer physico-chemical approach to the study of commercial starch hydrolysis products (SHPs). Carbohydr. Polym. 6:213-244.

Levine, H., and Slade, L. 1988. Water as a plasticizer: Physico-chemical aspects of low-moisture polymeric systems. Pages 79-185 in: Water Science Reviews. Vol. 3, Water Dynamics. F. Franks., ed. Cambridge University Press, New York.

Levine, H., and Slade, L. 1990. Influences of the glassy and rubbery states on the thermal, mechanical, and structural properties of doughs and baked products. Pages 157-330 in: Dough Rheology and Baked Product Texture. H. Faridi and J. Faubion, eds. Van Nostrand Reinhold, New York.

Ling, R. S., and Hoseney, R. C. 1977. Effect of certain nutrients on the gas produced in preferments. Cereal Chem. 54:597-604.

Lucena, C. V. 1955. Ice propagation in systems of biological interest. III. Effect of solutes on nucleation and growth of ice crystals. Arch. Biochem. Biophys. 55:217.

Mares, C. 1981. Test your I.Q. on retarded dough products. Bakery Prod. Manage. 16(5):190.

McMaster, G. J., and Bushuk, W. 1983. Protein-carbohydrate complexes in gluten: Fractionation and proximate composition. J. Cereal Sci. 1:171-184.

Panozzo, J. F., Bekes, F., Wrigley, C. W., and Gupta, R. B. 1994. The effects of bromate (0–30 ppm) on the proteins and lipids of dough. Cereal Chem. 71:195-199.

Payne, P. I., Holt, L. M., Jackson, E. A., and Law, C. N. 1984. Wheat storage proteins: Their genetics and their potential for manipulation by plant breeding. Philos. Trans. R. Soc. London B 304:359-371.

Payne, P. I., Corfield, K. G., Holt, M., and Blackman, J. A. 1981. Correlation between the inheritance of certain high-molecular weight subunits of glutenin and bread-baking quality in progenesis of six crosses of bread wheat. J. Sci. Food Agric. 32:51-60.

Payne, P. I., Corfield, K. G., and Blackman, J. A. 1979. Identification of a high molecular-weight glutenin whose presence correlates with bread making wheats of related pedigree. Theor. Appl. Genet. 55:153-159.

Ponte, J. G., Jr., Glass, R. L., and Geddes, W. F. 1960. Studies on the behavior of active dry yeast cells in breadmaking. Cereal Chem. 37:263-279.

Reid, D. S. 1990. Optimizing the quality of frozen foods. Food Technol. 44(7):78-82.

Reid, D. S. 1983. Fundamental physicochemical aspects of freezing. Food Technol. 37(4):110-115.

Stauffer, C. E. 1993. Frozen dough production. Pages 88-106 in: Advances in Baking Technology. B. S. Kamel and C. E. Stauffer, eds. Blackie Academic and Professional, Glasgow, UK.

Sutton, T., Olewnik, M., Boeckman, R., Breault, D., and Langmeier, J. 1994. Effect of glutathione in frozen dough yeast-raised baking products on soluble proteins, visco-elastic dough properties and finished quality characteristics (Abstr. 70). Cereal Foods World 39:602.

van den Berg, L. 1968. Physicochemical changes in food during freezing and subsequent storage. Pages 205-219 in: Low Temperature Biology of Foodstuffs. J. H. Hawthorn and E. J. Rolfe, eds. Pergamon Press, Oxford, UK.

Varriano-Marston, E., Hsu, K. H., and Mhadi, J. 1980. Rheological and structural changes in frozen dough. Baker's Dig. 54(1):32-34, 41.

Wolt, M. J., and D'Appolonia, B. L. 1984a. Factors involved in the stability of frozen dough. I. The influence of yeast reducing compounds on frozen-dough stability. Cereal Chem. 61:209-212.

Wolt, M. J., and D'Appolonia, B. L. 1984b. Factors involved in the stability of frozen dough. II. The effects of yeast type, flour type, and dough additives on frozen-dough stability. Cereal Chem. 61:213-221.

Wrigley, C. W., and Bietz, J. A. 1988. Proteins and amino acids. Pages 159-275 in: Wheat Chemistry and Technology, 3rd ed. Vol. I. Y. Pomeranz, ed. Am. Assoc. Cereal Chem., St. Paul, MN.

Zawistowska, U., Bekes, F., and Bushuk, W. 1984. Intercultivar variations in lipid content, composition and distribution and their relation to baking quality. Cereal Chem. 61:527-531.

Zawistowska, U., Bekes, F., and Bushuk, W. 1985. Involvement of carbohydrates and lipids in aggregation of glutenin proteins. Cereal Chem. 62:340-345

CHAPTER 5

Functional Role of Microingredients in Frozen Doughs

V. A. De Stefanis
Elf Atochem North America Fine Chemicals
Buffalo, New York 14240

When a processed dough is stored in the freezer for long periods, two problems often emerge: dough destabilization (weakness), resulting in a low loaf volume and coarse grain, and yeast inactivation, leading to long proofing. In reviewing the literature on frozen doughs, it becomes quite clear that yeast continues to receive the greatest attention. This may be explained by the fact that it was assumed that these problems were the result of yeast damage. However, recent research indicates that certain microingredients play a more important role in dough stabilization than yeast does, as is shown in this chapter.

Frozen Dough Quality

Practical experience, as well as the research reported in the literature, clearly indicates that certain measures must be considered to ensure a stable dough (Table 1). Frozen dough technology comprises two major steps: dough preparation (structure building) and dough processing (freezing and storing). In the past 20 years, a great deal of knowledge has been accumulated on how to freeze, package, and store doughs (Marston, 1978, 1979; Hsu et al, 1979; Lehmann and Dreese, 1981; Dubois and Blockcolsky, 1986b; Evenson, 1987; Inoue et al, 1991, 1994; Gelinas et al, 1993, 1994; Neyreneuf and Delpuech, 1993). However, our knowledge of how to achieve the best quality dough possible, *before freezing*, is somewhat limited.

Temperature of Dough Mixing

One area of research on frozen doughs that has received minimal attention is the preparation stage, particularly the temperature at dough mixing. Figure 1 illustrates the effect of temperature on loaf volume and proof time. This critical step has been treated lightly, and reports of mixing temperatures of 18–27°C have not been uncommon. Adopting the specific loaf volume as the index of dough quality (dough stability), it is obvious that a direct relationship exists between volume and temperature. However, if one were to plot the mixing temperature to proof time for the same doughs, an inverse relationship would be obtained. In other words, although the higher temperature produced a greater volume response, simultaneously, the proof time lengthened. The pat-

Table 1
Favorable Conditions for Processing Frozen Doughs

Reduced water absorption
Reduced dough mixing temperature
High level of shortening
High level of yeast
High level of surfactant
Straight-dough no-time baking method
Freezing of dough immediately after mixing
Suitable packaging having moisture and oxygen barriers
Freezer temperature of -23°C

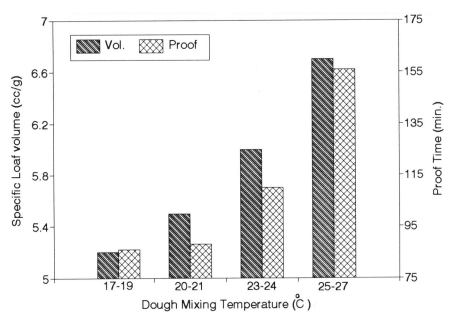

Fig. 1. Effect of dough mixing temperature on loaf volume and proof time. Doughs were mixed at 17–27°C, stored at -23°C for 16 weeks, retarded at 4°C (16–18 hr), proofed to 1 in. above the pan, and baked at 219°C (20 min). The dough-handling procedure out of the freezer was constant for all experiments. Oxidation system: potassium bromate (75 ppm) + fungal α-amylase (132 SKB/100 g of flour).

tern becomes worse as the freezer storage time increases (*data from author's laboratory*). This phenomenon is explained by the fact that, at higher mixing temperatures (above 21°C), incipient yeast fermentation occurs, rendering the yeast cell more susceptible to freezer damage during storage, while the structural integrity of yeast is retained at lower temperatures, with little or no fermentation occurring to 21°C. Therefore, dough mixing temperatures above 21°C are clearly discouraged.

Rest Time

The general practice in the industry is to freeze doughs immediately after mixing. However, if a dough were allowed to rest for at least 8–10 min immediately after mixing, a greater bread volume would be realized after storage (Fig. 2). In actual practice, this is easily accomplished by lowering the temperature from 20–21°C to 17–19°C or lower for 8–10 min, followed by direct freezing as normally done (*author's data*).

Flour

High-protein flours are normally used (13.5–14.0%). Both spring and winter wheats or blends are suitable (Lorenz, 1965). Lower-protein flours (11.5–12.5%) may be used; however, they need supplementation with vital wheat gluten. It is generally agreed by bakers that high-protein flours improve dough stability during storage. This practice has been confirmed in our laboratory, as is readily seen in Figure 3. Loaf volume fluctuated least when 13.8% protein flour was used, regardless of the temperature at mixing (18–27°C).

Shortening

It is well known that shortening in the formulation improves dough processing and the crumb properties of bread. At least 1% is required, with maximum benefits to 2% (Fig. 4). Saturated or partially saturated shortening is preferred in frozen dough. Unsaturated triglycerides (oils) are discouraged, unless formulations also include dough strengtheners, e.g. ethoxylated mono-diglycerides, sodium or calcium stearoyl lactylates, or diacetyl tartaric acid esters of mono- and diglycerides. Surfactants tend to suppress the ill effects of the oil in baking.

Surfactants

Surfactants generally modify dough and bread properties. They are categorized into two general classes: crumb softeners (e.g., monoglycerides) and dough strengtheners (e.g., ethoxylated mono- or diglycerides, sodium or calcium stearoyl lactylate, etc.), with a few exhibiting bifunctional properties (e.g., sodium stearoyl lactylate [SSL]). Dough strengtheners are highly desirable in frozen dough because they preferentially interact with the gluten proteins (De Stefanis et al, 1977). These proteins provide the architectural strength of the dough matrix, hence are important to freezer stability. It was shown previously (Fig. 3) that a high-protein flour is important in frozen dough. Formulations

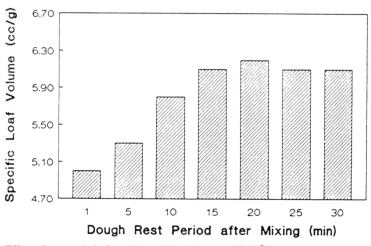

Dough Rest Period after Mixing (min)

Fig. 2. Effect of rest period after mixing. Mixed doughs (20–21°C) were cooled to 17–18°C and allowed to rest for 1–30 min, followed by freezing (-23°C). After three weeks, doughs were thawed (in a retarder), proofed, and baked (using the same procedure described in Fig. 2). Oxidation system: azodicarbonamide (45 ppm) + fungal α-amylase (132 SKB/100 g of flour). (De Stefanis, *unpublished data*)

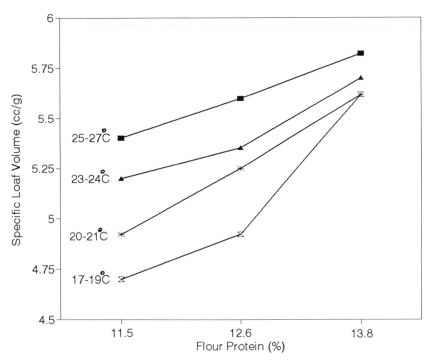

Fig. 3. Flour protein vs. loaf volume. Flours with different protein content (%) were used. Mixed oughs were frozen (-23°C) for one week. Oxidation: potassium bromate (20 ppm). (De Stefanis, *unpublished data*)

with high-protein flours and dough strengtheners increase dough stability and are therefore desirable in the production of frozen doughs (Dubois and Block-colsky, 1986a; Hosomi et al, 1992). In summary, formulations that include dough strengtheners, solid shortening, and high-protein flour with mixing at 17–19°C or lower provide the baker with a dough of much improved storage stability at -23°C.

Oxidation in Frozen Dough

Oxidants, whether of natural or chemical origin, exert an improving effect on dough rheology and the overall quality of the finished product. This effect is realized in all types of baking (Lorenz and Bechtel, 1965). Potassium bromate ($KBrO_3$) has been the oxidant of choice in the baking industry for at least 60 years. An oxidant exhibits its improving effect in baking by increasing the loaf volume during the first few minutes of baking (oven-spring). Volume response is often used as a measure of optimum oxidation, hence dough quality. Figure 5 illustrates the effect of bromate concentration, as a function of mixing temperature, on loaf volume (*author's data*). In general, the volume increased in proportion to concentration. However, it should be noted that doughs mixed at 17–19°C required a higher level of bromate than those mixed at 25–27°C to achieve similar volumes. These results suggest that a higher level of oxidation is required as the temperature of dough mixing decreases. Therefore, maximum volume response is realized when the level of oxidation is in balance with the temperature of dough at mixing. It will be shown later in the chapter that when a dough is treated at the optimum level of oxidation, it remains structurally stable in storage (at -23°C). Much research was conducted in the author's laboratory to identify key factors that were most responsible for volume response (oven-spring). A simple (lean) bread formulation (Table 2) was used to conduct this research. Conditions for dough preparation and thawing and bread evaluation are described in Table 3. Flour protein, mixing time, absorption, temperature of mixing, type of shortening, surfactants, type of yeast (compressed or instant dry), type of baking, oxidants, and yeast foods were all carefully scrutinized. Results of these experiments clearly identified two key ingredients, oxidant and yeast, as exercising the greatest effect on the behavior of frozen doughs during and after storage. Above all, results clearly identified dough destabilization and long proofing as being two distinctly different entities, although there were crossovers, as will be shown later.

This chapter focuses mainly on the functional role of the oxidant in frozen doughs and factors affecting its performance. Yeast is treated in detail in Chapter 2.

Requirements in Baking

Bread products are made for the consumer by many different methods. For example, some manufacturers use no fermentation time (no-time, the method most commonly used for frozen doughs), while others use the straight-dough or sponge and dough methods with varying sponge fermentation times (1–5 hr). Still others use extremely lean formulations, low yeast (1% or less), and long

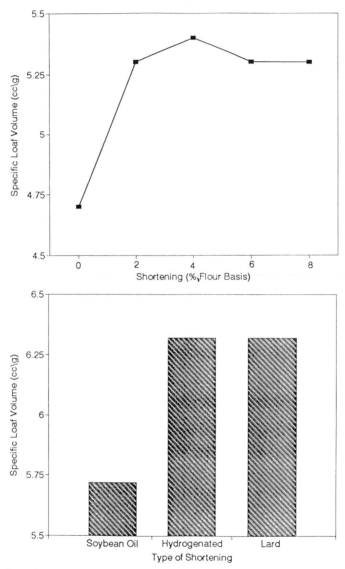

Fig. 4. Effect of shortening concentration (top) and type (bottom) on specific loaf volume. Top, doughs were formulated with 0–8% (flour basis) partially hydrogenated vegetable shortening. Oxidation: potassium bromate (20 ppm) Bottom, another group of doughs was prepared with 2% (flour basis) soybean oil, hydrogenated shortening, and lard and was stored at -23°C for four weeks. Oxidation: potassium bromate (75 ppm) + fungal α-amylase (132 SKB/100 g of flour). (De Stefanis, *unpublished data*)

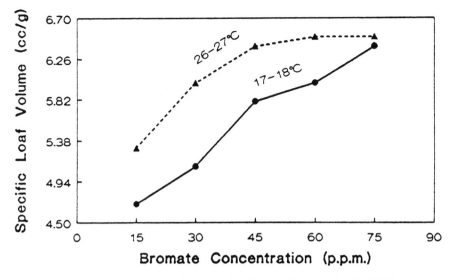

Fig. 5. Oxidant concentration vs. loaf volume. Doughs were formulated with 15–75 ppm potassium bromate, mixed at 17–18°C and at 26–27°C, and stored at -23°C for three weeks. (De Stefanis, *unpublished data*)

Table 2
Bread Formulation[a]

	Percent (flour basis)
Flour (13.5–14.0% protein)	100.0
Yeast (compressed)	5.0
Shortening (hydrogenated vegetable)	2.0
Dextrose (Cerelose)	4.0
Water (variable)	6–8 less than conventional

[a] Laboratory formulation (lean) used in frozen dough baking experiments.

fermentation (16–18 hr). It is generally agreed that different baking methods require different levels of oxidation to achieve a consumer-acceptable product and processing ease in the bakery. Frozen dough baking, by far, requires the highest level of oxidation, while considerably less is needed for the straight-dough and sponge and dough methods.

Different Oxidants

Potassium bromate ($KBrO_3$), potassium iodate (KIO_3), azodicarbonamide (ADA), and ascorbic acid (AA) are the oxidants (bread improvers) most commonly used by the baking industry for the improvement of loaf volume and overall dough and bread quality. These oxidants perform at different rates: $KBrO_3$ is slow-acting, ADA and KIO_3 fast-acting, and AA intermediate. Since their rates are different, it is logical to assume that they would also behave differently in dough; hence, they are not interchangeable in certain types of baking. Frozen doughs are prepared and processed under extremely rigid conditions, i.e., below conventional mixing temperatures, with low water absorption, and subjected to freezing and thawing cycles. Therefore, the rate of action is important. For instance, Figure 6 shows that fast-acting ADA produced a higher loaf volume than slow-acting bromate. The concept of speed can be illustrated in another way. Several years ago, De Stefanis et al (1988) reported the catalytic effect of the vanadium ion on bromate. Bromate in the presence of vanadium is transformed from a slow- to a fast-acting oxidant, so much so that the mixing time must be reduced to prevent overmixing (Fig. 7). Bromate alone is not very effective in frozen doughs, but its effectiveness is greatly improved with additions of ascorbic acid. Tsen (1965) suggested that the two oxidants operate in synergy. Reports in the literature indicate that the bromate action can be increased by lowering the operating pH. Using predetermined levels of HCl, doughs were adjusted to pH 4.50, 5.03, and 5.72 (as is) in the author's laboratory, mixed at 20–21°C, frozen for a week, then assessed by the procedure described previously. Results (Table 4) clearly show that the dough pH had little effect on the action rate of bromate. Potassium bromate is indeed a slow-acting oxidant, and the cold mixing temperature appears to lower its oxidative action even further.

The dough structural properties set at the mixing stage (with optimum oxidation) are critical to freezer stability. This concept is easily demonstrated. After mixing (20–21°C), one group of doughs was processed "fresh" (no freezing), while another was stored at -23°C for up to 16 weeks. Doughs were sampled at regular intervals (during weeks 4–16) and evaluated. Results (Fig. 8) indicate virtually no loss of volume up to 16 weeks; hence, the dough had good stabil-

Table 3
Standard Baking and Evaluation Methods Used in Studies

"No-time" baking method (20–21°C)
Flour + dry ingredients
Yeast suspension
Mixed (1 min) (low speed)
Salt + dextrose solution
Mixed to development (high speed)
Floor time (10 min)
Frozen (-23°C)
Thawing and bread evaluation
Frozen doughs placed in baking pans
Retarded (16–24 hr/2–4°C)
Proofed (time or height)
Baked (219°C/20 min)
Cooled (1 hr/ambient temperature)
Loaf volume measured

ity. A destabilized dough normally yields low volume and coarse grain. These results are valuable because several conclusions can be drawn: 1) structural properties are set at the mixing stage, 2) stability depends on oxidation, and 3) quality can be assessed on a "fresh" dough without needing to wait for long storage periods. Table 5 illustrates the effect of oxidant concentration on dough stability. An underoxidized dough exhibited poor stability (low volume, coarse grain), compared to one mixed at the optimal level. These results show that destabilization (low volume, open grain) is largely caused by underoxidation. This situation is aggravated when the temperature of mixing is lowered (Table 5). Again, the concentration of the oxidant in the formulation is inversely correlated with the temperature of dough mixing. Following this line of thinking, Autio and Sinda (1992) reported that the addition of dead yeast cells (glutathione) did not effect the structural properties of frozen doughs. They

No treatment   45 ppm ADA

150 ppm   75 ppm bromate
ascorbic acid

Fig. 6. Comparison of different oxidants in frozen dough. Separate doughs were prepared with potassium bromate (75 ppm), ascorbic acid (150 ppm), and azodicarbonamide (ADA, 45 ppm). All doughs contained fungal α-amylase (132 SKB/100 g of flour). Doughs were mixed at 20–21°C, followed by storage at -23°C for two weeks. (De Stefanis, *unpublished data*)

| Vanadyl acetate, 50 ppm | $K_{BR}O_3$, 75 ppm | Vanadyl acetate, 50 ppm $K_{BR}O_3$, 75 ppm |

Fig. 7. Change in bromate from slow- to fast-acting. Doughs were prepared with potassium bromate (75 ppm), vanadyl acetate (50 ppm), and potassium bromate (75 ppm) + vanadyl acetate (50 ppm). The mixing time of the last dough was reduced by 30%. Fungal α-amylase (132 SKB/100 g of flour) was added to all doughs. Doughs, mixed at 20–21°C, were frozen (-23°C) for one week. (Reprinted, with permission, from De Stefanis et al, 1988)

Table 4
Performance of Doughs[a] Containing Bromate (75 ppm)
at Various pH Levels

Dough pH[b]	Specific Loaf Volume (cc/g)
4.50	5.9
5.03	6.0
5.72 (as is)	5.9

[a] Doughs mixed at 20–21°C, followed by 10-min rest. Stored at -23°C for one week, retarded at 4°C (16–18 hr), proofed to height (1 in. above pan), and baked (219°C/20 min).
[b] Dough pH adjusted with HCl (predetermined); 13.8% protein flour.

stated further that dough weakness upon thawing was not caused by reducing substances released by the yeast cell but by reduced cross-linking action in the gluten network. Bruinsma and Gieselschlag (1984) also reported that the dough weakening phenomenon could occur independently of yeast.

Bromate Replacers

The state of California lists bromate as a carcinogen under California's Safe Drinking Water and Toxic Enforcement Act of 1986 (Proposition 65). The carcinogenicity is related to bromate *per se* and not to the type of salt. Therefore, neither the calcium nor the sodium form is considered a replacement for potassium bromate. Frozen doughs, as mentioned previously, require the highest level of oxidation. The need is so great that it often approaches the highest

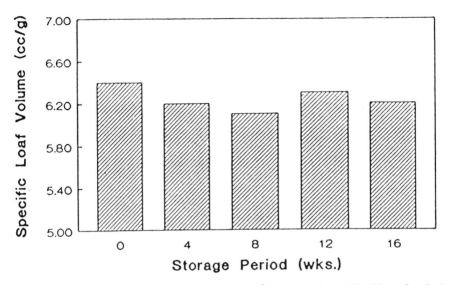

Fig. 8. Dough stability at -23°C. Mixed doughs (20–21°C) were evaluated "fresh" (no freezing), and after 4, 8, 12, and 16 weeks at -23°C. Oxidation system: potassium bromate (40 ppm) + ascorbic acid (70 ppm) + fungal α-amylase (132 SKB/100 g of flour). (De Stefanis, *unpublished data*)

Table 5
Oxidant Concentration vs. Loaf Volume

Temperature of Dough Mixing[a] (°C)	ADA Concentration (ppm)	Specific Loaf Volume (cm³/g)
17–19	0	3.3
	20	4.3
	45	5.8
20–21	0	4.3
	20	5.3
	45	6.4

[a] Doughs allowed to rest 10 min after mixing. Stored at -23°C for four weeks.

level permitted by law, whether used alone or in combination with other oxidants. What other oxidants can the baker use successfully in place of bromate? Currently, ADA and AA are the only alternatives. Iodate salts are not too appealing to the baker; hence, little emphasis is placed on this oxidant in this chapter.

The baking industry has been inundated with bromate replacers, causing a great deal of confusion. The numerous products in the marketplace are blends of ADA and AA, whether used alone and in combination with enzymes and surfactants. Before attempting to replace bromate, one should focus on the baker's requirements for a replacer, i.e., high dough-mixing tolerance, processing ease, improved loaf volume, and improved bread quality.

Typical practice by manufacturers of bromate replacers is to blend ADA,

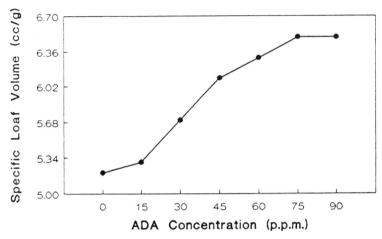

Fig. 9. Effect of azodicarbonamide (ADA) concentration on specific loaf volume. Doughs were formulated with 0–90 ppm ADA, mixed at 20-21°C, and frozen for one week. (De Stefanis, *unpublished data*)

Yeast A   Yeast B
2% active dry yeast

Fig. 10. Effect of yeast quality on doughs containing azodicarbonamide (ADA). Doughs were prepared with two commercial samples of active dry yeast (2% flour basis), mixed at 20–21°C, and frozen for four weeks. Oxidation system: ADA (45 ppm) + fungal α-amylase (132 SKB/100 g of flour). (De Stefanis, *unpublished data*)

AA, enzymes, and surfactants and offer them for sale to the baker. Often, the finished product is not analyzed before shipping because of limited analytical methodology. One approach to creating successful bromate replacers is to develop quantitative methods applicable to flour, doughs, and bread systems first, in order to learn the functional behavior of the oxidants in breadmaking.

Since ADA and AA operate differently from bromate, it is important to know how to use them most effectively as bromate replacers.

Azodicarbonamide

ADA is a fast-acting oxidant. The legal limit in the United States is 45 ppm, while for bromate it is 75 ppm. Replacement of bromate would be felt less if a higher concentration of ADA were permitted (Fig. 9). Unlike bromate, ADA is extremely sensitive to yeast quality (Fig. 10). Glutathione and other reducing substances react readily through a redox mechanism. Therefore, ADA gives a variable response in baking, depending on the concentration of these yeast substances. Since natural biological systems release glutathione to protect the cell from attack by free radicals, it seemed logical to utilize this concept by combining benzoyl peroxide (BPO) and ADA in baking (Fig. 11). Under the conditions of the experiment, BPO alone reacted only slightly with glutathione.

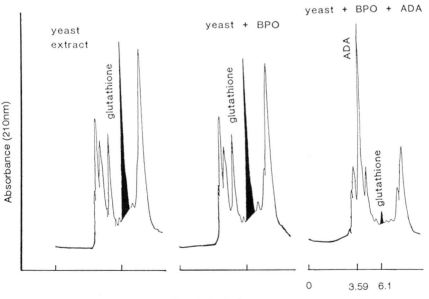

Fig. 11. Improved performance of azodicarbonamide (ADA) combined with benzoyl peroxide (BPO). Compressed yeast suspension (5%) was combined either with BPO (150 ppm) or BPO (150 ppm) + ADA (45 ppm) and held at pH 5.2–5.50 for 15 min (30°C). Each extract was analyzed by liquid chromatography at 210 nm. (De Stefanis, *unpublished data*)

The simultaneous addition of BPO and ADA catalyzed the oxidation, which caused the disappearance of glutathione. This concept is also demonstrated in actual baking (Table 6). The performance of ADA was affected by the form of

Table 6
Effect of BPO[a] on Doughs Containing ADA[b]

Yeast (type)	BPO (ppm)	Specific Loaf Volume[c] (cm³/g)
Compressed[d]	0	6.7
	150	7.0
Instant dry[e]	0	5.7
	150	6.8

[a] Azodicarbonamide, 45 ppm.
[b] Benzoyl peroxide.
[c] Flour contained 13.8% protein. Doughs stored one week at -23°C.
[d] 5%, flour basis.
[e] 2%, flour basis.

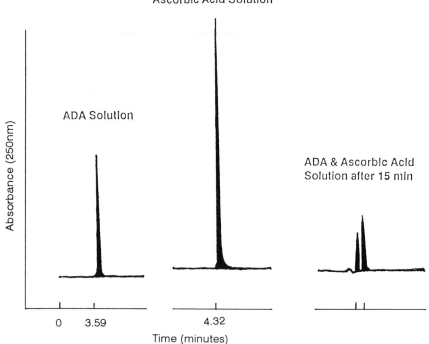

Fig. 12. Reaction between azodicarbonamide (ADA) and ascorbic acid (AA) in water. Aqueous solutions of ADA (0.004%), AA (0.010%), and ADA (0.004%) + AA (0.010%) were adjusted to pH 5.20–5.50 and held at 30°C for 15 min. The solutions were analyzed by liquid chromatography at 250 nm. (De Stefanis, *unpublished data*)

the yeast product. The instant dry yeast in this experiment contained a higher level of glutathione than the compressed yeast. Additions of BPO improved ADA performance. Later studies showed that BPO also improves the oxidative action of AA, bromate, and iodate (De Stefanis, 1994). Enhanced oxidation is desirable in frozen doughs.

At times, 45 ppm of ADA is not sufficient for frozen doughs. The baker often combines ADA and AA to meet the oxidation requirement. One word of caution on this practice: ADA and AA react with one another through a redox mechanism, which is rapid in water (Fig. 12). Therefore, products containing blends of ADA and AA should not be added to water slurries (without flour). In dough systems, the reaction is greatly reduced, possibly because AA undergoes transformation from the reductant to the oxidant state (dehydroascorbic acid), which is more compatible with ADA.

Encapsulated ADA. ADA is extremely reactive, hence classified as a fast-acting oxidant. One way to reduce its reactivity is by encapsulation. Several encapsulating agents have appeared in the marketplace (modified starch, hydrocolloids, proteins, fats, etc.). Fat encapsulation was preferred in our laboratory because the operation was compatible with the existing equipment. Various fat sources (hydrocarbons, triglycerides, phospholipids, monoglycerides, and surfactants) were carefully screened for properties that met our criteria. In general, results showed that the oils and saturated fats with melting points above 64°C performed poorly, while those within the 40–57°C range were effective. Dough strengtheners were superior because they interact favorably

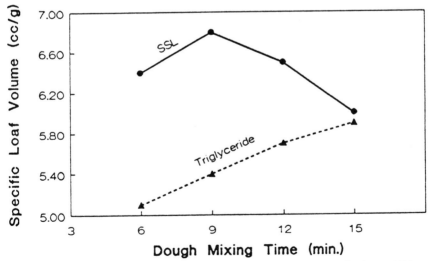

Fig. 13. Effect of fat-encapsulated azodicarbonamide (ADA) on specific loaf volume. ADA was encapsulated with saturated high-melting-point (63–65°C) triglycerides and with sodium stearoyl lactylate (SSL) under similar conditions. Finely pulverized product (through 60 mesh) was added to flour; doughs were mixed at 20–21°C and frozen for one week. Oxidation system: ADA (45 ppm) + fungal α-amylase (132 SKB/100 g of flour). (De Stefanis, *unpublished data*)

with the proteins. Figure 13 compares the effect of ADA encapsulated with saturated triglycerides (melting point 63–66°C) or with SSL. Triglyceride encapsulation prevented the complete release of ADA during mixing; hence, the obtained bread appeared underoxidized and of poor quality. The opposite pattern was obtained with SSL, which released ADA completely because of its melting point (40–43°C). The overall criterion for encapsulation is to delay the action of ADA toward the end of the mixing cycle, with quantitative release at end of the cycle.

ADA vs. SSL-ADA. Encapsulation with dough strengtheners, e.g., SSL, improves the performance of ADA in baking. SSL-ADA produced a larger volume than ADA alone (Fig. 14). SSL seems to perform several functions: it protects ADA from side reactions, promotes greater oxidant response, and accelerates dough development (reduces mixing time by 10–15%). Once again, a fast-acting oxidant is desirable in frozen doughs. It is postulated that the mechanism of SSL encapsulation may involve protecting ADA, as well as promoting direct transport of the oxidant to the gluten proteins.

Ascorbic Acid

AA is used extensively as a bread improver, especially in countries where bromate was never permitted. In frozen dough, AA is as effective as bromate but less effective than ADA. Doughs containing AA require slightly longer mixing times than those with bromate. The improving effect of AA largely de-

45 ppm ADA   45 ppm coated ADA

Fig. 14. Azodicarbonamide (ADA) vs. encapsulated ADA in frozen doughs. ADA was encapsulated with sodium stearoyl lactylate (SSL) under standardized conditions. The powdered product (through 60 mesh) was added to flour; doughs were mixed at 20–21°C and frozen for one week.. Oxidation system: ADA (45 ppm) + fungal α-amylase (132 SKB/100 g of flour). (De Stefanis, *unpublished data*)

pends upon the flour and the type of mixer. Bakeries that use mixers that re-
strict the flow of air will not benefit greatly from its use. Chamberlin and Collins (1979) found that the improving action of AA was related to the amount of
oxygen (air) entrained during dough mixing.

Dehydroascorbic Acid

AA is a reductant. It is generally believed that the improving action in bread
is due to its oxidized form, dehydroascorbic acid (DHA). The transformation of
AA to DHA is accomplished through a mechanism that requires both oxygen
(air) and the enzyme ascorbic acid oxidase. DHA is very unstable and highly
reactive. Other mechanisms (e.g., chemical) for the transformation of AA to
DHA provide alternate approaches. Strong oxidants, such as ADA, potassium
iodate, and hydrogen peroxide (H_2O_2) can oxidize AA. For example, H_2O_2
oxidizes AA slowly; however, addition of catalytic ions (Fe^{2+}, Fe^{3+}, Cu^{2+}) accelerates the oxidation, with the catalyst's concentration controlling the rate.
Using balanced reactant concentrations, the transformation of AA to DHA can
be induced in aqueous media, flour brews, and plastic doughs. DHA is highly
unstable (1–2 hr) and therefore must be prepared fresh before use in baking.
Dry preparations are much more desirable in a bakery operation. One preparation that seems to have strong possibilities is a mixture of calcium peroxide and
AA. Product ingredients remain inactive, and thus stable, in the dry state. Reactions are activated with the addition of water. One possible pathway is described in Figure 15. Figure 16 illustrates the transformation occurring in a
flour brew. Encapsulated ADA + DHA mixtures provide the baking industry
with a powerful oxidative system.

Azodicarbonamide-Ascorbic Acid Mixtures

The legal limit for ADA in the United States is 45 ppm. There is no legal
limit for AA, although benefits greatly diminish above 150 ppm in frozen

$$CaO_2 \xrightarrow[\text{medium}]{\text{acid}} H_2O_2 + HOH$$

$$Fe^{2+} + H_2O_2 \underset{\longleftarrow}{\overset{\longrightarrow}{}} FeOH^{2+} + OH$$

$$OH + H_2O_2 \longrightarrow HOH + HO_2$$

$$HO_2 + H_2O_2 \longrightarrow HOH + O_2 + OH$$

$$AA + O_2 + OH + HO_2 \longrightarrow DHA + HOH$$

Fig. 15. Chemical oxidation of ascorbic acid (AA). Speculated oxidation mechanism of AA to
dehydroascorbic acid (DHA), when water is added to a product mixture of AA, calcium peroxide
(CaO_2), and ferrous sulfate ($FeSO_4$).

doughs. Often, ADA and AA are combined to meet the oxidation requirements of a particular type of baking. Caution is required in using such mixtures in baking. Additions to flour at mixing are preferred (Table 7), to minimize reactions between ADA and AA. When such reaction occurs, the oxidative potentials of both AA and ADA are reduced.

Iodate Salts

Either the calcium or potassium salt of iodate has been used by the baking industry for at least 70 years. Iodate is a fast-acting oxidant similar to ADA. When used above 15–20 ppm, the oxidant tends to alter the dough rheology greatly. Iodated doughs containing above 20 ppm have a negative effect on loaf volume compared to bromate when mixed to the same time. This effect on volume is reduced by simply decreasing the mixing time of a dough. Iodate not only accelerates dough development but also accelerates dough breakdown (producing doughs with low mixing tolerance). Blends of ADA and iodate are successfully used in frozen doughs and continuous-mix baking. Use of ADA-

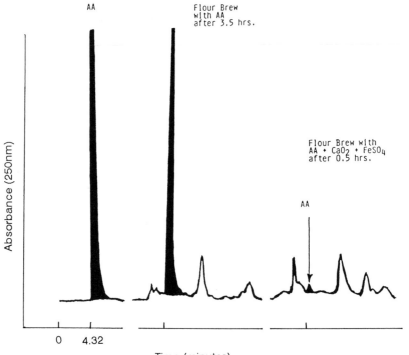

Fig. 16. Oxidation of ascorbic acid (AA) in a flour brew. AA and AA + CaO_2 + $FeSO_4$ (product) were added to a 40% flour brew. Fermentation was permitted to 3.5 hr at 30°C. Pure AA solution and the brews were analyzed by liquid chromatography at 250 nm. (De Stefanis, *unpublished data*)

iodate mixtures in frozen doughs is particularly attractive because they shorten the proof time, especially when doughs are stored for long periods (at -23°C).

Iodates in breadmaking raise the level of iodine intake, which may have repercussions on health. Hence, caution in its use is stressed.

Copper Compounds

In 1988, De Stefanis et al reported that cupric compounds (Cu^{2+}) exhibited the same oxidative properties as bromate in baking. Finney et al (1992) reported similar observations. Presently, these compounds are not permitted in baking. However, they are worth discussing because they exhibit functional properties similar to those of bromate. Cupric sulfate ($CuSO_4$), as a flour improver, dates back to 1860 (Jorgensen, 1945). The author found that 5–40 ppm cupric sulfate gives the same effect as 10–75 ppm $KBrO_3$, in different types of baking. Cupric gluconate, at slightly higher concentrations, functions as well as cupric sulfate. Cupric compounds are slow-acting oxidants similar to bromate.

Oxidation Mechanism

How an oxidant improves the baking properties of flour is not clearly understood. Several hypotheses have been proposed during the past several decades. Jorgensen (1945) promoted the concept that the oxidant inhibited the deleterious action of proteolytic enzymes on the dough structure. Sullivan et al (1940) suggested that the mechanism involved the oxidation of protein sulfhydryls to disulfide bridges (cross-links). This theory was helpful in explaining the strengthening action of the oxidants in dough systems. Flour water-solubles (Finney, 1943), a salt-soluble material from gluten (Baker et al, 1942), and phosphoric acid (Hoseney et al, 1972) have also been implicated in the mechanism. Most cereal chemists today seem to adhere to Sullivan's hypothesis. Iodometric methods have been proposed for bromate (Hlynka et al, 1953; Cunningham et al, 1956; Thewlis, 1977; AACC, 1983). However, iodometric titration does not discriminate between oxidants (hence, it is not selective) and is not sensitive in the parts-per-million range. Quantitative liquid chromatographic procedures have been developed for ADA and AA in the author's

Table 7
Azodicarbonamide (ADA)-Ascorbic Acid (AA) Mixtures in Frozen Dough

ADA (ppm)	AA (ppm)	Point of Addition	Specific Loaf Volume[a] (cm³/g)
0	0	0	5.3
45	100	Flour	6.5
	100	Water[b]	5.8

[a] Flour contained 13.8% flour protein. Stored one week at -23°C.
[b] Oxidants held in water for 15 min before addition to flour at mixing. (DeStefanis, *unpublished data*)

laboratory, as well as a colorimetric procedure for bromate (De Stefanis, 1992). These methods work well on flour, dough, and bread matrixes. One way of furthering the understanding of the oxidation mechanism is to apply previous methodology to determine at what point of the frozen dough process the oxidant shows its greatest loss (that is, when consumption of the oxidant is the highest). This information would be extremely useful in the formulation of bromate alternatives. Figure 17 compares the consumption of ADA, AA, and bromate. Major losses of ADA and AA occurred at the mixing stage, with minor losses at the retarder and proofing stages. At the time the proofed dough entered the oven, only 5–8% of the starting ADA and AA concentrations remained active. Bromate followed a totally different pattern; little consumption occurred during mixing, followed by major losses after proofing and baking. Approximately 45–50% of the original concentration of bromate added to flour remained active at the baking stage. These results illustrate two points—that bromate is a slow-acting oxidant, in agreement with bakery experience, and that ADA and AA operate differently from bromate, which makes it difficult to mimic bromate properties totally. It is interesting to note that although ADA, AA, and bromate were consumed at different points of breadmaking, they had similar effects on the improvement of loaf volume. Conventional wisdom tells us that bromate, being a slow-acting oxidant, exerts its improving effect during

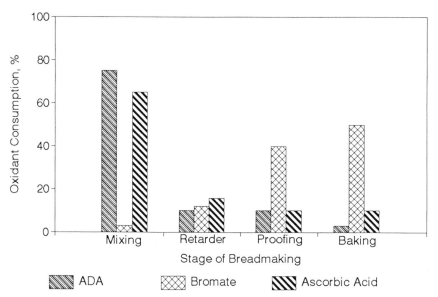

Fig. 17. Consumption of bromate, azodicarbonamide (ADA), and ascorbic acid (AA) during breadmaking. Doughs were prepared with ADA (45 ppm), AA (200 ppm), and potassium bromate (75 ppm). Fungal α-amylase (132 SKB/100 g of flour) was added to each dough. Samples of dough or bread were evaluated for residual oxidant at various stages of frozen dough baking. ADA and AA were analyzed by liquid chromatography (250–300 nm) and bromate by colorimetry. (Reprinted, with permission, from De Stefanis et al, 1992)

the latter stages of proofing and, particularly, during baking. Baking experiments focused on the consumption (loss) of bromate in the oven (Fig. 18). Clearly, the oxidant lost its activity in proportion to baking time, in agreement with conventional wisdom. Assuming that bromate exerts its improving action during baking by reacting with the proteins, then a different consumption profile would be expected when wheat flour is replaced by wheat starch. It is obvious that both profiles are the same, indicating that the phenomenon is common to both systems. This area was explored further using vanadium, which transforms bromate from a slow- to a fast-acting oxidant (De Stefanis et al, 1988), as illustrated in Figure 7. Assuming that one uses sufficient levels of bromate and vanadium to yield a typical oxidant response in bread while leaving no detectable bromate after proofing, then it could be said that the oxidant really exerts its effect well *before* baking. Following this line of reasoning, bromate (25 ppm) and ammonium vanadate (50 ppm) were added to flour doughs and processed by the no-time baking method. Results of this experiment appear in Table 8. By the end of proofing, bromate was reduced to trace levels (if any). Although no bromate was present at the oven stage, the volume-improving effect was still obtained. It is suspected that the bromate at the baking stage is of little importance to the bread-improving mechanism. The loss occurring during baking is most likely due to thermal decomposition of bromate. This is an important point to consider when analyzing for residual bro-

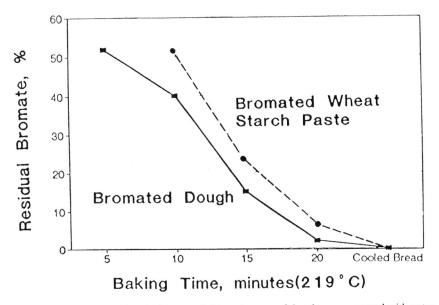

Fig. 18. Bromate consumption during oven baking. A group of doughs was prepared with potassium bromate (75 ppm) + fungal α-amylase (132 SKB per 100 g of flour). In another group, prime wheat starch was substituted for wheat flour. At baking, doughs were baked for 5–20 min and analyzed immediately for residual bromate. (De Stefanis, *unpublished data*)

mate in a baked product. Excessive levels of bromate (75 ppm and higher) in the formulation, combined with underbaking, could lead to high residual bromate in the bakery product. Previous results clearly show that bromate's improving action occurs *before* baking, similar to that of ADA and AA. Hopefully, these findings improve our understanding of the oxidation mechanism, as well as how to formulate better bromate alternatives.

Relationship Between Enzymes and Oxidants

Enzymes have found a place in a wide range of industrial applications (Reed, 1975). In baking, α-amylases and proteases have received the most attention (Kruger et al, 1987). We have looked at many commercial products, and our experience with enzymes indicates that they do not duplicate the action of the oxidants (ADA, AA, and bromate). In other words, enzymes alone do not replace the functional role of the oxidant in frozen doughs. They may, however, be effective in types of baking where the oxidation demand is much lower.

α-Amylase

We have observed, as have other researchers, that the simultaneous addition of the enzyme and the oxidant to dough yields greater loaf volume and a more uniform crumb structure than when either one is used alone. The improving action is enhanced with additions of high levels of α-amylase (110–220 SKB/100 g of flour). Fungal α-amylase is preferred because of its low temperature of inactivation (63–66°C).

Glucoamylase

Frozen doughs, at times, are formulated very leanly (with no sweetener). Most of the natural sugars in the flour become fermented during the retarding period (16–24 hr at 2-4°C), leaving little or no fermentables at the proofing

Table 8
Bromate Action During Breadmaking[a]

Bromate[b] Concentration (ppm)	Ammonium Vanadate (ppm)	Stage	Residual Bromate (ppm)	Specific Loaf Volume (cm³/g)
0	0	Bread	0	5.1
0	50	Bread	0	5.2
25	50[c]	End of mixing	23	0
		End of proofing	Trace (?)	0
		Beginning of baking	Trace (?)	0
		Final bread	0	7.1

[a] No-time baking method.
[b] Potassium bromate.
[c] Dough mixing time reduced by 25%.

stage. When this situation occurs, proof times become undesirably long. This problem is alleviated with the addition of glucoamylase to the oxidation system. Glucoamylases digest dextrins, produced by the α-amylase, and damaged starch to glucose during the retarding period and proofing. Glucose is utilized by the yeast to sustain normal proofing (Table 9).

Other Enzymes

Cellulases, glucanases, pentosanases, and oxidoreductases (lipoxygenases, glucose oxidases, catalases, and peroxidases) have been recommended as bromate replacers. Again, we have found that enzymes alone do not replace the action of the oxidant in frozen doughs.

Proteases tend to depolymerize and weaken the gluten structure of doughs. This type of hydrolysis is irreversible and permanent. Proteolysis works contrary to the action of the oxidant, in that a weak gluten structure is generally responsible for poor bread quality (low volume, open grain, loaf collapse in the oven, etc.). Proteolytic activity should be kept to a minimum in frozen doughs.

Standardization

Commercial enzyme products should be standardized before use in frozen doughs. Addition on a weight basis is strongly discouraged. Lastly, the enzyme concentration must be in balance with the oxidant concentration for optimum performance in baking.

Relationship Between Oxidant and Yeast

A comprehensive report on yeast is given in Chapter 2. This section discusses the relationship between oxidant and yeast performance (proof time) when doughs are frozen for long periods. In general, long proof times may result from insufficient yeast, sugar, or oxidation and combination of these in the processed dough. When these ingredients are optimally used, the time in storage (-23°C) exercises a negative effect on proofing (Fig. 19). The type of oxidant used in the formulation can also exert an affect on proof time (*author's data*) (Fig. 19). In general, slight differences were obtained up to 10–12 weeks

Table 9
Glucoamylase in Lean Frozen Doughs[a] with ADA[b] as Oxidant

Added α-Amylase[c] (SKB/100 g)	Added Glucoamylase (GU/100 g)	Proof Time (min)	Specific Loaf Volume (cm³/g)
0	0	520	4.8
88	0	400	5.3
88	33	73	6.7

[a] No sweetener, no shortening. Frozen four weeks at -23°C. Proofed to height.

[b] Azodicarbonamide (45 ppm).

[c] Fungal.

in storage. The effect of the oxidant became clearly evident after 12 weeks. Bromate increased proofing the most, followed by ascorbic acid, iodate, and ADA. The profiles in Figure 19 were obtained with yeast of excellent quality. However, when doughs were formulated with yeast of inferior quality, the inhibitory effect of bromate appeared earlier than 12 weeks. Bakers generally proof doughs either to a predetermined height or time. Table 10 compares the effect of oxidants on proof time, for doughs stored to 43 weeks in the freezer. When proofed to time, the bromated dough had a specific loaf volume of 3.5 cm³/g compared to 6.4 for the ADA dough. At a glance, these results appear misleading. One could rationalize that bromate failed to stabilize the dough structure during storage, thus producing a lower volume than ADA. However, when doughs were proofed to height, rather than to time, the results followed a different pattern. While no difference in loaf volume was obtained between bromate and ADA doughs, the time to reach the height (proof time) was greatly different. Therefore, one can say that bromate and ADA equally stabilized the dough structure during storage (-23°C), except that bromate affected yeast in a negative manner. The deleterious effect of bromate was not alleviated by varying the yeast food. When doughs were formulated without a sweetener and

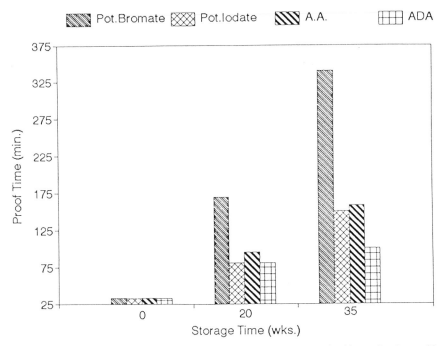

Fig. 19. Comparison of oxidants on proof time. Doughs were prepared with azodicarbonamide (ADA, 45 ppm), ascorbic acid (AA, 200 ppm), KIO_3 (40 ppm), and $KBrO_3$ (75 ppm). Fungal α-amylase (132 SKB/100 g of flour) was added to all doughs. Doughs were held in the freezer (at -23°C) for up to 35 weeks.

mixed above 21°C, the adverse effect of bromate was clearly discernible after one week in storage. In general, proof times were unusually long, regardless of the oxidant used, if prefermentation occurred before dough mixing (Table 11). Again, prefermentation has a negative effect on the yeast, yielding doughs with long proof times. Prefermentation should be avoided in frozen dough preparation.

Conclusions

Frozen dough is more sensitive to ingredients and processing conditions and is, therefore, more complex than conventional dough. There are many parameters to consider in order to ensure success. Yeast is not the only element re-

Table 10
Effect of Oxidants on Proof Time After Long Storage

		43 Weeks in Freezer			
Oxidant	α-Amylase[a] (SKB/100 g)	Proofed to Time (min)	Specific Loaf Volume (cm³/g)	Proofed to Height (min)	Specific Loaf Volume (cm³/g)
Bromate,[b] 75 ppm	132	120	3.5	452	6.2
ADA, 45 ppm	132	120	6.4	120	6.3
Ascorbic acid, 150 ppm	132	120	5.4	170	6.0
Iodate,[b,c] 45 ppm	132	120	5.7	142	6.0

[a] Fungal.
[b] Potassium salt.
[c] Dough mixing time reduced by 25–30%.

Table 11
Effect of Prefermented Brew on Oxidant Performance in Frozen Doughs

		Proof Time (min)			Specific Loaf Volume (cm³/g)		
Oxidant[a]	Prefermentation[b,c]	Fresh	One Week	Six Weeks	Fresh	One Week	Six Weeks
KBrO³, 75 ppm	Yes	66	62	240+	⋯	5.1	1.9
	No	36	50	49	5.9	5.8	5.8
ADA, 45 ppm	Yes	67	58	240+	⋯	5.4	2.1
	No	37	47	46	6.2	5.8	6.0
AA, 150 ppm	Yes	67	59	240+	⋯	5.2	1.8
	No	36	49	49	5.9	5.7	5.9

[a] Oxidant + fungal α-amylase (132 SKB/100 g).
[b] No fermentation: H_2O (15°C) + salt + dextrose + yeast food + compressed yeast added directly to flour.
[c] Prefermentation: same as previous, held 1 hr at 27°C, then added to flour.

sponsible for such success, as conventionally thought. Oxidants, of the bread improver type, exercise a major influence on dough stability during storage (-23°C). Furthermore, choosing oxidants judiciously helps to ensure short proof times. Both the oxidant and the yeast play a crucial role in frozen dough. Optimum performance of these two ingredients is realized when the baker 1) carefully selects ingredient (e.g., high-protein flour, saturated shortening, surfactants, oxidants, enzymes, yeast, etc.), 2) mixes dough at 21°C and lower (with no prefermentation), and 3) allows mixed dough to rest at least 8–10 min before freezing.

Acknowledgment

P. M. Ranum, R. W. Erickson, Kathleen Donohue, and Kathy DelZoppo are acknowledged for their assistance with deep gratitude.

Literature Cited

American Association of Cereal Chemists. 1983. Approved Methods of the AACC, 8th ed. Method 48-42, approved April 1982, reviewed October 1982. The Association, St. Paul, MN.

Autio, K., and Sinda, E. 1992. Frozen doughs: Rheological changes and yeast viability. Cereal Chem. 69:409-413.

Baker, J. C., Parker, H. K., and Mize, M. D. 1942. The action of an oxidizing agent in bread dough made from patent flours. Cereal Chem. 19:334-346.

Bruinsma, B. L., and Gieselschlag, J. 1984. Frozen dough performance: Compressed yeast— Instant dry yeast. Baker's Dig. 58(6):6-7, 11.

Chamberlin, N., and Collins, T. H. 1979. The Chorleywood bread process: The role of oxygen and nitrogen. Baker's Dig. 53(1):18-24.

Cunningham, D. K., and Anderson, J. A. 1956. Decomposition of bromate in fermenting and nonfermenting doughs. Cereal Chem. 33:290-299.

De Stefanis, V. A. 1992. Analysis of potassium bromate in flour, dough, and bread. Cereal Chem. 69:683-685.

De Stefanis, V. A., Ponte, J. G., Jr., Chung, F. H., and Ruzza, N. A. 1977. Binding of crumb softeners and dough strengtheners during breadmaking. Cereal Chem. 54:13-24.

De Stefanis, V. A., Ranum, P. M., and Erickson, R. W. 1988. The effect of metal ions on bromate oxidation during breadmaking. Cereal Chem. 65:257-261.

De Stefanis, V. A. 1994. Benzoyl peroxide to improve the performance of oxidants in breadmaking. U.S. patent No. 5,318,785.

Dubois, D. K., and Blockcolsky, D. 1986a. Frozen bread dough: Effect of additives. AIB Tech. Bull. Vol. VIII, issue 4.

Dubois, D. K., and Blockcolsky, D. 1986b. Frozen bread dough: Effect of dough mixing and thawing methods. AIB Tech. Bull. Vol. VIII, issue 6.

Evenson, M. 1987. New developments in frozen dough technology. Pages 85-89 in: Proc. 63rd annual meeting. American Society of Bakery Engineers, Chicago, IL

Finney, K. F. 1943. Fractionating and reconstituting techniques as tools in wheat flour research. Cereal Chem. 20:381-396.

Finney, K. F., Bruinsma, B. L., and Natsuaki, O. 1992. Copper (II) vs. zinc inorganic salts as oxidizers in breadmaking. Cereal Chem. 69:347-348.

Gélinas, P., Lagimonière, M., and Dubord, C. 1993. Baker's yeast sampling and frozen dough stability. Cereal Chem. 70:219-225.

Gélinas, P., Lagimonière, M., and Rodrique, N. 1994. Performance of cream or compressed yeast in frozen and nonfrozen doughs. Cereal Chem. 71:183-186.

Hlynka, I., Templin, P. R., and Anderson, J. A. 1953. Decomposition of bromate in dough. Cereal Chem. 30:391-403.

Hoseney, R. C., Finney, K. F., and Shogren, M. D. 1972. Functional (breadmaking) and biochemical properties of wheat flour components X. Fractions involved in the bromate action. Cereal Chem. 49:372-378.

Hosomi, K., Nishio, K., and Matsumoto, H. 1992. Studies on frozen dough baking. I. Effects of egg yolk and sugar ester. Cereal Chem. 69:89-92.

HSU, K. H., Hoseney, R. C., and Seib, P. A. 1979. Frozen dough II. Effects of freezing and storing conditions on the stability of yeasted doughs. Cereal Chem. 56:424-426.

Inoue, Y., and Bushuk, W. 1991. Studies on frozen doughs. I. Effects of frozen storage and freeze-thaw cycles on baking and rheological properties. Cereal Chem. 68:627-631.

Inoue, Y., Saperstein, H. D., Takayanagi, S., and Bushuk, W. 1994. Studies on frozen doughs. III. Some factors involved in dough weakening during frozen storage and thaw-freeze cycles. Cereal Chem. 71:118-121.

Jorgensen, H. 1945. Studies on the nature of the bromate effect. Oxford University Press, London.

Kruger, J. E., Lineback, D., and Stauffer, C. E., eds. 1987. Enzymes and Their Role in Cereal Technology. Am. Assoc. Cereal Chem., St. Paul, MN.

Lehmann, T. A., and Dreese, P. 1981. Stability of frozen bread dough—Effects of freezing temperatures. AIB Tech. Bull. Vol. III, issue 7.

Lorenz, K., and Bechtel, W. G. 1965. Frozen dough variety breads: Effect of bromate level on white bread. Baker's Dig. 39(4):53-59.

Lorenz, K. 1965. Frozen bread dough. Baker's Weekly, Feb. 22, p. 52.

Marston, P. E. 1978. Frozen dough for breadmaking. Baker's Dig. 52(5):18.

Marston, P. E. 1979. Frozen dough for breadmaking. Bull. No. 213. American Society of Bakery Engineers, Chicago, IL.

Neyreneuf, O., and Delpuech, B. 1993. Freezing experiments on yeasted dough slabs. Effects of cryogenic temperatures on the baking performance. Cereal Chem. 70:109-111.

Reed, G. 1975. Enzymes in Food Processing, 2nd ed. Academic Press, New York.

Sullivan, B., Howe, M., Schmalz, F. D., and Astleford, G. R. 1940. The action of oxidizing and reducing agents on flour. Cereal Chem. 17:507-528.

Thewlis, B. H. 1977. The estimation of potassium bromate in bread. J. Sci. Food Agric. 28:85.

Tsen, C. C. 1965. The improving mechanism of ascorbic acid. Cereal Chem. 42:86-97.

CHAPTER 6

Microbiological Considerations in Freezing and Refrigeration of Bakery Foods

Daniel Y. C. Fung
Department of Animal Sciences and Industry
Kansas State University
Manhattan, Kansas 66502

Microorganisms are ubiquitous in our environment, and they affect our daily lives by their prolific biochemical activities under ideal growth conditions. All living things less than 0.1 mm in diameter fall into the world of microbes, since the human eye cannot resolve matters that small without the aid of magnification. The microbial world includes viruses, bacteria, yeasts, molds, protozoa, algae, and other organisms that at different growth stages are too small to be seen. On the one hand, microorganisms are beneficial to humans by virtue of their roles in metabolic cycles of matters (phosphorous cycle, carbon and oxygen cycles, nitrogen and sulfur cycles). They are also important in various fermented foods such as bread, wine, cheese, beer, and vinegar. They can even be eaten as foods such as mushroom, yeast, and single-cell protein. On the other hand they can spoil foods and cause foodborne diseases, and even death in extreme cases.

From the standpoint of the microorganisms, however, they are simply trying to fulfill their biological need to grow and to perpetuate by sexual and asexual reproduction. They need water, carbohydrate, protein, fat, minerals, vitamins, and the right combination of gases, temperature, pH, and other conditions in order to grow and multiply. This is similar to the human being's need to survive.

Therefore there are no "good" microorganisms or "bad" microorganisms in nature; it is according to how they affect us that we consider them harmful or beneficial.

A general review of microbiology was published by Fung (1992d). Various

119

topics related to food microbiology, food fermentation, and foodborne diseases were detailed in three articles by Fung (1992a; 1992b; 1992c) in the *Encyclopedia of Food Science and Technology* (Hui, 1992). In addition, excellent books on the subject include *Modern Food Microbiology* by Jay (1992), *Microbiology of Foods* by Ayres et al (1980), and *Techniques d'Analyse et de Controle dans les Industries Agro-Alimentaires* by Bourgeois and Leveau (1991).

Origin of Microorganisms in Bakery Products

The most logical starting point to discuss the origin of microorganisms in bakery products is with the ingredients: flour, spices, milk, eggs, and water.

Flour

Microorganisms in flour come from plant materials, soil, storage environment, processing equipment, and personnel. Sinha and Muir (1973) published an excellent review of the physical, chemical, biochemical, and microbiological interactions of grain storage and processing, which ultimately affect the microbial quality of flour. Since the water activity (a_w) of flour is low, most organisms will not grow during storage. However, if flour becomes wet, microorganisms will grow. The number of microorganisms in flour varies from a few hundred per gram to millions per gram, depending on the source of the flour and the conditions of processing and storage of the products. In general, the bacterial number decreases and mold number increases, the rate being dependent on moisture content and storage temperature (Fung 1983).

Bacteria found in flour include *Bacillus*, enterics, *Lactobacillus, Pseudomonas, Streptococcus, Achromobacter, Flavobacterium, Micrococcus, Alcaligenes*, and others. Yeasts and molds found include *Torula, Rhizopus, Nucor, Aspergillus, Fusarium, Penicillium, Alternaria, and Cladosporium*.

Spores of *Bacillus* in flour are of particular interest because they can survive for a long period in flours. When flour is deliberately or inadvertently hydrated, these spores germinate and the organism grow and cause spoilage of products. *Bacillus* species produce amylase and a variety of enzymes that enable them to utilize flour as an energy source for growth. A moisture content of 13% and above may permit the growth of molds and bacteria. A moist flour may undergo acidic fermentation, alcoholic fermentation, or acetic acid production, depending on the numbers and kinds of organisms present at the time of spoilage. Many molds grown on flour produce a variety of observable spoilage symptoms, including "moldiness"—black, blue, and gray spots and discolorations in the products. It is therefore important that flour not be exposed to high humidity during storage and handling.

Spices

One of the most overlooked ingredients in food preparation and processing as far as microbial contamination is concerned is spice. Many spices carry high numbers of bacterial, yeast, and mold spores as well as vegetative cells. Addition of spice to food can occur at any point along the food processing chain. When the spice is added after the food is processed or cooked, the organisms carried in the spice may spoil the food. They may even cause foodborne infection and intoxication. Pruthi (1980) made a detailed study of microbial profiles of selected spices and condiments in terms of chemistry, microbiology, and technology.

Heat treatment and cooking reduce the total bacterial load on spices. A study of the effect of boiling of curry powder with and without salt and citric acid indicated that 0.5% citric is highly effective in destroying microorganisms in curry even without heating, but 5% salt in curry did not show significant reduction of bacteria after boiling compared with curry powder alone. Prolonged heating reduced counts in all systems (Pruthi, 1980).

Inactivation of 99.9% of microflora in spices can be achieved by 300–400 krad of irradiation. For sterilization of spices, levels of 1,600–2,000 krad are necessary. Fumigation using ethylene oxide with or without added CO_2 has been shown to be very effective in pasteurization of spices. Heating at 15 psi pressure at 121°C for 15 min reduced flora from 8×10^6 to 1 per gram (Pruthi, 1980). However, such high heat caused deterioration in the flavor and quality of the spices.

Milk (Liquid and Dry)

The microbiology of milk is well known. Organisms enter the milk supply from the farm environment, udder, dirt from animals, handlers, equipment, and dust. The number of bacteria in raw milk usually is less than log 4/ml when the cow, utensils, and environment are clean, but the number can exceed log 5/ml if the conditions are dirty. Storage time and temperature have a profound influence on microbial growth in milk.

The kinds of bacteria isolated from milk include *Bacillus, Micrococcus, Proteus, Streptococcus, Lactococcus, Lactobacillus, Microbacterium, Clostridium, Pseudomonas, Leuconostoc, Escherichia, Klebsiella,* and many others.

Pasteurization time and temperature are designed to kill pathogenic organisms with minimum alteration of flavor and quality of milk. The organisms designed to be destroyed are *Mycobacterium tuberculosis* and *Coxiella burnetii.* However, thermoduric organisms (*Bacillus, Streptococcus, Micrococcus, Brevibacterium,* and *Clostridium*) will survive the treatment and then grow and spoil the milk if it is not properly refrigerated.

Milk left at room temperature turns sour due to the activities of lactic acid bacteria. However, when it is stored at refrigerated temperature for a long time, milk turns putrid due to the growth of psychrotrophs, microorganisms that grow in cold environments.

Dry milk products pose a different problem. In these dry products, organisms, if present, are mainly in a dormant state. They start to grow as soon as the dry milk is rehydrated. After addition of water, the problems for rehydrated milk are the same as for liquid milk. During storage, it is imperative to avoid allowing moisture to contact dry milk products.

Excellent discussions on the microbiology of milk and milk products are given in *Standard Methods for the Examination of Dairy Products,* published by the American Public Health Association (Marshall, 1993).

Egg (Liquid and Dry)

The microbiology of eggs is also well known. Whereas milk is extremely perishable, eggs in the shell are not. The egg in the shell has natural protection through the cuticle, shell, shell membranes, lysozyme, conalbumin, avidin, high pH, etc. Once the egg is broken, the liquid egg is as perishable as milk.

Salmonella is a constant concern when eggs and egg products are used. With the recent increase in isolation of *Salmonella enteritidis* in the northeastern United States and in other countries, closer scrutiny of *Salmonella* has been advocated by food microbiologists nationally and internationally. Other bacteria found in dry and liquid eggs include *Pseudomonas, Streptococcus, Alcaligenes, Staphylococcus, Bacillus, Flavobacterium, Proteus, Serratia, Arthobacter, and Micrococcus.* Molds and yeast found include *Penicillium, Cladosporium, Sporotrichum, Alternaria,* and *Mucor.* Liquid eggs should be properly refrigerated and used without delay. Dry egg products once rehydrated have the same problems as liquid eggs.

Water

Water is used as an ingredient and for the general purpose of sanitation for food processing plants. The number and kinds of microorganisms in water are extremely diverse, depending on the source and effectiveness of treatment of water in various locations. It is assumed that water used in the bakery is from city water that has been treated. Such water does not pose a problem unless gross negligence occurs either in the water treatment plant or the food processing plant.

Other Ingredients

Other ingredients used in bakery products are so varied and diverse that it is impossible to discuss all possible ingredients and the microbes therein. It is important to realize that all food items have their particular intrinsic parameters (pH, a_w, oxidation-reduction potential, nutrient contents, antimicrobial compounds, and biological structure) and extrinsic parameters (relative humidity, temperature of storage, gasses, mechanical stresses, and time), which must be considered. All these factors individually and collectively influence microbial growth and spoilage and the disease-producing potential of foods, including bakery products.

Producers of food and consumers both must realize the importance of the intrinsic and extrinsic factors of foods, such that bakery products and other daily food items can be manufactured, stored, transported, handled, and used in a safe manner.

Spoilage Potential of Bakery Products

Bakery products go through a variety of processing steps. The most important and usually the final step is baking. Because of the high heat used in baking, the product freshly out of the oven is essential a sterile product. However once the product is exposed to the environment, contamination occurs. The most serious contamination in a bakery is, of course, mold spores. Due to the high humidity and warm temperature of the environment, it is not possible to completely eliminate mold spores from a bakery. It is common knowledge that *Rhizopus stolonifer* and *R. nigricans* regularly contaminate bread and cause "moldy bread" syndrome. A large number of other molds such as *Neurospora sitophila* (red bread mold), *Mucor, Geotrichum, Saccharomycopsis, Trichosporon, Penicillium,* and *Aspergillus* also contaminated bread. Spoilage of bakery products by bacteria is much less common due to the low a_w of bakery products. Occasionally spoilage by *Bacillus subtilis* in bread may lead to a condition known as "ropiness."

The situation changes dramatically if "toppings," "fillings," and other ingredients are added to the baked products. In those situations, it is entirely possible that foodborne pathogens such as *Salmonella, Staphylococcus aureus,* and a host of potential pathogens such as *Listeria* and *Clostridium perfringens* may grow and pose a problem. In these cases, the quality of the ingredients added to the baked products must be closely monitored to ensure safe bakery products.

Control of contamination is best done through a sanitary environment, clean equipment and processing steps, and the use of antimicrobials such as benzoic, sorbic, and propionic acids. Addition of citric acid, acetic acid, and other organic acids can be helpful as well. The book *Antimicrobials in Foods* edited by Davidson and Branen (1993) provides up-dated information on the use of antimicrobials for preservation of bakery products.

Effects of Refrigeration on Microbes

Refrigeration is defined as holding the storage temperature of foods at 1–10°C. Most household refrigerators are around 4–7°C if left undisturbed. The temperature can fluctuate greatly due to usage or malfunction of units. Bakery products are no different from other food products in terms of microbial growth under refrigeration conditions. The group of organisms that spoils foods at refrigeration temperature is called psychrotrophs. A summary of important attributes of psychrotrophs is presented in Table 1 (Fung, 1986).

At refrigeration temperature, the microorganisms essentially have a retarded metabolism. Their growth and the concomitant spoilage potential of food are reduced. However, these psychrotrophs can also grow at a higher temperature such as 21°C. They nevertheless can grow, albeit slowly, at refrigeration temperature and eventually cause spoilage of foods as listed in Table 1. Since bakery products have a low a_w, spoilage under refrigeration is mostly by molds. Again *Rhizopus, Mucor*, and *Penicillium* are predominant in this type of spoil-

Table 1
Characteristics of Psychrotrophs and Their Effects on Foods[a]

Definition	Psychrotrophs (*psychros* = cold, *trephein* = to nourish upon or to develop). Microorganisms able to grow at refrigeration temperature (0–10°C). In suitable agar medium, they form visible colonies, sometimes extremely small, after incubation at 7°C for 10 days. Most psychrotrophs grow much faster at higher temperatures.
Types of psychrotrophs	Bacteria: *Pseudomonas* (by far the most important), *Flavobacterium, Alcaligenes, Enterobacter, Micrococcus, Lactobacillus*. Many more Gram-negative bacteria involved than Gram-positive. Yeasts: *Candida, Torulopsis, Saccharomyces, Rhodotorula*, etc. Molds: *Mucor, Rhizopus, Penicillium, Geotrichum, Aspergillus*, etc. *Note*: Psychrotrophs usually do not pose a public health problem since most of them are not pathogens.
Source of psychrotrophs in foods	Soil and vegetation (grass, hay, etc.) Water (treated and untreated) Air (dust particles, etc.) Equipment (one of the major sources) Humans (not well studied)
Conditions for psychrotrophs to proliferate	Depends on the type of foods Number of psychrotrophs Kinds of psychrotrophs (some are more active than others) Conditions of food processing Storage temperature, time, environment
Effects of pasteurization on psychrotrophs	Pasteurization destroys most psychrotrophs. Spore-forming psychrotrophs can survive pasteurization. High numbers of psychrotrophs in pasteurized products, such as milk, indicate post-pasteurization contamination. Good sanitation will reduce the problem.
Alterations in food by psychrotrophs during cold storage	*Lipolysis*: lipolytic enzymes (lipases) cause rancid flavor and odor, increase free fatty acids. *Proteolysis*: Proteolytic enzymes (proteases) cause flavor and odor changes; in advanced cases cause putrification of food products. *Saccharolysis*: Breakdown of sugars (relatively less important activity for psychrotrophs as a group). This will cause souring of food products. *Pigment production*: At refrigerated temperature, psychrotrophs tend to produce more pigments than at a higher temperature. Pseudomonas fluorescens produces a fluorescent compound in foods. *Production of polysaccharides*: Some psychrotrophs produce large amounts of polysaccharides, resulting in slime formation in foods (highly undesirable). *Some undesirable results*: Fruity, rancid, putrid, ropy, discoloration, cheesy, soapy, bitter, "sweaty feet" odor, skunk-like, potato odor, fishy, taint, etc.

[a] Source: Fung (1986); used with permission.

age. Other molds such as *Cladosporium, Botrytis,* and *Geotrichum* can also cause problems. Yeasts, including *Candida, Torulopsis, Debaryomyces,* and *Rhodotorula,* can also grow at refrigeration temperature. Depending on the ingredients of the bakery products, bacteria can also spoil the products. The most important psychrotrophic bacterium is *Pseudomonas.* About 90% of psychrotrophic bacteria are *Pseudomonas.*

Other psychrotrophic bacteria include *Micrococcus, Acinetobacter, Alcaligenes,* and *Flavobacterium.* Recently there has been great concern because of the growth of food pathogens with psychrotrophic potential such as *Listeria monocytogenes* and *Yersinia enterocolitica.* These potential pathogens should not be a problem in bakery products unless unpasteurized or undercooked high-protein foods are added to the baked products (milk, meat, bacon, ham, nut meats, etc.). If the food is vacuum packaged, a new set of problems may arise. *Pseudomonas* is an aerobic organism and will not spoil vacuum-packaged products. The group of organisms spoiling the food will be the lactic acid bacteria. Under anaerobic cold stored conditions, the food will turn "sour," as opposed to food under aerobic cold stored conditions, which will turn "putrid" due to the metabolic activity of the proteolytic *Pseudomonas.*

A comprehensive summary of *Psychrotrophic Bacteria in Foods: Disease and Spoilage* was published recently by Kraft (1992). Major chapters were devoted to psychrotrophic spoilage bacteria in fresh meat, cured and cooked meat, poultry products, eggs, fish, dairy products, vegetables, and fruits. Interestingly enough, bakery products are not listed as a major food group spoiled by psychrotrophs, indicating that bakery products are very stable (microbiologically) under refrigerated temperatures. Of course, if the bakery products contain the other ingredients mentioned above, the spoilage potential exists even under refrigeration.

Effects of Freezing on Microbes

By definition, freezing of water occurs at 0°C. Since food contains a great variety of compounds, freezing of a food depends on its composition. Metabolic activities of most living systems are related to water. When water freezes, metabolic activities cease or at most progress at a very slow rate. The end result is that microbes do not grow into large numbers during prolonged freezing. From the standpoint of food quality, freezing has a profound effect on the structure, texture, flavor, rheology, and chemistry of the food, and at the same time suppresses the growth of microbes. Although a portion of the microbes die or are injured, a large number survive and remain dormant. Once the food is thawed and brought to room temperature or higher temperatures, the surviving organisms start to grow and spoil the food in question. As stated earlier, bakery products are quite stable in regard to microbial spoilage. Frozen bakery products definitely have very little microbial problems unless gross negligence occurred in the processing step or after the bakery products were thawed.

If the bakery products are good and safe in terms of microbial quality, then freezing maintains and prolongs their microbial safety under frozen conditions.

Quick freezing (to -20°C within 30 min) is less damaging to food components and microbial cells than is slow freezing (to -20°C in 3–72 hr) due to the formation of small ice crystals, which are less disruptive to biological membranes than the large crystals formed during slow freezing. Rapid thawing is also more advantageous than slow thawing from the standpoint of quality of food.

An excellent review on refrigeration and freezing of foods relative to microbial considerations is by Kraft (1992). Also, Jay (1992) discusses the issues related to low temperature effects on microbes and quality of foods.

Specific Considerations Concerning Bakery Products

It is well established that baked goods are microbiologically safe. In an article detailing foodborne disease outbreaks between 1983 and 1987, Bean et al (1990) indicated that baked foods accounted for only eight outbreaks of bacterial origin. The total number of outbreaks of bacterial origin during that period was 600.

According to Vanderzant and Splittstoesser (1992), normal microflora expected from baked goods (breads, cakes, pie shells, and pastries) for molds, yeasts, and yeast-like fungi are less than $10–10^3/g$; the aerobic bacteria plate count is less than $10^2–10^3/g$; and the coliform group plate count is less than $10–10^2/g$.

To extend the shelf life of bakery products, addition of organic acids was mentioned. One way to prevent mold growth is by the use of an oxygen scavenger to modify the atmosphere and prevent mold growth on whole wheat ready-to-eat wrapped bread (Powers and Berkowitz, 1990). The authors found that a proprietary desiccant added in a wrapper with baked, whole wheat, ready-to-eat bread prevented growth of a mixed mold inoculum on the surface of the bread for 13 months. Without the scavenger, *Aspergillus* and *Penicillium* were visible on the bread within 14 days. The bread samples were stored at 25°C for 13 months during the study.

English-style crumpets (a chemically leavened bakery product) had a shelf-life of 14 days when packaged in a $CO_2:N_2$ (3:2) gas atmosphere (Smith et al, 1983). The initial flora in crumpets was *Bacillus licheniformis*, but after seven days at 25°C, lactic acid bacteria accounted for almost 100% of the flora. *Leuconostoc mesenteroides* was identified as the major CO_2 producer in this type of packaging. The number of molds remained low throughout the study at a $10^2–10^3/g$ range, whereas the bacterial number went from 10^4 to $10^8/g$. This study was done at 25°C.

The aforementioned examples illustrate the fact that modification of gases in the packages can make a great difference in storage stability of bakery products. Had the studies been done under refrigerated temperatures, the products would have been microbiologically safe even longer.

The production of refrigerated, unbaked biscuits started in Kentucky around 1930. This concept—refrigerated dough—gradually expanded to include many products such as refrigerated rolls, cookies, and pizzas (Hesseltine et al, 1969). Because of the great expansion of the market and the concern for food safety and food spoilage potential, a large-scale study of aerobic and facultative microflora of fresh and spoiled refrigerated dough products was made by Hesseltine et al (1969). They found that, except for two special cases in which yeast and *Penicillium roqueforti* were the spoilage organisms (Tables 2 and 3), all the samples deteriorated because of bacterial growth. In the deliberately spoiled products, 92% of the isolates were from the family *Lactobacillaceae*. More than half (53%) of these were *Lactobacillus* and 36% were *Leuconostoc*, with *L. mesenteroides* being predominant. *Streptococcus* accounted for 3% of the isolates (Table 4).

In the same study, the authors evaluated 1,132 bacterial isolates, in which no

Table 2
Microbial Counts of Various Fresh Refrigerated Dough Samples[a]

Product	Total Number of Samples	Number of Microorganisms per Gram			
		Total Count at 32°C	Lactic Acid Bacteria	Psychrophilic Bacteria	Fungi
Buttermilk biscuits					
Brand A	3	2,100,000	2,300,000	...	430
		130,000,000	240,000,000	3,200,000	180
		160,000,000	200,000,000	4,800,000	280
Brand B	4	440	0	40	700
		120	0	55	530
		12,000	11,000	0	10
		120,000	110,000	0	10
Brand C	1	5,100	1,700	0	280
Biscuits					
Brand A	2	81,000	76,000	14,000	1,800
		3,400,000	3,300,000	220,000	960
Brand D	2	3,800	1,200	1,200	100
		6,800	4,000	6,400	120
Dinner rolls					
Brand B	2	150	25	0	50
		160	65	80	190
Sweet rolls					
Brand B (cinnamon)	2	470	25	360	100
		320	35	260	110
Brand B (Danish)	2	560	20	150	1,100
		520	15	200	940
Brand B (caramel)	2	210	5	150	890
		1,800	20	2,400	980
Pizza dough	2	680,000	710,000	280,000	110
		1,600,000	1,900,000	710,000	70

[a] Source: Hesseltine et al (1969); used by permission.

fecal indicators were isolated and no toxin-producing organisms were found. They also found in moist, fresh products up to 2×10^8 lactic acid bacteria per gram in buttermilk biscuits and a psychrophilic count as high 1.8×10^6. In spoiled samples, the highest total counts were $8.2 \times 10^8/g$ in buttermilk biscuits. Mold counts were no higher than 1,800/g except in the sample ruined by *P. roqueforti,* where the count was $1.3 \times 10^5/g$.

In another study on microbiological quality of biscuit dough, snack cakes, and soy protein meat extender, Swartzentruber et al (1984) found that the geometric mean of aerobic plate counts was 34,000 and that counts of yeasts and molds, coliforms, *Escherichia coli,* and *Staphylococcus aureus* were 46, 11, 3, and 3/g, respectively.

Sugihara (1978a) was very interested in the problem of soda cracker proc-

Table 3
Microbial Counts of Various Spoiled Refrigerated Dough Products[a]

Product	Total Number of Samples	Number of Microorganisms per Gram			
		Total Count at 32°C	Lactic Acid Bacteria	Psychro-philic Bac-teria	Fungi
Buttermilk biscuits					
Brand A	2	>0.3	>0.3	0	290–920
	5	9.6–28.0	7.9–42.0	0	65–240
	4	31.0–61.0	30.0–58.0	0	100–160
Brand B	1	0.14	0.13	0	30
	4	3.9–7.6	3.3–7.5	0	10–45
	1	4.7	11.0	4,400	130,000
Biscuits					
Brand A	1	9.2	8.1	0	110
	1	820	6.4	0	45
	1	82.0	89.0	0	75
Brand D	3	3.1–5.1	3.2–4.5	0	15–35
	1	0.52	0.56	0	20
Dinner rolls					
Brand B (sesame)	4	3.4–6.8	3.6–7.0	0	25–2,200
Brand B (bread end)	3	0.77–5.4	0.7–1.9	0	15–65
	1	0.04	0.04	0	25
Sweet rolls					
Brand B (cinnamon)	1	1.8	1.6	0	0
Brand B (Danish)	3	0.75–3.2	0.6–1.1	0	10–25
Brand B (caramel)	1	(250)[b]	(5)[b]	…	10
Pizza dough	2	10.0–11.0	13.0–20.0	0	10–920
Doughnuts	2	0.94	0.79	…	0
		30.0	32.0	0	240,000

[a] Source: Hesseltine et al (1969); used by permission.
[b] Absolute count.

Table 4

Incidence of Bacteria in Spoiled Refrigerated Dough Products[a]

Organism	Total Number of Isolates	Percentage of Isolates	Buttermilk Biscuits A[b] (11)[c]	B (6)	C (2)	Biscuits A (3)	D (4)	Dinner Rolls B[d] (3)	B[e] (4)	Cinnamon Rolls B (1)	Danish Rolls B (3)	Caramel Rolls B (1)	Pizza Dough (2)	Doughnuts (2)
Leuconostoc mesenteroides	390	34.5	8	6	0	0	4	0	1	0	1	0	1	0
L. dextranicum	21	1.9	0	0	0	0	0	0	0	0	1	0	0	0
Lactobacillus sp.	597	52.7	9	5	2	2	2	3	4	0	3	0	2	2
Streptococcus sp.	45	3.1	0	0	1	1	0	0	1	0	1	0	0	0
Bacillus sp.	15	1.3	0	0	0	0	0	0	0	0	0	1	0	0
Micrococcus sp.	51	4.5	0	0	0	0	0	0	0	1	0	1	0	0
Gram-negative rods	13	1.1	0	0	0	0	0	0	0	0	0	1	0	0

[a] Source: Hesseltine et al (1969); used by permission.
[b] Brand designated by capital letter.
[c] Total number of samples given in parentheses.
[d] Sesame.
[e] Bread ends.

essing. In the manufacture of soda crackers, a chance contaminant was relied upon for the fermentation of this popular product, since no starter cultures were used. He found that *Saccharomyces cerevisiae, Lactobacillus plantarum, L. delbrueckii, and L. leichmannii* were present in these products and that *L. plantarum* was the predominant organism responsible for the fermentation process.

With this information, Sugihara (1978b) developed a pure culture fermentation process for the soda cracker process. He found that stable, pure-culture, frozen concentrates of *L. plantarum, L. delbrueckii, and L. leichmannii* can be used to replace the conventional process and that the entire process can be reduced to 8 hr compared to the conventional 24-hr soda cracker process.

Due to the popularity of frozen pizza, Dickson (1987) studied survival of selected indicator and pathogenic bacteria in refrigerated pizzas. He inoculated pizzas with *Escherichia coli, Staphylococcus aureus*, and *Salmonella typhimurium*, then froze the pizzas and stored them at 3 and 10°C. Microbiological profiles were determined every two days for 14 days. There was a significant increase of *E. coli* between 8 and 10 days at 10°C. There were no significant differences in the populations of *S. typhimurium* and *S. aureus* with either temperature. Dickson (1987) concluded that the inoculated pathogens did not increase in number but did not decrease either. Therefore, it is essential to eliminate or minimize the populations of potential pathogens during the production phase of pizzas that are to be frozen and later thawed and processed by consumers.

Data obtained in the author's laboratory indicated that raw pizzas with meat, cheese, and other toppings had about 1.0×10^7 total bacteria per gram, with less than three per gram of coliform and *Staphylococcus aureus* and less than one per 25 g of *Listeria*. After baking the pizzas, the total count decreased to 6.1×10^3/g with no pathogens detected (*unpublished data*).

From the aforementioned examples and discussions, it is abundantly clear that frozen and refrigerated bakery products and doughs are microbiologically safe. These products, when treated with heat such as baking or microwave processing before consumption, are very safe products for consumers.

There is yet another important area dealing with frozen doughs for bakery technology—that is the viability of yeast in frozen doughs. This topic is important because it has been advocated that frozen dough with active yeast be prepared and sold to bakeries for on-site thawing of the dough and subsequent proofing and baking. The bake-off system costs less than a complete bakery in terms of operation, labor, and space requirements.

The viability and activities of the yeast in frozen dough become a matter of great concern in this new technology. Al-Eid (1993) made a detailed study of the effect of various common bread ingredients on yeast viability and bread quality in frozen doughs. He prepared an excellent review of the literature of the topic. Jackel (1991) predicted that the frozen dough business would reach $1.5–2.0 billion annually by 1995 in the United States. In 1994, Palmer reported that frozen dough accounted for about $10 billion of business. The main concern in frozen dough is the performance of the yeast, which is related to dough formulation, yeast type and quality, fermentation before freezing, duration of storage, freeze-thaw rates, and sulfhydryl compounds released by the yeast (Al-Eid, 1993).

In terms of dough formulation, Pyler (1988) suggested an increase of yeast level from 4 to 6%, an increase in shortening to 5%, and a slight decrease in absorption. Lorenz (1974) found that maintenance of sugar level at 6% and keeping nonfat dry milk at 4% were advantageous. Flour having a protein content of 11–13% and low starch damage is preferred (Matz, 1989).

The use of fresh compressed yeast, dry yeast, and instant active dry yeast in frozen dough was studied by Wolt and D'Appolonia (1984a; 1984b) and by Bruinsma and Giesenschlag (1984) with mixed results, although all three types seem to perform satisfactorily if they have the correct cryoprotection and nutrients.

The physiology of yeast during freezing and thawing cycles is complex and is related to the genetic makeup of the particular strain under consideration as well as the compounds surrounding the yeast cells during freezing and thawing. Ideally, the cell should be able to withstand freezing and, after thawing, be able to resume maximum activity during the proofing stage.

The general conclusion of Al-Eid's work was that the effects of ingredient level on gassing power correlated better with proofing times than did the total yeast count.

From this angle, it would be interesting to introduce a new procedure of stimulating the gassing power of yeast by the use of bacterial membrane fractions, which have been developed in the author's laboratory.

It has been established in the author's laboratory that membrane fractions from *Escherichia coli* can stimulate the growth of a variety of facultative anaerobic bacteria, including starter cultures (Yu and Fung, 1991; Park, 1992). Recently Tuitemwong (1993) made a detailed study of the affect of membrane fractions on food fermentation and concluded that membrane fractions can stimulate gassing power of yeast in breadmaking and in beer and wine fermentation. Furthermore, Tuitemwong (1993) was able to isolate membrane fractions from "food grade" bacteria such as *Acetobacter* and *Gluconobacter* and to use these membranes to stimulate the gas production of yeast in rye dough.

It is, therefore, conceivable that addition of food grade membrane fractions to frozen dough may help the production of gas after thawing of the dough during the proofing stage. The feasibility of this process remains to be tested and, of course, the quality of the bread must be evaluated as well. However, the possibility exists that membrane fractions can be a great enhancer of yeast fermentation in frozen dough technology.

Conclusion

Bakery products are, in general, excellent food products with good microbiological stability. Refrigeration and freezing further enhance the stability of these products in regard to food spoilage and foodborne diseases. The maintenance of viability and activity of yeast in refrigerated and frozen doughs remains an exciting and important area of research.

Acknowledgment

This is contribution No. 94-398-B from Kansas Agricultural Experiment Station, Manhattan, KS.

Literature Cited

Al-Eid, S. M. 1993 The effect of various common bread ingredients on yeast viability and bread quality in frozen doughs. M.S. thesis. Kansas State University, Manhattan, KS.

Ayres, J. C., Mundt, O., and Sandine, W. E. 1980. Microbiology of Foods. W. H. Freeman and Co., San Francisco.

Bean, N. H., Griffin, P. M., Goulding, J. S., and Ivey, C. B. 1990. Foodborne disease outbreaks, 5-year summary, 1983–1987. J. Food Protect. 53:711-728.

Bourgeois, C. M., and Leveau, J. Y. 1991. Techniques d'Analyse et de Controle dans les Industries Agro-Alimentaires. Lavoisier-Tec Doc., Paris.

Bruinsma, B. L., and Giesenschlag, J. 1984. Frozen dough performance, compressed yeast—Instant dry yeast. Baker's Dig. 58(6):6-7.

Davidson, P. M., and Branen, A. L., eds. 1993. Antimicrobials in Foods, 2nd ed. Marcel Dekker, New York.

Dickson, J. S. 1987. Survival of selected indicator and pathogenic bacteria in refrigerated pizzas. J. Food Protect. 50:859-861.

Fung, D. Y. C. 1983. Microbiology of butter and breading. Pages 106-109 in: Technology of Batter and Breading. D. Suderman and F. E. Cunningham, eds. AVI Publishing Co., Westport, CT.

Fung, D. Y. C. 1986. Microbiology of Meats: MF-792. Publ. no. MF-792. Kansas State Univ. Coop. Ext. Serv., Manhattan, KS.

Fung, D. Y. C. 1992a. Food diseases. Pages 984-990 in: Encyclopedia of Food Science and Technology. Vol. 3. Y. H. Hui, ed. John Wiley & Sons, Inc., New York.

Fung, D. Y. C. 1992b. Food fermentation. Pages 1034-1041 in: Encyclopedia of Food Science and Technology, Vol. 3. Y. H. Hui, ed. John Wiley & Sons, Inc., New York.

Fung, D. Y. C. 1992c. Food microbiology. Pages 1097-1102 in: Encyclopedia of Food Science and Technology, Vol. 3. Y. H. Hui, ed. John Wiley & Sons, Inc., New York.

Fung, D. Y. C. 1992d. Microbiology. Pages 1770-1772 in: Encyclopedia of Food Science and Technology, Vol. 3. Y. H. Hui, ed. John Wiley & Sons, Inc., New York.

Hesseltine, C. W., Graves, R. R., Rogers, R., and Burmeister, H. R. 1969. Aerobic and facultative microflora of fresh and spoiled refrigerated dough products. Applied Microbiol. 18:848-853.

Hui, Y. H, ed. 1992. Encyclopedia of Food Science and Technology. John Wiley & Sons, Inc., New York.

Jackel, S. S. 1991. Frozen dough opportunities keep heating up. Cereal Foods World 36:529.

Jay, J. M. 1992. Modern Food Microbiology, 4th ed. Van Nostrand Reinhold, New York.

Lorenz, K. 1974. Frozen dough: Present trend and future outlook. Baker's Dig. 48(2):14-22.

Kraft. A. A. 1992. Psychrotropic bacteria in foods: Disease and spoilage. CRC Press, Boca Raton, FL.

Marshall, R. T. 1993. Standard methods for the examination of dairy products. Am. Public Health Assoc., Washington, DC.

Matz, S. A. 1989. Bakery Technology: Packaging, Nutrition, Product Development. Pan-Tech International, Inc., McAllen, TX.

Palmer, E. 1994. Food companies are buying into frozen dough. Milling Baking News 73(34):28.

Park, H. Y. 1992. The effect of Oxyrase™ on starter cultures. M.S. thesis. Kansas State University, Manhattan, KS.

Powers, E., and Berkowitz, D. 1990. Efficacy of an oxygen scavenger to modify the atmosphere and prevent mold growth on meal, ready-to-eat pouched bread. J. Food Protect. 53:767-771.

Pruthi, J. S. 1980. Spices and Condiments: Chemistry, Microbiology, Technology. Academic Press, New York.

Pyler, E. J. 1988. Baking Science and Technology, 3rd ed., Vol. II. Sosland Publishing Co., Merriam, KS.

Sinha, R. N., and Muir, W. E. 1973. Grain Storage: Part of a System. AVI Publishing Co., Westport, CT.

Smith, J. D., Jackson, E. D., and Ooraikul, B. 1983. Microbiological studies on gas-packaged crumpets. J. Food Protect. 46:279-283.

Sugihara, T. F. 1978a. Microbiology of the soda cracker process. I. Isolation and identification of microflora. J. Food Protect. 41:977-979.

Sugihara, T. F. 1978b. Microbiology of the soda cracker process. II. Pure culture fermentation studies. J. Food Protect. 41:980-982.

Swartzentruber, A., Schwab, A. H., Wentz, R. A., Duran, A. P., and Read, R. B., Jr. 1984. Microbiological quality of biscuit dough, snack cakes and soy protein meat extender. J. Food Protect. 47:467-470.

Tuitemwong, K. B. 1993. Characteristics of food grade membrane bound enzymes and applications in food microbiology and food safety. Ph.D. dissertation. Kansas State University, Manhattan, KS.

Vanderzant, C., and Splittstoesser, D. F. 1992. Compendium of methods for the microbiological examination of foods. Am. Public Health Assoc., Washington, DC.

Wolt, M. J., and D'Appolonia, B. L. 1984a. Factors involved in stability of frozen dough. I. The influence of yeast reducing compounds on frozen dough stability. Cereal Chem. 61:209-212.

Wolt, M. J., and D'Appolonia, B. L. 1984b. Factors involved in stability of frozen dough. II. The effects of yeast type, flour type, and dough additives in frozen dough stability. Cereal Chem. 61:213-221.

Yu, L. S. L., and Fung, D. Y. C. 1991. Effect of oxyrase enzyme in *Listeria monocytogenes* and other facultative anaerobes. J. Food Saf. 11:163-176.

CHAPTER 7

Freezing of Doughs for the Production of Breads and Rolls in the United States

K. Lorenz
Department of Food Science and Human Nutrition
Colorado State University
Fort Collins, Colorado 80523

K. Kulp
Cereal Chemistry and Technology Consultant
Manhattan, Kansas 66502

A significant development in bakery operations is the use of frozen doughs in the distribution of breads and rolls and similar yeast-leavened products. The doughs are generally fully mixed in central bakeries and shipped frozen to retail outlets, mostly located in large supermarkets, for final bake-off. This method of distribution is beneficial to both the bakeries and the supermarkets since it offers freshly baked, high-quality products to consumers and a well-operated in-store bakery attracts customers to the store for general shopping.

The main shortcoming of frozen dough is its relatively short shelf life. Baking quality tends to deteriorate after a few weeks of frozen storage. Although most manufacturers of frozen dough attempt to move the dough from the central plant freezer within a week and utilize it at the retail or institutional level within 90–120 days, a longer shelf life would provide more flexibility. Also, extended shelf stability of frozen doughs would be desirable in retail distribution for use in the home, where a much longer period of stability is demanded.

Frozen dough manufacturers probably place more emphasis today on quality control than on any other factors in their production-marketing program. The frozen dough industry has spent much effort in the last few years to educate supermarket managers and consumers on correct storage temperatures and proper preparation procedures. Quality has been enhanced by dating of the products and quicker sales due to improved merchandizing techniques. The home baker, however, still finds it quite frustrating at times trying to prepare a "home-baked" loaf of bread from frozen dough that fails to rise in the bread pan.

Instructions for proper handling must be provided to distributors and customers. For that reason, frozen dough companies must be staffed with service technicians who must constantly advise, instruct, and monitor customers and distributors on the proper use and handling of frozen doughs.

Effects of Ingredients on Frozen Dough Quality

The typical formulation for frozen doughs (Table 1) differs somewhat from that of unfrozen doughs, but the basic dough characteristics are essentially the same. The following sections give ingredient percentages and how they affect the quality of frozen dough.

Flour

The flour used in a frozen dough formulation can be from a spring or winter wheat with a protein content in the range of 12–14% (Marston, 1978; Sideleau, 1987; Anonymous, 1990). The flour may be bleached, bromated, and malted. Somewhat higher than usual protein levels (above 11%) are generally recommended to ensure sufficient dough strength for gas retention during thawing and final proof. Flour starch damage should not be above 7% (Marston, 1978), and flour should not be overmalted. The amylograph reading should be between 400 and 500 BU. High levels of amylase accelerate the fermentation process during makeup and have an adverse effect (Sideleau, 1987). Flour ash contents within the range of 0.4–0.5% are acceptable.

Table 1
Frozen Bread Dough Formula and Procedure

Ingredients	Percent Flour Basis
Patent flour (11.5% protein)	100.00
Water	59.00
Yeast (compressed)	4.50
Acid type yeast food	0.50
Salt	2.00
Sucrose	6.00
Milk replacement	3.00
Shortening, nonemulsified	4.00
Potassium bromate[a]	(50 ppm)
Ascorbic acid[a]	(120 ppm)
Procedure	
Mix to development at dough temperature	65–70°F (18–21°C)
Fermentation	None
Floor time	0–10 min

[a] Quantities based on 100 pounds of flour.

Absorption

Absorption levels in the range of 55–60% are recommended. Lower levels of absorption than are normal in unfrozen preparations are desirable for frozen doughs since low levels limit the amount of free water in the system. A high level of free water is damaging to the dough and yeast during freezing and thawing cycles (Javes, 1971; Sideleau, 1987; Anonymous, 1990). It is important to get complete hydration of flour particles with a minimum amount of free water. Lower absorption also helps the dough to maintain its shape during freezing and thawing cycles (Anonymous, 1990). Actual water absorption depends on the product variety desired, the formulation, and the proper machining requirements (Sideleau, 1987). Chilled dough water is used to reduce the dough temperature to less than 70°F (~20°C). This slows the yeast activity and accelerates freezing of the dough piece (Javes, 1971; Anonymous, 1990).

Mineral Yeast Food, Oxidation, and Reducing Agents

The normal level of yeast food required for a flour (0.5% flour basis) in conventional baking is satisfactory for frozen doughs. When yeast food was omitted from a bread formula for preparation of frozen straight doughs made with an unbromated winter wheat flour, the bread had low volume and poor grain and texture (Lorenz and Bechtel, 1964). Oxidation level and type of oxidants are very important in the production of frozen dough. Addition of potassium bromate produced some improvement in loaf volume and a definite improvement in bread quality (Lorenz and Bechtel, 1965). Ascorbic acid and potassium bromate together bring about an even greater improvement (Anonymous, 1990).

Potassium bromate levels of 15–45 ppm in addition to the normal levels (0.5% based on flour) of bromated yeast food in the formulation were found to be beneficial for frozen doughs (Lorenz and Bechtel, 1965; Dubois and Blockcolsky, 1986). Experiments by Lorenz and Bechtel (1965) were conducted with both a spring wheat and a winter wheat flour.

With the winter wheat flour, loaf volumes increased and grain improved with addition of potassium bromate after four weeks of storage of the dough. Bread made with spring wheat flour had improved grain. Although there was no change in volume after the first week of storage, after four weeks the volume increased as bromate was increased to 30 ppm, then decreased at 45 ppm. At this level, a slight effect of overoxidation was noticeable.

As the frozen storage period became longer, loaf volumes decreased and the overall quality of the bread deteriorated. However, the bread prepared with the higher levels of bromate had higher volume and better grain than the control bread without added bromate. The bread with 45 ppm added bromate was by far the best in overall quality. The volume was highest, the grain best, and the texture smoothest. Also, the slight effect of overoxidation, observed after four weeks, was no longer noticeable (Lorenz and Bechtel, 1965).

After 12 weeks of storage, quality of external and internal bread characteristics decreased with all levels of oxidation, although the loaves with higher bromate levels had slightly higher volumes.

In summary, addition of bromate above the amounts in bromated yeast food may improve the volume, grain, and texture of white bread from frozen dough. However, it does not appear to increase storage stability. Storage time of 12 weeks still appears to be the maximum, since there was an abrupt change in external and internal bread characteristics at the 14th week (Lorenz and Bechtel, 1965).

Kline and Sugihara (1968) also reported that potassium bromate (35–60 ppm) improved the performance of frozen dough after 15 weeks of storage, loaf volume being considerably greater when as much as 35 ppm of potassium bromate was added. However, the higher bromate levels extended the proof time by 45% compared to that of the dough containing no potassium bromate. Also, the addition of 35 ppm of potassium bromate appeared to decrease gas production after 15 weeks of frozen storage as measured by a pressure meter (Kline and Sugihara, 1968; Dubois and Blockcolsky, 1986). Dubois and Blockcolsky (1986) also state that doughs containing higher level of potassium bromate (43 ppm) require longer proofing time than those with lower potassium bromate at each storage time. The addition of ascorbic acid in addition to potassium bromate appeared to decrease the proofing time, indicating that the ascorbic acid improved dough gas retention properties (Varriano-Marston et al, 1980).

All proof times increased with age of the frozen dough, with the greatest increase occurring between the 8th and 12th weeks of storage. The proofing time then leveled off to an approximately constant figure between 12 and 20 weeks of storage, as seen in Figure 1.

Reducing agents frequently used in normal breadmaking to soften the gluten are not generally applied to frozen doughs, although there might be some exception (Marston, 1978). Reducing agents are used to shorten dough mixing time and produce more pliable, workable doughs. Reducing agents are used to supplement the mixing action when the flour is too strong to perform satisfactorily. The action of the reducing agent occurs rapidly in the dough mixer. Some dough conditioners contain reducing agents to produce a shorter mixing time and also an oxidizing agent to counteract this reducing action at a later stage in the baking cycle (Anonymous, 1990).

L-Cysteine, which is quite popular, aids in effectively reducing the mixing time for frozen doughs. The use levels of this ingredient should be adjusted so as to give a maximum 15–20% mixing time reduction. Levels that cause a greater decrease in mixing time produce excessive dough softening or weakness, causing flat or misshapen dough pieces and possible collapse of the dough at the final proofing stage or in the oven. Use of products containing a combination of reducing and oxidizing agents provides optimum mixing, machining, and maturing properties by means of direct biochemical action on the flour protein.

Yeast

Higher levels of yeast (5–6% flour basis) are normally used in frozen dough formulations to compensate for losses in yeast gassing power during extended storage (Merritt, 1960; Drake, 1970; Javes, 1971; Lorenz, 1974; Marston, 1978).

As reported by many investigators (Merritt, 1960; Kline and Sugihara, 1968; Hsu et al 1979a, 1979b), the major problem of frozen doughs is the performance of the yeast. Yeast is necessary to provide proper gas production for dough leavening. In any yeast-leavened dough, the aroma, taste, and texture of the final product are dependent on yeast fermentation (Merritt, 1960). When dough is frozen and thawed, the yeast's viability and capacity to produce gas are decreased, resulting in bread with lower loaf volume and inferior quality.

Because of its importance, yeast is the single most studied ingredient in frozen dough (Bruinsma and Giesenschlag, 1984). Freezing yeast in a dough system is different from direct freezing of yeast. Yeast in a dough system is under osmotic pressure and is in a state of active fermentation, which may increase its susceptibility to damage when frozen. On the other hand, the physical nature of the dough may protect yeast cells during the freezing process. Using a plate-count method, Kline and Sugihara (1968) reported substantial losses in the number of viable cells in frozen dough. The first problem that must be solved with frozen unbaked doughs is the retention of sufficient yeast viability and gassing power during frozen storage to avoid excessive proofing times or even a virtual loss of proofing power after thawing. Minor improvements in the quality of the thawed product can be achieved by formulation and ingredient changes, type of yeast, dough conditioners, decreasing absorption, oxidizing agents, or reworking the dough after thawing (Lorenz and Bechtel, 1964, 1965; Davis, 1981; Bruinsma and Giesenschlag, 1984).

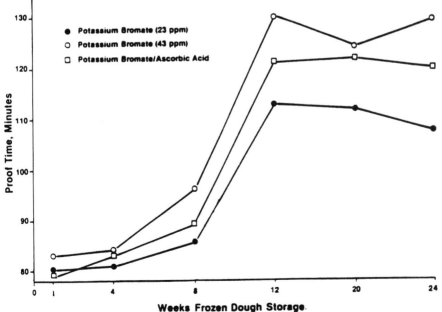

Fig. 1. Effects of additives on frozen-dough proof time. (Adapted, with permission, from Dubois and Blockcolsky, 1986)

Three different types of yeast are available to the frozen dough producer. These are compressed yeast, instant dry yeast, and active dry yeast. Fresh compressed yeast performed better than active dry yeast and instant active dry yeast when used at comparable activity levels (Wolt and D'Appolonia, 1984a, 1984b; Sideleau, 1987). Some workers, however, have suggested that dry yeast may be superior to compressed yeast in maintaining shelf life in frozen dough (Zaehringer et al, 1951; Merritt, 1960). Theoretically, the longer lag period with dry yeast should minimize fermentation before freezing and thus give a more stable frozen dough. Kline and Sugihara (1968), however, found that doughs made with dried yeast had somewhat longer proof times than doughs made with compressed yeast. These workers suggest that the release of reducing agents from active dry yeast could be the cause of the longer proofing time.

The tripeptide glutathione has been isolated from dry active yeast and is associated with marked effects on the rheological and baking properties of dough (Ponte et al, 1960). These effects include shorter mixing time, increased extensibility, decreased loaf volume, and a greater requirement for oxidizing improvers. Lorenz (1974) and Kline and Sugihara (1968) reported better overall bread quality with increased levels of potassium bromate in frozen-dough formulation. Both bromate and ascorbic acid are capable of counteracting the adverse effects of glutathione (Freilich and Frey, 1944; Johnston and Mauseth, 1972).

The recommended usage of active dry yeast is generally at a concentration of one-half the normal compressed yeast level. If conversion ratios of dry yeast are very low, then proof times are longer. As more dry yeast is added, proof times decrease such that they may be consistently shorter than those of doughs prepared with compressed yeast samples. However, it may not be economically feasible to use higher levels of instant dry yeast in frozen dough to decrease proof time (Bruinsma and Giesenschlag, 1984).

Sweeteners

Sugar levels in frozen dough depend on the type of product and crust characteristics required, but they are slightly higher than in freshly baked products (Heid, 1968; Dubois and Dreese, 1984). Levels of 8–10% are recommended. Products that are higher in sugar generally show greater freezer stability due to the sugar's hygroscopic properties, which bind with water to help keep the level of free water low, reducing its damage to the yeast cell (Bruinsma and Giesenschlag, 1984).

Most research studies report the use of sucrose in frozen doughs. However, in recent years, high-fructose corn syrup (HFCS) has replaced sucrose and corn syrup as the predominant sweetener in commercial bread production.

A study of different sweeteners in frozen dough by Dubois and Dreese (1984) indicated that increased sweetener level (from 6 to 10%) did not increase dough proof time for fresh dough. In the frozen dough, breads with three levels of corn syrup (6, 8, and 10%) had about the same proof time at each test period. However, increasing the sucrose or HFCS from 8 to 10% produced a definite lengthening of the proof time over the 6 and 8% levels at each test period. The experiments were conducted for 26 weeks.

At higher use levels (8 and 10%), corn syrup doughs had shorter proof times than the corresponding sugar and HFCS doughs. Proof times increased with dough age to 14 weeks of storage, then decreased for six weeks, after which the time increased, but not to the 14-week level.

Corn syrup doughs generally produced lower-volume bread than HFCS or sucrose. Sweetener level and dough age did not appear to have any effect on loaf volume. Sucrose and HFCS produced bread having a darker crust color than that of bread produced with corn syrup. Increased sweetener levels produced darker crusts. Corn syrup produced bread having poorer crumb grain than was produced by sucrose or HFCS, which were about equal. These differences narrowed with dough age, and after 20 weeks of storage, the crumb grain in breads from all sweeteners was about equal and poor.

Salt

Since salt retards yeast activity as well as serving as a flavor enhancer, the suggested level is 1.5–2.0% (Anonymous, 1990). It is usually added late in the mixing process to minimize the effect of salt on mixing time.

Shortening

Shortening at a 4–5% level is recommended for fine grain quality and tender texture. An emulsifier of the mono-diglyceride type benefits volume and crumb quality (Lorenz and Bechtel, 1964, 1965; Heid, 1968; Anonymous, 1990).

Milk

Nonfat dry milk at levels of 2–4% enhances the crust color but has little effect on the internal characteristics of the crumb (Heid, 1968; Javes, 1971). Merritt (1960) and Anonymous (1990) suggest using dried sweet dairy whey and soy for the nonfat dry milk because the high lactose content in whey contributes to crust color but is not utilized by the yeast.

Nonfat dry milk, in addition to improving flavor and crust color, also plays an important role as a buffering agent to counteract the effects of fermentation acids during long storage periods (Javes, 1971).

Dough Additives

The surfactants sodium stearoyl lactylate (SSL) and diacetyl tartaric acid esters of monoglycerides (DATEM) have been shown to be effective in maintaining both volume and crumb softness in bread produced from dough subjected to extended frozen storage (Marston, 1978; Varriano-Marston et al, 1980; Davis, 1981; Dubois and Blockcolsky, 1986). Davis (1981) reported data showing that SSL provides a longer period of dough stability in terms of loaf volume; however, the study did not include information on proof-time stability, which is a critical parameter in judging the overall shelf life of the dough.

In a study by Wolt and D'Appolonia (1984b), the effect of SSL and DATEM on proof-time and loaf-volume stability were analyzed over 20 weeks of frozen storage. The role of SSL and DATEM in counteracting rheological changes that occur in frozen storage were studied with the extensigraph. The additives were not effective in reducing the time needed to proof doughs to a specific height. Breads from frozen doughs with SSL had greater loaf volumes than doughs without SSL, because of a greater oven-spring. The use of diacetyl tartaric acid was less effective than SSL in counteracting rheological changes and in maintaining loaf volume. In all these studies, the experiments were conducted with yeasted dough. Thus, it is difficult to dissociate the changes in the dough rheology from the effects of yeast and its deterioration.

Addition of glutamic acid to frozen dough was claimed to be beneficial in a U.S. patent issued to Taguchi et al (1975). The formula and procedure used in this patent were somewhat different from those used by the bread industry in the United States. Also, four weeks was the maximum storage time covered in the patent. Dubois and Blockcolsky (1986) did not see any improvement of quality of frozen bread dough using glutamic acid added at 0.5% based on flour.

Glycerol at 0.75–1.5% (flour basis) had relatively little effect on loaf volume of bread baked from frozen dough, but it may have slightly improved the crumb grain after 20 weeks of frozen storage (Dubois and Blockcolsky, 1986). The crumb grain of the glycerol doughs and the standard doughs was comparable during the first 16 weeks of storage. These results suggest that glycerol has no improving effect on frozen dough at the levels used in these tests.

When xanthan gum was added to formulas for frozen doughs at 0.5% (flour basis), the water absorption was increased (Dubois and Blockcolsky, 1986). Even with this higher absorption, the xanthan gum produced somewhat tighter doughs that had less tendency to spread in the pan during the early stages of final proof. The xanthan gum did not appear to affect proof time or the rate of gas production during final proof. Also, xanthan gum had little effect on loaf volume of the bread.

Xanthan gum had a slightly adverse effect on the internal characteristics of the loaf, the crumb grain being judged slightly poorer than that of the control at each storage time during a 20-week storage study. No improvement in reducing crust blistering during frozen storage was observed (Dubois and Blockcolsky, 1986).

Mixing

Research reports conflict regarding selection of the best mixing method for the production of frozen dough. Lorenz and Bechtel (1964) reported that frozen dough with the best storage life was made by the continuous-mix process. Javes (1971), however, indicated that the process was unsatisfactory when the liquid sponge was fermented for 2.5 hr. In his experiments, resultant bread exhibited young dough characteristics that became more pronounced as its frozen storage time was extended. When the preferment received a 3-hr fermentation, the results were normal. Not enough testing has been done, however, to justify any definite conclusions concerning the suitability of the liquid ferment process for frozen-dough production.

Sugihara and Kline (1968) and Hsu et al (1979a) reported good quality of frozen doughs prepared by the sponge and dough method and stored for up to 15 weeks. Bread quality improved with increasing sponge time. Frozen samples showed good yeast stability with sponge times up to 90 min. Sponge times longer than 90 min gave longer proof times than normal.

Dubois and Blockcolsky (1986) studied the effects of several mixing methods (Table 2) on the quality of bread produced from frozen dough (Table 3). Mixing procedures 1 and 2 appeared to produce the greatest rate of gas production, and this increased rate was maintained throughout the 24 weeks of storage.

An important observation is that the delayed salt method in common use pro-

Table 2
Mixing Procedure Variations

Mixing Stage	Mixing Procedure[a,b]			
	1	2	3	4
1	All ingredients except salt and yeast. Mix to partial development.	All ingredients. Mix to full development.	All ingredients except salt. Mix to partial development.	All ingredients except salt and yeast. Mix to partial development.
2	Add yeast. Mix to partial development.		Add salt. Mix to full development.	Add salt and yeast. Mix to full development.
3	Add salt. Mix to full development.			

[a] Source: Dubois and Blockcolsky (1986), used with permission.
[b] Final dough temperature after mixing was 70°F (21°C) with each procedure.

Table 3
Effect of Dough Mixing Methods on Gas Production[a] in Doughs After Frozen Storage[b]

Frozen Dough Storage[c] (weeks)	Mixing Procedure[d]			
	1	2	3	4
1	2.10	2.21	2.19	1.56
4	2.20	2.19	2.25	1.64
8	1.52	1.51	1.51	1.07
12	1.87	1.81	1.80	1.38
16	1.95	1.85	1.77	1.40
20	1.33	1.18	0.92	1.13
24	1.56	1.36	0.97	1.15

[a] Gas production of thawed dough after 90 min of fermentation at 86°F (30°C). One gasograph unit is equivalent to 2.38 cm^3 of gas.
[b] Source: Dubois and Blockcolsky (1986); used with permission.
[c] Doughs were frozen to a core temperature of 18–20°F and stored in plastic lined cardboard boxes at -10°F.
[d] Final dough temperature after mixing was 70°F with each procedure.

duced a reduced rate of gas production (method 3). The gas production rate for this method was satisfactory for the first 16 weeks of frozen dough storage but dropped to a low rate as the storage time was extended to 20 and 24 weeks. However, a variation of the delayed salt method (method 1) produced doughs having good gas production. The lowest rate of production occurred when salt and yeast were withheld until the dough had been partially mixed and then both ingredients were added at the same time late in the mixing stage (method 4) (Dubois and Blockcolsky, 1986).

The effects of the dough mixing procedure on proof time are reflected in Table 4. The shortest proof times after 24 weeks of storage were produced using mixing methods 1 or 2, which also produced the greatest gas production. Doughs produced with method 3, delayed salt, maintained a relatively short proof time for the first 16 weeks, then deteriorated rapidly at 20 and 24 weeks. No explanation is offered for this. Long proofing times at all storage periods indicate that mixing method 4 would be unsatisfactory for frozen-dough production.

The effects of dough mixing procedures on loaf volume are shown in Table 5. Volume is affected by the dough mixing procedure, with procedure 1 producing consistently the best loaf volume during 24 weeks of frozen dough storage. It is noted that loaf volume tends to improve during the first 8 to 14 weeks of storage for all mixing methods, with some deterioration in loaf volume thereafter. This indicates a loss of gas retention properties after 14 weeks of frozen dough storage (Dubois and Blockcolsky, 1986).

The frozen dough industry seems to prefer the straight-dough procedure (Sideleau, 1987). Twenty-three of the 26 firms surveyed by the U. S. Department of Agriculture used the straight-dough mixing method, with fermentation times ranging from none to well over 1 hr (Anonymous, 1967).

Two points about the mixing procedure should be emphasized:

1. Use a high-speed dough mixer with a refrigerating jacket to keep the dough

Table 4
Effect of Dough Mixing Procedure on Proofing Time[a] of Frozen Dough[b]

Frozen Dough Storage (weeks)[c]	Mixing Procedure			
	1	2	3	4
1	76	69	74	107
4	81	78	67	103
8	88	86	90	123
12	103	104	99	128
16	101	101	103	124
20	104	109	120	127
24	98	107	149	133

[a] Proof time: minutes for dough piece to rise 5/8 in. above pan when proofed at 90°F (32°C) and 70% RH.

[b] Source: Dubois and Blockcolsky (1986); used with permission.

[c] Doughs were frozen to a core temperature of 18–20°F (-7.8 to -6.7°C) and stored in plastic-lined cardboard boxes at -10°F (12.2°C).

temperature at about 65–70°F (18–21°C). This retards fermentation, produces a plastic dough that handles easily, and induces fast freezing. Dough temperature control is critical, and standards should be maintained at all times. Digital probe thermometers and mixer bowl temperature indicators should be installed on each mixer.

2. Mix the dough to full development. Undermixing results in sticky doughs with ingredients unevenly dispersed and gluten inadequately developed. The result is poor volume and appearance and a coarse grain in the baked product. Overmixed doughs are difficult to handle; they are sticky and runny in character; they yield a baked product with essentially the same faults as the undermixed doughs. Several factors influence the optimum time of mixing: flour strength, dough temperature, ingredients, type of mixer, and speed of mixing. Delayed salt and fat methods are preferred to reduce mixing times and improve dough development and extensibility. This procedure eliminates excessive use of no-time dough agents (reducing compounds, proteolytic enzymes), which are detrimental to gluten strength and the gas retention properties of the flour.

Fermentation

Dough fermentation before freezing may be the most important factor affecting the stability of frozen dough (Godkin and Cathcart, 1949; Meyer et al, 1956; Merritt, 1960; Kline and Sugihara, 1968; Sugihara and Kline, 1968). Many workers believe that fermentation before freezing is detrimental to the viability of yeast. They attribute the greater stability of the unfermented dough to the relatively dormant condition of the yeast (Merritt, 1960; Kline and Sugihara, 1968; Sugihara and Kline, 1968).

Godkin and Cathcart (1949) and Merritt (1960) demonstrated that the stability of a frozen dough is inversely related to the amount of fermentation before

Table 5
Effect of Dough Mixing Methods on Loaf Volume[a] of Bread Produced from Frozen Dough[b,c]

	Mixing Procedure			
Loaf Volume	1	2	3	4
Lowest, ml	2,583	2,417	2,400	2,492
After weeks of storage	4 and 24	24	24	18
Greatest, ml	2,750	2,650	2,808	2,692
After weeks of storage	14	12	10	8
Average, ml, for all storage times	2,650	2,581	2,615	2,517

[a] Loaf volume in milliliters.
[b] Source: Dubois and Blockcolsky (1986); used with permission.
[c] Doughs were frozen to a core temperature of 18–20°F and stored in plastic lined cardboard boxes at -10°F.

freezing. With more than 1 hr of fermentation, the stability during frozen storage was reduced to a few weeks. With a half hour of fermentation, the stability might be satisfactory for three to four months. When no fermentation was given, the dough was stable for up to 12 months, provided proper formulation, mixing, freezing, packaging, and storage practices were carefully observed (Merritt, 1960). Today's producers of frozen dough cannot achieve a 12-week stability of frozen doughs, however.

There is general agreement that during the fermentation process certain physical and chemical changes occur in the dough that give the dough maturity and mellowness. Flavor precursors are developed that account for the delightful flavor in the freshly baked rolls and bread. The key problems are the limitation of storage stability of fermented doughs and the unreasonable proofing periods required after several weeks of frozen storage. Those who recommend the fermentation step also advise a limit of 10–12 weeks of storage (Heid, 1968). The choice of method must be resolved by the ultimate disposition of the frozen dough. Where bake-off at a point-of-sale outlet in supermarket, retail bakery, or food-service institution is the goal after short storage of a week or two, and all handling is done by personnel trained in the temperature limitations of the product, there is no problem with product quality if stable freezer temperatures can be assured. If the retail frozen food cabinet is the ultimate channel of distribution, the producer can anticipate some temperature abuse during transportation and handling and in the supermarket and no control whatsoever over the duration or temperature of storage once the product reaches the hands of the customer (Heid, 1968).

Dough Makeup

After mixing, all doughs should be immediately transferred to the make-up equipment, either by hoist, dough pump, or conveyor. After scaling, short intermediate proofs are required before the sheeting and molding of the product. This is to ensure that the product is extensible enough for proper sheeting and molding. Longer intermediate proof times will shorten the freezer storage period of the product (Sideleau, 1987).

Since most doughs are stiff in consistency, uniform scaling may be difficult. It is extremely important that the machine operators consistently monitor the scaling weights and make adjustments. Dough degassing equipment should be used where and if possible. Product integrity and uniformity during makeup is totally dependent upon correct formulation and mixing, correct fermentation times, and no mechanical down-time. Mechanical down-time is the frozen dough nightmare.

Air-conditioned make-up areas are recommended to maintain a year-round temperature of 70°F (21°C) so that the product has more tolerance to any manufacturing delays and is more pliable for machining. Older doughs at warm ambient temperatures tend to sweat and become sticky, requiring excessive use of dusting flour and production line stoppages due to dough jam-ups on the manufacturing equipment (Sideleau, 1987).

Freezing

The made-up dough units should be frozen immediately if the freezer dough storage life is to be maintained for the 8–12 weeks practiced by most commercial operations. The most effective and efficient operations use a fast-freezing chamber in addition to a low-temperature holding or equilibrium room. The dough piece should be frozen to a core temperature of approximately 20°F (-7°C) in the fast freezer and kept at 0°F (-18°C) to equilibrate and for storage (Lehmann and Dreese, 1981).

Studies (Nei, 1964; Nei et al, 1967; Mazur and Schmidt, 1968; Mazur, 1971) on the preservation of microorganisms by freezing have shown that freezing and thawing rates affect yeast viability. Slow freezing is generally believed to allow cells to adjust to the freezing environment by transferring intracellular water to the external ice. Fast freezing, on the other hand, causes intracellular freezing because temperatures change much faster than water permeates cell membranes. The small ice crystals formed during intracellular freezing are likely to recrystallize into larger crystals during thawing and hence become lethal to the cells (Hsu et al, 1979b).

Freezing to an internal core temperature of 20°F (-7°C) gives a raw center to the dough piece. It is highly recommended not to freeze solidly, since this will shorten the freezer storage life of the product and eventually lengthen proof times when the product is used by the retail baker. The remaining freezing of the product occurs during what is called the equilibration period. Thus, the dough is thoroughly frozen at the point where yeast activity is least. This process occurs during the packaging and frozen storage of the product (Sideleau, 1987). Internal core temperatures of products must be monitored by supervision and adjustments made to the dwell time in the freezer to maintain the proper freezing of products. It is also extremely important that the products be indexed properly before entering the freezer to ensure that there is separation between items for proper freezing. Products that touch each other will not freeze properly. By utilizing the two-stage freezing operation, the dwell time in the main freezing chamber is reduced and both the productivity of the plant and the product quality are improved.

Products are stored in a warehouse freezer at a temperature of 0 to -10°F (-18 to -23°C). Storage temperatures should be kept as consistent as possible, with a minimal amount of fluctuation. Fluctuation of the temperature of the product during cold storage or shipment minimizes dough performance and shortens the freezer life of the product due to ice crystal formation and movement. Yeast, even at these temperatures, is not totally dormant, and extreme temperature fluctuations are detrimental to product quality and performance (Sideleau, 1987).

Changes in the temperature between freezing and storage clearly affect yeast viability (Hsu et al, 1979b). Storage temperatures lower than freezing temperatures were more harmful than freezing and storing at the same temperature. For instance, yeast activity, as judged by proofing time, was significantly lower in samples of dough frozen at 0°F (-18°C) and stored at -30°F (-34°C) than in samples frozen and stored at 0°F. The damage from freezing at 0°F and storing at

-30°F was even more pronounced than from freezing and storing at -30°F. Damage seemed to result from transferring a frozen sample to a lower temperature. Yeast damage caused by slow freezing to -30°F was similar to that caused by freezing at 0°F and storing at -30°F. Change of storage temperature to a higher level did not cause much additional yeast damage (Table 6) (Hsu et al, 1979b).

Packaging

Packaging designed for frozen doughs must perform a number of functions, such as contain, protect, identify, and merchandize the food. One of the factors responsible for the decline in product quality during frozen storage is the loss of moisture. Cold air has a low moisture content and therefore dehydrates any unprotected product with a higher moisture content. A good packaging material must keep this loss of moisture to a minimum (Klein, 1971a, 1971b).

Films to be used for frozen dough should possess the following characteristics: 1) good moisture protection, 2) good oxygen-barrier characteristics, 3) physical strength against brittleness and breakage at low temperature, 4) stiffness to work on automatic machinery, and 5) good heat sealability.

Packaging materials for frozen dough are discussed in detail in Chapter 13.

Distribution

For shipment, the product is transferred into refrigerated trailers. The entire trailer should be thoroughly insulated to prevent heat penetration into the trailer and product thawing. The product should be loaded onto the trailer in such a way that the proper temperature and air circulation can be maintained during the distribution of the product to the consumer. The trailer temperature should be the same as that of the storage freezer warehouse, with minimal temperature fluctuation (Sideleau, 1987).

Table 6
Effect of Temperature Change Between Freezing and Storage
on Frozen Dough Quality[a]

Freeze Temperature		Store Temperature		Proof Time	Volume
(°F)	(°C)	(°F)	(°C)	(min)	(cm³)
0	-18	0	-18[b]	69	920
		-30	-34[b]	98	85
-30	-34	-30	-34[b]	89	910
		0	-18[b]	80	875
0	-18	-30/0	-34, -18[c]	100	880

[a] Adapted from Hsu et al (1979b).
[b] Samples were frozen at the given temperatures for 20 hr and stored at the given temperatures for one week.
[c] Samples were frozen at 0°F (-18°C) for 20 hr, transferred to -30°F (-34°C) for 36 hr, and stored at 0°F for one week.

Cost-effective systems are necessary for maintaining the quality of frozen dough throughout the "cold chain"—from exit of the freezer through transportation, distribution, warehousing, and the final transport to the retail or institutional outlet. Storage temperature is a primary consideration, as well as the integrity of packaging and inventory control.

Frozen doughs are often mishandled while being loaded, transported, or kept in display freezers. The dough may be partially or even completely thawed and then refrozen later. Because temperature changes are involved, the quality of the frozen doughs may be affected.

Thawing, Proofing, and Baking

Operations in In-Store Bakeries

Processing of frozen doughs into baked products at in-store bakeries involves frozen storage, thawing under refrigeration (called *retarding* by bakers), proofing, and baking. Bakers who have never used frozen doughs and are accustomed only to "fresh" dough operations may not appreciate the differences between the methods of handling these types of doughs. This lack of experience with frozen doughs may become a serious source of production difficulties, especially at the thawing and proofing stages.

Frozen Storage

This is essentially the first production step in in-store baking. The doughs are delivered from a central bakery's frozen storage to an in-store bakery. At that point, they are transferred to a freezer maintained at a temperature of 0 to -10°F (-18 to -23°C). Ideally, this freezer should be dedicated to frozen dough storage in order to give the baker full control over its operating conditions. Since in-store baking generally takes place in grocery supermarkets, frozen doughs are often kept in a common freezer. In this case, temperature control of the shared freezer is almost nonexistent, which often results in serious operating and quality problems.

Another factor affecting proper storage is the keeping of frozen dough inventory. Proper storage of frozen dough must be well planned and organized, so that the doughs can be easily stored according to product variety, rotated, and then used according to their age in the freezer. To facilitate this operation, the frozen-dough suppliers assign to each carton a "product code number" and a "pull date code." Most suppliers also use product color-codes for quick and easy identification (e.g., bread cases are green, Danish cases are red, etc.).

Thawing (Retarding)

The second step in frozen dough processing is thawing. This operation takes place in the retarder, an enclosed area closely maintained at a temperature within the range of 33–40°F (1–4°C). A bakery provides either a "cabinet" or "walk-in" type of retarder, with the "walk-in" being the preferred type. This latter permits the storage of racks each containing 20–30 pans. On the other hand, the "cabinet" retarder requires placing of individual pans on shelving, which is time-consuming and also causes a loss of cold air from the retarder and temperature fluctuations.

When frozen dough is being removed from the freezer, the individual dough units are removed from the shipping cartons and positioned on sheet pans, allowing sufficient space between units for expansion during retarding. The panned units must be covered to prevent skin formation and crusting by dehydration. This operation is called bulk-panning, or "break-out."

In walk-in retarders, entire racks filled with pans of frozen dough units are enclosed in tent-like zippered, open-ended poly-bags. To minimize dehydration of the dough-surface units in cabinet-type retarders, the individual pans are covered with plastic bags. The latter practice is less desirable since in individually bagged trays, airspace above the frozen dough units is limited and can readily become oversaturated with humidity. This condition may cause the plastic to adhere to dough surfaces, which results in difficulties (surface damage) when the covers are removed from fully proofed doughs. Excessive moisture condensation also causes dough softening and excessive dough flow during proofing. In extreme cases, the moisture condensation is responsible for blistering and/or discoloration of the external surfaces of baked products.

In-store bakeries normally retard (thaw) a day's production for 12–18 hr, placing bulk-panned frozen dough into the retarder for overnight defrosting. Retarding times vary for different items. Small dough units like 1¾-oz (50-g) ring doughnuts may require only 3–4 hr of retarding, whereas 18-oz (510-g) bread dough units need 12–16 hr. Retarding of ring doughnuts for the 12- to 16-hr internal, however, does not result in over-retarding but may shorten the proof time slightly. During retarding, fermentation proceeds at a very slow rate. If the dough is kept in the retarder longer than 24 hr, a sour flavor may be generated by the action of flour microorganisms, which may adversely affect the flavor of the finished product.

Dough Proofing

At the end of the retarding period, the dough temperature is essentially the same as that of the retarder. Consequently, the next processing step, proofing, takes place with doughs of lower moisture, humidity, and temperature levels than for fresh doughs. These factors affect physical and biochemical dough properties such as extensibility, rate of fermentation, enzyme activity, and rate of oxidative and reducing reactions. In view of this condition, the proofing must be conducted differently than for fresh dough.

Frozen-dough proofing at in-store bakeries requires relative humidity within the range of 70–75%, substantially lower than for proofing of fresh dough. The temperature of the proof box should be adjustable between 90 and 110°F (32–43°C). This range is necessary for accommodating different dough sizes and weights. Doughnuts will, in most cases, withstand 110°F (43°C), whereas 20-oz (570-g) retarded bread doughs require a 90°F (39°C) proofing temperature.

Proof times are significantly longer for retarded than for fresh dough units. An 18-oz (510-g) fresh bread dough generally requires 50–60 min of proof time. A retarded unit of the same weight typically requires 75–90 min. The extended proof time is due to the cooler temperature at the core of the dough piece (retarded temperature = 33–40°F [1–4°C], compared to that of fresh dough, 80–82°F [26.7–27.8°C]) when it enters the proofer.

Baking

Baking conditions for fully proofed doughs from frozen doughs are essentially the same as in conventional bread production. The fully proofed doughs from the frozen dough operation have a significantly lower internal temperature than those from a fresh dough system, which may result in slightly different oven-spring. However, this difference is due more to the different action of various oxidizing agents than directly to the cooler core of the dough in retarded-dough operation.

Home-Use Procedures

Full instructions for the handling of the product for "home use" should be included in the package. In most situations, conditions for proofing of dough in the home kitchen are not readily controllable, and improvisation to regulate temperature and humidity will usually be necessary. The baking pan should be greased before the piece of dough is placed in it, and the dough should be allowed to rise above the rim of the baking pan, to at least double its original volume, in an enclosed and moderately warm area where it can thaw and proof before being put into the oven (Heid, 1968; Marston, 1978). This will take several hours, at least.

This rather lengthy period required for thawing and proofing the frozen dough has often proved to be a deterrent to home bakers, who expect to have a baked loaf of bread ready for eating within an hour or two.

Thawing of the dough overnight in the refrigerator, followed by proofing in a warm place is an alternative procedure. The bread resulting from this treatment usually has the best loaf volume and crumb texture, yet the actual proof is relatively short (Lorenz and Bechtel, 1964, 1965).

A moderate oven temperature of 400–425°F (200–220°C) is usually most suitable for the baking of frozen dough in the home kitchen. This allows for some extension of "proofing" and further expansion of the dough before the structure sets, and it avoids too dark a crust color (Marston, 1978).

Literature Cited

Anonymous 1967. Potentials for frozen dough. Bull. 787. Econ. Res. Serv., U.S. Dep. Agric., Washington, DC.

Anonymous 1990. Frozen dough production, Lesson 45, correspondence course-Baking Science. American Institute of Baking, Manhattan, KS.

Bruinsma, B. L., and Giesenschlag, J. 1984. Frozen dough performance. Compressed yeast-Instant dry yeast. Baker's Dig. 58(6):6.

Davis, E. W. 1981. Shelf-life studies on frozen doughs. Baker's Dig. 55(3):12.

Drake, E. 1970. Up-to-date review of freezing. Baker's Dig. 44(2):65.

Dubois, D. K., and Dreese, P. 1984. Frozen white bread dough-Effects of sweetener level. AIB Tech. Bull. Vol. VI, Issue 7. American Institute of Baking, Manhattan, KS.

Dubois, D. K., and Blockcolsky, D. 1986. Frozen bread dough, effect of additives. AIB Tech.

Bull. Vol. VIII, Issue 4. American Institute of Baking, Manhattan, KS.

Freilich, J., and Frey, C. N. 1944. Dough oxidation and mixing studies. VI. Effects of oxidizing agents in the presence of reducing matter. Cereal Chem. 21:241.

Godkin, W. J., and Cathcart, W. H. 1949. Fermentation activity and survival of yeast in frozen fermented and unfermented doughs. Food Technol. 3(April):139.

Heid, M. 1968. Frozen batters and doughs. Pages 360-385 in: The Freezing Preservation of Foods, Vol. 4. D. K. Tressler, W. B. van Arsdel, and M. J. Copley, eds. AVI Publ. Co., Westport, CT.

Hsu, K. H., Hoseney, R. C., and Seib, P. A. 1979a. Frozen dough. I. Factors affecting stability of yeasted doughs. Cereal Chem. 56:419.

Hsu, K. S., Hoseney, R. C., and Seib, P. A. 1979b. Frozen dough. II. Effects of freezing and storing conditions on the stability of yeasted doughs. Cereal Chem. 56:424.

Javes, R. 1971. Frozen bakery foods—The ingredients and the processes—Effect on shelf-life of frozen, unbaked yeast leavened doughs. Baker's Dig. 45(2):56.

Johnston, W. R., and Mauseth, R. E. 1972. The interrelations of oxidants and reductants in dough development. Baker's Dig. 46(2):20.

Klein, M. G. 1971a. Packaging—Special requirements for frozen bakery products. Baker's Dig. 45(2):58.

Klein, M. G 1971b. Problems in baking. Baker's Dig. 45(6):64.

Kline, L., and Sugihara, T. F. 1968. Factors affecting the stability of frozen bread dough. I. Prepared by the straight dough method. Baker's Dig. 42(5):44.

Lehmann, T. A., and Dreese, P. 1981. Stability of frozen bread dough—Effects of freezing temperatures. AIB Tech. Bull. Vol. III, Issue 7. American Institute of Baking, Manhattan, KS.

Lorenz, K., and Bechtel, W. G. 1964. Frozen bread dough. Baker's Dig. 38(6):59.

Lorenz, K., and Bechtel, W. G. 1965. Frozen dough: Variety breads—Effect of bromate level. Baker's Dig. 39(4):53.

Lorenz, K. 1974. Frozen dough—Present trend and future outlook. Baker's Dig. 48(2):14.

Marston, P. E. 1978. Frozen dough for breadmaking. Baker's Dig. 52(5):18.

Mazur, P. 1971. Physical-chemical basis of injury from intracellular freezing in yeast. Page 171 in: Cellular Injury and Resistance in Living Organisms. E. Asahina, ed. Institute of Low Temperature Science, Hokkaido University, Sapporo, Japan.

Mazur, P., and Schmidt, J. 1968. Interactions of cooling velocity, temperature, and warming velocity on the survival of frozen and thawed yeast. Cryobiology 5:1.

Merritt, P. P. 1960. The effect of preparation on the stability and performance of frozen, unbaked, yeast-leavened doughs. Baker's Dig. 34(4):57.

Meyer, B., Moore, R., and Buckley, R. 1956. Gas production and yeast roll quality after freezer storage of fermented and unfermented doughs. Food Technol. 10(April):165.

Nei, T. 1964. Freezing and freeze-drying of microorganisms. Cryobiology 1:87.

Nei, T., Araki, T., and Matsusaka, T. 1967. The mechanism of cellular injury by freezing in microorganisms. Page 157 in: Cellular Injury and Resistance in Living Organisms. E. Asahina, ed. Institute of Low Temperature Science, Sapporo, Japan.

Ponte, J. G., Jr., Glass, R. L., and Geddes, W. F. 1960. Studies on the behavior of active dry yeast in breadmaking. Cereal Chem. 37:263.

Sideleau, P. 1987. Freezing and thawing of unbaked products. Proc. Am. Soc. Bakery Eng., p. 89.

Sugihara, T. F., and Kline, L. 1968. Factors affecting the stability of frozen bread doughs. II. Prepared by the sponge and dough method. Baker's Dig. 42(5):51.

Taguchi, K., Tabata, H., and Yoshizaki, T. 1975. Process for the preparation of a frozen dough for bakery products. U.S. patent no. 3,801,975.

Varriano-Marston, E., Hsu, K. H., and Mahdi, J. 1980. Rheological and structural changes in frozen dough. Baker's Dig. 54(1):32.

Wolt, M. J., and D'Appolonia, B. L. 1984a. Factors involved in the stability of frozen dough. I. The influence of yeast reducing compounds on frozen-dough stability. Cereal Chem. 61:209.

Wolt, M. J., and D'Appolonia, B. L. 1984b. Factors involved in the stability of frozen dough. II.

The effects of yeast type, flour type, and dough additives on frozen-dough stability. Cereal Chem. 61:213.

Zaehringer, M. V., Mayfield, H. L., and Odland, L. M. 1951. The effect of certain variations in fat, yeast, and liquid on the frozen storage of yeasted doughs. Food Res. 16:353.

CHAPTER 8

Bread and Rolls from Frozen Dough in Europe

J.-M. Brümmer
Federal Center for Cereal, Potato and Lipid Research
Detmold, Germany

Storage of frozen yeast-leavened dough pieces (interruption or retardation of fermentation) for baked products has gained considerable importance in Western Europe. Freezing of doughs has become popular because it makes it possible to provide the consumer at all times with an assortment of crisp breads and rolls. Other reasons for the introduction of this new process in baking technology have been the increase in the number of bakery items and consumer demand for product freshness.

Doughs with low fat and sugar contents (bread and rolls) present more difficulties than baked products made from richer formulations. For years, the principles of freezing yeast-leavened dough pieces have been under investigation, since satisfactory baking results could not be immediately demonstrated. It became apparent that disruption of the proofing process, in comparison with other fermentation-slowing processes or the storage of baked frozen rolls, could provide the consumer not with a substitute product, but with a product of equal quality and a better flavor. In general, however, rolls from frozen dough are still described as being lower in volume, dark and uneven in crust color, and occasionally having a blistered surface. On the other hand, the taste can be more aromatic and the crumb coarser and thereby more elastic than in rolls produced by the conventional process.

Even though there are flaws in shape and appearance, consumers appreciate these products, probably because of the pleasant taste (possibly due to reduced volume) and the freshness of the product, since crisp rolls and bread are fresh for only a few hours. Rolls and breads prepared from proof- and fermentation-interrupted doughs are more frequently consumed within the period of optimum freshness in comparison with products produced once daily by conventional manufacturing processes. Thus far, there is no indication that baked products produced from frozen doughs are not purchased because of external flaws.

Initially, dough pieces were frozen without proofing, but more frozen storage of fully proofed dough pieces is being investigated. This would meet the demands of the consumer more rapidly. The demand for frozen dough is steadily increasing.

Even though there are many different small baked products, there are few variations in dough composition and preparation when using the frozen dough process. The greatest difficulties are encountered with doughs for small crisp baked items. Because of that, recommendations given in this chapter are especially designed for freezing of dough pieces for rolls. Principally, the chosen combination of wheat and rye flours or meals has no influence on fermentation and, therefore, established dough formulations can be used. Furthermore, recommendations are given for the storage of a few days up to a week. With longer storage periods, differences in product quality become more apparent, but storage times of even one month and more are used.

The Frozen Dough Process in Europe

The use of frozen doughs is popular in Western Europe, especially in France, Belgium, The Netherlands, Luxembourg, and Great Britain. This technology is being applied in Scandinavia, especially in Denmark and Sweden and less frequently in Norway and Finland. The situation is similar in Spain, Italy, and to some extent in Portugal, although the climate in countries of southern Europe presents some problems. The technology is under consideration in Eastern European countries. However, lack of proper raw materials, energy, and needed equipment present some difficulties there.

The principles of freezing and the possibilities for use of this technology are essentially the same in all regions of Europe in spite of the great differences in product variety. Doughs are frozen primarily for wheat-based products with limited diameter such as rolls or baguettes intended for faster bake-off in the bakery. Of course, there are specific recommendations for different products such as baguettes, rolls, and other baked products. Doughs for larger baked products such as breads are seldom frozen because of high energy cost.

Central production of small frozen dough pieces requires a longer storage period and different ways of distribution. The problems here are the same as those in other areas of the world. Therefore, this type of baking technology is used only in regions with highly developed bakery technology and with sufficient and available raw materials and energy.

Principal Requirements for Freezing

The freezing point of water in dough is not 0°C; the freezing point of doughs made with flour and water only is approximately -4°C. Doughs for rolls containing fat, sugar, salt, and yeast have a freezing point of about -7 to -9°C. These are core temperatures of individual dough pieces, which must be maintained. So temperatures of at least -10 to -15°C are recommended for satisfactory frozen conditions for short-time storage. This requires a certain freezing capacity and control of temperatures at several points during the interruption of fermentation. Not only computer-controlled freezing installations, but also conventional freezing cabinets or rooms with sufficient freezing capacity can be used. Since temperature changes during the interruption of fermentation are not uniform and are influenced by the sensitivity of the control mechanisms of the freezing installation, the above-mentioned temperatures must be considered the highest acceptable limit. Sensitivity of temperature-control mechanisms should be not more than 5°C, since storage at temperatures outside the recommended range can be a disadvantage.

Quality of Raw Materials and Formulations

Wheat Flours

Flours with an ash content of 0.55 (db), good to very good gluten quality, protein content of about 12.5%, wet gluten of about 30%, a sedimentation value of greater than 35, a falling number of 300 sec or higher, and low starch damage are important for doughs that are to be frozen without prior proofing. Quality requirements for doughs that are proofed before freezing are more stringent. Flours should receive at least a normal oxidation treatment with ascorbic acid. Higher than normal treatment is not necessary since dough conditioners used in the formulation will meet the higher oxidation requirement.

Dough Conditioners and Other Ingredients

Several dough conditioners for use in frozen doughs have recently been developed. Products containing diacetyl esters of tartaric acid with low amylase activity are preferred. In the selection of the conditioner, consideration should be given not only to good volume response but also to good crumb characteristics of the product after baking. Most conditioners and their recommended dosage level are designed to provide optimum volume response. For Central Europe, selection should also make sure that the breads and rolls have the proper crumb elasticity. Studies have been initiated using additive-free formulations since the demand for "natural foods" is increasing.

A volume difference of 10–15% between fresh rolls made by the direct process and those produced from fermentation-interrupted doughs should be expected. Fat levels of 1–2% give doughs of good machinability and gas-holding capabilities and have a positive effect on crumb characteristics. Preliminary experiments with peanut fat (oil) containing a certain amount of nitrogen gas have produced small baked products with volumes equal to those of doughs frozen after proofing.

Yeast and Sourdough

Commercially available yeast has been shown to be acceptable for doughs with interrupted fermentation with and without proofing before freezing. However, occasional problems result from the physiological condition of the yeast, caused not only by the time of storage between yeast manufacture and dough preparation, but also by manufacturing variables. It is not yet known which variations in manufacturing conditions have the greatest effects on freezing characteristics of the yeast. Different batches of yeast have shown differences in freezing tolerance. At present, the relationship between oxygen supply during propagation (and, therefore, the formation of mitochondria and their activity) and the influence of foam inhibitors is being investigated. These differences, however, affect only doughs that are frozen without preproofing. Also, active dry yeasts, because of slow gas formation, have been found to be suitable for doughs to be frozen without preproofing. Yeasts with rapid or high gas production are not recommended for doughs frozen without prior proofing, but they can be used if doughs are proofed before freezing. Several experiments with German normal or rapid-gas-production yeasts have shown that, during freezing of doughs without preproofing, every increase in yeast activity decreases the freezing tolerance of the yeast. There is no final explanation for this as yet, but it seems to be due to accumulations of metabolism products in and around the yeast cells. Our research data (Fig. 1) should be of interest because

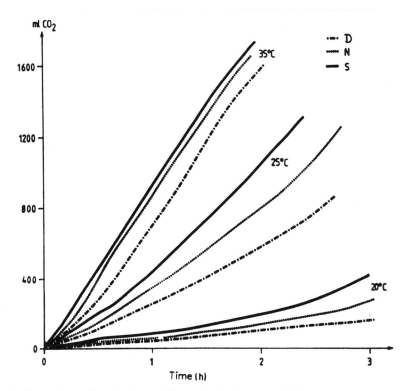

Fig. 1. Comparison of gassing power of normal (N), dry (D), and high-gas-production (S) yeasts as affected by temperature.

they show that yeasts of higher gas production provide greater fermentation capabilities than normal yeasts even at lower temperatures. This becomes apparent during freezing of doughs without preproofing, in that high-gas-production yeasts are more strongly activated until freezing temperatures are reached. The suitability of dry yeast is also apparent in Figure 1. Less gas is being produced as dough temperatures decrease.

Van der Plaat (1989) attributes the reduction in gas production capacity in doughs to a loss in trehalose. New attempts to develop yeasts for non-preproofed frozen doughs have concentrated on dry yeast; however, they have not shown increased sales (Neyreneuf and Nitsche, 1989). Such yeasts will be indispensable as more preproofed doughs are frozen, since yeast activation is not required during the bake-off. For interesting reviews about the research on freezing-tolerant yeasts, see Dunaas (1991) and Gelinas et al (1991).

If sourdough is used in addition to yeast, the customary sourdough amounts should be somewhat reduced. Too much acidification, especially in doughs to be frozen without prior proofing, should be avoided, since it affects yeast activity after frozen storage and tends to produce a sour taste.

Mixing

Thus far, research on doughs for wheat flour rolls has indicated the importance of good dough development and, therefore, proper mixing. To obtain good dough characteristics, mixing is more important than the availability of raw materials of the best quality. It is established that doughs in the temperature range of 24–26°C, which, with normal mixing, produce a dry dough surface and normal to pliable dough characteristics, are very acceptable. For doughs not proofed before freezing, it is sometimes necessary to reduce absorption. To reach the desired dough temperature, the temperatures of the flour and the water must be taken into consideration. Doughs that come out of the mixer too cool (18–20°C) have not shown any advantage in Europe. Experiments with late addition of salt and/or yeast during the mixing process to improve conditions for the interruption of fermentation have not shown improvements in end-product quality when using formulations established in Central Europe. If any adjustments are to be made at all, late addition of yeast, but only for doughs frozen without preproofing, might be considered. This, however, cannot be done in the form of a yeast suspension since dough development will be influenced by the additional liquid. A homogeneous distribution of the yeast must be assured. Continental normal yeasts ferment more slowly than those available in North America and the United Kingdom.

Dough Handling

Dough rest periods, intermediate proof, and make-up time should be as short as possible for dough pieces frozen before or after proofing. The total time should be between 10 and 20 min. After final shaping, dough pieces are frozen immediately or are given the desired proof before freezing.

Proofing

Production of small wheat-based baked products that are not frozen requires normal proofing times of about 40 min. Yeast levels are 5%, based on flour. Because of the different requirements for the final preparation of frozen dough pieces, proof times of 0, 25, or 75% of the normal 40 min should be considered. Proof times of 50% of the normal proof times do not yet produce the characteristics of shorter, nor the advantages of longer proof times. A 40-min proof time of individual dough pieces produced frozen roll doughs that are too sensitive and could not be stored and baked without serious quality reduction. Short proofing times (0–25% of the normal 40 min), in comparison with a 75% proofing period, produce several advantages. The shorter the proof time, the easier, more precise, and more uniform are the freezing, defrosting, and final baking processes. At the same time, baked products are more uniform, especially products such as small rolls and Kaiser rolls.

Dough pieces that had little proof and therefore are lower in volume require a storage and transport capacity that is 30–40% less than that required by pre-proofed doughs. Optimally, preproofed dough pieces can be baked faster after frozen storage, however, since reactivation of the yeast is no longer required and the baker must wait only for the dough pieces to thaw. Even this time is not necessary if special oven types are used.

Freezing Process

The freezing of small dough pieces should reduce considerably not only fermentation activities, but also enzymatic, microbial, and oxidative processes. At the same time, a fast and if possible high yeast reactivation capability should be maintained. To accomplish this, the core temperature of the small dough pieces should be below -10°C. This, however, still leaves a rather high percentage of unbound or free water, as has been shown in recent studies using thermo-difference analysis (K. Münzing, *personal communication*, 1990). It is, therefore, recommended that core temperatures of -15 to -18°C should be reached, mainly for long-time dough storage.

Obtainable freezing rates depend on several factors. The most important of these are:

- size of dough piece (weight),
- geometry of dough piece (the largest diameter),
- ingredients (absorption, salt level),
- proofing boards and screens (location of control thermometer),
- packaging, and
- freezer capabilities (temperature and air movement).

The rate of freezing not only affects cell structure but also determines the percentage of viable yeast cells. The literature gives different opinions about how to obtain optimum results. Some experts recommend fast, while others suggest slow freezing of dough pieces (Neyreneuf and Nitsche, 1989). The terms "fast/slow" have, in most instances, been arbitrarily selected or are used in a comparison. Terms such as "fast/slow" should be avoided, and precise information about dough composition, dough sizes, freezer temperatures, and freezing rates at the center of the dough should be presented.

Our investigations with dough slices (2 cm thick) on the Rheofermentometer (Chopin, Paris) have shown that slow freezing (90 min to -20°C) results in faster and stronger gas production after thawing than does fast freezing (20 min to -20°C). This indicates that there are disadvantages when doughs are frozen too rapidly.

Microbiological tests on those doughs showed the following percentages of surviving yeast cells after one day of frozen storage: freezing to -20°C over 90 min = 77% and freezing to -20°C over 20 min = 62%. After storage of seven days, these percentages were 61 and 51%, respectively. The smaller number of yeast cells explains the observed 30% reduction in gas production after one week and 48% reduction after four weeks of storage. Whenever these dough slices were frozen even faster and at a lower temperature, which can be accomplished with cryogenic gases, even greater damage to yeast activity resulted. The lower the frozen temperature of the dough pieces, the smaller the number of surviving yeast cells and the smaller the gas-forming capacity with less elasticity of the dough itself. In addition, as storage time increased, a longer time was required for the yeast cells to regenerate and be fully active, but then the dough resisted extension. Yeast cells that remained active developed nearly the same fermentation capabilities as were present in cells that were not frozen (W. Röcken, B. Antuna, and J.-M Brümmer, *unpublished*, 1992).

According to Gelinas et al (1991), the optimal freezing rates for yeast of 7–10°C decrease per minute cannot be achieved in doughs. Blast freezers can produce only temperature reductions of 1–2°C/min in wheat bread doughs. Wheat doughs are poor conductors. Doughs that have been given some proofing are somewhat warmer, but they freeze faster, as our experiments have shown (Fig. 2).

To accomplish a fast heat exchange, for doughs to be stored frozen for a longer time, the use of cryogenic gases is suggested. Calculations for the use of CO_2 indicated that 0.5 metric ton of CO_2 is needed per metric ton of dough. Our investigations showed clearly that the yeast itself, even during rapid freezing to temperatures of -20 to -30°C, does not lose its gas-forming capability. Slower freezing and lower temperatures (-35 to -40°C) caused damage, however. Therefore, yeast in doughs seems mainly affected when freezing rates are too slow during dough freezing.

Storage and Transport

Separate facilities for freezing and storage are always recommended, especially for continuous and long-term storage. Frequent opening of freezer doors and adding of unfrozen dough pieces should be avoided. Storage conditions should be changed as little as possible even for packaged products. Tight storage of dough and/or packages to minimize temperature changes has advantages. To assure a rapid and uniform temperature reduction, dough pieces on perforated screens should be placed into the freezer as a single layer and core temperatures should be reduced to at least -15°C. To make this possible, conventional freezers must be at a temperature of -30°C and storage facilities must be at least at -15°C to -20°C. CO_2 installations could be considered (Brümmer, 1990). As mentioned before, one must realize when using such shock freezing that the lowest temperatures do not necessarily produce the best quality products.

After the core temperature of -15°C has been reached, dough pieces appear to be mechanically sturdy, but they still should be treated carefully. For further frozen storage, packaging in synthetic bags, sacks, or containers is recommended to prevent dehydration on the surface. Intense freezing in conjunction with high air velocity causes such dehydration of the surface of dough pieces. Packaging is also recommended for shorter storage periods of dough pieces, especially if storage facilities are frequently opened, causing temperature fluctuations. For very short-time storage, covers or curtains for the transfer equipment are sufficient. However, these should not interfere with the freezing operation of the doughs.

Physical as well as enzymatic processes take place during frozen storage and cause changes in the dough. Especially affected are the gluten proteins and the yeast cells. Starch is affected less, but damage could occur because of ice breakage due to expansion of the water (ice) that penetrated into the starch during

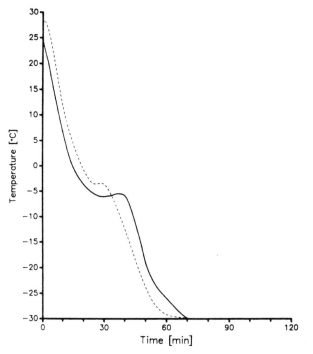

Fig. 2. Freezing curves of 50-g preproofed (- - -) and 50-g non-preproofed (——) doughs.

freezing. This might be a reason why sponge doughs, long fermentation times, and high amylase activity are detrimental.

The gluten matrix changes, especially with increasing frozen-storage time. These changes are greater if there are high fluctuations of the storage temperatures and if storage temperatures are close to the freezing point of water in this special system. It should be kept in mind that even at a -15°C dough temperature, a significant amount of water is not frozen and can participate in various reactions. During frozen storage, incorporation of the starch into the protein matrix is reduced. While complete enclosure or coverage of the starch is achieved during mixing, freezing exposes the starch granules, which are then subjected to the severe conditions of the freezing process (Berglund et al, 1990). The extensibility of the doughs in response to CO_2 formation is reduced, but the doughs seem to be gas-tight, according to rheofermentometer studies. Gas pressure is smaller because of less CO_2 production (Brümmer, 1990).

The effect of frozen storage on yeast cells is due to changes in the stability of the pores and the composition of fatty acids in the membrane of the yeast cells. Phospholipids (P) and free sterols (S) are affected (Neyreneuf and Nitsche, 1989). A high P:S ratio seems favorable. We know from our experiments that extractability of lipids in flour as well as that of any added fats and emulsifiers is reduced. Polar lipids, especially galactosyl lipids, seem to decrease during frozen storage, which not only affects the extensibility of the dough, but also reduces the functionality of the wheat gluten.

Optimum conditions during storage must be maintained during transport as well, especially if there is additional storage after delivery.

Thawing and Baking

For best quality of small baked products from dough pieces that were not given any proof before freezing, it is ideal if core temperatures at the time they are placed into the oven are the normal temperatures for the dough (~25°C). The minimum satisfactory core temperature is 15°C. For this reason, the increase in temperature in the center of the dough must be uniform, i.e., not too fast and not too slow. If the temperature increases too rapidly, the outer regions of the dough piece are ready for proofing while the center is still at too low a temperature. However, a certain temperature differential within the dough can never be completely avoided. A step-wise or continuous temperature increase always assures a uniform quality in rolls (Brümmer, 1990). The core temperature increase from -5°C to 5°C should occur in less than 1 hr. Shorter bake-off procedures are being tried by the industry.

Doughs also are colder than the surrounding air, and so water condenses on the dough surface. The greater the temperature difference between dough and air, the wetter the dough surfaces will be. Doughs that are too wet cause stickiness, whereas doughs that are too dry affect crust characteristics and cause lower volumes. Doughs should be thawed quickly but should not be forced. The insulation effect of proofing boards or screens can make a difference in product

Table 1
Proofing Times for Dough Pieces With and Without Preproofing

| | Proof Before Freezing | | |
| | No Proofing | 75% Proof | |
	Normal Oven	Normal Oven	Special Oven
Final proof, min at room temperature	60	40	0
Final proof, min in proofing cabinet	60	20	0
Total time, min	120	60	0[a]
Time difference, min	+60 ←	+60 ←	

[a] Somewhat longer baking time.

quality. Materials that hinder transfer of heat slow the increase in dough temperature and cause wetness on doughs. Later, during baking, surface wetness produces undesirable discoloration of the crust. For thawing, proper microwave conditions can be used. Low energy for a longer time (70 W for 7–9 min/50 g of dough) are recommended over high energy for a shorter time.

Preproofed dough pieces are frequently placed into the oven when the core temperature is still much too low. Depending on the time interval between removal from frozen storage and the time into the oven, dough pieces are either still frozen or just thawed. For preproofed dough pieces for which the core temperature during thawing is not automatically controlled, we recommend that dough pieces be kept at room temperature for about 40 min to avoid excessive condensation. Such dough pieces will have a core temperature of about 5°C. These then should be placed into a conventional proofing cabinet for 20 min. When the dough pieces are placed into the oven, the core temperature should be around 15°C.

In the case of direct production of rolls, convection ovens (with air movement) have given good bake-off results, since they provide proper conditions for desirable crust characteristics. Normal baking times of about 20 min at a somewhat reduced baking temperature (~10–20°C lower than conventional) with less steam injection into the oven at the beginning of the baking step lead to good quality baked products. This reduces undesirable bread characteristics due to condensation on the cold surfaces of the dough.

Dough pieces frozen before and after proofing show a tremendous time difference in thawing, final proofing, and total process time (Table 1). Use of special ovens, called bake-off stations, frequently cuts the thawing and proofing times. After removal from frozen storage, dough pieces are subjected to an intense warming process, which also can be provided in special baking ovens. These special ovens are different in that the actual baking process does not start immediately. At a base temperature of 110–140°C and considerable pulsating steam injections (10–20 steam impulses per minute), a thawing process is initiated. After this first warming phase of 6–8 min, dough temperature in the core is still around 0°C. The oven temperature is continuously raised. Baking thereafter is done at 170–190°C. The total warming period and baking time is 24–28 min.

This technique has become rather popular and will probably dominate in the future, at least for doughs frozen for very short periods.

If a bakery uses interruption of fermentation and experiences differences in baked product quality, these are most frequently the results of different processing methods. For this reason, we recommend that every user of frozen dough pieces insist upon the utmost uniformity in ingredients, dough characteristics, processing times, and proofing times. Freezing installations and conditions must be proper, and storage times must not be too long.

Literature Cited

Berglund, P. T., Shelton, D. R., and Freeman, T. P. 1990. Comparison of two sample preparation procedures for low-temperature scanning electron microscopy of frozen bread dough. Cereal Chem. 67:139-140.

Brümmer, J.-M. 1990. Chilling and deep freezing of baked goods in the Federal Republic of Germany (Kühlen und Tiefgefrieren von Backwaren in der Bundesrepublik Deutschland). Pages 135-145 in: Chilled Foods. The State of the Art—London and New York. T. R. Gormley, ed. Elsevier Applied Science Publishers, London.

Dunaas, F. 1991. Yeast in frozen bread doughs. Ph.D. thesis. University of Lund, Lund, Sweden. p. 104.

Gelinas, P., Fiset, G., Willemot, C., and Goulet, J. 1991. Lipid content and cryotolerance of baker's yeast in frozen doughs. Appl. Environ. Microbiol. 57:463-468.

Neyreneuf, O., and Nitsche, G. 1989. Tiefgefrieren von Hefeteigen und -teiglingen. Anforderungen an Rohstoffe und Verfahren. Getreide Mehl Brot 43:298-303.

Van der Plaat, J. B. 1989. Baker's yeast in frozen dough—The state of the art. Pages 110-120 in: Cereal Science and Technology in Sweden. N.-G. Asp, ed. Proc. Int. Symp. June 1988, Ystad, Sweden. University of Lund, Lund, Sweden.

CHAPTER 9

Freezing and Refrigeration of Cake and Muffin Batters in the United States

K. Lorenz
Department of Food Science and Human Nutrition
Colorado State University
Fort Collins, Colorado 80523

Batters in frozen form can make possible more efficient batch scheduling, with larger batch runs and tighter control over production labor and inventory in the bakery. A supply of batters helps to balance shortages and excesses, and the small operator could possibly offer a greater daily assortment of fresh merchandise. With frozen batters in reserve, items that sell out early in the day can be replenished for late shoppers. For the large operator, there may be untapped potential for distribution of cakes in frozen batter form for bake-off as needed at the point of sale in supermarkets, restaurants, institutions, and hospitals, whose variable needs are not easily accommodated by their own baking facilities (Heid, 1968). Frozen batter products are already mixed and, in some instances, prescaled. For this reason, the operator does not need any equipment other than an oven. The size of the operation can be reduced, as less equipment and fewer individual ingredients require less space. Since the batters are already prepared, the need for skilled help to finish processing the products is eliminated (Heiney, 1989). However, such batters perform well only if stored for very short periods of time.

Research on frozen cake batters started in the early 1940s at several universities (Sunderlin et al, 1940; Graul and Lowe, 1947). During the 1940s and early 1950s, interest was directed toward applications for homemakers in home freezers (Heid, 1968). By 1966, over half the retail bakers in the United States were freezing some products at one or more stages of processing (Pillsbury, 1966) to extend the shelf life of highly perishable bakery products. Very few, however, froze batters. A survey by Rollag and Enochian (1964), which included 109 bakeries, indicated that only 6% were freezing cakes at the batter stage, partly because baked cakes freeze so well and frozen batters require a larger inventory of cake pans. The baking industry had learned that distribution of frozen batters through retail outlets and supermarkets to consumers for bake-off in the house is a risky operation because frozen batters are very susceptible to damage from temperature fluctuations, and simply do not perform well if stored for extended periods of time. Frozen muffin batters emerged in the 1980s (Anonymous, 1990) and have increased in popularity since they often include high-fiber ingredients for nutrition-conscious consumers.

As we learn more about freezing of cake batters, we might see more frozen cake batters produced by the baking industry.

Formulation

Any well-balanced cake batter can be frozen for short periods of time with satisfactory results and but slight modifications in formulation and mixing. The leavening agent and shortening are critical ingredients in batters to be frozen.

Chemical Leavening

The amount, the type, and the ratio of acid to soda are all extremely critical to the production of a frozen batter that will perform up to expectations when thawed. Batters held in frozen storage evidence a progressive decrease in baked volume as the storage period increases, due to loss of air from the batter.

An explanation of why air is lost from cake batters during frozen storage was offered by Mackey (1955). In freshly prepared batters, microscopic examination depicted the fat dispersed in aerated particles as thin patches. Closely packed air bubbles clustered within the fat particle. Globules of fat appeared only occasionally. As frozen storage at 0°F (-18°C) progressed over a period of 12 weeks, the fat tended to pull away from the aqueous phase and form globules with distinct boundaries. The tiny air bubbles seemed to coalesce into larger bubbles, which escaped from the warm batter during the early stages of baking. This redistribution of air bubbles in the stored batters was reflected in increasingly coarse texture and steadily diminishing volume in the test cakes after baking as storage period progressed. These observations were supported during storage tests by Heid (1968).

Observations of progressive decrease in volume of cakes baked from frozen batters as storage periods increased led to several comparisons by early researchers of the performance of the available types of leavening agents in cake batters that were to be held in frozen storage for later bake-off. Under comparable conditions of frozen storage, similar cake formulations retained better volume with sulfate-phosphate leavening agents than with tartrate (Zaehringer and Mayfield, 1951; Mackey et al, 1952). During identical frozen storage situations, cake batters containing phosphate leavening agents were observed to release carbon dioxide at a slower rate than similar batters with either sulfate-phosphate or tartrate leavening agents.

In general, sodium-aluminum phosphate performs well in frozen cake batters. It is delayed during the makeup. It does not release its CO_2 until the oven;

therefore, it optimizes the level of CO_2 available after the frozen batter is placed in the oven to bake. Because it releases CO_2 in the oven only, the only air cells available to be lost during preparation, freezing, and storage are those from cavitation (B. Heidolph, *personal communication*). Other leavening acids that have been used in frozen batters are shown in Table 1.

Research conducted by Pickens (1955) and Heid (1968) demonstrated the need to increase the leavening in commercial cake batters to be held in frozen storage by 0.2–0.25% above the level required in the same batters when baked immediately after mixing, and possibly to whip in more air during mixing. This partially compensates for the loss of air from batters during frozen storage and baking (Pickens, 1955).

Shortening

Shortening type and emulsifier content are critical in the production of "hi ratio" frozen cake batters. Frozen muffin batters, having a leaner formulation, are more tolerant to varying shortening types and levels. The inclusion of butter in a frozen batter contributes to improved flavor of the baked cake but at the same time results in a lower volume. Although butter was given higher ratings on texture and cell characteristics in some studies (Graul and Lowe, 1947; Mackey et al, 1952), others reported better results with hydrogenated vegetable shortening (Zaehringer and Mayfield, 1951) in batters stored at freezing temperatures for later bake-off. Butter is generally not used today in frozen batters. Butter oxidized in frozen batters during storage for six months at -34°C and developed rancid odors and flavors (Mackey et al, 1952). Hydrogenated vegetable shortening is the one strongly recommended for commercial production. Heid (1968) obtained satisfactory results with liquid shortening when it was used with an emulsifier (sorbitan monostearate with polyoxyethylene sorbitan monostearate) in yellow cake batters that were held in frozen storage at -23°C over a 12-week period. Improved cell structure was reported in white and chocolate cakes baked from frozen batters made with hydrogenated vegetable oil when an emulsifier (glycerol monostearate) was used at levels of 5 and 10%

Table 1
Leavening Acids in Frozen Batters

Baking Acid	Comparative Rate of Reaction
Anhydrous monocalcium phosphate	Delayed
Dicalcium phosphate	Very slow
Sodium acid pyrophosphate	Slow
Sodium aluminum phosphate	
Hydrous	Slow
Anhydrous	Very slow
Sodium aluminum sulfate	Very slow
Glucono delta lactone	Delayed
Monocalcium phosphate	Fast

(Mackey et al, 1952). Heid (1968) noted greater air inclusion during mixing, more uniformity in cell structure and grain, and better volume in yellow and chocolate cakes baked from frozen batters when an emulsifier (sorbitan monostearate with polyoxyethylene sorbitan monostearate or glycerol monostearate) was used at levels up to 4%.

Hydrogenated vegetable oil is now the recommended shortening. A high shortening level and high sugar ratio give better results in cakes baked from frozen batters than do the leaner formulations. An emulsifier increases the potential air inclusion during mixing and thus improves volume, cell structure, and symmetry in the baked cake. It helps stabilize the air distribution in the frozen batter during storage. The optimum level of emulsifier is dictated by the kind of emulsifier, the type or brand of shortening, and the particular formulation. The commercial manufacturers of the shortenings or emulsifiers are best qualified to make recommendations for their own products. However, glycerol monoesters and mono- and diglyceride emulsifiers in a plastic or liquid vegetable shortening seem to be used most frequently. Typical frozen cake batter formulations and preparation procedures are given in Tables 2–5.

Packaging

Cake batters should be packaged immediately after mixing and frozen without delay. The container has several specific requirements: rigidity to shape the

Table 2
Frozen Yellow Layer Cake Batter[a]

	Percent
Stage I	
Cake flour	100.0
Sugar, granular	120.0
Salt	3.75
Baking powder (sodium acid pyrophosphate)[b]	4.5
Cake shortening	59.0
Emulsifier (polysorbate/sorbitan monostearate)[b]	2.5
Nonfat dry milk solids	8.0
Water	50.0
Stage II	
Whole eggs	59.0
Water	50.0
Flavor	2.5
Procedure	
Stage I: Mix 5 min at low speed.	
Stage II: Mix 2 min at low speed.	
Batter temperature: 65–70°F (18–21°C)	

[a] Adapted from Heid (1968).

[b] Use of a different type of baking powder or emulsifier may require adjustment in the level indicated here.

cake during baking, both low and high temperature tolerances, and prevention of moisture and volatile odor transfer to or from the batters. It must be capable of an airtight seal. Aluminum foil pans fulfill these requirements and are good heat conductors both in the freezer and in the oven.

Freezing and Frozen Storage

The method and speed at which a batter product is frozen can greatly affect the end product's quality. Several investigators reported on the relationships of rate of freezing, storage temperature, and rate of deterioration of frozen batters (Graul and Lowe, 1947; Mackey et al, 1952; Pickens, 1955; Heid, 1968; Heiney, 1989).

Cakes baked from batters stored at -23°C up to four months showed no significant differences from freshly baked cakes, whereas similar batters stored at -18°C were inferior in aroma, flavor, color, and volume (Graul and Lowe, 1947). Batters stored at -34.5°C retained good volume up to six months (Mackey et al, 1952). Pickens (1955) recorded a time-temperature curve to demonstrate graphically the stages through which a cake batter passes at various temperatures down to -18°C. At -7°C, the batter was still pliable. It became firm between -12 and -18°C but was actually only 65–70% frozen at this stage. It was not completely frozen until it reached a temperature of about -29°C.

Table 3
Frozen Devils Food Cake Batter[a]

	Percent
Stage I	
Cake flour	100.0
Sugar, granular	175.0
Nonfat dry milk solids	25.0
Cocoa, light Dutch	25.0
Salt	2.0
Baking powder (sodium acid pyrophosphate)[b]	6.0
Cake shortening	83.0
Emulsifier (polysorbate/sorbitan monostearate)[b]	3.0
Water	80.0
Stage II	
Whole eggs	93.0
Water	66.0
Vanilla	4.0
Procedure	
Stage I: Mix 6 min at low speed.	
Stage II: Mix 3 min at low speed.	
Batter temperature: 65–70°F (18–21°C)	

[a] Adapted from Heid (1968).
[b] Use of a different type of baking powder or emulsifier may require adjustment in the level indicated here.

Pickens' cake batter curve was very similar to his curve depicting the gradual absorption of latent heat at falling temperatures in the freezing range, and with the freezing point of a sugar solution having the same sugar-liquid ratio as he used in his cake batter. The high sugar content is responsible for the long heat-of-fusion period and the low freezing point of cake batters, as well as for rapid defrosting when batters are exposed to temperatures above their freezing point (Heid, 1968; Heiney, 1989).

Studies by Heid (1968) support rapid freezing at a temperature well below the freezing point of the cake batter, with subsequent storage at -23°C or below if batters are to be stored more than a few weeks. Table 6 shows results of a four-month storage test. Cakes baked from stored batters maintained quality comparable to those of freshly prepared batters during the period noted for each temperature (Heid, 1968).

Temperature stability is essential to quality maintenance in stored frozen batters. Volume, grain, and texture are damaged by fluctuations in storage temperatures, especially in angel, sponge, and chiffon batters, which are highly aerated in comparison with regular cake batters. They quickly break down; air bubbles escape; and water separates from the batters, settling to the bottom of the pans and causing an unbaked layer at the bottom of the baked cake (Heiney, 1989). The texture of the baked cake is coarse. Although batters con-

Table 4
Frozen Angel Cake Batter[a]

	Percent
Stage I	
Cake flour	100.0
Salt	3.3
Powdered sugar	57.5
Sugar, granular	76.0
Stage II	
Dried egg white	6.8
Sugar, granular	150.0
Cream of tartar	1.0
Water	173.0
Stage III	
Water	75.0

Procedure
  Stage I: Sift together.
  Stage II: Whip 1 min at low speed, scrape down;
    continue whipping for 3 min at medium speed.
  Stage III: Add slowly to stage II while whipping
    at medium speed to a soft peak. Fold stage I
    into whipped whites.
  Batter temperature: 65–70°F (18–21°C)

[a] Adapted from Heid (1968).

taining shortening show more tolerance to temperature fluctuations than the sponge-type batters, their period of quality preservation can also be rather short. Because of their high sugar content, cake batters thaw rapidly when exposed, for even short periods, to temperatures above -18°C. Air, which was incorporated during the mixing, is released. Decreasing volume, coarsening of texture, and irregularity in cell structure parallel the amount of air lost (Heid, 1968).

Chemically leavened muffin batters may be frozen, providing they are reasonably high in sugar and shortening, are mixed by the emulsion or cake method (not by the standard muffin method), and not more than 10–12 weeks of storage is planned. Batters that are prepared by the standard muffin method have no tolerance for freezing, as they break down during the freezing process and develop an extremely coarse texture and undesirably large and uneven cell structure. Because these mixtures are lower in shortening and sugar than cake batters, muffin batters are not as stable for prolonged frozen storage periods (Anonymous, 1990).

Presently, the standard storage life of frozen, batter-type products is 16 weeks (four months). Manufacturers of these products usually include storage information in or on the case in which the product is packed (Heiney, 1989).

Table 5
Frozen Chiffon Cake Batter[a]

	Percent
Stage I	
Cake flour	100.0
Baking powder	4.0
Sugar	89.0
Salt	2.7
Stage II	
Egg whites	104.0
Cream of tartar	0.5
Sugar	48.6
Stage III	
Salad oil	51.0
Egg yolks	51.0
Water	78.0
Vanilla	1.5

Procedure
Stage I: Dry blend together.
Stage II: Whip to a stiff peak.
Stage III: Combine and add to stage I, mix
  smooth; then fold into whipped whites.
Batter temperature: 65–70°F (18–21°C)

[a] Adapted from Heid (1968).

Thawing and Baking

Foam-type batters such as angel, sponge, and chiffon batters bake quite successfully from the frozen state. However, if these highly aerated frozen batters are thawed before baking, the air emulsion may be lost. White, yellow, and chocolate cake batters, on the other hand, achieve better volume, cell structure, and symmetry if they are thawed before baking. The high sugar content induces rapid thawing. Usually 20–30 min is a sufficient time for batters up to 2.5 cm in depth. Some bakers, however, prefer to bake frozen cake and muffin batters without thawing. They use slightly lower than normal baking temperatures. Thawing adds time to the overall preparation time (B. Heidolph, *personal communication*).

A frequent problem in the thawing of frozen batter products is that of condensation and evaporation. This phenomenon is a result of water that was once in crystal form melting and collecting on the surface of the batter or underneath a prepackaged product cover (condensation). This water, now removed from the batter, cannot be reincorporated into the product. The water then evaporates. Generally, when evaporation occurs, the batter develops a dry "crust," which, in turn, affects the overall quality of the end product (Heiney, 1989).

There are several ways to thaw frozen batter products. The ambient method is the typical method of choice for most bakers. The product is left at room temperature to thaw and then is baked. Some control points should be considered here. This method will most likely result in the occurrence of the condensation/evaporation phenomenon as well as a loss of leavening. To combat the condensation/evaporation problem, simply place a cover over the batter when it has been deposited into its appropriate baking container. It is very important to limit the air space between the cover and batter surface as much as possible. By limiting this space, the tendency for condensation/evaporation is greatly reduced. Convection ovens as well as infrared and microwave ovens have been used with some success for defrosting of cake batters (Heiney, 1989).

To combat the loss of leavening, it is suggested that frozen muffin batters be thawed in a retarder where the temperature is between 0 and 4°C. Depending upon the size of the container and the temperature of the retarder, this will, in

Table 6
Storage Time (Weeks) of Frozen Cake Batters[a]

Cake Type	Storage Temperature (°C)		
	-34.5	-23	-18
Yellow	18	14	14
Chocolate	18	14	14
Angel food			
Dried whites	10	10	8
Liquid whites	10	8	6
Chiffon	14	9	6

[a] Adapted from Heid (1968).

most cases, take somewhere between 12 and 24 hr. The practice of placing the frozen batter at room temperature and allowing it to thaw tends to generate leavening activity on the outer extremities of the container with no activity or warming of the batter in the inner portion of the container, which results in poor quality and, in some cases, unsalable products. It is also helpful if the temperature of the oven is reduced 10–15°C during baking and the baking time is increased as needed in order to obtain optimum leavening activity that coincides with the starch gelatinization in the batter (Heid, 1968).

General Guidelines for Freezing of Cake Batters

To ensure the best possible quality of frozen batters, the following rules should be adopted:

1. Use a well-balanced formula.

2. For chemically leavened batters, use high-ratio sugar and shortening levels.

3. Choose the proper leavening agent, one designed specifically for use in frozen batters. Increase the amount of leavening by 0.2–0.25% above the level required for immediate bake-off.

4. Include an emulsifier.

5. Store batters in tightly covered containers made from a material that prevents moisture and odor migration and has both low and high temperature tolerance.

6. Lose no time in packaging and freezing batters.

7. Freeze batters as rapidly as possible to -29°C or below. Store at temperatures below -18°C. Avoid temperature fluctuations.

8. Retard cake batters (0–4°C) before baking. Bake sponge-type batters such as angel, sponge, and chiffon batters directly from the frozen state.

9. Decrease normal baking temperature 10–15°C and adjust the baking period as needed.

10. Dating frozen products to guard against quality losses resulting from prolonged storage is highly recommended. The consumer is entitled to complete package information describing the temperature and storage requirements of the product as well as detailed directions for thawing and baking (Heid, 1968).

Literature Cited

Anonymous 1990. Frozen dough production. Lesson 45, correspondence course–Baking Science. American Institute of Baking, Manhattan, KS.

Graul, L. S., and Lowe, B. 1947. How storage affects frozen cakes and batters. Food Ind. 19:330-332.

Heid, M. 1968. Frozen batters and doughs. Pages 360-385 in: The Freezing Preservation of Foods, Vol. 4, D. K. Tressler, W. B. van Arsdel, and M. J. Copley, eds. AVI Publ. Co., Westport, CT.

Heiney, J. H. 1989. Frozen batters. Baker's Tech Talk. Ph. Orth Co., Oak Creek, WI.

Mackey, A. O. 1955. Microscopic structure of frozen batter. Food Technol. 9(5):261-263.

Mackey, A. O., Jones, P., and Dunn, J. 1952. The effect of ingredient variations on the quality of white and chocolate cake batters baked prior to freezing or baked from frozen batters. Food Res. 17:216-224.

Pickens, O. 1955. The freezing of cake batters. Baker's Dig. 29(6):181-185.

Pillsbury Co. 1966. Frozen bakery foods. Baking Ind. 126(1594):45-47; (1597):33-35.

Rollag, N. L., and Enochian, R. V. 1964. The freezing of commercial bakery products; current practices, problems and prospects. U.S. Dept. Agric., Mark. Res. Rep. 674.

Sunderlin, G. L., Collins, O. D., and Acheson, M. 1940. Frozen batters and doughs. J. Home Econ. 32:381-382.

Zaehringer, M. A., and Mayfield, H. L. 1951. The effect of leavening and shortening combinations on the frozen storage of cakes and batters prepared at high altitudes. Food Technol. 5(4):151-154.

CHAPTER 10

Freezing of Confectionery Dough Units in Germany

G. Brack
U. Hanneforth
Federal Center for Cereal, Potato, and Lipid Research
Detmold, Germany

In Germany, breads are distinguished from confectionery products by their fat and/or sugar levels. Confectionery products are richer than breads, containing more than 10 parts of fat/sugar ingredients per 90 parts of cereals and/or starches (Deutsche Landwirtschafts-Gesellschaft, 1994; Seibel, 1991; Deutsches Lebensmittelbuch Leitsaetze, 1992). They are further classified into doughs (yeasted and unyeasted) and batters (whipped and unwhipped). Of these products, mainly the yeasted and puff pastry doughs are frozen as dough units. Freezing technology has the advantage of making dough units available whenever they are needed.

Since the introduction of fermentation retardation procedures, the period between the production and distribution steps has undergone a significant change, permitting the time between completion of baking and time of sales to be reduced to a minimum. Production by baking from frozen bakery units has become a common practice.

Unyeasted Frozen Confectioneries

Production of frozen short-crust doughs (*Muerbteige*) does not offer special problems. Fresh doughs for these products can be simply produced by consumers or retail bakers and, due to their relative stability in storage, these types of bakery doughs are infrequently frozen. Additionally, many products with long-term stability, e.g., cookies, are widely marketed in Germany. Frozen puff pastry, as small plate units, is commonly offered directly in the retail market for home use. Defrosting and baking of these units in homes is simple and does not require any special skill.

For economic reasons, frozen puff pastry doughs with sweet or seasoned fillings/coatings are produced. These types of doughs are manufactured in special food plants and distributed in the frozen state by middlemen. They are stable for several months and can be baked in ovens directly in the frozen condition, or after partial or complete defrosting. The best results are generally obtained using fully defrosted units.

Yeasted Frozen Confectioneries

The important factor in interruption of fermentation by freezing is the state of fermentation, e.g., whether the dough units have received fermentation before freezing or not. Four parameters are especially important in production of frozen doughs (Fig. 1): dough development, fermentation of dough units, freezing process, and baking conditions. The dough preparation must be adjusted for the selected fermentation interruption method. Fermented frozen dough units, which require no fermentation between the frozen storage period and baking (contrary to nonfermented dough units), can be placed into an oven for baking directly after defrosting. This procedure eliminates appreciable differences in product handling by the sales personnel and also determines the time required to produce baked products. For yeasted products, this time is substantially longer than that for unyeasted ones. In preparation of the latter products, the manufacturer can respond more quickly to the sales demand. The most apparent difference between yeasted confectioneries prepared with or without freezing is the lower volume of products made from frozen doughs, especially when they have been frozen without fermentation (Brack and Hanneforth, 1991). This difference is attributed to the lower gassing power of yeast in frozen doughs or to their reduced gas-holding capacity (Wassermann, 1990). This is an area that attracts significant technological research interest.

Methods of Fermentation Interruption

The activity of yeast and the rate of fermentation are reduced by application of low temperatures. Depending on the objective of the retardation, the yeast activity can be retarded or stopped. In the latter case, it is important to determine whether the dough pieces are to be frozen with or without prior fermentation (Sluimer, 1981).

Cooling of Dough Pieces (Fermentation Retardation)

During dough cooling, a series of biochemical reactions is slowed down and concomitant retardation of the yeast activity takes place. The proof times of retarded doughs are extended as compared with the conventional duration of proof times. This extension of conventional dough fermentation times is caused by temperature reduction and can also be considered, irrespective of its duration, to be fermentation retardation. The cooling temperature generally applied in industrial conditions varies from 8 to -2°C.

Freezing of Dough Units (Fermentation Interruption)

In freezing of dough units, the temperature is reduced to such an extent that the yeast activity is almost arrested. Considering this fact, the reduction of yeast activity is not time dependent, whereas, in practice, bakers mainly use the term "fermentation interruption" to refer to the duration of the interruption period. In practice, this interruption period may vary from several days to a few months.

It is essential that yeasted unfermented frozen dough units retain a sufficient level of yeast activity to produce adequate leavening gas within a reasonable time. In fermented dough units, where gas development has produced the necessary leavening action before freezing, no further gas formation by yeast reactivation takes place. Therefore, it is essential for this dough to receive full fermentation before freezing and to the retain this gas in the dough during baking.

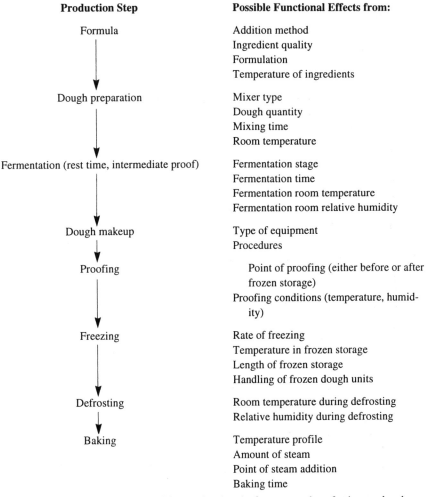

Production Step	Possible Functional Effects from:
Formula	Addition method Ingredient quality Formulation Temperature of ingredients
Dough preparation	Mixer type Dough quantity Mixing time Room temperature
Fermentation (rest time, intermediate proof)	Fermentation stage Fermentation time Fermentation room temperature Fermentation room relative humidity
Dough makeup	Type of equipment Procedures
Proofing	Point of proofing (either before or after frozen storage) Proofing conditions (temperature, humidity)
Freezing	Rate of freezing Temperature in frozen storage Length of frozen storage Handling of frozen dough units
Defrosting	Room temperature during defrosting Relative humidity during defrosting
Baking	Temperature profile Amount of steam Point of steam addition Baking time

Fig. 1. Flow sheet of manufacturing of frozen dough units from yeasted confectionery doughs. (Adapted from Seibel, 1991)

The basic requirement for conservation by freezing (i.e., retention of essential product characteristics) is the storage of food products at or below -18°C temperature. In spite of the low temperature used, chemical and biochemical changes in the products may take place. Consequently, frozen storage is possible for a limited period only. The frozen products change more quickly, and to a larger extent, when they are unpackaged or improperly packaged. Suitable packaging for frozen food is therefore essential.

Production of Frozen Dough Units

When considering the entire field of fermentation interruption, it is essential to view the complex interrelationships taking place in the doughs. Thus, all possible variations of the production processes and the effects of individual ingredients can be recognized and properly adjusted. Figure 1 presents a flow diagram for production of doughs from yeasted confectionery formulas. It includes the most important parameters for practical application of fermentation interruption.

Production of Confectionery Products from Unfermented Frozen Dough

Dough development. Proper dough development is essential in dough preparation. The dough development is affected by, besides flour quality, the type of mixer used, the mixer load, and mixing time. Changes of these variables influence the degree of dough development, which causes variations in product volume and quality characteristics. Optimally developed doughs yield best results.

Dough rest times and fermentation before freezing. The effects of the length of the dough rest periods on doughs designed for fermentation interruption are compared with an unfrozen dough control in Figure 2. The experiment used croissant doughs. It is evident that the normal rest period is beneficial for the conventionally processed control. For frozen doughs, shorter or no rest periods were found to produce the best results, provided the frozen units were fermented after freezing.

For dough units that have not been proofed before freezing, the freezing step should proceed immediately after dough preparation. These doughs must be carefully monitored during both defrosting and fermentation. Initially, when the doughs are still cold, the relative humidity of the ambient air in the proof cabinets should be relatively low to prevent excessive condensation on the dough surfaces. Surface condensation reduces product quality by forming blisters and causing spreading of products. The subsequent baking step then proceeds as usual.

Freezing conditions (rates, times, and temperature). The freezing rate depends on various factors, which, in practical applications, are difficult to adjust. For instance, the freezing capacity is generally provided by an available freezing unit in a plant. Also other existing parameters, specifically given by the production plant design, indirectly influence the freezing rates, e.g., the freezer load (the higher the load, the lower the freezing rate). Similarly, the product unit size, formula, fermentation state, ambient temperature, etc., are more or less given. The adjustable variables are freezing temperature, temperature control, air velocity within limits of the freezer design, and initial dough temperature of the units.

Model experiments were conducted in our laboratory in which the freezing temperature and freezing environment were varied. Freezing in carbon dioxide gas with all other variables kept constant produced quick freezing. The determined freezing times are recorded in Table 1. In addition, freezing rate measurements for freezing at -60°C in carbon dioxide are presented. This temperature is neither common nor practically achievable in commercial production but can be achieved in our laboratory, due to low load and high evaporator perform-

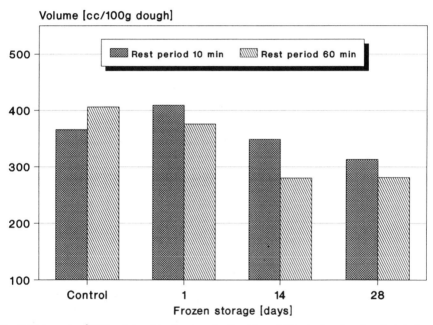

Fig. 2. Volume (cm³/100g of dough) of croissants after 10- and 60-min dough rest periods before makeup at different frozen storage times. Control = without frozen storage. (Reprinted, with permission, from Hanneforth et al, 1994)

Table 1
Freezing Times of Yeasted Confectionery[a]

Freezing Temperature (°C)	Freezing Medium	Freezing Time 10 to -10°C (min)	Freezing Time 15 to -20°C (min)
-20	Air	48	>150
-30	Air	24	37
	Carbon dioxide	12	20
-60	Carbon dioxide	5	10

[a] Source: Hanneforth et al (1994); used by permission.

ance in the freezing chamber. These data illustrate the effects of temperature conditions on freezing time. In these experiments, the freezing time/rate was defined as the time (minutes) necessary to reduce the center temperature in a round dough piece from 10 to -10°C or from 15 to -20°C.

Effects of freezing time variations on croissant doughs are described in Table 1, and the same variations appear in Figure 3. As evident from Figure 3, freezing rate imparted no appreciable differences and no product volume differences were detected for units kept in 14-day frozen storage. Also, variation in fermentation times had little effect on the quality of this product.

Appreciable volume decrease was observed for samples frozen at -60°C in carbon dioxide gas. This deterioration was attributed to lowered yeast activity, which appreciably diminished the gassing power. This observation demonstrates that a temperature of about -30°C may be considered optimal. On the other hand, freezing in a -60°C environment, even when stopped at -20°C center temperature of the unit, is detrimental because it damages some yeast cells in the external layers of the dough unit.

Dough units frozen for more than one day must be packaged (e.g., in plastic bags) to protect their surfaces from drying out. In spite of this precaution, the product volumes diminish with progressing storage time. Frozen storage of one to two days causes a relatively minor volume loss when compared with unfrozen controls. After three- and four-day frozen storage, a noticeable loss of volume is observed. After the fourth day, volume reduction continues consistently, but at a relatively slow rate.

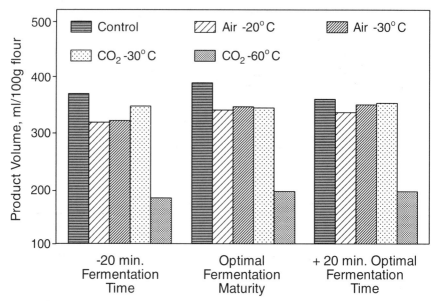

Fig. 3. Volumes of croissants frozen at different temperatures and in different atmospheres and using doughs of varied maturity. Volumes determined after 12 days of frozen storage. (Authors' unpublished data)

Defrosting conditions. Frozen doughs can be defrosted by various procedures, for instance, 1) using a so-called programmable fermentation retarder (*Gaerunterbrecher*), 2) defrosting dough units in a room at 20–22°C and 40% RH, 3) defrosting in a fermentation cabinet at, e.g., 32°C and 80–100% RH, or 4) defrosting in a temperature- and humidity-programmable fermentation cabinet.

In the fermentation retarder, the temperature can be set and, above about 10°C, the relative humidity also can be set. When defrosting is programmed for stepwise temperature increases, small differences are set between the temperature of the dough and of ambient air to avoid excessive surface condensation. Defrosting according to this procedure takes several hours.

Defrosting in a room environment proceeds relatively quickly (e.g., 40 min). The relatively dry air causes initially less condensation on the cold dough surfaces than in the more humid environment of the fermentation cabinet. The defrosted dough units are fermented in a proof box.

Defrosting in a conventional fermentation cabinet proceeds relatively quickly, being affected by a high temperature differential and a high humidity level. These conditions are conducive, however, to formation of excessive condensation on dough surfaces, which subsequently, during baking, produce adverse quality effects: surface blisters, dough spreading, and irregular crust browning.

In programmable fermentation cabinets, the temperature is adjusted by heating and/or cooling. The air humidity is also regulated at the same time by controlled humidification and dehumidification to eliminate excessive surface

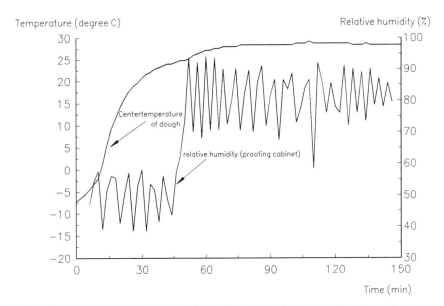

Fig. 4. Center temperature and relative humidity in proof box at 32°C during defrosting and proofing. (Authors' unpublished data)

condensation during the initial defrosting phases. The temperature differential in respect to the dough is initially set as high as possible for a maximum rate of defrosting; the relative humidity in the initial phase (from frozen temperature to about 20°C) is adjusted to 75% RH and is subsequently raised to 85% RH at the fully fermented dough stage. Dough defrosting from -10 to 10°C at the center of the unit is accomplished by this procedure within approximately 20 min (Fig. 4). A definite advantage of this defrosting procedure is the relatively higher crumb grain uniformity in contrast to that of products defrosted in retarders. The latter procedure tends to produce two types of crumb grain: a relatively fine grain in lower parts of the baked units and a coarse grain in the upper crumb section, which shows a tendency to overbake. As is evident from

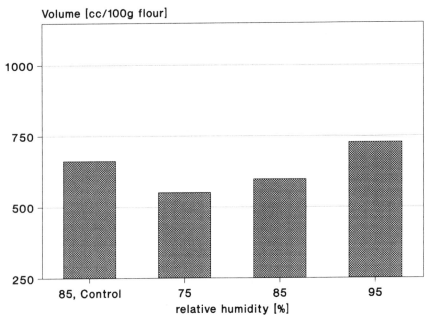

Fig. 5. Volume of yeasted buns after one-day frozen storage, defrosting, proofing at different relative humidities, and baking. Control = without frozen storage. (Authors' unpublished data)

Table 2
Baking Quality Index (points[a]) of Yeasted Rolls/Buns After One- and Seven-Day Frozen Storage and of Unfrozen Controls[b]

Quality Index	Control	One-Day	Seven-Day
Appearance	98	95	98
Crumb structure	70	75	85
Crumb texture	81	93	90
Volume, ml/100 g of flour	833	685	656

[a] Maximum rating for each index = 100 points.
[b] Source: Hanneforth et al (1994); used by permission.

Figure 5, unit volumes consistently increase with relative humidity increments from 75 to 95% RH. To evaluate baked products, it is advisable to judge the various quality parameters and to compare them with those of conventionally produced controls. The characteristics generally evaluated include appearance (shape, surface), crumb structure (cell distribution and size), and crumb quality (crumb properties, elasticity, chewability/tenderness). These parameters are rated using a numerical scale, ranging from 0 (lowest) to 100 (highest). The values of these parameters for the unfrozen control and for products baked after one- and seven-day frozen storage are presented in Table 2. When frozen products are compared with the unfrozen control, it is evident that product volumes were diminished by freezing but that crumb quality values apparently improved.

Wheat flour quality. Wheat flour, with an ash content of ≈0.55% (range, 0.51–0.63%; Table 3), is generally used. This flour is relatively high in protein (12.5–13,0%, $N \times 5.7$ or higher), with a falling number >300 sec. When dough improvers are included in the formulas, ingredients containing proteolytic activities are to be avoided.

Dough consistency. Doughs to be frozen without fermentation should be somewhat stiffer than normal. To achieve this consistency, the dough water absorption should be reduced by 1–2% (flour basis).

Effects of sugar and fat level. Sugar and fat levels were varied in the formula (control) for yeast-leavened products given in Table 3. The doughs were frozen and tested for volumes after 14-day frozen storage.

Additions of fat increased the volumes (Fig. 6). The products of this experimental series were baked at the same baking conditions to permit direct com-

Table 3
Flour and Formula Used in Experiments[a]

Average flour analytical indices	
Ash, % dry basis	0.53
Protein ($N = 5.7$), % dry basis	12.7
Wet gluten, %	31
Sedimentation value	35
Falling number, sec	380
Water absorption	58.2

Basic experimental yeasted confectionery formula	
Ingredient	Percent, flour basis
Flour	100
Water	51
Shortening	10
Sugar	10
Yeast, compressed	6
Salt	1.25
Ascorbic acid	0.002

[a] Adapted from Arbeitsgemeinshaft Getreideforschung (1994).

parisons (200°C for 25 min). This baking formula was not optimal for one of the tested ingredient variables (0% fat/0% sugar).

Additions of gluten, diacetyl tartaric acid esters (DATA-esters), and whole eggs increased the product volume. The use of egg whites, however, had no effect. Other additives showed only minor improvements in products baked from frozen doughs. The DATA-esters were most effective as volume improvers in this application.

Preparation of Confectionery Products from Prefermented Frozen Doughs

The parameters given in Figure 1 also exhibit marked influences on the baking results of this type of product. Of special significance are: dough preparation, the fermentation stage before freezing, defrosting, and baking method. To bake this type of product directly in the frozen condition, an oven equipped with a special environmental control in the baking chamber is required. In these ovens, steam is injected uniformly for a selected period. This is in contrast to conventional ovens, in which steam is supplied only once at the beginning of baking.

Mixing procedures. If the dough is optimally developed, the mixing procedure has no significant effect on the baked product.

Dough preparation and rest time. The factors that should be carefully observed in dough preparation are dough consistency, dough temperature, and dough rest time after mixing.

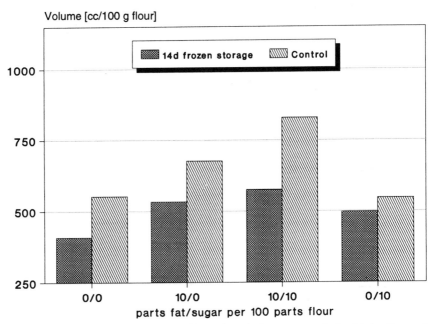

Fig. 6. Volumes of yeasted buns from different formulations, measured after 14-day frozen storage. Fat/sugar is according to the basic recipe. (Authors' unpublished data)

The relationships between product volume, dough temperature, and dough rest time for doughs with a constant normal consistency are represented in the contour map in Figure 7. The product volumes for each isoline are constant. Considering the trend of the lines from left to right, it is evident that the product volumes increase consistently with rising temperature. Volume also increases with increasing rest time up to 40 min, then decreases as rest time increases to 60 min.

The rest periods have an appreciable effect on dough consistency and product properties. Shorter rest periods (below 30 min) produce doughs of normal to slightly firmer consistency, which then yield slightly higher volumes than the softer doughs. When longer rest periods (above 30 min) are used, this trend is reversed: the softer doughs produce products of higher volumes than the firmer doughs.

Also products from softer doughs have a tendency to have better surface and crumb quality characteristics than those from firmer doughs.

In general, dough consistency does not have a significant effect on appearance, surface, and crumb properties. This observation shows that the total effect of dough consistency is either relatively minor or that it is overcome by interaction with other variables.

Temperatures around 29°C (normal) are favorable for appearance characteristics (symmetry, shape, surface without blisters, and adequate volume), and crumb with good properties (soft).

The rest period durations have different effects on individual product quality

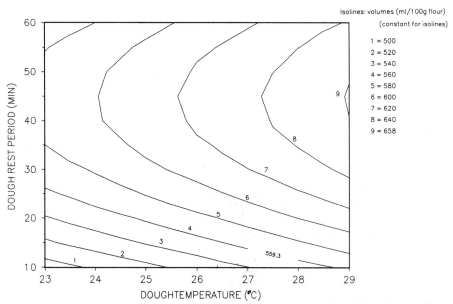

Fig. 7. Contour plot of volume at constant dough consistency as a function of dough rest period and dough temperature. (Reprinted, with permission, from Hanneforth et al, 1994)

parameters. Dough rest times between 30 and 40 min are favorable for crumb quality. On the other hand, for the best surface and crumb properties, the shortest possible rest periods are desirable.

In Figure 8, the effects of dough consistency and rest time on crumb grain uniformity are presented. It is evident that the crumb grain is only slightly influenced by the dough consistency at short rest times (approximately up to 26 min). The rest period itself can be considered to have a negative effect on grain uniformity, as is evident from the decreasing trend of the isoline with increasing dough consistency values (i.e., nonuniform crumb grain). This effect is especially pronounced for stiffer doughs. Long rest periods used in connection with a soft dough still produce crumb with good cell distribution, uneven cell sizes, and no or very few holes. This texture is desirable.

State of dough fermentation at the point of freezing. The state of fermenting dough (degree of fermentation maturity) is judged empirically by a finger test. Actually the fermentation time depends on the dough's fermentation state. Fermentation is judged as one-half, three-fourths, and fully fermented. According to this definition, a half-fermented dough has not necessarily received half of the optimal (full) fermentation time.

It has been established that the fermentation state has a special role in determining end-product quality, especially the crumb grain uniformity of yeasted rolls. With increasing fermentation state, holes are formed in the upper sections

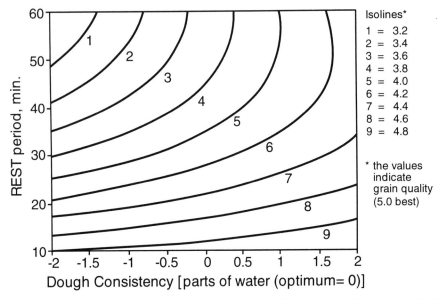

Fig. 8. Contour plot of crumb structure as a function of dough rest period and constant optimal dough consistency. Dough consistency units: 0.0 = normal level of water absorption resulting from normal sensorial dough consistency, 2.0 = normal level of water absorption plus two parts water per 100 parts flour, resulting in "soft" dough consistency, -2.0 = normal level of water absorption minus two parts water per 100 parts flour, resulting in "firm" dough consistency. (Reprinted, with permission, from Hanneforth et al, 1994)

of the crumb area or the crust has tendency to overbake. The reason for this occurrence may be the solubility behavior of carbon dioxide. With longer fermentation times, more carbon dioxide is formed, which simultaneously causes a gradual weakening of the gluten film. During subsequent cooling, the carbon dioxide dissolves, since its solubility increases at lower temperatures (Sluimer, 1981). A substantial temperature differential exists between the center and the surface of dough pieces during defrosting/heating in the oven. Measurements show that the center temperature increases from about -15 to 100°C within 8–10 min. As expected, the temperature rise is much quicker on the surface, which causes again a rapid transition of carbon dioxide from the dissolved into the gaseous form. The concomitant volume increase under these conditions leads to a more or less apparent disruption of crumb cell walls. Consequently, crumb holes are formed and/or the crust is overbaked. Half-fermented dough definitely produces products with the best properties (high quality crumb grain, fewer holes, and less overbaked crust).

Defrosting and baking. The combination of abundant steam, high temperature, and short baking time has a positive effect on product volume. Increasing the baking time, with other factors constant, yields lower volumes. Figure 9 shows the relationship of product volume to dough temperature and the amount of steam while a constant defrosting/heating phase of 5 min is maintained. The product volumes increase with more steam, especially at high oven temperatures. Further, it is noteworthy that low steam levels (up to 0.5 L) with rising temperatures cause volume reduction. This relationship is reversed when the steam increases above 0.5 L; in that case, higher temperatures produce higher volumes.

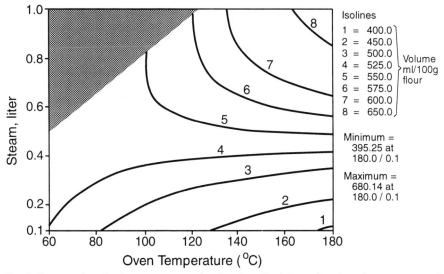

Fig. 9. Contour plot of volume at constant thawing time (5 min) as a function of temperature and steam (blacked out area was not investigated). (Reprinted, with permission, from Hanneforth et al, 1994)

Finally the product appearance, mainly the external overall characteristics consisting of surface, shape, and crust browning/sheen are generally affected positively by high oven temperatures. High steam values, above 0.5 L, reverse this trend. These conditions, especially at high oven temperatures, increase the product volume.

High temperatures along with low steam produce little surface blistering. On the other hand, high steam levels (above 0.5 L) are required to produce good crust surface sheen.

All these observations are based on experiments with a baking oven equipped with a special control that is operated during the defrosting/heating phase. When these control variables are varied, one must consider the effect of steam in connection with time and set temperature because the control mechanism alters the oven climate from that produced by normal oven settings. It is also imperative to be aware that specifically set conditions, e.g., higher temperatures or steam values, do not always affect all the target values (product properties) positively and simultaneously. Consequently, experimental baking results carried out under optimally set conditions represent only the best possible approximations for achieving the most desirable overall properties of the baked products.

Optimization of experimental conditions. It is evident from the presented relationships that the control setting of certain variables, e.g., high dough temperatures and longer dough rest times, does not always produce simultaneously positive effects on product quality. For instance, a longer fermentation time increases the product volume but also causes formation of crumb holes. Experimental baking results provide only a guide in establishing the best conditions for production of optimal quality products.

Optimal variables for dough production and fermentation are given in Table

Table 4
Optimal Experimental Conditions for Production of Preproofed Frozen Doughs[a]

Variable	Optimal Range
Dough consistency	One to two parts water
Dough temperature	28–29°C
Dough rest time	25–40 min
Proof time	1/2 to 2/3 of normal proof time
Defrosting conditions in oven	
Defrosting/heating time	6–8 min
Amount of steam	0.8–1.0 L water after full load
Defrosting temperature	155–170°C at full load
Baking conditions in oven	
Baking time	23 min, including defrosting and heating periods
Baking temperature	172°C
Air draft	Open vents during last 8 min

[a] Adapted from Brack and Hanneforth (1991) and Hanneforth et al (1994).

4; optimal conditions for defrosting and baking are shown in the same table. Experiments made under these optimized conditions confirmed the expectations, producing high-quality products.

Summary

The following conclusions can be made on the basis of the presented experiments:

1. It is advantageous for the production of unfermented yeasted dough units to use cold dough temperatures and short dough rest periods after mixing. Defrosting of the frozen dough units should be done in a low-humidity environment to avoid water condensation on the dough surface. Subsequent baking proceeds as usual.

2. Prefermented frozen dough units are produced from normal to slightly soft doughs. Dough temperature should be about 29°C. Rest periods should be 25–40 min. The fermentation state at the point of freezing should be within one-half to two-thirds of full normal fermentation. The defrosting/heating time in the oven is about 6–8 min; the steam amount range is 0.8–1 L; and the set oven temperature during the defrosting step is 155–170°C. These results indicate only a general trend, which may need to be modified for other production conditions.

Literature Cited

Arbeitsgemeinschaft Getreideforschung e. V., ed. 1994. Standard-Methoden fuer Getreide Mehl und Brot (Standard methods for grain, flour and bread, 7th ed.) Schaefer, Detmold.

Brack, G.,and Hanneforth, U. 1991 Herstellung von tiefgefroren Teiglingen aus Hefefeinteigen (Production of frozen dough units from yeasted confectioneries). Getreide Mehl Brot 10:309-315.

Deutsche Landwirtschafts-Gesellschaft, ed. 1994. Brot und Feine Backwaren: Eine Systematik der Backwaren in der Bundesrepublik Deutschland (Bread and confectioneries: A systematic handbook of bakery goods in the German Federal Republic). Deutscher Fachverlag, Frankfurt (Main).

Deutsches Lebensmittelbuch. Leitsaetze, ed. 1992. Leitsaetze fuer Feine Backwaren (Regulations for flour confectionery). Bundesanzeiger Verlagsges. mbh., Koeln.: 301-318.

Hanneforth, U., Brack, G., and Valerius, U. 1994. Herstellung von Hefefeingebaeck aus vorgegaerten Tiefkuehlteigen (Production of confectioneries from frozen prefermented doughs). Getreide Mehl Brot 48(4):36-42.

Seibel, W., ed. 1991. Feine Backwaren (Confectioneries) Berlin and Hamburg. Grundlagen Fortschr. Lebensmittelunters. Lebensmitteltechnol. 21:285.

Sluimer, P. 1981. Prinzipien der Gaerunterbrechung bei der Weizenbrotherstellung (Principles of fermentation interruption in wheat bread production). Getreide Mehl Brot 1:18-21.

Wassermann, L. 1990. Gefrostete Teiglinge (Basis Wasserwaren): Rezepturen (Frozen dough units [basic water products]: Formulations). Getreide Mehl Brot 44:7, 218-220.

CHAPTER 11

Principles of Heat Transfer

R. Paul Singh

Department of Biological and Agricultural Engineering
University of California
Davis CA 95616

Heating and cooling processes represent some of the more commonly encountered operations in the food industry. Many important physical and biochemical reactions depend on the temperatures used during processing. Several desirable quality attributes in processed foods are obtained by controlling the rate of heat transfer. Undesirable effects of heating and cooling processes must also be considered. Therefore, a quantitative understanding of how foods heat or cool is necessary.

Thermal processes can be understood by examining the physical and thermal properties of foods. These properties, with unique magnitudes, are useful in determining how a food will heat or cool when it is exposed to different environments. For example, the rapidity with which a food material equilibrates with the surrounding environment is influenced by the internal resistance to heat transfer, or its thermal conductivity.

The important principles of heat transfer are discussed in this chapter with illustrative examples. We first consider the physical and thermal properties that influence thermal processes. Then, we examine different modes of heat transfer. Several important mathematical expressions are reviewed that are useful in calculating the rate of heat transfer in food materials. Definitions of variables are provided in Appendix I.

A thermal process may be divided into two stages: unsteady state and steady state. During the unsteady state, the temperature of an object changes with time and location within the object, whereas during the steady state, the temperature in an object does not change with time, although it may be different from one location to another. For example, consider a food undergoing heating in an oven. At the beginning of the process, there are unsteady-state conditions because the temperature at every location within the object changes with time. A steady-state condition is reached when the temperature of the object no longer changes with time.

Thermal Properties

Although several physical and thermal properties influence the rate of heat transfer in foods, the following discussion focuses on three of the most important properties, namely, thermal conductivity, specific heat, and thermal diffusivity.

Thermal Conductivity

Thermal conductivity of a food is a measure of how well a food material conducts heat when it is subjected to a temperature gradient. In quantitative terms, thermal conductivity is a measure of the amount of heat (in joules) transferred across a known thickness of a material (meters) in a given time (seconds) and for a known temperature difference (°C) across the material. The commonly used units for thermal conductivity are J/sec^{-1} m^{-1} °C^{-1}. Since 1 J/sec equals 1 W, thermal conductivity is also expressed as W/m°C or W/mK.

Foods are generally poor conductors of heat, especially when compared with metals. Thermal conductivity values of dough and bread are shown in Appendix II, as compiled by Rask (1989). The thermal conductivity of foods may be several orders of magnitude lower than that of common metals such as steel or copper. Since foods generally contain a significant amount of water, their thermal conductivity is strongly influenced by the presence of water. The thermal conductivity of water is 0.597 W/mK at 20°C. In the case of bread, thermal conductivity of the crumb portion is about 0.3 W/mK. For the crust layer, where the water content is much lower than in the crumb, the thermal conductivity is about 0.05 W/mK. In addition, the thermal conductivity of a material changes with temperature. Data obtained for dough by Lind (1988) (Appendix II) show the dependence of thermal conductivity on temperature.

Thermal conductivity is measured using either steady-state or unsteady-state procedures. Reidy (1968) provided a review of the advantages and limitations of these methods. Measurement techniques for thermal conductivities have been discussed by Nesvadba (1982), Ohlsson (1983), and Rao and Rizvi (1994). A line source probe method developed by Sweat and Haugh (1974) has been used extensively in measuring thermal conductivities of foods. Unkelsbay et al (1981) and Bakshi and Yoon (1984) used this probe to measure the thermal conductivity of white bread and bread rolls, respectively. During the baking process, water content and density of the bread decrease. Bakshi and Yoon (1984) suggested the following expression to relate thermal conductivity of bread to changes in density and moisture content:

$$k = 0.6792 - 0.0551\, X_{wb} + 0.0020\rho + 0.0000\, X_{wb}^{2} - 0.000024\, X_{wb} , \qquad (1)$$

where k is thermal conductivity (W/mK); ρ is density (kg/m^3); and X_{wb} is moisture content, wet basis (kg/kg).

Figures 1 and 2 (Rask, 1989) show the relationship between thermal conductivity and moisture content and density, respectively, using the data of Bakshi and Yoon (1984) and Unklesbay et al (1981). It is evident that decreases in moisture content and density result in decreases in thermal conductivity of the product. Near the end of the baking process, there appears to be a slight increase in thermal conductivity with decreasing moisture content (Fig. 1). As noted by Rask (1989), the influence of porosity and orientation of pores must be given due consideration. Any errors associated with measuring density would influence the estimation of thermal conductivity. The density values of bread and other bakery products are shown in Appendixes II and III, respectively. The values of density for these products change over a large range. As the baking process proceeds, decreasing moisture content and increasing bread volume result in decreasing density.

In general, the thermal conductivity of foods can be estimated if the composition of the food is known. For example, Sweat (1974) has suggested the following equation to determine thermal conductivity of fruits and vegetables when the water content is greater than 60%.

$$k = 0.148 + 0.00493\, X, \tag{2}$$

where X is water content (percent).

The thermal conductivity of ice is 2.22 W/mK at 0°C; this value is almost

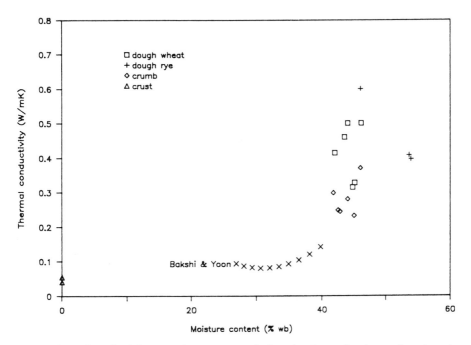

Fig. 1. Thermal conductivity vs. moisture content of wheat dough, rye dough, crumb, and crust. (Reprinted, with permission, from Rask, 1989; ©ElsevierScience Ltd.)

four times that of water (0.597 W/mK) at 20°C. During freezing of foods, because of the presence of water, as the temperature is lowered below freezing point, we observe dramatic changes in the thermal conductivity of frozen foods. For example, as seen in Figure 3, the thermal conductivity of lean beef increases significantly when the temperature is lowered below 0°C.

Specific Heat

The specific heat of a material provides an estimate of the amount of heat (in joules) needed to raise the temperature of a known mass of a material (kilograms) by a known temperature difference (°C). In other words, specific heat is a measure of how much heat is required to heat (or cool) a food. Materials with high specific heat require a much larger amount of heat than those with lower specific heat to experience the same change in temperature.

Specific heat is usually measured by a calorimetric method. A procedure developed by Hwang and Hayakawa (1979) involves an indirect method of mixing. This method was used by Bakshi and Yoon (1984) to measure the specific heat of bread. Differential scanning calorimetry (DSC) has been used to measure the specific heat of foods. Johnsson and Skjöldebrand (1984) used DSC to measure the specific heat of crust and crumb portions of bread at different moisture contents and temperatures. They obtained the following expressions that relate specific heat at constant volume to water content,

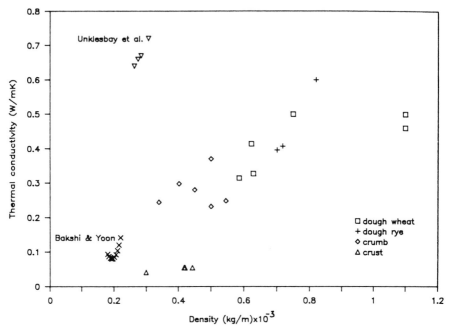

Fig. 2. Thermal conductivity vs. density of wheat dough, rye dough, crumb, and crust. (Reprinted, with permission, from Rask, 1989; ©ElsevierScience Ltd.)

for crust:

$$c_v = 2.62(1 - X_{wb})T + X_{wb}c_w + 1,263(1 - X_{wb}) ,\qquad(3)$$

where c_v is specific heat at constant volume (J/kgK); c_w is specific heat of water (J/kgK), assumed to be 4,200 J/kgK; and T is temperature (°C);
for crumb:

$$c_v = 1.60(1 - X_{wb})T + X_{wb}c_w + 1,373(1 - X_{wb}) .\qquad(4)$$

For dried doughs , Polak(1984) suggested the following relationship:

$$c_p = (1.114 + 0.004867) \times 10^3 ,\qquad(5)$$

where c_p is specific heat at constant pressure (kJ/kg°C).

In general, the specific heat of foods can be estimated when the water content of the food is known. For example, for meat products in the range of 26–100% moisture content, and for fruit juices with a moisture content greater than 50%, the following expression is useful:

$$c_p = 1.675 + 0.025 X .\qquad(6)$$

Values of specific heat for dough and bread are shown in Appendix II (Rask, 1989). As noted in the table, some of the values were obtained experimentally, while others were calculated by Rask (1989) from the mathematical relationships given by the original researchers. From the data in Appendix II, it is evident that the water content of bread and bread dough has a marked influence on the specific heat. For example, the specific heat of crumb and dough,

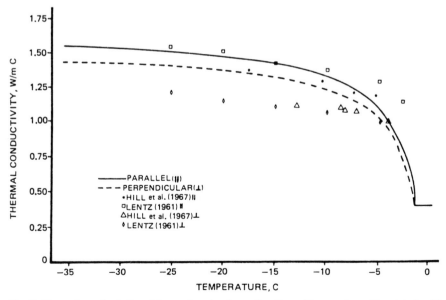

Fig. 3. Thermal conductivity of frozen lean beef as a function of temperature. (Reprinted, with permission, from Heldman and Gorby, 1975)

which have a high moisture content, is around 2,800 J/kgK, whereas dried crust has specific heat of about 1,680 J/kgK. Figure 4 is a plot drawn by Rask (1989) to show specific heat of dough, crust, crumb, and intact bread as a function of moisture content. The specific heat of bread decreases as the moisture content is reduced during the baking process.

The specific heat of a food material can also be estimated if more detailed composition of the material is known, using the following expression (Heldman and Singh, 1981):

$$c_p = 1.424 \, m_c + 1.549 \, m_p + 1.675 \, m_f + 0.837 \, m_a + 4.187 \, m_m , \qquad (7)$$

where m = mass fraction, and the subscripts indicate carbohydrate (c), protein (p), fat (f), ash (a), and moisture (m). The specific heat is calculated as kJ/kgK.

When foods are frozen, both latent heat and sensible heat must be removed. One can express an apparent specific heat that involves both sensible heat and latent heat. Figure 5 shows the predicted values of apparent specific heat of frozen sweet cherries as a function of temperature. The peak in the curve is due to the additional latent heat that must be removed to freeze a product.

Thermal Diffusivity

During the unsteady-state period of heat transfer, thermal diffusivity pro- vides a measure of how rapidly heat can transfer through a material. It is a

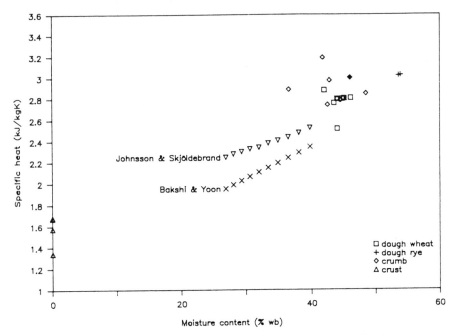

Fig. 4. Specific heat of dough, crust, crumb, and intact bread as a function of moisture content. (Reprinted, with permission, from Rask, 1989; ©ElsevierScience Ltd.)

combination of thermal conductivity, specific heat, and the density of a material. It is expressed as:

$$\alpha = \frac{k}{\rho c_p} \, ,$$ (8)

where α is thermal diffusivity (m²/sec).

Thermal diffusivity values of selected bakery foods are given in Appendixes II and III. They are low in comparison with the values for metals. Thermal diffusivity values are usually obtained by substituting thermal conductivity, density, and specific heat values in equation 8. Therefore, the calculated values of thermal diffusivity are highly dependent upon how accurately the three properties are determined. Rask (1989) has plotted the thermal diffusivity of dough, crumb, and crust against density, as shown in Figure 6. As expected, the thermal diffusivity for crust is lower than that for crumb.

During the freezing process, dramatic changes take place in thermal diffusivity, as seen in Figure 7 for a food model system. These changes are associated with a large increase in thermal conductivity and a decrease in apparent specific heat with decreasing temperature.

The preceding discussion on thermal properties emphasizes that foods have property values that are uniquely different from those of several nonfood ma-

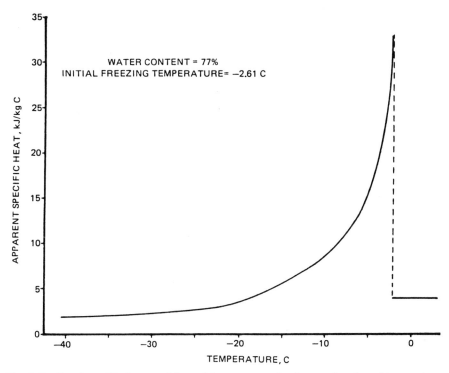

Fig. 5. Predicted specific (apparent) heat of frozen sweet cherries as a function of temperature. (Reprinted, with permission, from Heldman, 1982)

terials. Since foods are mostly composed of water, their thermal properties can be estimated if their composition, particularly the water content, is known. Mathematical relationships for estimating the thermal properties of bakery products (Table 1) were compiled by Rask (1989). A computerized database of food properties is useful in gaining access to published values for numerous foods (Singh, 1993).

Next, we consider important principles governing steady-state heat transfer and determine how physical and thermal properties can be incorporated into mathematical expressions that are useful in determining the rate of heat transfer through a food material.

Steady-State Heat Transfer

Conductive Heat Transfer

Steady-state conditions are established when a food object is exposed, for a sufficiently long period of time, to an environment that is at a temperature different from that of the object's initial temperature. Once the steady-state conditions are reached, the temperature of the object does not change with time. The temperature may, however, vary from one location to another.

The rate of heat transfer under steady-state conditions is dependent on the temperature difference between the object and the surrounding environment,

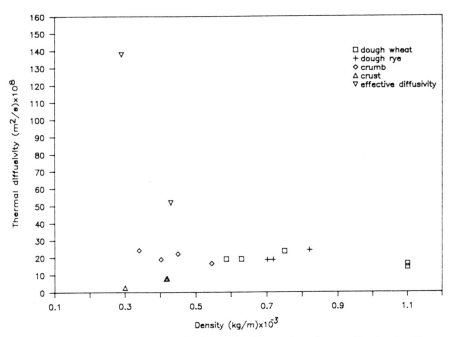

Fig. 6. Thermal diffusivity of wheat dough, rye dough, crumb, and crust. (Reprinted, with permission, from Rask, 1989; ©ElsevierScience Ltd.)

the area perpendicular to the direction of heat flow, and the thermal conductivity. These relationships can be combined into a simple mathematical expression called Fourier's law:

$$q = -kA \frac{dT}{dx} ,$$ (9)

where q is the rate of heat transfer (W), A is area (m²), and dT/dx is the temperature gradient in the direction of the heat flow (°C/m).

Fourier's law provides the mathematical basis for describing the rate of heat transfer due to the conduction mode in solid materials. Equation 9 may be solved for different geometrical shapes. For example, for a rectangular slab, considering heat flow in one dimension, we get,

$$q = kA \frac{(T_2 - T_2)}{(X_2 - X_1)} .$$ (10)

Thus, for a 1-cm thick material with a thermal conductivity of 0.7 W/m°C, subjected to a temperature of 80°C on one side and 40°C on the other, if the area perpendicular to heat flow is 1 m², then the rate of heat transfer is 2,800 W.

Convective Heat Transfer

Heat transfer from a solid surface into the surrounding fluid occurs by convection. The surrounding fluid may be liquid or gas (air). For such cases, the rate of heat transfer is described by the following expression:

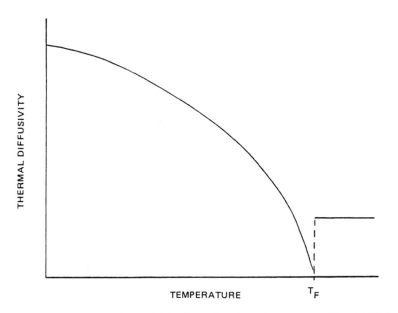

THERMAL DIFFUSIVITY

TEMPERATURE T_F

Fig. 7. Thermal diffusivity of a model food as a function of temperature. T_F = initial freezing temperature of the food. (Reprinted, with permission, from Heldman, 1983)

$$q = hA(T_s - T_a) , \tag{11}$$

where q is the rate of heat transfer from the solid surface into the surrounding fluid, T_s is the surface temperature of the solid object (°C), T_a is the surrounding temperature of the fluid (°C), and h is the convective heat transfer coefficient (W/m²°C).

The convective heat transfer coefficient is a measure of the ease with which heat can transfer from the surface of an object into the fluid. Indirectly, it expresses the boundary layer resistance to heat transfer. For example, if there is a forced airflow around a solid object instead of stagnant air, then the convective heat transfer coefficient would be high, indicating that the resistance to heat transfer at the surface is low. For such a case, the rate of heat transfer would be high. Magnitudes of the convective heat transfer coefficient for commonly encountered situations in food processing are given in Table 2.

As would be expected, if the processing conditions involve little or no fluid

Table 1
Selected Mathematical Models to Calculate Moisture Content, Density,
and Thermal Properties of Bakery Products[a]

Reference	Product	Equations[b]
Bakshi and Yoon (1984)	White bread	$X_{wb} = 41.53 \times 10^{-0.0189\tau}$ $\rho = 225 \times 10^{-0.0095\tau}$ $c_p = 30.56X_{wb} + 1130.44$ $k = 0.6792 - 0.0551X_{wb} + 0.002\rho + 0.0009X_{wb}{}^2$ $\quad - 0.000024X_{wb}\,\rho$
Johnsson and Skjöldebrand (1984)	Bread crumb Bread crust	$c_v = 1.60(1-X_{wb})T + X_{wb}c_w + 1{,}373(1-X_{wb})$ $c_v = 2.62(1-X_{wb})T + X_{wb}c_w + 1{,}263(1-X_{wb})$ $\alpha_{eff} = 0.000031e^{(-0.06783T_{mv})}$
Metel et al(1986)	Dough wheat 20–90°C	$\rho = 2{,}272.2 - 4.97(T + 273)$ $k = -0.23 + 0.178 \times 10^{-2}(T + 273)$ $k = 1.38 - 0.023X_{wb}$ $k = 0.31 - 0.82 \times 10^{-2}X_{wb} + 0.13 \times 10^{-2}(T + 273)$ $\alpha = [15.41 + 0.134 \times 10^{-1}(T + 273)] \times 10^{-8}$ $\alpha = [16.15 - 0.113 \times 10^{-1}X_{wb} + 0.126 \times 10^{-1}(T + 273)] \times 10^{-8}$ $\alpha = [17.65 - 0.84 \times 10^{-3}\rho - 0.49 \times 10^{-2}X_{wb} + 0.89 \times 10^{-2}(T + 273)] \times 10^{-8}$
Polak (1984)	Dough, dry	$c_p = (1.114 + 0.00486\,T) \times 10^3$ $c_p(\text{average}) = (1.114 + 0.00243\,T) \times 10^3$
	Dough, wet	$c_p(\text{average}) = [(c_{pdm} + X_{wb}c_w)/(1 + X_{wb})] \times 10^3$

[a] Source: Rask (1989); used by permission.
[b] See the appendix for explanations of the variables.

flow around an object, the overall rate of heat transfer from the object is small. This type of condition is referred to as natural convection. On the other hand, vigorous fluid flow around an object, caused, for example, by moving air around the object with a fan, minimizes the resistance to heat transfer and results in an increased rate of heat transfer from the object. This type of situation is referred to as forced convection.

While internal properties of a food material are important in determining how well it heats or cools, a thin stagnant layer of the fluid surrounding the food material can have a dominant influence on heat transfer. Since the thickness of the boundary layer is influenced by a variety of factors, dimensional analysis is used to determine the magnitude of the convective heat transfer coefficient for a given situation. Usually, when the flow of fluid around an object is caused by some mechanical means, such as a fan, blower, or pump, the surface heat transfer coefficient is expressed by:

$$h = f(N_{Re}, N_{Pr}) , \tag{12}$$

where N_{Re} is Reynolds number and N_{Pr} is Prandtl number.

Both Reynolds number and Prandtl number are dimensionless. The Reynolds number is influenced by the viscous and inertial forces in the fluid surrounding the object, and the Prandtl Number contains various thermal properties of the fluid.

When there is no forced movement of fluid around the object, the surface heat transfer coefficient is computed from the following expression:

$$h = f(N_{Gr}, N_{Pr}) , \tag{13}$$

where N_{Gr} is the Grashoff number.

In equation 13, N_{Gr} contains necessary parameters that influence the buoyant movement of a fluid around an object. Functional relationships shown in equations 12 and 13 can be obtained from engineering handbooks and from Singh and Heldman (1993).

Table 2
Some Approximate Values of the Convective Heat-Transfer Coefficient[a]

Fluid	Convective Heat-Transfer Coefficient
Air	
Free convection	5–25
Forced convection	10–200
Water	
Free convection	20–100
Forced convection	50–10,000
Boiling water	3,000–100,000
Condensing water vapor	5,000–100,000

[a] Source: Singh and Heldman (1993); used by permission.

Radiative Heat Transfer

The third mode of heat transfer is radiation. It plays a significant role in the heating processes occurring inside an oven. Radiative heat transfer involves emission of heat from an object at high temperature such as a heating element inside the oven, and the absorption of heat by an object placed inside the oven such as a loaf of bread. The mathematical expression useful for calculating the rate of heat transfer due to radiation is given by the Stefan-Boltzmann law:

$$q = \sigma \varepsilon A T_A^{\ 4} \ , \tag{14}$$

where σ is the Stefan-Boltzmann constant (5.8779×10^{-8} W/m^2 K^4), ε is emmissivity, and T_A is absolute temperature (Kelvin).

Emmissivity values of common materials are listed in Table 3. The preceding discussion on steady-state heat transfer has provided a quantitative description of conductive, convective, and radiative modes of heat transfer. Next, we consider the unsteady-state heat transfer processes.

Table 3
Emissivity of Selected Materials[a]

	Wavelength (μm) and Temperatures (approximate)			
	9.3 (38°C)	5.4 (260°C)	3.6 (540°C)	1.8 (1,370°C)
Aluminum				
Polished	0.04	0.05	0.08	0.19
Oxidized	0.11	0.12	0.18	...
Iron				
Polished	0.06	0.08	0.13	0.25
Cast, oxidized	0.63	0.66	0.76	...
Galvanized, new	0.23	...	...	0.42
Galvanized, dirty	0.28	...	...	0.90
Steel plate, rough	0.94	0.97	0.98	...
Stainless steel				
18-8, polished	0.15	0.18	0.22	...
18-8, weathered	0.85	0.85	0.85	...
Brick				
Red	0.93	...	...	...
Fire clay	0.90	...	~0.70	~0.75
Enamel, white	0.90	...	...	...
Paints				
Aluminized lacquer	0.65	0.65	...	...
Lacquer, black	0.96	0.98	...	...
Red	0.96	...	...	...
Yellow	0.95	...	0.50	...
White	0.95	...	0.91	...
Ice, at 0°C	~0.97	...	...	...
Water	~0.96	...	...	...

[a] Adapted from Kreith (1973).

Unsteady-State Heat Transfer

During unsteady-state heat transfer, the temperature of an object changes with time and location. The mathematical analysis to solve for temperature becomes more complicated. The governing equation that describes the change in temperature is:

$$\frac{\partial T}{\partial t} = \alpha \frac{\partial^2 T}{\partial x^2} , \qquad (15)$$

where T is temperature (C), t is time (sec), x is location coordinate (m), and α is thermal diffusivity (m²/sec).

The solution of the preceding equation is mathematically complex. Charts and computer-aided spreadsheets have been developed for simple geometrical shapes that allow easy calculations. In order to calculate the temperature inside

	A	B	C	D	E	F	G	H	I
1									
2		SPHERE - Negligible Surface Resistance to Heat Transfer							
3		Temperature Ratio at the center of a sphere for a known Fourier Number							
4									
5		Domain: 0<r<D							
6									
7		**Example**				Terms of Series	=((-1^(E9+1))/E9*EXP(-		
8		Fourier Number =	0.3		n	term_n	E9*E9*PI()*PI()*C8)*SIN(E9*PI()*C9))		
9		r/D =	0.00001		1	1.62651E-06			
10		**Results**			2	-2.25721E-10			
11		Temperature Ratio =	0.104		3	8.39653E-17	Steps:		
12					4	-8.37219E-26			
13		=SUM(F9:F38)*2/PI()*(1/C9)			5	2.23764E-37			
14					6	-1.60306E-51	1) Enter numbers 1 through 30 in		
15					7	3.07839E-68	cells E9 through E38.		
16					8	-1.58455E-87			
17					9	2.1863E-109	2) Enter formula in cell F9, then		
18					10	-8.0855E-134	copy it into cells F10 to F38.		
19					11	8.0154E-161			
20					12	-2.1299E-190	3) Enter formula in cell C11.		
21					13	1.517E-222			
22					14	-2.8963E-257	4) Enter Fourier Number in cell C8		
23					15	1.4822E-294	and radial location/(Characteristic		
24					16	0	Dimension) in cell C9. For a sphere,		
25					17	0	characteristic dimension is radius.		
26					18	0			
27					19	0	If temperature ratio is desired at the		
28					20	0	center of the sphere, do not use r=0		
29					21	0	instead enter a very small number		
30					22	0	(e.g. 0.00001) for cell C9.		
31					23	0			
32					24	0	5) The result is shown in Cell C11.		
33					25	0			
34					26	0			
35					27	0			
36					28	0			
37					29	0			
38					30	0			

Fig. 8. Computer spread sheet to calculate center temperature in a sphere. (Reprinted, with permission, from Singh and Heldman, 1993)

a solid object, the mathematical analysis involves a ratio of temperatures and the Fourier number. The Fourier number, containing the time variable t, is given by:

$$N_{\text{Fo}} = \frac{\alpha t}{r^2} , \qquad (16)$$

where r is radius of the sphere.

The temperature ratio, $(T_a - T)/(T_a - T_i)$, is the unaccomplished temperature ratio, where T is temperature at any instant of time, T_i is the initial temperature, and T_a is the temperature of the surrounding medium. If there is resistance to heat transfer at the surface of the object, then the Biot number, N_{Bi}, must be known. It is determined as:

$$N_{\text{Bi}} = \frac{hr}{k} , \qquad (17)$$

The Biot number is a ratio between the amount of internal resistance to heat transfer and the resistance to heat transfer present at the surface of an object. The magnitude of the Biot number provides an indication of the location where the resistance to heat transfer is significant. For example, a Biot number smaller than 0.1 indicates that there is negligible resistance to heat transfer inside the object, whereas a Biot number greater than 40 signifies that there is negligible resistance to heat transfer at the surface of the object. A Biot number between 0.1 and 40 is indicative of finite resistance to heat transfer both inside the object and in the surrounding fluid.

The method used to determine temperature at any location within an object involves calculating the Fourier number and the Biot number. When the surface resistance to heat transfer is negligible, or the Biot number is greater than 40, then the spreadsheet shown in Figure 8 may be used to determine the temperature ratio. This spreadsheet is written in EXCEL. Similar spreadsheets for other geometrical shapes such as infinite cylinder or infinite slab are available (Singh and Heldman, 1993). As shown in Figure 8, a Fourier number of 0.3 gives a temperature ratio of 0.104.

Heat Transfer During Freezing of Foods

In describing the rate of heat transfer during a freezing process, we usually need to know how much heat must be removed and how much time is needed to remove the required amount of heat.

The freezing process involves removal of both sensible and latent heat. As latent heat is removed, the water present in the food changes into ice. In Figure 9, the enthalpy of two types of bread is shown at several temperatures normally encountered in the freezing range. The use of this graph can readily provide the heat content (or enthalpy) that must be removed to lower the temperature of a food to a desired temperature in the freezing range. For example, to lower the temperature of white bread from 0 to -18°C, we must remove 98 J/kg of product (from 137 J/kg to 39 J/kg). While this calculation is easily done, the time during which the heat is removed, another important calculation, is obtained from the following equation, referred to as Planck's equation.

$$t = \frac{\rho H_L}{T_F - T_a}\left(\frac{Pa}{h} + \frac{Ra^2}{k}\right),$$ (18)

where t = time for freezing (sec); ρ = density of food (kg/m³); H_L = latent heat of fusion, T_F = initial freezing temperature of the food, T_a = temperature of the surrounding medium, a = characteristic size, h = convective heat transfer coefficient (W/m²°C), and k = thermal conductivity of the material (W/m°C). The constants P and R are used to account for the influence of the product shape. For a sphere, $P = \frac{1}{6}$, $R = \frac{1}{24}$; for infinite plate, $P = \frac{1}{2}$, $R = \frac{1}{8}$; for infinite cylinder, $P = \frac{1}{4}$, $R = \frac{1}{16}$.

For more realistic geometrical shapes, computer methods have been developed to predict temperature in foods during freezing. These methods can be used to predict temperature with good accuracy (Singh and Mannapperuma, 1990), using desktop computers.

The material presented in this chapter is a brief overview of the selected principles of heat transfer that are important in heating and cooling of food materials. For more discussion on these and related topics, the reader is referred to textbooks such as Singh and Heldman (1993), Heldman and Lund (1992), Holman (1986), and Heldman and Singh (1981).

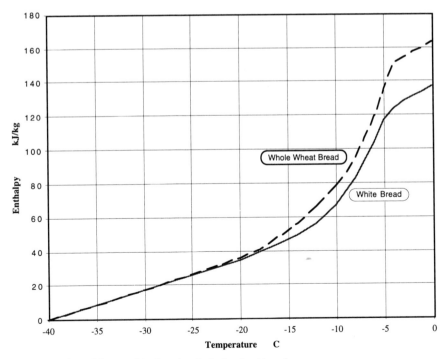

Fig. 9. Enthalpy of frozen white bread and whole wheat bread.

Literature Cited

Bakshi, A. S., and Yoon, J. 1984. Thermophysical properties of bread rolls during baking. Lebensm. Wiss. Technol. 17:90-93.

Griffith, C. L. 1985. Specific heat, thermal conductivity, density, and thermal conductivity of Mexican tortillas dough. J. Food Sci. 50:1333-1337.

Heldman, D. R. 1982. Food properties during freezing. Food Technol. 36(2):92.

Heldman, D. R. 1983. Factors affecting food freezing rates. Food Technol. 37(4):103-109.

Heldman D. R., and Gorby, D. P. 1975. Prediction of thermal conductivity in frozen food. Trans. ASAE 18:740.

Heldman, D. R., and Lund, D. B. 1992. Handbook of Food Engineering. Marcel Dekker, Inc., New York.

Heldman, D. R., and Singh, R. P. 1981. Food Process Engineering, 2nd ed. Van Nostrand Reinhold, New York.

Hill, J. E., Litman, J. D., and Sunderland, J. E. 1967. Thermal conductivity of various meats. Food Technol. 21:1143.

Holman, J. P. 1986. Heat Transfer, 6th ed. McGraw Hill Book Co., New York.

Hwang, M. P., and Hayakawa, K. I. 1979. A specific heat calorimeter for foods. J. Food Sci. 44:435-438, 448.

Johnsson, C., and Skjoldebrand, C. 1984. Thermal properties of bread during baking. Pages 333-342 in: Engineering of Food, Vol. 1. B. M. McKenna, ed. Elsevier Applied Science Publishers, London.

Kafiev, N. M., Lekhter, A. E., Leites, R. Y., Klokacheva, O. A., Panin, A. S., Ribakov, A. A., and Didenko, I. A. 1987. Thermophysical characteristics of certain bread dough improvers (in Russian). Maslo Zhir. Promst. 1:20-21. Cited in Rask (1989).

Kriems, P., and Reinhold, M. 1980. Das Backen von Mischbrot (VI)—Schlussfolgerungen zur Verbesserung des Backeffektes und der Brotqualität Zusammenfassung (in German). Bäcker Konditor 34:356-359. Cited in Rask (1989).

Krieth, F. 1973. Principles of Heat Transfer, 3rd ed. Harper and Row Publishers, New York.

Kulacki, F. A., and Kennedy, S. C. 1978. Measurement of the thermo-physical properties of common cookie dough. J. Food Sci. 43:380-384.

Lentz, C. P. 1961. Thermal conductivity of meats, fats, gelatin gels and ice. Food Technol. 15:243.

Lind, I. 1988. Thawing of minced meat and dough: Thermal data and mathematical modelling. In: Progress in Food Preservation Processes, Vol. 1. Center for Education and Research of Food and Chemical Industries (CERIA), Brussels.

Makljukow, I. I., and Makljukow, W. I. 1983. Thermophysikalische Charakteristika für das Backstück (in Russian). In: Industrieofen der Backwarenproduktion, Verlag Leicht und Lebensmittelindustrie, Moskow. Translated by H.-D. Tscheuschner; cited in Rask (1989).

Mannheim, H .C., Steinberg, M. P., Nelson, A. I., and Kendall, T. W. 1957. The heat content of bread. Food Technol. 7:384-388.

Metel, S. N., Mikrukov, V. V., and Kasparov, M. N. 1986. Thermophysical characteristics of yeast dough (in Russian). Izv. Vyssh. Uchebn. Zaved. Pishch. Tecknol. 4:107-108. Cited in Rask (1989).

Nebelung, M. 1979. Model der Wärmeübertragung in kontinuerlich und diskontinuer-licharbeitenden Kammeröfen unter Berücksichtigung von Wärmeleitung, Stofftransport und Reaktionen in einem feuchten kapillarporosen Körper (Backprozess). Ph.D. thesis, T.U., Dresden, DDR. Cited in Rask (1989).

Nesvadba P. 1982. Methods for measurement of thermal conductivity and diffusivity of foodstuffs. J. Food Eng. 1:93-113.

Neznanova, N. A., Panin, A. C., Puchova, L. L., and Skverchak, V. D. 1978. Thermophysical properties of dough and bread from grade I wheat flour during baking (in Russian). Khlebopek. Konditer. Promst. 8:13-14. Cited in Rask (1989).

Ohlsson, T. 1983. The measurement of thermal properties. In: Physical Properties of Foods, Vol.

1. R. Jowitt et al, ed. Applied Science Publishers, London.

Ordinanz, W. O. 1946. Specific heats of foods in cooking. Food Ind. 18(12):101.

Polak, M. 1984. Specific heat capacity of dough (in Czech). Mlyn. Pek. Prum. Tech. Skladovani Obili. 30(2):42-4. Cited in Rask (1989).

Rao, M. A., and Rizvi, S. S. H. 1994. Engineering Properties of Foods, 2nd ed. Marcel Dekker Inc., New York.

Rask, C. 1989. Thermal properties of dough and bakery products: A review of published data. J. Food Eng. 9(3):167-193.

Reidy, G. A. 1968. Thermal properties of foods and methods of their determination. M.S. thesis. Michigan State University, E. Lansing, MI.

Singh, R. P. 1993. Food Properties Database. CRC Press Inc., Boca Raton, FL.

Singh R. P., and Heldman, D. R. 1993. Introduction to Food Engineering. Academic Press, San Diego.

Singh R. P., and Mannapperuma, J. D. 1990. Developments in food freezing. Pages 309-358 in: Biotechnology and Food Process Engineering. H. Schwartzberg and A. Rao, eds. Marcel Dekker Inc., New York.

Standing, C. N. 1974. Individual heat transfer modes in band oven biscuit baking. J. Food Sci. 39:267-271.

Sweat, V. E. 1973. Experimental measurement of the thermal conductivity of a yellow cake. Pages 213-216 in: Proc. Int. Conf. on Thermal Conductivity, 13th.

Sweat, V. E. 1974. Experimental values of thermal conductivity of selected fruits and vegetables. J. Food Sci. 39:1080.

Sweat, V. E., and Haugh, C. G. 1974. A thermal conductivity probe for small food samples. Trans. ASAE 17(1):56-58.

Tadano, T. 1987. Thermal conductivity of white bread (in Japanese). Bull. Coll. Agric. Vet. Med. Nihon Univ. 44:18-22. Cited in Rask (1989).

Tichy, O. 1974. Matematick'y model sdileni tepla a hmoty pri peceni (in Czech). Potravin. Chladici Tech. 5(1):20-7. Cited in Rask (1989).

Tschubik, I. A., and Maslow, A. M. 1973. Wärmephysikalische Konstanten von Lebensmitteln und Halbfabrikaten (in German). VEB Fachbuchverlag, Leipzig, p. 28. Cited in Rask (1989).

Unklesbay, N, Unklesbay, K., Nahaisi, M., and Krause, G. 1981. Thermal conductivity of white bread during convective heat processing. J. Food Sci. 47:249-253, 259.

Appendix I
Nomenclature Used in This Chapter

Variable	Name
A	Area (m^2)
a	Characteristic size
α	Thermal diffusivity (m^2/sec)
c_p	Specific heat at constant pressure (kJ/kg°C)
c_{pdm}	Specific heat of dry matter (kJ/kg°C)
c_v	Specific heat at constant volume (J/kg°C)
c_w	Specific heat of water (J/kg°C)
ε	Emmissivity
h	Convective heat transfer coefficient, (W/m^2°C)
H_L	Latent heat of fusion
k	Thermal conductivity (W/m°C)
m	Mass fraction (with subscripts c = carbohydrate, p = protein, f = fat, a = ash, m = moisture)
N_{Bi}	Biot number
N_{Gr}	Grashoff number
N_{Pr}	Prandtl number
N_{Re}	Reynolds number
P	A constant used in equation 18
q	Rate of heat transfer (W)
R	A constant used in equation 18
r	Radius of the sphere
ρ	Density (kg/m^3)
σ	Stefan-Boltzmann constant, 5.8779×10^{-8} W/m^{2}K^4
t	Time (sec)
τ	Dimensionless time
T	Temperature (°C)
T_A	Temperature, absolute (K)
T_a	Temperature of the surrounding fluid (°C)
T_{mv}	Mean volume temperature (°C)
T_F	Initial freezing temperature of the food
T_s	Surface temperature of the solid object (°C)
X	Water content (%)
X_{wb}	Water content, wet basis (%)
x	Location coordinate (m)

Appendix II
Thermal Properties of Bread and Dough[a]

Product	Temperature (°C)	Moisture Content (%, wb)	Density (kg/m³)	Specific Heat (J/kgK)	Thermal Conductivity (W/mK)	Thermal Diffusivity (×10⁻⁸[m²/sec])	Reference
Dough	...	...	...	...	0.386	...	Bakshi and Yoon (1984)
Bread solids	...	...	...	1,130.44	0.309[b]	...	
Bread							
5 min	...	33.4[b]	202[b]	2,151.42[b]	0.085[b]	...	
10 min	...	26.9[b]	181[b]	1,951.77[b]	0.093[b]	...	
Bread							Johnsson and Skjöldebrand (1984)
Crumb	...	34[c]	...	...	...	40.7	
	30	41	...	2,560[b]	...	...	
	100	41	...	2,626[b]	...	...	
Crust	100	...	...	...	...	3.67[b]	
	150	0	...	1,656[b]	...	...	
Dough	35	...	...	1,500–1,900[d,e]	0.5–0.6[d]	...	Kafiev et al (1987)
Bread							Kriems and Reinhold (1980)
Rye/wheat							
100/0, 10 min	...	...	...	...	...	24	
40 min	...	...	430[d]	...	...	52[d]	
0/100, 10 min	...	...	...	...	...	43[d]	
40 min	...	...	290[d]	...	...	138	

							Reference
Dough	-43.5	43.5	1,100	1,760	0.920	47.8[b]	Lind (1988)
	-28.5	43.5	1,100	1,940	...	39.5[b]	
	-22.0	43.5	1,100	...	0.880	...	
	16.5	43.5	1,100	2,760	...	...	
	23.0	43.5	1,100	...	0.460	14.5[b]	
	-38	46.1	1,100	1,760	1.030	53.0	
	-28	46.1	1,100	1,880	...	...	
	-16	46.1	1,100	...	0.980	43.5[b]	
	19	46.1	1,100	...	0.500	16.3[b]	
	21	46.1	1,100	2,810	...	...	
Dough, wheat							Makljukow and Makljukow (1983)
Bread crumb	28	42	623	2,883	0.414	13.3–22.2	
Loaf	18	41.8	402	3,190	0.298	16–22.3	
Tin loaf	18	42.8	340	2,975	0.244	24.2	
Crust	120–160	0	300	1,470–1,680	0.066–0.43	2.68	
Bread solids	1–24	36.6	...	1,558	...	...	Mannheim et al (1957)
	<0	35.6–37.0	...	657	...	...	
Dough							Nebelung (1979)
Wheat	...	44.4[f]	750	2,800	0.5	23.75	
Rye	...	45.9[f]	820	3,000	0.6	24.34	
Crust							
Wheat	...	0	417	1,680	0.055	7.85	
Rye	...	0	443	1,680	0.055	7.39	
Crumb							
Wheat	...	44.4[f]	450	2,800	0.28	22.2	
					0.315[b]		
Rye	...	45.9[f]	500	3,000	0.37	24.7	
					0.356[b]		

Appendix II (continued)

Product	Temperature (°C)	Moisture Content (%, wb)	Density (kg/m³)	Specific Heat (J/kgK)	Thermal Conductivity (W/mK)	Thermal Diffusivity (× 10⁻⁸[m²/sec])	Reference
Dough	...	41.7	...	1,600[b,d]	0.6[d]	...	Neznanova et al (1978)
Dough	...	...	...	1,880–2,180	...	...	Ordinanz (1946)
Bread							
White	0–100	44–45	...	2,720–2,850	...	...	
Brown	0–100	48.5	...	2,850	...	...	
Dough							Polak (1984)
Dry	30	0	...	1,260[b]	...	...	
Wet	0–30	44.4[f]	...	2,516[b]	...	...	
Bread solids	3	...	...	...	0.361	...	Tadano (1987)
	24	...	...	...	0.378	...	
Bread, rye/wheat	...	46.7[f]	...	...	...	55.8	Tichy (1974)
Dough							Tschubik and Maslow (1973)
Wheat	...	44.8	586	2,801	0.314	19.16	
	...	45.1	629	2,805	0.327	19.16	
Rye	...	53.6	718	3,023	0.407	18.75	
	...	53.9	701	3,027	0.396	18.75	
Bread							
Loaf	...	42.5	545	2,742	0.248	16.66	
Tin loaf	...	45.0	500	2,805	0.232	...	
Crust							
Loaf	...	0	420	1,675	0.055	8.00	
Tin loaf	...	0	300	1,675	0.041	...	

Unklesbay et al (1981)

Bread, white						
8 min	...	...	307.3	...	0.72 ± 0.04	...
16 min	...	...	284.6	...	0.67 ± 0.02	...
24 min	...	...	275.1	...	0.66 ± 0.03	...
32 min	...	...	263.6	...	0.64 ± 0.02	...

[a] Source: Rask (1989); used by permission.
[b] Calculated.
[c] Added amount of water as percent of total weight.
[d] Estimated from diagram.
[e] Volumetric specific heat ($C_p\rho$).
[f] Calculated from moisture content on dry basis (%).

Appendix III
Thermal Properties of Bakery Products Other Than Bread[a]

Product	Temperature (°C)	Moisture Content (%, wb)	Density (kg/m³)	Specific Heat (J/kgK)	Thermal Conductivity (W/mK)	Thermal Diffusivity (×10⁻⁸[m²/sec])	Reference
Biscuit		3.15 [b]		1,875.7			Hwang and Hayakawa (1979)
		3.53 [b]		1,942.7			
		3.87 [b]		1,934.3			
Cracker		2.72 [b]		1,595.2			
		2.55 [b]		1,570.1			
Biscuit dough							Kulacki and Kennedy (1978)
AACC		4.1 [c]	1,252.3 ± 17.6	2,940 ± 170	0.405 ± 0.022	8–12	
Hard-sweet		8.5 [c]	1,286.6 ± 8.8	2,804 ± 380	0.390 ± 0.037	8–12	
Biscuit					0.07		Standing (1974)
					0.16		
Yellow cake							Sweat (1973)
Batter		41.5 [d]	693.5	2,950	0.233	10.9	
Edge, ¼ done		40 [d]	815 [d]		0.239	8.6	
Center, ¼ done		40 [d]	815 [d]		0.228	8.6	
Edge, ½ done		39 [d]	360 [d]		0.147	21.4	
Center, ½ done		39 [d]	290 [d]		0.195	16.1	
Edge, ¾ done		36.5 [d]	265 [d]		0.132	18.5	

Center, ¾ done	37.5 [d]	265 [d]			0.135	16.9	
Edge, done	34 [d]	285 [d]			0.119	15.0	
Center, done	35.5 [d]	300 [d]	2,800		0.121	14.3	
Tortilla dough	55, 65, 75	50, 55, 60	1,102–1,173	298–317	0.0366–0.1079	10.5–30.8	Griffith (1985)

[a] Source: Rask (1989); used by permission.
[b] Calculated from moisture content on dry basis (%).
[c] Added amount of water as percent of the total weight.
[d] Estimated from diagram.

CHAPTER 12

Cryogenic and Mechanical Food-Freezing Equipment for the Baking Industry

Jim M. Venetucci
Liquid Carbonic Industries Corporation
Chicago, Illinois 60629

Throughout history, people in all parts of the world have continually made efforts to develop new, successful techniques or processes to extend the length of time that food could be preserved while retaining its original quality.

Eating food raw or cooking it slightly over an open fire eventually gave way to the drying, salting, and pickling of food. In the late 1700s, the first canning process using containers was developed to help feed Napoleon's conquering army, which was on the move throughout the European continent. Pressure cooking became a reality in 1860, and in 1923 Clarence Birdseye developed the basic mechanical freezing system that enabled food to be preserved for long periods of time. This type of freezing system became widely accepted and was basically the only commercial method used for the next 30–40 years. The use of mechanical freezing equipment changed the method of food preservation and preparation to a high degree and contributed to the increase in the standard of living in the United States and other countries.

Cryogenic freezing, which takes place at temperatures substantially lower than mechanical freezing of foods, became a reality in the 1960s, and commercial freezers made their entry into food processing plants during that period of time. Companies that produce cryogenic, low-temperature gases established a defined cryogenic freezing program in early 1960. Although cryogenic freezing of foods is only half as old as mechanical freezing, the process has taken a firm and successful position in the industry because of the many benefits that it offers. More than a quarter of a century later, the industry continues to develop new, more effective, and highly efficient commercial freezing equipment.

Cryogenic freezing equipment has dramatically changed during the past 25–30 years, leading to increased performance and decreased operating costs. Freezers such as the vintage 1958 vibrating hooded conveyor seen in Figure 1 were used to freeze diced chicken and diced, whole, or sliced fruit such as berries, apples, and strawberries, using carbon dioxide snow that was injected into the hood of the freezer. It was a low-cost and effective freezing method for that time and allowed food processors who supplied such items to bakeries to introduce individually quick-frozen (IQF) fruit for bakery products.

The IQF method of freezing eliminated the use of a frozen "block" of fruit, which had to be thawed out before use and generally could not be refrozen if not completely used. Cryogenic freezing enabled the fruit or other product to

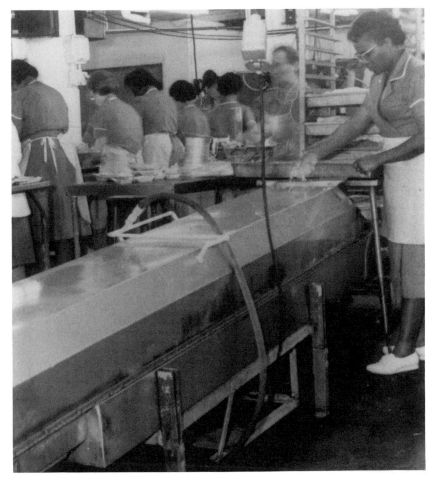

Fig. 1. Vibrating hooded conveyor from 1958. (Courtesy Liquid Carbonic Industries Corporation, Chicago, IL)

be quick-frozen in individual pieces that did not freeze together. IQF products could be used in the amount required and the excess placed back into storage for use at a later date. IQF became a tremendous convenience to the food processor.

In the early 1960s, the vacuum-insulated liquid-nitrogen freezing tunnel (Fig. 2) was introduced. This far exceeded the performance of the early vibrat-

Fig. 2. Vacuum-insulated liquid nitrogen freezing tunnel. (Courtesy Liquid Carbonic Industries Corporation, Chicago, IL)

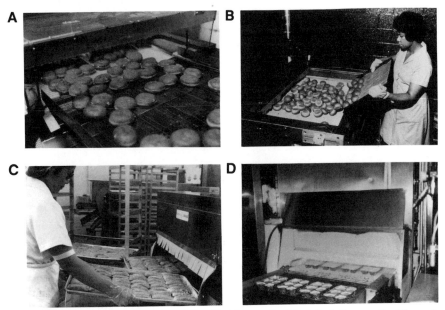

Fig. 3. Several bakery items such as jelly filled bismarcks (A), baked dinner rolls (B), apple-filled tarts (C), and raw blueberry muffin mix (D) being frozen in cryogenic freezers. (Courtesy Liquid Carbonic Industries Corporation, Chicago, IL)

ing conveyor for the efficient use of a cryogen for freezing, and it further improved the quality of the IQF food product because of the extremely low temperature of liquid nitrogen and the extremely short time that it took to freeze the food product.

Continuous design improvements produced systems that circulated the overflow of the cryogenic liquid and introduced blower systems and specially designed low-temperature modified control valves, all of which further improved cryogenic freezing equipment.

The use of cryogenics, both CO_2 (carbon dioxide) and LN_2 (liquid nitrogen), and the purchase of cryogenic freezers have shown a sizable and continued increase in the past few years and are expected to continue to grow in the United States and other countries throughout the world. This is a clear indication that cryogenics has become established as a alternative to mechanical freezing. It is used for freezing a variety of products, including bakery items (Fig. 3).

Cryogenic Freezing Equipment

The faster the temperature of a food product is reduced, the smaller the frozen crystal will be and less product damage will occur. Cryogenic freezing produces a relatively small frozen crystal (Fig. 4). Slow freezing; which occurs in a mechanical freezer, produces large crystals, and "weepage" of product occurs when the food is thawed (Fig. 5). Cryogenic freezing offers the fastest way to reduce the temperature of the food item while still maintaining the high initial quality.

Mechanical freezers generally have an operating temperature between -37.2 and -40°C. This is the temperature range used to freeze the food. Compared to the temperatures used in cryogenics, this "bottom out" temperature is not very cold. The cryogen CO_2, which is sometimes referred to as "dry ice," can produce a freezing temperature of -78.3°C, and LN_2 has a freezing temperature of -195.5°C.

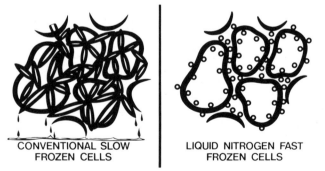

CONVENTIONAL SLOW FROZEN CELLS   LIQUID NITROGEN FAST FROZEN CELLS

Fig. 4. Model of frozen food cell structure. (Courtesy Liquid Carbonic Industries Corporation, Chicago, IL)

Cryogenic freezing is used in various types and sizes of freezing equipment, which enables processors to enter the frozen food market at any size level with a low capital investment and low risk factor. Generally, the smallest commercial type of cryogenic freezer available is a single- or double-door cabinet freezer (Fig. 6). A cart with trays is used to hold the food; the entire unit is placed into the cabinet; and a predetermined freezer cycle is set. A cryogen such as CO_2 or LN_2 is sprayed into the cabinet and, with the aid of high-capacity fans, the temperature of the cabinet quickly drops below the freezing

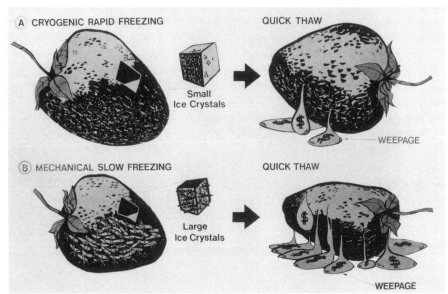

Fig. 5. Cryogenic and mechanical freezing. (Courtesy Liquid Carbonic Industries Corporation, Chicago, IL)

Fig. 6. Cabinet freezer. (Courtesy Liquid Carbonic Industries Corporation, Chicago, IL)

temperature. The food product is subjected to a "blizzard" condition, which quickly freezes the crust of the product. This is similar to encapsulating the food within a frozen enclosure, thereby reducing moisture loss and locking in the flavor until the product is completely frozen. This batch-type freezer is suitable for small production operations. As one batch is being frozen, a second batch is being prepared. It can generally be used in a small bakery or other small food processing plant.

For larger and continuous production, a straight-belt cryogenic freezing tunnel can be used (Fig. 7). This type of freezer is suitable for bread dough, cakes, cookies, pies, rolls, croissants, doughnuts, etc. The bakery product can be placed directly on the moving conveyor belt, where it then passes under a cryogenic spray and series of fans. Once again, a blizzard effect is created in the tunnel to freeze the product. The operating temperature of the tunnel, the fan speed, spray zone, etc., are critical and are different for various types of bakery products.

For large production rates for food items that can be tumbled, such as blueberries, strawberries, and sliced apples, a cryogenic flighted freezer can be used (Fig. 8). The flighted freezer is designed to "crust freeze" the product on a short horizontal belt at the freezer entrance. Then the product is allowed to pile up on the incline belts while it freezes solid. The product does not clump together and remains IQF. The incline belts move at a slower speed than the inlet belt. This allows the product to pile up, turn over, and continuously expose the surface to the extremely cold tunnel temperatures. This unique design results in a shorter freezer than a comparable straight-belt freezer. For the equivalent production rate, a straight-belt freezer would have to be more than twice the length of the flighted freezer.

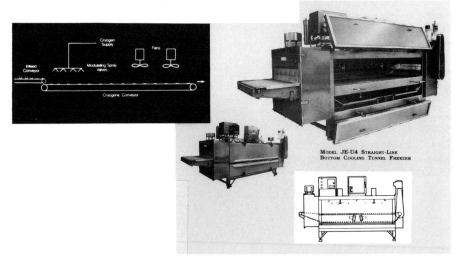

Fig. 7. Straight-line cryogenic freezing tunnel. (Courtesy Liquid Carbonic Industries Corporation, Chicago, IL)

The cryogenic immersion freezer is available for products that can be dropped directly into a pool of LN_2 (Fig. 9). This design, which takes full advantage of the extremely low -195.5°C liquid nitrogen temperature, is the fastest way to commercially freeze a food item. The immersion time is adjustable, and final freezing can be done in the downstream tunnel, if that is required. Although it may have limited use in the bakery industry, it is a method used for berries, diced and sliced fruit, etc.

As production rates increase, making cryogenic tunnels too long and not practical because of the required floor space, a spiral freezer can be used (Fig. 10). This is a large-capacity freezer that has a circular conveyor generally moving from the bottom to the top of the freezer. The cryogen is sprayed on the product at the inlet, as well as into the freezer area. This concept allows the product to be crust-frozen as soon as it enters the spiral, thereby minimizing

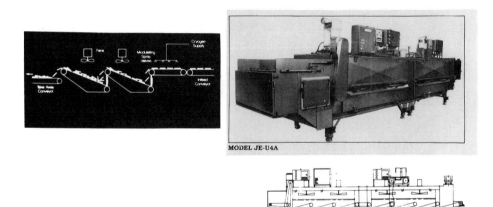

MODEL JE-U4A

Fig. 8. Flighted tunnel freezer. (Courtesy Liquid Carbonic Industries Corporation, Chicago, IL)

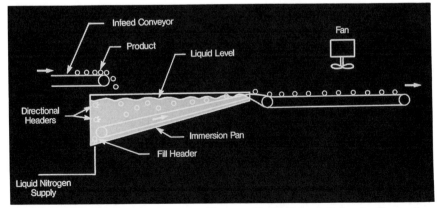

Fig. 9. Liquid nitrogen immersion operation. (Courtesy Liquid Carbonic Industries Corporation, Chicago, IL)

dehydration, and to continue to freeze as it travels through the remainder of the freezer, again in a "blizzard" type of atmosphere.

If a mechanical-type spiral freezer is "peaked out" in freezing capacity and bakery production must be increased, the use of a cryogenic freezing tunnel in front of the mechanical spiral is a possible and very low-cost solution to increasing the productivity of existing equipment (Fig. 11). The cryogenic freezing tunnel can be used to crust-freeze the product before it enters the mechanical freezer. Crust-freezing the product first substantially reduces dehydration loss and increases the efficiency and capacity of the existing mechanical freezer.

Advantages of Cryogenic Freezing

Numerous advantages are available when cryogenic, rather than mechanical, freezing is used (Table 1).

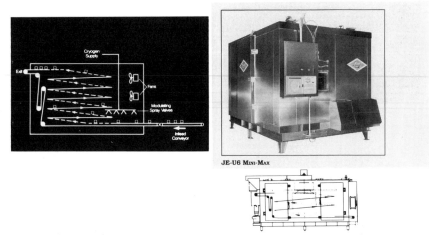

Fig. 10. Spiral freezer. (Courtesy Liquid Carbonic Industries Corporation, Chicago, IL)

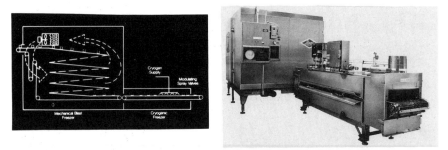

Fig. 11. Combined use of cryogenic and mechanical freezing. The cryogenic tunnel crust-freezes the product, thereby reducing dehydration, while the mechanical freezer continues the freezing process. (Courtesy Liquid Carbonic Industries Corporation, Chicago, IL)

Product dehydration. Dehyration is substantially less with cryogenics due to the quick crust-freezing of the product surface. The amount of the savings in U.S. dollars per pound can be quickly determined from Figure 12.

Cost savings. This savings of 2–3 cents (U.S. dollars) per pound easily offsets part of the cost of the cryogen.

Freezing costs. Initial comparison may indicate a higher cryogen freezing cost. However, larger floor space and high investment cost for the mechanical system tends to reduce the cost difference between the two systems.

Flavor. No change or loss in flavor occurs in a cryogenically frozen product due to the instantaneous freezing of the crust.

Quality. Cryogenic freezing retains the original high quality of the product, which is especially important in cooked entrees.

Shelf life. The shelf life is frequently increased because of the rapid drop in product temperature, which decreases growth of bacteria.

Convenience. Short cryogenic freezing tunnels can be made portable and quickly moved from one processing line to another during the working day, making it an extremely versatile freezer.

Operating power costs. Cryogenic freezers have only a few motors, which require low horse power and very little electrical power. Mechanical freezers, in contrast, require motors with high horse power and substantial electrical power to operate comparable systems.

Risk factors. Very low risk is involved with cryogenic freezers, which are compact, lower in cost and easily removed and have excellent resale value.

Quick installations. Tunnels are shipped assembled in one piece and in-

Table 1
Comparison of Freezing Systems[a]

	Cryogenic	Mechanical
Product dehydration	0.25–0.5%	2–10%
Cost savings	2–3¢/lb (U.S. $)	3–5 ¢/lb (U.S. $)
Freezing costs	3–6¢/lb (U.S. $)	Avg. 1¢/lb (U.S. $) + floor space and high investment cost
Flavor	No change	Loss on surface
Quality	Same as original	Lower
Shelf life	Frequently increased	No change
Convenience	High	Low
Operating power costs	Very low	High
Risk factor	Very low	High
Quick installation	Yes	No
Turn-up capability	Yes	No
Low operating temperature	-195.5°C	-37.2/-40°C
Defrost downtime	None	Required

[a] Courtesy Liquid Carbonic Industries Corporation, Chicago, IL.

stalled overnight. Spirals are also shipped, assembled, and installed over a weekend. The cryogenic system is very simple (Fig. 13), whereas the mechanical system requires extensive piping, controls, auxiliary equipment, and usually a separate room for the large compressors, etc. (Fig. 14).

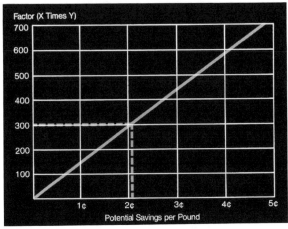

Fig. 12. Shrinkage savings potential, showing saving in U.S. dollars. X = blast freezer shrink loss in percent, Y = product value in cents per pound. Example: if X = 4% and Y = 75 cents per pound, the factor = 4 × 75 = 300. Potential savings is 2.1 cents per pound. (Courtesy Liquid Carbonic Industries Corporation, Chicago, IL)

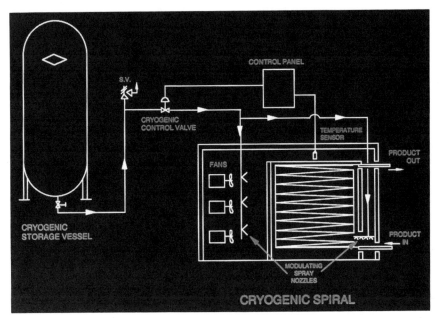

Fig. 13. Basic diagram of cryogenic freezing. (Courtesy Liquid Carbonic Industries Corporation, Chicago, IL)

Turn-up capability. It is very easy and simple to turn up the freezing capacity of a cryogenic freezer by lowering the operating temperature setpoint when an increase in output capacity is required. Lowering the temperature of the cryogenic freezer increases the cost but can achieve an increase in production within minutes.

Lower temperature. Cryogenics can provide the user with freezing temperatures as low as -195.5°C if and when that is needed. However, average cryogenic freezing equipment temperatures are between -62.2 and -101.1°C, which is far colder than any mechanical system.

Defrost downtime. No downtime is experienced in a cryogenic freezer to defrost the ice buildup on the coil because no coil exists and there is no wet ice buildup in the freezer. Defrost downtime can be a very high cost factor in many plants. Also, a large portion of the ice buildup on the coil is moisture that has been removed from the product.

Since each product and formulation is different for each processor, some cryogenic freezer manufactures provide in-depth studies, laboratory testing, and freezing sizings for individual food products.

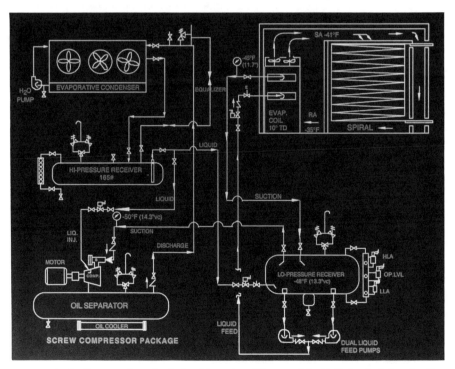

Fig. 14. Basic diagram of mechanical refrigeration. (Courtesy Liquid Carbonic Industries Corporation, Chicago, IL)

Mechanical Freezing

Simple Basic Refrigeration System

Refrigeration means to make something "cold." We can cool food by placing it near something that is colder or in a box that is colder than the food. Heat always travels from a warm or hot object to a colder object. This change is called heat transfer. For years, people used "ice" boxes, which had a block of ice as the cold object. Heat from warm food placed into the box flowed to the block of ice, thereby melting the ice and simultaneous cooling the food. With the advent of commercial refrigerators, the "box" temperatures could be controlled and reduced if required.

The basic mechanical refrigeration principle on which the modern home refrigerator and freezer work is shown in Figure 15.

The transformation of a liquid into a gas or vapor absorbs heat and cools whatever is around it. A refrigerator or freezer contains tubes or hollow plates filled with a liquid. This liquid, the refrigerant, can be a fluorocarbon gas such as freon gas, ammonia, or carbon dioxide. Each has different properties and "boiling" temperatures. Regardless of the gas used, it flows into the tubes or plates in the freezer while under a lower pressure. The low-pressure liquid quickly changes into a gas; that is, it "boils," while in the tubes or plates and absorbs heat from the food inside the freezer chamber.

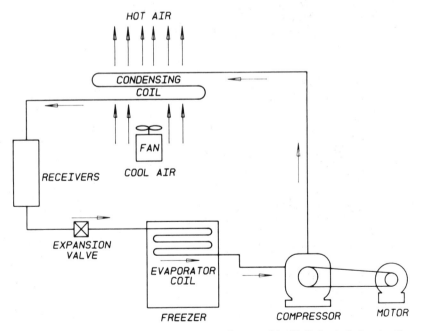

Fig. 15. Simple mechanical refrigeration system. (Courtesy Liquid Carbonic Industries Corporation, Chicago, IL)

The vapor or gas is then drawn from the freezer coil by a compressor, which is like a pump driven by a motor. The compressor forces the vapor into a "condenser," a bundle of tubes normally exposed to open air. As the vapor passes through the tubes, it is cooled by the air and changes back into a liquid again. As a liquid it is now slowly sent back into the tubing located in the freezer, which can now be called an evaporator. Here it once again vaporizes to a gas and repeats its cycle. This operation continues as long as the motor and compressor run.

A thermostat in the freezer is used to maintain the freezer. The thermostat automatically starts and stops the motor and compressor, which, in turn, keeps the freezer at the correct preset temperature.

Frost that collects on the surface of the evaporator coils in the freezer acts as an insulator and reduces the efficiency of the system, preventing proper freezing. The evaporator coils must be defrosted to remove the ice buildup, which returns the system to its peak operating condition. On some large commercial-sized freezers, the defrost cycle can be needed several times a day. A large amount of lost production time can result from downtime caused by defrost cycles.

Airflow

A simple but extremely important factor in effective heat removal in a freezer is the effect that airflow around the food item has on the rate at which the heat transfer takes place. The faster the cold air moves, the faster the surface temperature of the food drops until the rate of heat being transferred eventually reaches its maximum. As an everyday example, if a person stands outside on a cold winter day, he or she is colder when the wind blows than when no wind is blowing, and becomes even colder when the wind is at blizzard conditions, even if the outside temperature is the same in each situation. This is sometimes referred to as wind chill. Therefore, the velocity of the air in a freezer has a definite effect on the rate of freezing.

Usually, high fan velocity produces the most efficient freezing. However, a low fan velocity may be necessary for some food such as bakery products, for which it may be desirable to have a slower freeze to prevent the killing of yeast. Preventing the killing of the yeast is directly related to the rate of freezing for some bakery products.

Standard Mechanical Freezing Equipment

There are several advantages in a "standard" mechanical system and conversely there are some disadvantages.

The advantages include the fact that this system:
- Is a widely accepted, proven system.
- Operates similarly to a household refrigerator or freezer.
- Consists of a simple enclosure, compressors, and evaporative and cooling coils.

- Uses fluorocarbon or ammonia gas as the refrigerant.
- Has operating temperatures of -37.2° to -40°C.
- Needs only turnkey installation.
- Has high production capacity.

Among the disadvantages are its:

- High initial cost.
- High electrical energy costs.
- Fixed maximum freezing capacity.
- Potentially high dehydration of food.
- Dedicated floor space.
- Fixed low temperature and production rate.
- Need for a defrost cycle.
- Use of fluorocarbon, which is being phased out due to environmental regulation.
- Usual need for a separate room for the large compressor.
- High potential maintenance factor.

Airflow Design

Currently two types of airflow are being used and several modifications of the two basic types, which are horizontal and vertical.

Horizontal airflow simply means that the cold air is moved horizontally across (parallel to) the surface of the food product. This method is illustrated in Figure 16, which shows the air movement in a commercial spiral freezer. Air passes horizontally through the conveyor belt tiers, removing surface heat from the food on the conveyor belt. It then passes across the evaporator coil located in the spiral freezer and transfers the heat to the refrigerant in the coil, which then goes through the compressor cycle.

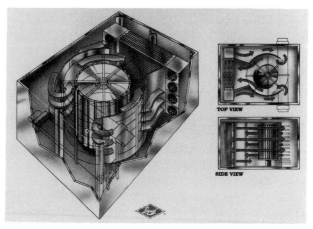

Fig. 16. Horizontal airflow design of a mechanical freezer. (Courtesy Liquid Carbonic Industries Corporation, Chicago, IL)

The same phenomenon occurs in the vertical airflow design. However, cold air is directed vertically downward through the spiral conveyor (Fig. 17). Once again, the air flows across the evaporator coil, transferring heat to the coil refrigerant, which becomes cold, and then recirculates over the food product, eventually freezing the item.

Turbo freeze airflow design, as illustrated in Figure 18, improves the performance of a freezer. This design uses the coldest air at the inlet of the freezer, where the incoming product is the warmest, thereby obtaining a high heat removal rate and improved performance. The flow of air is upward through the center of the freezer, passing the top plenum and flowing outward as well as downward through the evaporator coil and horizontally across the food product

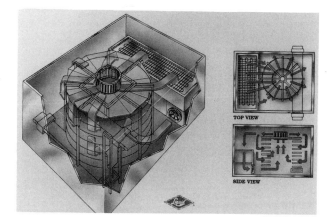

Fig. 17. Vertical airflow design of a mechanical freezer. (Courtesy Liquid Carbonic Industries Corporation, Chicago, IL)

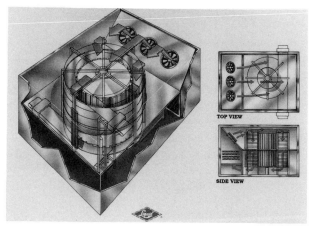

Fig. 18. Turbo-freeze airflow design of a mechanical freezer. (Courtesy Liquid Carbonic Industries Corporation, Chicago, IL)

on the conveyor belt. Several benefits can be achieved with this type of air-flow:

- The operating cost is between those of the horizontal and vertical air-flow designs.
- Energy cost is between those of the horizontal and vertical design air-flow designs.
- Dehydration is reduced.
- The evaporative coil performance is improved.
- Airflow over the food products is independent of the coil.
- It has good cleanability and accessibility.

Subcooled CO_2/Mechanical Freezing

A recently innovated patented method that shows promise and is available for commercial use is the combined use of CO_2 and the available fluorocarbon or ammonia refrigerants.

This system uses low-temperature liquid CO_2 in a closed loop to produce colder freezer temperatures than are otherwise available. Freezers with lower temperatures are able to freeze the food faster, thereby increasing production rates while decreasing dehydration of the product. Freezer temperatures in the range of -48°C are now attainable with this new system.

There are several benefits available from this freeze, which:

- Has lower (-48°C) freezer operating temperature.
- Is 10–15°C colder than ammonia.
- Has a higher heat transfer rate.
- Uses a smaller-size pressure piping system in place of large-size vacuum piping.
- Can use a smaller evaporative coil.
- Does not require fluorocarbons or ammonia to be used in the work area.
- Has a closed CO_2 loop system.

Figure 19 illustrates how the system works. Cold liquid CO_2 at -53.8°C is pumped from the CO_2 receiver to the in-plant refrigeration heat exchanger. After passing through the heat exchanger, the CO_2, now a mixture of liquid and vapor, returns to the CO_2 receiver. CO_2 vapor is drawn off the top of the receiver to a compressor, then through an ammonia-fluorocarbon heat exchanger, where the vapor CO_2 is condensed to a liquid and returned to the CO_2 receiver. Using a refrigerant loop, the heat picked up by the ammonia-fluorocarbon in the CO_2 heat exchanger creates a vapor, which is compressed and condensed in a normal evaporative condenser. This refrigerant loop can be handled by the in-plant refrigeration system, if it has excess capacity.

SECO$_2$ Freezing System

Another patented freezing method is available as a commercial freezing method. "SECO$_2$" is the trademark for the "Stored Energy Carbon Dioxide" system, which is designed to substantially reduce energy cost while providing a -53.8°C freezing temperature in the enclosure.

Reduced chiller capacity. The chiller can be sized for the average instead of the peak load, reducing new chiller capacity requirements or increasing the effective output of existing chillers.

Reduced electric costs. On-peak kWhr electric charges and on-peak kW demand charges are reduced by a smaller chiller shifting the load to off-peak hours. Compressors operate at the high-efficiency full-load condition, minimizing power consumption per ton of refrigeration.

High cooling rates. Rapid-burst or spot cooling can be provided to handle peaks or occasional loads using the efficient, direct-contact, $SECO_2$ heat transfer.

Backup refrigeration. The stored -56.6°C CO_2 liquid can be used as an expendable refrigerant for backup refrigeration or for additional burst-cooling. Replacement CO_2 is easily and economically obtained from carbon dioxide suppliers.

Simple operation. Thermal storage is provided in one simple, compact vessel that contains no moving parts. The entire system operates under positive pressure, eliminating vacuum problems. Conventional refrigeration system controls are used.

High reliability. Chiller maintenance is reduced and reliability is improved due to uniform full-load compressor operation. Conventional vapor compression equipment with proven reliability is selected to match the optimized operating loads.

Inherent safety. CO_2 is a colorless, odorless, nontoxic, noncorrosive, nonabrasive, nonexplosive, nonflammable, naturally occurring compound used

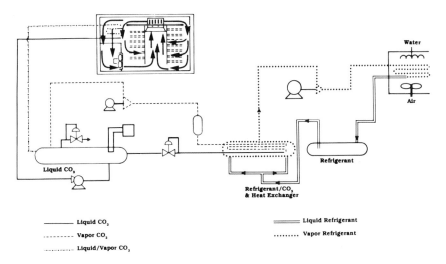

Fig. 19. The sub-cooled CO_2 system. (Courtesy Liquid Carbonic Industries Corporation, Chicago, IL)

throughout the world for many applications such as direct-contact food freezing and beverage carbonation.

Figure 20 shows how the $SECO_2$ system works. It is a low-temperature thermal storage system that uses the latent heat of CO_2 (21,411 I.T. Cal. [84 BTU/lb]) at its triple point. The triple point is the unique thermodynamic state at which solid, liquid, and vapor all coexist, occurring at -56.6°C and 4.08 atm.

$SECO_2$ storage differs from conventional CO_2 liquid storage at -28.8°C or solid dry ice storage at -78.3°C. In the $SECO_2$ system, solid CO_2 is formed with a conventional cascade chiller and is accumulated in a storage vessel that initially contained all liquid. The chiller, operating at full load, draws CO_2 vapor directly from the vessel vapor space as the low-stage refrigerant. Ammonia or freon is used as the high-stage refrigerant. Cooling is supplied from the vessel on demand by circulating CO_2 liquid from the vessel through a process heat exchanger. The vaporized CO_2 returns to the vessel and condenses directly against the solid/liquid slush, thereby melting the solid.

During the freezing of food items, low-temperature CO_2 is withdrawn from the storage vessel and passes through the evaporator coil in the freezer, where the heat of the product is transferred to the CO_2. This changes the CO_2 to a two-phase warmer combination of liquid and gas, which is then returned to the storage vessel. The cycle of refrigerating the contents of the storage vessel is repeated during the off-peak power period.

Consideration must be given to the volume of triple point CO_2 stored in the vessel. The storage volume must be adequate to supply the entire refrigeration required by the freezer during the period when the compressors do not operate. Generally speaking, the compressors would operate at night, producing enough triple point CO_2 to be used during the following day.

However, if plant conditions dictate that more triple point CO_2 is needed during the day, the compressor can be operated. The cost of the operation would then be based on the higher electrical power rate cost.

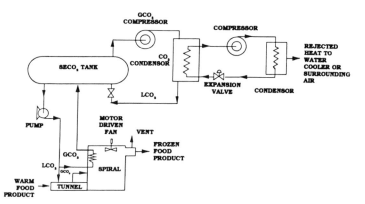

Fig. 20. The $SECO_2$ system. (Courtesy Liquid Carbonic Industries Corporation, Chicago, IL)

Table 2
Freezer Systems Comparisons

	Cryogenic	Mechanical	Duo System	Sub-Cooled CO_2	$SECO_2$
Auxiliary equipment	Cryogenic storage vessel	Refrigeration system	Refrigeration system and cryogenic vessel	Refrigeration system	Large storage vessel
Electrical power	Extremely low	High	Moderate	High	Moderate
Maintenance	Very low	Moderate	Moderate	Moderate	Moderate
Installation time	Days	Weeks	Weeks	Weeks	Weeks
Moisture loss	Extremely low	High to moderate	Low	Moderate	Moderate
Production rate	Variable	Fixed	Variable	Fixed	Fixed
Initial cost	Low	Moderate	Moderate	Moderate	High
Turn-up capabilities	High	None	Moderate	None	None
Dwell time	Very short	Long	Short	Moderate	Moderate
Monthly operating costs	Moderate	Moderate	Moderate	Moderate	Low
Capital	Low	High	High	High	Very high

Comparison of Freezing Systems

Before freezing equipment is selected, it is beneficial to compare each type of system available and evaluate its use for the products to be frozen. Based on several factors, one freezing process may provide advantages not available with other systems. Table 2 compares freezer systems. This comparison is a guide, and a complete study should be made to assure the processor of the correct selection of equipment. A list of manufacturers of freezing equipment, both cyrogenic and mechanical, is given in the Appendix.

Appendix
Manufacturers of Freezing Equipment

Names and Addresses	Air Blast Tunnel (A)	Belt/ Contact (B)	CO$_2$ (C)	Fluid- ized Bed (F)	Immer- sion (I)	Nitro- gen (N)	Plate (P)	Spiral (S)
AGA Gas, Inc. P.O. Box 94737 Cleveland, OH 44101 216/642-6600								
Air Products & Chemicals, Inc. 7201 Hamilton Blvd. Allentown, PA 18195-1501 215/481-4911	X	X			X			X
Alard Equipment Corp. 6483 Lake Ave., Box 57 Williamson, NY 14589 201/812-1066	X			X			X	X
Alamo Refrigeration Corp. P.O. Box 12370 San Antonio, TX 78212	X			X			X	X
American Cryogas Ind. 1695 Hylton Rd. Pennsauken, NJ 08110 609/486-1117			X			X		X
APV CREPACO, Inc. 9525 W. Bryn Mawr Ave. Rosemont, IL 60018	X						X	
Bakery Machinery Dist., Inc. 1365 Lakeland Ave. Bohemia, NY 11716 516/567-2222								X
Barliant & Co. 4701 W. Augusta Blvd. Chicago, IL 60651 312/378-7090			X	X			X	X
Barr Equipment Co. Inc. 7701 County Road FF Pickett, WI 54964 414/589-2721	X							
The BOC Group, Inc. 575 Mountain Ave. Murray Hill, NJ 07974 08/771-1375			X	X				X

(continued)

Names and Addresses	A	B	C	F	I	N	P	S
Cardox Div. Liquid Air Corp. 2121 N. California Blvd. Walnut Creek, CA 94596 510/977-6500		X	X	X		X		X
The Cardwell Machine Co. Box 34588 Richmond, VA 23234 804/275-1471	X	X						X
Cloudy & Britton Inc. 6202 214th SW Mountlake Terrace, WA 98043 206/775-7424	X	X					X	X
Esquire Gas Products Co. 156 Spring St., Box 281 Enfield, CT 06083 203/745-2477			X					
Freestech International Ltd. Box 1657 Lancaster, PA 17603 717/569-8251	X	X						X
Freezing Systems Inc. 17625 130th Ave. NE, #101 Woodinville, WA 98072 206/486-8852	X	X						X
Frigoscandia Food Process System Box 3984 Bellevue, WA 98009 206/883-2244	X	X		X		X	X	X
Fujitetsumo U.S.A., Inc. Box 1238 Lodi, CA 95241 209/339-9317		X	X			X		X
Gram Equipment of America 1212 N. 39th St., Suite 438 Tampa, FL 33605 813/248-1978	X	X					X	X
Greerco Corp. (A) Executive Dr., Box 187 Hudson, NH 03051	X							
Howe Corp. 1650 N. Elston Ave. Chicago, IL 60622 312/235-0200	X							

(continued)

Names and Addresses	A	B	C	F	I	N	P	S
O.G. Hoyer Inc. 201 Broad St. Lake Geneva, WI 53147 414/248-8950	X	X	X					
O.G. Hoyer Inc. Packaging Div. 1104 Industrial Blvd. Albion, MI 49224 517/629-2166	X							
InTec Inc. 6631-J Commerce Pkwy. Dublin, OH 43017 614/792-5833	X							
Kelly Trailer & Container Inc. Box 1132 West Springfield, MA 01090 413/788-0917	X							
King Air Systems Box 287 Owatonna, MN 55060 507/455-7400	X							
The King Co. 1001 NW 21st Ave. Owatonna, MN 55060 507/451-3770	X							
Koach Engineering & Mfg. Inc. 8950 Glenoaks Blvd. Sun Valley, CA 91352 818/768-0222	X	X	X		X	X		X
Koppens Machinefabriek B V P.O. Box 1 Bakel 5760 AA Holland 09/31-4924-2530								X
Krack Corp. 401 S. Rohlwing Road Addison, IL 60101 708/629-7500	X							
T. W. Kutter Inc. Alfa-Laval 91 Wales Ave., Box 358 Avon, MA 02322 508/588-2600								X
Liquid Air/Cardox 2121 N. California Blvd. Walnut Creek, CA 94596 510/977-6576			X		X	X		

(continued)

Names and Addresses	A	B	C	F	I	N	P	S
Liquid Carbonic Industries 810 Jorie Blvd. Oak Brook, IL 60521-2216 708/572-7500	X	X	X			X		X
Master Bilt Products Hwy. 15 N. New Albany, MS 38652 601/534-9061	X							
McCormack Mfg. Company, Box 1727 Lake Oswego, OR 97035 503/639-2137		X						x
MPBS Industries, Meat Packers & Butchers Supply Co. Philadelphia, PA 19136 2820 E. Washington Blvd. Los Angeles, CA 90023								X
Niagara Blower Co. 673 Ontario St., Box 67 Buffalo, NY 14207-0067	X							
Northfield Freezing System Inc. 1325 Armstrong Rd., Box 98 Northfield, MN 55057 507/645-9548								
Nova & Company 64 Main Street Gloucester, MA 01930 617/281-1222	X							
Odenberg, Inc. 6890 Luther Dr. Ste. E Sacramento, CA 95823 916/422-8396	X							X
PRAXAIR Linde Division 777 Old Sawmill River Rd. Tarrytown, NY 10591-6799 914/789-3353						X		X
Production Line Equipment 21 Pine St., Box 392 Rockaway, NJ 07866 708/629-7500		X						X
Pulver Systems, Inc. 10255 S. Ridgeland Ave. Chicago Ridge, IL 60415 708/424-2500								X

(continued)

Names and Addresses	A	B	C	F	I	N	P	S
Refrigeration Engineering Corp. Box 3C San Antonio, TX 78217	X			X			X	X
Refrigeration Systems Co. 1770 Genessee Ave. Columbus, OH 43211	X			X			X	X
RF-Custombilt Machinery & Conveying Ltd. 3947 Graveley St. Burnaby, BC, Canada V5C 3T4								X
Ross Industries Inc. Rt. 610 Midland, VA 22728-0070 800/336-6010	X							
Sandvik Process System Inc. Food Processing Div. 409 Minnisink Rd. Totowa, NJ 07512 201/812-1066	X	X						
SFB Plastics Box 533 Wichita, KS 67201 800/343-8133	X							
W. C. Smith Inc. 4773 Tolbut St. Philadelphia, PA 19136 215/624-3200						X	X	X
Standard Metal Products 1559 St. Paul Ave., Box 67 Gurnee, IL 60031 708/249-8900								X
The Stellar Group 2900 Hartley Rd. Jacksonville, FL 32257 904/260-2900	X							
Thrune Corp./Peerless Metals 8585 S. 77th Ave. Bridgeview, IL 60455 708/598-0100			X			X		
Tippmann Construction Inc. 3711 Rupp Dr. Fort Wayne, IN 46815 219/482-2519	X							

(continued)

Names and Addresses	A	B	C	F	I	N	P	S
Victory, A Div. of Hussmann Foodservice Co. P.O. Box 507 Cherry Hill, NJ 08003			X			X		
Vilter Export Corp. 2217 S. 1st St. Milwaukee, WI 53207 414/744-0111	X							
Vilter Manufacturing 2217 S. 1st St. Milwaukee, WI 532 414/744-0111	X							
I. J. White Corp. 20 Executive Blvd. Farmingdale, NY 11735 516/293-2211						X		X
WSE, Inc., Cryo-genic/Carbonic Craftsmen Co. Div., Western Springs Engrg. (CR) Box 471 LaGrange, IL 60525			X			X		
York Food System 361 NE Gilman Blvd., Ste. B Issaquah, WA 98027 206/391-5600	X	X		X				X

CHAPTER 13

Packaging Materials for Frozen and Refrigerated Doughs

E. Varriano-Marston

E. V. Marston & Associates
Windham, NH 03087

Selecting packaging materials for frozen and refrigerated doughs involves considering packaging material barrier properties, mechanical and physical properties, and cost. The goal is to maximize product quality and shelf life while minimizing costs. Package eye appeal and other aesthetic characteristics determine the product's potential sales and can affect packaging costs.

Unlike breads and other heat-processed bakery foods, frozen and refrigerated doughs are active biochemical systems. The enzymes in flour cells carry out biochemical reactions that alter the pH, produce browning pigments, and generate gas, water, and other metabolites. In addition, microorganisms, either natural or added, contribute their own by-products of biochemical reactions, including acid and gas. In the case of fermenting doughs, living yeasts produce CO_2 and other fermentation products that affect quality and shelf life and could compromise package integrity.

To match packaging materials to product requirements for frozen and refrigerated doughs, an analysis of product and package requirements is needed, followed by empirical studies to determine the effects of packaging materials on product quality.

What Are the Requirements?

Product Requirements

The first step in the selection of packaging materials for frozen or refrigerated doughs is to do an analysis of the product. A list of criteria is developed by asking the following questions:

- What type of product is it? Is it chemically leavened or yeast-leavened?

• What is the viscosity of the product, and will that dictate the package selection?

• What are the ingredients that limit shelf life? Fat? Moisture? O_2? Viable yeast cells? What are the product limits for relative humidity? Does light affect its quality?

• What are the storage requirements in terms of temperature, relative humidity, storage time, O_2, absence of light?

• How much shelf life is needed to make the product commercially viable?

Package Requirements

Packaging limitations are determined by answers to the following questions:

• What physical form will the package take? Bulk or single serve? Rigid or flexible container?

• What aesthetic properties are needed? Opaque or clear container? High-resolution graphics?

• What special features are necessary? Microwavability? Minimal flavor scalping and no odor transfer into the product? Direct or indirect food contact, as defined by the Food and Drug Administration (FDA)? Does the food need to be packed in a modified atmosphere?

• Are high barrier materials required? Must the materials be recyclable? What are the cost considerations?

• What temperature will be used to store and distribute the product?

• Can existing packaging equipment be used or must a new equipment investment be made?

Material Selection Affects Product Quality

The packaging goals for frozen and refrigerated doughs center on preventing moisture loss, oxidative changes, and microbial growth in the product during storage. To attain these goals, packaging materials that limit O_2 ingress and water vapor egress from the package are selected. In addition, materials with good mechanical properties are needed to survive the rigors of the distribution system.

Gas Transmission Rates

Technically, all plastic packaging materials can be considered breathable. That is, they do not completely prevent gases in the atmosphere from penetrating their walls. The range of gas transmission rates for films is large (Table 1). The barrier properties needed for a product are dependent on the effects of moisture loss or O_2 level on shelf life.

When selecting packaging materials, we must understand that the gas composition inside a package is a function of both product and package characteristics. The composition of the atmosphere inside the package during storage is determined by:

- the initial atmosphere inside the package,
- the biochemical activity of the food inside the package,
- the film gas transmission rates (O_2, CO_2, and water vapor),
- the package surface area, and
- the storage temperature.

As with all active biochemical systems, the rates at which these biochemical reactions occur are dependent on storage temperature. As a general rule, for every 10 degree C (18 degree F) rise in storage temperature there is a two- to threefold increase in reaction rates. Therefore, packaging materials selected for storing doughs and batters at 4°C (39°C) often will be different from those used to store them at 0°C (32°F) or below, and it is important to select packaging materials based on storage temperature.

Once the appropriate film gas transmission rates have been selected for a specific item, weight, and storage temperature, it is a simple task to determine what gas transmission rates are needed for smaller or larger weights of that product. Package surface area is a key variable, as it affects the barrier properties of the packaging materials. High ratios of package surface area to product volume mean greater gas transmission rates and less barrier protection. This implies that smaller packages often require better barrier materials than larger packages.

Mechanical and Physical Properties of Film

Although gas transmission rates are very important factors in packaging material selection, mechanical and physical properties of materials also must be

Table 1
Oxygen Transmission Rates (O_2TR) and Water Vapor
Transmission Rates (WVTR) of Plastic Films

Material	O_2TR at 23°C, 0% RH (cm³/mil/100 in²-day-atm)[a]	WVTR at 38°C, 90% RH (g/100 in²-day)[b]
EVOH (ethylene vinyl alcohol)	0.01–0.09[c]	1.4–3.8
Nylon 6	5[c]	13
PET (polyethylene terephthalate)	2.3	1.2
OPP (oriented polypropylene)	160	0.4
PVDC (polyvinylidene chloride)	0.2	0.2
PVDC/OPP	0.7	0.3
HDPE (high-density PE)	140	0.4–0.5
LDPE (low-density PE)	460	1.0–1.6
EVA (ethylene vinyl acetate)	780	7–10
Metallized 80 ga OPP	3.4	0.1
Metallized 125 ga LDPE	17	0.3

[a] To convert cm³/mil/100 in² to cm³/m₂, multiply by 15.5; 1 mil = 25.4 microns.
[b] To convert g/100 in² to g/m², multiply by 15.5.
[c] O_2TR increases with relative humidity.

considered. What good is it to use a barrier material if it is easily punctured during handling? Check out these important properties before selecting packaging materials:

- machinability (coefficient of friction/slip, blocking tendencies),
- print quality,
- clarity,
- sealability (heat seal temperature range, seal strength, hot tack),
- strength (tear and tensile strength, puncture resistance),
- recyclability, and
- cost.

All materials have advantages and disadvantages. Oriented polypropylene (OPP) has better transparency and gloss than low-density polyethylene (LDPE), higher heat resistance, and twice the tensile strength. LDPE has higher oxygen transmission rates than OPP. Films made with linear low-density polyethylene (LLDPE) have higher tear strength and greater puncture resistance than LDPE, but they have lower clarity. Recycling centers exist for rigid polyester containers, while most plastic bags are not being recycled.

Packaging materials used for foods in the United States must be approved by the FDA. Flexible polymer films for food contact are regulated under FDA regulation Part 177 (Table 2). The regulation does not state specifications for the use of recycled materials, but this does not mean that FDA will prohibit the use of recycled plastic materials for food packaging. The agency intends to publish regulations and protocols for demonstrating the safety of recycled plastics for food contact.

Performance Testing

Once potential packaging materials are selected, the next step is to test the performance of those materials made into packages containing the product and

Table 2
Common FDA Regulations (21 CFR) for Flexible Packaging[a]

Part and Section Number	Title
175.105	Adhesives
175.125	Pressure-sensitive Adhesives
175.300	Resinous and Polymeric Coatings
175.320	Resinous and Polymeric Coatings for Polyolefin Films
176.170	Components of Paper and Paperboard in Contact with Aqueous and Fatty Foods
176.180	Components of Paper and Paperboard in Contact with Dry Foods
177.1200	Cellophane
177.1390	High Temperature Laminates
177.1630	Polyethylene Phthalate Polymers
178.1005	Hydrogen Peroxide Solution

[a] Source: Anonymous (1988).

used at the expected storage temperature. Are the gas transmission properties adequate to obtain the desired quality and shelf life? Do the materials have good seal strength and are they puncture resistant?

The film selection process must include testing the structures on packaging equipment to be sure that it will perform satisfactorily on the particular equipment at the required speeds.

Packaging Costs and Product Quality

Selecting packaging materials based entirely on cost without consideration of the gauge and barrier properties required can compromise shelf life (Marsili, 1993). For example, a 1-mil (25.4-μm) polypropylene ($0.415/1,000 in.[2]) film gives better barrier properties but is more expensive than a 1.5-mil (152.4-μm) LLDPE film ($0.062/1,000 in.[2]).

Evaluations of packaging costs cannot be based solely on the cost of materials. Consider the entire packaging operation when calculating unit cost: labor productivity, shipping charges, in-plant leaker rates, and cost of returns.

Many packers are switching from polymer blends to more costly multilayer films because of their superior printability and the ease with which they run on automated packaging equipment. Coextrusions can be designed to provide specific heat seal properties on one side and optimum conditions for ink or laminating adhesives on the other.

A single-ply material may not always meet a number of performance requirements. However, you should ask whether paying the cost of the multilayer structure will make a significant difference in the quality of the packaged product. For example, if the laminate runs well on the equipment but its water vapor transmission rate is not any better than that of a single-ply film, what benefit would it have for product quality and shelf life?

Many packers have the impression that the properties of individual layers in a laminate or coextrusion are additive. That's not necessarily so. The oxygen transmission rate of a OPP/LDPE coextrusion is determined mainly by the permeability of the OPP, which is lower than that of a single layer of LDPE.

Frozen-Dough Packaging

Selection of packaging materials in the frozen-dough industry is driven mainly by cost. Many packaging materials used for frozen-dough products are based on coextrusions of ethylene vinyl acetate (EVA) and LLDPE or blends of LLDPE with high-density polyethylene (Table 3). LLDPE is preferred over LDPE because of its improved physical properties. LLDPE films are stronger and tougher and have higher abrasion and puncture resistance than comparable LDPE films. This translates into excellent seal strength and reduced leakers.

LLDPE films can be downgauged while still maintaining strength and toughness. This offers benefits in source reduction of packaging material, an environmental plus. However, packaging films made with LLDPE have some disadvantages compared to those made with LDPE—they are less clear than LDPE and they cost more.

Packaging equipment used in the frozen-dough industry is not sophisticated. Frozen-dough products are packaged in premade bags using common bagging machines made by such companies as Formost Packaging Machines (Woodinville, WA) and United Bakery Equipment (Compton, CA). Bagging machines have attached closure-applying equipment. Closures are made with wire ties, or, more frequently, plastic clips are used since they can carry regulatory coding and dating requirements. Clip closure speeds of 120 bags per minute are not uncommon. Such closures are not hermetic; the bags leak at the clip. Large pieces of frozen dough for bread may be placed in a thermoformed tray before being placed in the bag and sealed with a plastic clip.

Bag-in-box packaging is used for boiled, quick-frozen bagel dough. Bagel dough pieces are packed in LDPE-lined corrugated boxes. The bag is sealed with a clip, and the box is taped shut.

Some frozen pie crusts are wrapped using a horizontal form-fill-seal machine. The frozen shells, in aluminum pans, are pushed into the filling tube. The packaging machine folds the film and pushes the shells into the formed tube; the bottom is lap-sealed; and the sides are heat-sealed.

Weighing, metal detection, checkweighing, and case-packing operations in the frozen-dough industry are similar to those found in most packing operations.

Refrigerated Doughs

Table 3 lists the film structures commonly used for refrigerated doughs. Packaging refrigerated doughs is more complicated and costly than packaging frozen doughs. It often requires barrier materials and specialized packaging

Table 3
Typical Film Structures for Frozen and Refrigerated Doughs

Product	Film Structure[a]
Frozen bread dough, bagel dough, and pie crusts	EVA/LLDPE/EVA LDPE/LLDPE/LDPE LLDPE-HDPE blends
Refrigerated pie dough	LLDPE/EVA
Refrigerated cookie doughs	EVA/nylon/EVA OPP/adhesive/OPP
Refrigerated fresh tortillas	Nylon/PE
Refrigerated, canned doughs	Fiberboard/foil/paper composite with metal ends

[a] EVA = ethylene vinyl acetate, PE = polyethylene, LLD = linear low density, LD = low density, HD = high density, OPP = oriented polyethylene.

equipment. Often, some form of modified atmosphere packaging (MAP), such as gas-flushing or vacuum packaging, is used. Preservation relies on the synergy of packaging technology, control of the microbial condition of raw ingredients, and impeccable sanitary procedures in the process environment. Reducing the water activity (a_w) and lowering the pH are common manufacturing techniques used to control microbial growth in these products.

The goal of MAP is to change the atmosphere surrounding the product so that oxidative, enzymatic, and organoleptic changes are reduced and microbial growth is retarded. The air in the package is replaced by a mixture of CO_2 and N_2 or N_2 only. Often, a modified atmosphere consisting of 20–50% CO_2/80–50% N_2 is injected into the package before sealing. High CO_2 levels in the package can lead to the formation of carbonic acid ($CO_2 + H_2O \rightarrow H_2CO_3$), which reduces the pH and thereby slows microbial growth.

MAP of refrigerated doughs requires materials that provide a good barrier to O_2, CO_2, and moisture. Ethylene vinyl alcohol (EVOH) and polyvinylidene chloride (PVDC) are the leading barrier resins. Ideally for MAP, O_2 and CO_2 transmission rates of packaging materials should be less than 1 cm^3/100 in^2-day-atm (15.5 cm^3/m^2-day-atm). Moisture vapor transmission rates should be <1 g/100 in^2-day (15.5 g/m^2-day). These stringent requirements often lead to the selection of laminated structures, such as polyester/PVDC/LDPE or nylon/-PVDC/LDPE structures, which can provide maximum barrier properties at the least possible cost. Whichever packaging materials are selected, they must form strong, hermetic seals to maintain the desired atmosphere.

MAP and gas flushing have often been used interchangeably. However, MAP may not necessarily involve gas flushing. Instead, sachets that absorb O_2, CO_2, or moisture vapors may be placed in the package before sealing. The chemicals included in these sachets control the atmosphere in the package. Table 4 lists some common absorbers used to modify the atmosphere in packages.

Oxygen absorbers can reduce headspace O_2 to less than 0.01%. The oxygen scavengers in these sachets can be one of a number of metallic reducing agents such as powdered iron oxides, ferrous carbonate, ferrous compounds, or metallic platinum. Oxygen scavengers may reduce the need for high-barrier packaging materials, allowing the packer to use less expensive, moderate oxygen barriers.

Table 4
Commercial Gas Scavengers Used in Sachets
for in-Package Atmosphere Control

Type	Composition
O_2	Iron oxides
	Ferrous salts
CO_2	Iron oxides + $Ca(OH)_2$ (absorbs O_2 and CO_2)
H_2O	CaO
	NaCl

New films that incorporate oxygen scavengers directly into the film are being introduced by American and Japanese companies. In addition, films containing antimicrobial agents are being sold in Japan (Anonymous, 1986; Littman, 1993). None of these films, at present, is being used in refrigerated or frozen-dough packaging.

A modified atmosphere can be established in a package by one of two methods: drawing a vacuum on the package and then back-flushing with the desired gas composition, or continuous flushing with the desired gas mixture. In both cases, an injection lance is used to inject the gas mixture into the package. Packages may be gas-flushed in two areas along the line to ensure replacement of air by CO_2 and N_2. Residual O_2 levels of 0.1–0.3% have been reported by some horizontal form-fill-seal equipment manufacturers after gas-flushing. More often, residual O_2 levels of 1% persist in the package after gas-flushing.

Premixed gases can be purchased for use with gas-flushing horizontal-form-fill-seal equipment, but these tend to separate over time, resulting in the injection of an inconsistent mixture into the packages. To avoid the expense of premixed gases as well as the delivery lead times, inventory space, and record keeping, companies have invested in in-house gas mixing and generating systems. These systems allow the packer to dial-in varying gas mixtures for different products.

Horizontal fill-seal and vertical fill-seal equipment or vacuum packaging units are used to produce flexible MAP pouches for refrigerated doughs. MAP requires that a hermetic seal be produced to maintain the atmosphere inside the package. Therefore, a method to detect leaks is a crucial part of any MAP system.

Chemically Leavened Doughs

Chemically leavened fresh refrigerated doughs were probably the first doughs sold in a modified atmosphere package. These doughs are sold in spiral-wound composite cans with metal ends. The 90-day shelf life of canned doughs would not be possible without this specially designed package. From the outside in, the can is made of a foil/Kraft paper label, a center layer of cylinder board, and inner layer of foil/Kraft paper. The label holds the inner and middle layers together so that when the label is removed the can pops open.

Dough is packed in the can to about 80% capacity, and metal ends are forced into the side walls of the can. The false seam created by the metal ends allows gas to escape. An anaerobic atmosphere is produced in the can during the "proofing" step of dough production. During proofing, the sealed cans of dough are held at 90°F (32°C) for a few hours until enough CO_2 is generated by the leavening agents to expand the dough and push it up against the metal ends. The can must withstand internal pressures of 10–25 psi caused by continual CO_2 generation throughout storage (Anonymous, 1979; Chen, 1979; Gajderowicz, 1979).

Cookie Doughs

Refrigerated cookie doughs have a small amount of leavening action and a low water activity (a_w about 0.8). The main objectives are to prevent desiccation of the dough during storage and to retard deteriorative changes in the fat. The high solute content of these doughs helps to retard microbial growth.

The most common way to package cookie dough is in chubs. The cookie chubs are made from two layers of PVDC or OPP film. Alternatively, an EVA/nylon/EVA structure may be used. The film is fed to the chub packaging machine from a roll, formed around a mandrel, and heat-sealed along the length to form a tube. A metal clip is used to close one end of the tube, and the cookie dough is forced into the tube. Another metal clip is used to seal the top end of the tube.

Pie Doughs

A major problem in extending the shelf life of refrigerated pie doughs is graying of the dough, caused by enzymatic browning reactions. Enzymatic browning is reduced through product formulation and packaging. The doughs are usually packaged in unprinted barrier material such as polyethylene terephthalate/PVDC and are N_2-flushed before the pouch is heat sealed. Pouches are then placed in printed paperboard boxes.

Tortillas

The refrigerated shelf life of fresh uncooked tortillas has been extended to 60 days by vacuum packaging in gas-barrier reclosable-zipper pouches made of PVDC/nylon/polyethylene (Rice, 1990).

Fresh Pizza Doughs

Gas flushing doughs with 100% N_2 or 60% N_2/40% CO_2 retards mold growth and delays discoloration. A typical recommendation for packaging fresh pizza is 20–35% CO_2 and the remainder N_2. This gives a shelf life of 15–21 days. An alternative to gas flushing to prevent mold growth is to include a sachet that emits ethanol vapor inside the package (Smith et al, 1987).

Literature Cited

Anonymous. 1979. Advances in packaging of refrigerated doughs. Cereal Foods World 24:50.

Anonymous. 1986. What are today's trends in Europe and Japan? Packaging 31(2):72-74.

Anonymous. 1988. A guide to FDA regulations of adhesives and coatings for flexible packaging. TAPPI J. Sept., pp. 125-128.

Bakker, M. 1986. Wiley Encyclopedia of Packaging Technology. John Wiley & Sons, New York. pp. 185-186.

Chen, R. W. 1979. Refrigerated doughs. Cereal Foods World 24:46-47.

Gajderowicz, L. J. 1979. Progress in the refrigerated dough industry. Cereal Foods World 24:44-45.

Littman, M. 1993. Foreign frontiers. Prep. Foods 162(12):13-14.

Marsili, R. 1993. Optimizing the value and benefits of packaging films. Food Prod. Des. 3(8):63-75.

Rice, J. 1990. Fresh, uncooked tortillas in recloseable zipper packs. Food Process. 51(11):48-49.

Smith, J. P, Ooraikul, B., Koersen, W. J., Van de Voort, F. R, Jackson, E. D., and Lawrence, R. A. 1987. Shelf life extension of a bakery product using ethanol vapor. Food Microbiol. 4:329-337.

CHAPTER 14

Selected Patents for Frozen Dough, 1983–1993

Ronald L. Wirtz
American Institute of Baking
Manhattan, Kansas 66502

Although the practice of freezing yeast-raised breads dates from the 1930s in the United States (Marx, 1932), the freezing of yeast doughs was not generally practiced until the mid-1940s. This was first done on a small scale by retail bakers for the interrupted production of rolls and other small goods and was seen as a means to reduce the need for night work and to provide goods that might be "baked off" with a minimum of notice to meet unexpected customer demand (Anonymous, 1946).

The freezer equipment of that period was limited in size and capabilities, and there were quality problems associated with the production and freezing of yeast-raised bakery goods larger than rolls. As a result, direct consumer use of frozen yeast-raised doughs was not widespread until the development of grocery store and supermarket distribution of frozen foods in the late 1940s and early 1950s (Anonymous, 1951, 1963a; McPherson and Lamb, 1948).

Improvements in freezing technology and the development of large-capacity commercial freezers following World War II led to the advent of practical means of retail distribution of frozen foods. The result was the emergence of a wide range of frozen food products, of which frozen doughs were only a relatively small segment.

Frozen yeast doughs were first marketed for direct consumer preparation by such companies as Rhodes Refrigeration, Inc., with its Bake-N-Serve franchise, the J. L. Jarman Co., the William Freihofer Baking Co., and the Homade Bread Co. (Anonymous, 1961, 1963b, 1964; Teiser and Harroun, 1963; Wheeler, 1961). By 1963 there were at least a dozen companies engaged in this commerce (Williams, 1963).

Frozen dough allowed home baking of fresh bread without the investment in time and labor that had previously been required, and this "convenience" aspect of frozen bread dough was important throughout the early 1960s. However, as increasing numbers of women entered the general workforce, the tradition of home baking began a long decline that has shown no sign of significant reversal.

The market for frozen dough products began a shift away from direct consumer sales in the early 1960s (Anonymous 1960, 1984; Howard, 1960) with the emergence of the in-store bakery concept. Growth of this market segment has continued, and today in-store bakeries constitute the most significant single market for frozen dough products. The retail bakery and general food-service industries are also making increased use of a growing variety of frozen dough products.

The level of activity in the development of new frozen dough patents indicates that interest in the application of this concept to the commercial production of bakery goods continues to be very strong. It is significant that this is not solely a North American phenomenon but that important developments are being made as well in Europe, especially in France and Germany, and in Japan.

European interest in frozen dough technology is stimulated by a continuing decline in the number of trained retail bakers. This is also the basis for the popularity of industrially produced frozen dough in North America. Japanese interest is substantially related to the emergence of new types of wheat-based bakery foods as a growing part of the Japanese diet and to the highly competitive role of Japanese baking and food equipment companies on the world market.

In view of the "internationalization" of the frozen dough concept, patents discussed in this chapter were selected by the use of a number of international on-line databases as "finding aids," including the DIALOG databases *C.A. Search, World Patents Index, Food Science Technology Abstracts, Foods Adlibra, Claims: U.S. Patents*, and the French-language database *Pascal*. Other sources of patents included the FROSTI food technology and science database on CD-ROM, produced by Leatherhead Food R.A. in the United Kingdom, and the FINDER databases maintained in-house by the library staff of the American Institute of Baking.

The patents selected for discussion were granted over a period of 10 years, from 1983 through 1993. They include patents issued to inventors from the United States, Europe, and Japan. Although the present discussion is limited to a selected group of these patents, the original search found reference to more than *100* patents issued during that decade.

Those chosen for this brief review reflect the significant changes in industrial bakery production taking place outside North America. They do not indicate the considerable developmental activity that occurred both on this continent and in Europe in previous decades, since that activity has been discussed previously in other publications.

Yeast Technology in Improvement of Frozen Doughs

As noted in preceding chapters, one of the more serious problems associated with the industrial production of frozen doughs has been that of yeast mortality under freezing and storage conditions. A number of different approaches have been developed to optimize the survival of the yeast used in frozen doughs. The customary means of providing a sufficient number of viable yeast cells in the thawed dough to assure fermentation has been to supplement the normal yeast level in the formulation by 30–50%, with attention being given to freezing conditions that would tend to reduce yeast mortality.

A method that takes a somewhat different approach to addressing the matter of yeast mortality involves "stabilization" of the yeast by deep freezing. The procedure, patented in the United States and subsequently assigned to Grandes Boulangeries Associées of Paris, France (Nourigeon, 1983), involves a multi-stage process in which the yeast is first frozen for 48 hr at -15°C or for 24 hr at -20°C . This has the result of killing the yeast cells that are the least cold-resistant. The temperature of the yeast is then brought to 10–15°C before being mixed with the other dough ingredients. Mixing is done at a preferred speed of 30 rpm for 5 min, followed by kneading at 60 rpm for 15–20 min. Salt is then incorporated and the dough again kneaded at 60 rpm for 2–7 min. Temperature-controlled water and/or flaked ice may be used in the mixing to arrive at a final dough temperature of less than 20°C at the center of the dough mass. The weighing, dividing, and forming stages are conventional in nature.

The resulting dough pieces are then frozen under conditions of high humidity to assure that they will be coated with a layer of ice, which allows them to be stored for periods up to six months. After freezing, the dough pieces are packed in wrappings that are impermeable to water vapor, and preservation may be aided by either vacuum or inert gas packaging. The packaged dough pieces are stored in conventional freezers at temperatures between -15 and -18°C.

Dough pieces manufactured according to this method are prepared for baking by being removed from their wrappings and placed in a moisture-saturated oven maintained at 90–100°C for 3–7 min, preferably for 5 min. The dough pieces are then removed to an oven or proofing chamber maintained at 25°C for 20 min, the core of the dough reaching a temperature of 19°C at the end of this period. Conventional fermentation under standard conditions of humidity and temperature is then maintained for 20–40 min before baking.

The stated advantages of the Nourigeon method is that the flour used may be a lower-quality non-bread-making flour, and that a six-month shelf life may be achieved without appreciable loss in quality of the finished product.

A more technologically sophisticated means of "pretreating" the yeast used for frozen dough is described in a European patent developed by J. Goux and P. Clément and assigned to Lesaffre et Cie of Paris, France (Goux and Clément, 1987). The primary purpose of this invention is to produce a freeze-dried form of conventional bread yeast that has superior handling and storage characteristics when compared to standard yeasts. A further advantage of this method of yeast pretreatment is that the resulting product offers excellent performance in frozen doughs.

Conventional baker's yeast is extruded as granules or particles up to 3 mm in diameter but preferably in the form of "vermicelli" less than 1 mm in diameter. The yeast "vermicelli" is then pretreated by drying to a preferred dry matter level of 74%. The dried yeast is further processed by freezing in a fluid-bed drier, using a current either of inert gas or of air maintained at -25°C. The resulting product is then packaged in sacks of 1–25 kg under either conventional atmosphere or an inert gas.

The freezing process used in this method, at temperatures from -18°C to -30°C, permits good heat transfer between the gas and the yeast particles. There is no need to use temperatures so low as to cause damage to the yeast. For optimum results, the temperature should be lowered no more than one degree per minute.

These conditions minimize the possibility of formation of ice crystals in the yeast, avoid damage to yeast cell membranes, and thus provide the largest possible percentage of viable yeast cells for fermentation of the dough after thawing. Yeast survival may be further enhanced by the use of additives commonly used in drying, such as sorbitan monostearate, polyglyceride esters, or citric esters of monoglycerides and diglycerides. Alginates, gums, or cellulose derivatives may also be used for this purpose. Cryoprotective substances that may be utilized include lactose, whey or defatted milk, sorbitol, glycerol, or gelatin. Packaging under inert gas atmosphere in multilayer polyethylene-aluminum-vinyl acetate film permits a frozen storage life of up to three months at -20°C.

Testing of gas production of frozen yeast produced according to this method has shown no significant loss of fermentative ability. Comparison with frozen doughs produced from U.S. fresh yeast and commercial European dry yeast showed that the freeze-dried yeast produced by the method described above was clearly superior in producing loaves of a given volume in terms of required proof time. The freeze-dried yeast described was also found to offer advantages in the production of standard Danish pastry.

For both bread and yeast-raised pastry, the freeze-dried yeast may be incorporated into the mixed dough just before the end of dough development, mixing being continued just until the yeast is evenly distributed throughout the dough. This has the effect of minimizing yeast activity before freezing and produces better and more uniform baking results after the frozen dough has been defrosted for use.

The European patent assigned to Uno et al (1986) describes the use of a novel yeast, *Saccharomyces cerevisiae* KYF 110, which is not susceptible to damage by freezing before fermentation or by the conditions of frozen storage. Another stated advantage is the ability to ferment maltose, making it particularly suited for use in lean bread doughs. The yeast may also be used in the preparation of other breads and pastries, including Danish pastry, yeast doughnuts, and Chinese steam bread.

This yeast is used in an amount of 1–5% by weight of flour, mixed conventionally with high-gluten wheat flour, sugar, salt, shortening, yeast food, and water for a total of 14 min. The optimal dough temperature after mixing and kneading is 20°C, in contrast to 28°C for a typical unfrozen dough. The dough is conventionally proofed, divided, rounded, fermented, molded, and frozen at -80°C.

The resulting dough pieces are stored at -20°C. They are prepared for use by thawing for 90 min at 30°C, then proofed at 40°C and a relative humidity of 85% to 1.5 cm above the baking pan. The proofed dough is then baked for 23 min at 210°C.

Bread produced using *S. cerevisiae* KYF 110 and conventional methods of makeup has been shown to be superior in specific volume to that made from frozen doughs produced with commercially available yeast for frozen dough or from conventional yeast. Doughs produced with this yeast require substantially less proofing time after freezing than doughs made with commercial yeast for frozen dough or commercial yeast for conventional bread. Tests also illustrate that use of this novel yeast is equally suitable in the production of pastries and in both low- and high-sugar bread doughs.

Another effort to produce a freeze-resistant yeast with the ability to ferment maltose is described in the U.S. patent issued to Nakatomi et al (1985). This patent is based on the development of *Saccharomyces* FD 612 (FERM BP-742), resulting from selective hybridizations of the conventional bread yeast *S. cerevisiae* AHU 3028 with *S. uvarum* IFO 0220 and *Saccharomyces* IFO 1426. The resulting yeast strain, which was selected from approximately 400 segregants, has excellent gassing power for dough fermentation and possesses improved ability to utilize both starch and maltose. The yeast is also highly freeze-resistant and has excellent frozen storage life, i.e., one year or more. In short-term laboratory testing of freeze resistance, *Saccharomyces* FD 612 achieved a yeast survival rate of 75%, in comparison with 29.8% for conventional baker's yeast.

Bread made with *Saccharomyces* FD 612 is produced in a conventional manner. The dough obtained is frozen at -40°C for 1 hr, then stored at -20°C for periods of one day to one year. It is prepared for use by thawing at 5°C for 15 hr, or at room temperature for 1–2 hr, before final proofing at 35°C. Baking is at 200–210°C for approximately 20 min.

Bread and sweet goods produced from *Saccharomyces* FD 612 frozen doughs were clearly superior to bread produced from frozen doughs leavened with conventional baker's yeast, especially as regards aroma of the finished products. Conventional (unfrozen) doughs for both bread and sweet goods leavened by *Saccharomyces* FD 612 were only slightly inferior to unfrozen doughs leavened with standard baker's yeast.

Another effort to produce a yeast having maltose fermentative ability and improved freeze resistance is described in the European patent developed by Takano et al (1990). This patent describes in detail the development of a diploid hybrid strain from two parent yeast strains of *S. cerevisiae*, notably *S. cerevisiae* KB-3, which exhibits good fermentative ability of low-sugar dough but lacks freeze-resistance, and *S. cerevisiae* FTY, which has strong freeze resistance but weak fermentative ability in low-sugar doughs. The resulting hybrid, termed *S. cerevisiae* FTY-3, combines both of these desired qualities.

Fermentation tests comparing ordinary baker's yeast, yeast for nonsugar dough, freeze-resistant yeast, and the hybrid strain indicate that the hybrid had higher levels of CO_2 production in no-sugar and low-sugar doughs both before and after freezing and thawing than the comparison yeasts. Actual baking tests of French bread using the *S. cerevisiae* FTY-3 strain in comparison with yeast for nonsugar dough and with a freeze-resistant yeast showed that the hybrid strain produced loaves of superior volume both before dough freezing and after seven and 14 days of frozen storage. Similar results were obtained in tests for white bread with 5% sugar content, rolls with 10% sugar content, buns of 15% sugar content, and buns of 20% sugar content, all based on flour weight.

In all cases except the last, the hybrid strain, *S. cerevisiae* FTY-3, provided greater bread volume. At the 20% sugar level, although performance of the hybrid strain was still superior after seven and 14 days of frozen storage, the yeast for nonsugar dough generated greater volume in unfrozen doughs. Testing of *S. cerevisiae* FTY-3 for long-term stability and fermentative ability were not noted in this patent.

Use of Additives in Improvement of Frozen Dough

Various types of additives have been suggested as means of improving the quality, convenience, performance, and storage characteristics of frozen doughs. These additives range from combinations of those used in conventional unfrozen doughs (emulsifiers, amylases, ascorbic acid, etc.) to less conventional substances such as sucroglycerides and alcohols or alcohol derivatives and amino acids.

Conventional practice in the manufacture of frozen doughs has long been that fermentation should be minimized, whether in bulk fermentation or bench fermentation after product makeup. However, in an effort to reduce or eliminate the time necessary to thaw and proof frozen doughs, some inventors have sought to produce a fully proofed frozen dough, either through the use of various additives, by special processing steps, or a combination of the two.

A European patent (Lindstrom and Slade, 1987) describes the production of a fully proofed frozen dough composition that may be baked immediately upon removal from the freezer, the finished product being available about 1 hr after removal from frozen storage. This method eliminates the usual thawing step, which may range from 2 to 12 hr, and also dispenses with proofing, which may take 2–4 hr.

The frozen dough composition described in this patent may include conventional dry ingredients, be either chemically leavened or yeast-leavened, and contain shortenings, emulsifiers, and other ingredients as traditionally used in the baking industry. The principal change involves the use of a "hydration medium" composed of water and a melting-point depressant to eliminate the need for the thawing and proofing steps necessary in conventional frozen dough processes. This hydration medium is composed primarily of water, but also includes 5–20% (based on water weight) of a melting point depressant consisting of monohydric or polyhydric alcohols. The most advantageous of these melting point depressants would seem to be ethanol, due to its status as a food additive. Furthermore, the low boiling point of ethanol, 78°C, ensures that it will not remain in the product after baking. The vaporization of ethanol during the baking stage also contributes to "oven-spring" of the baked product.

The food grade ethanol to be used in this application may be synthetically produced but may also be advantageously produced by means of a liquid preferment typically containing one part sucrose, 10 parts water, and 2.6 parts active dry yeast, along with some minor ingredients, and fermented until the sucrose has been converted to 5% aqueous ethanol. An ethanol-tolerant, fast-fermenting variety of *S. cerevisiae* known as gasohol yeast may be used to reduce fermentation time or to produce higher concentrations of ethanol in the slurry. An alternative method involves the production of ethanol in the dough, up to a level of 20% by weight of water in the dough, by the use of this same variety of gasohol yeast.

Doughs produced according to this process are mixed under ambient conditions but with an atypically low fermentation temperature of 30°C. The optimal fermentation is between 20 and 30°C, since higher temperatures may cause weakening of the dough cell structure. After fermentation in bulk, the dough is divided, rounded, molded, panned, and given "bench" or secondary fermentation as in conventional bread makeup. Total fermentation time is generally between 1 and 2 hr, and proofing beyond this point generally contributes to poor cell structure and dessication of the outer surface of the dough.

Specific volume and related rheological qualities of the dough are important to the quality of the final product. The formed and panned dough must be allowed to ferment until a specific gravity, preferably 1.98–2.86 cm^3/g of dough, is achieved. Fermentation beyond 3.08 cm^3/g of dough causes the dough to "fall" during baking due to weak gluten cell structure.

Dough that has reached the desired specific gravity is frozen so that a preferred core temperature of -6 to -25°C is reached, preferably within 1½ to 4 hr. The frozen dough is stored at -30 to -10°C.

The frozen dough is prepared for use by being removed from frozen storage and placed in a *cold* conventional oven, which is immediately heated to a temperature of 175°C. The baking process requires about 45 min from cold oven to finished bread. A comparison test of frozen dough containing ethanol, as described in the invention, with frozen dough without ethanol showed an almost twofold increase in oven-spring in the case of the ethanol-containing dough.

A U.S. patent, developed by Larson et al (1983) and assigned to General Foods Corporation, describes a method of preparing a fully proofed frozen bread dough that has good stability under frozen conditions, can be baked from the frozen state in about 1 hr, and has the desired flavor and aroma characteristic of yeast-leavened fresh bread.

This process consists of adding a combination of gums, surface-active agents, and film-forming proteins (dough strengtheners) to the normal ingredients used in the production of frozen bread dough, i.e., flour, water, yeast, sugar, salt, nonfat dry milk, and shortening. Suitable gums include xanthan, tragacanth, guar, carrageenan, carboxymethylcellulose, and others. Surfactants might include hydroxylated lecithin, mono- and diglycerides, diacetyl tartaric acid esters of mono- and diglycerides, calcium stearoyl-2-lactylate, and others, used at a level of 0.20–1.5% on a flour weight basis. Suitable dough strengtheners would include vital gluten, egg albumen, beef albumen, selected legume protein, or cereal grain protein isolates, typically used at a level of 0.3–3.3% by weight of flour.

Contrary to normal practice in the production of frozen doughs, mixing of ingredients may be done at ambient temperatures rather than in a chilled state. Total fermentation time before freezing is preferably 1.5 hr. Total proofing time should not exceed 2 hr, since prolonged fermentation weakens cell structure. Conventional steps are followed in the dividing, rounding, benching, molding, and final proofing of the dough. Final proofing should permit each 454-g loaf to reach an optimal volume of 1.98–2.86 cm³/g of dough.

The dough is frozen to a preferred core temperature of -6 to -25°C and stored within a range of -15 to -25°C. Frozen dough pieces produced according to this invention should be removed from frozen storage to a cold oven, which is then turned on and heated to a temperature of 175°C. Loaves are baked for approximately 60 min, yielding a loaf with traditional "homemade" taste and character.

A French patent, invented by Grandvoinnet et al (1986) and assigned to Grands Moulins de Pantin, S.A., describes the production of frozen proofed French bread dough that may be baked directly upon removal from the freezer. This procedure requires the use of a strong flour from selected wheat varieties, with a Chopin alveograph value of 300–350 as determined by AFNOR (1974), rather than the usual alveograph values of 150–200.

In addition to the use of high-protein bread flour, which is a departure from the usual French practice, there is also an addition of 0.7–1.0% gluten by weight of flour. Other additives include 500 ppm of ascorbic acid, rather than the 200–300 ppm generally in use. The authors also state that 0.2–0.3% lecithin is to be added and that this addition is "unusual because of the strength of the flour." Another significant change is a *reduction* in the amount of yeast used, to 2% by flour weight rather than the normal 2.5%.

There are also several departures from normal processing procedures: although mixing and first fermentation conform with standard French practice, the rest period after dough division is lengthened from 20 to 60 min, and the fermentation period following makeup and diagonal cutting is extended to around 2.5 hr. Dough pieces are frozen at -50°C, freezing of wrapped or covered dough being completed in 30 min to 1 hr. The frozen dough units are stored in airtight bags at -25°C.

Frozen French bread produced according to this invention is prepared for consumption by being removed from storage, taken from the airtight bags, and placed immediately into an oven preheated to 220–230°C rather than the normal baking temperature of 250°C. Baking under this reduced temperature is prolonged for approximately 10 min over normal baking time.

A U.S. patent (Benjamin et al, 1990), assigned to Kraft General Foods, discusses a method of producing a frozen proofed dough that has improved resistance to less-than-optimal frozen storage and handling conditions. This is accomplished through the use of a dough composition that includes wheat protein (gluten) at a level greater than 16%, but preferably 17–28%, based on the total weight of flour.

The flour used in this process may be a "naturally-occurring high-quality wheat flour" having 17–24% protein as measured by AACC standard methods. Another source might be commercially available flour having a protein content in the range of 12–15%, supplemented by high-protein wheat fractions and vital wheat gluten to reach the desired total protein level. The upper limit of wheat protein content of the flour will largely be determined by economic considerations, since addition of protein beyond the 16% level seems to have a cumulative positive effect on product quality, including improved organoleptic qualities and higher loaf volume.

Ingredients are mixed under ambient conditions. A typical formulation includes a protein-fortified wheat flour, a hydrocolloid gum, sugar, L-cysteine, potassium bromate, ascorbic acid, water, nonfat dry milk, activated dry yeast, and yeast food. The total fermentation is 1–3 hr within the temperature range of 20–30°C. After a bulk fermentation of approximately 15 min at 23°C, the dough is divided, rounded, molded, panned, and given a final proofing period of 120 min at 85% humidity and 26°C. Optimum specific gravity of the formed and proofed dough pieces is 1.98–2.86 cm³/g of dough, with each 454-g dough piece attaining a volume of approximately 1,100 cm³. Proofed dough pieces are then frozen at -35°C for 2 hr, packaged, and transferred to freezer storage at -18°C.

Frozen dough produced according to this method is finish-baked by being placed in a thermostatically controlled *cold oven*, which is immediately turned on and heated to 180°C. Total baking time is approximately 55–60 min. Frozen storage life of products prepared using this method is considered to be at least 16 weeks.

Additional examples are included in this patent description for the use of a "naturally occurring high protein varietal flour with a measured protein content of 20% based on weight of the flour," production of yeast-leavened dough that is not proofed before freezing, chemically leavened frozen dough, unleavened frozen dough, and variety breads including bran bread, wheat bread, and French and Italian breads.

Le Duff (1987c), a French patent assigned to the Société Générale de Pâtisserie Armoricaine, discusses a method of preparing a frozen "French" bread dough that, after frozen storage for six months, has structural and other characteristics similar to bread baked immediately after dough makeup and that possesses notably good resistance to firming.

Frozen bread dough produced according to this patent is made from a standard French type 55 bread flour (0.5–0.6% ash, 75–78% extraction) with a protein level between 10 and 12%, a standard fresh or dehydrated variety of *S. cerevisiae*, water, sodium chloride, and several improving agents. These include ascorbic acid at a level of 0.01–0.025% and amylolytic enzymes, sometimes with the addition of soy lecithin. The amylolytic enzymes that may be used include α-1,6-amylase, α-1,4 amylase, and amyloglucosiadase. The authors state that the ascorbic acid helps to resolve the problem of gas cell permeability, which may occur as a result of frozen storage, and permits the reestablishment of disulfide bonds in the gluten, giving good oven-spring even after several months of frozen storage.

After an initial 2-min mixing of the flour, water, ascorbic acid, and enzymes at slow speed, and 5 min of high speed mixing, the yeast is added to the mixture. Following an additional 10 min of mixing, the salt is added, and the dough is mixed for an additional 5 min, at which time the temperature of the dough should be between 20 and 24°C. After dividing, the dough pieces are allowed to rest for 10–25 min, depending on the type of dough and the size of the dough pieces. They are then formed into baguettes, flutes, or rolls; placed on screens or forms; and immediately inserted into a freezing tunnel. Depending on the size of the dough piece and the temperatures used, freezing is completed in 20–80 min, the temperature at the heart of the dough piece reaching -7°C. Dough pieces are then placed in airtight packaging and stored in a freezer maintained between -15 and -25°C.

Frozen dough made according to this method is prepared for consumption by thawing at ambient temperature, followed by conventional baking. Bread thus produced possesses a fine and crisp crust, the irregular alveolar structure characteristic of "French" bread, and a soft crumb that is resistant to firming.

An international patent assigned to the Kama Danish Pastry A/S of Denmark (Larsen, 1991) also describes a method of preparing a fully fermented bread product. The method, which is equally effective in the production of bread or of Danish-type pastry, is obtained by omitting the addition of fermentable carbohydrates such as saccharose, glucose, or maltose, and adding amylase, specifically 0.05–0.1% (flour weight) of Fungamyl MG 35000 and 0.1–0.2% (flour weight) of AMG 300 MG. (Both products are available from Novo Nordisk, Copenhagen).

The action of the amylases on the flour produces sufficient fermentable carbohydrates to ensure the desired leavening effect but is effectively interrupted under freezing conditions. The action of many commercially used amylases ceases during the first part of baking, and complete deactivation of the amylase Fungamyl MG 35000 generally occurs between 50 and 55°C. However, the formation of a satisfactory brownish crust color will not occur, and the resulting product is too pale. The authors state that this problem is resolved by the addition of AMG 300 MG, an amyloglucosidase that is inactivated at 80–85°C. This avoids the need to add fermentable mono- or disaccharides to the formula and thus eliminates the negative effects of such addition on the frozen storage life of the frozen dough products, since the liberation of gluten-decomposing proteinases is limited.

In both cases, the amounts of the enzymes used are approximately 100 times greater than customarily used in the production of bakery products. Because both enzymes are effectively deactivated under baking temperatures, the authors state that the "final product has a 'natural' composition without use of chemical preservatives," and that even if some enzymatic activity were present there would be no health risk involved. Acceptability of such high levels of additives under European Community food regulations is not addressed.

The dough is laminated with a roll-in margarine, using a three-doubled three-fold method to obtain 27 layers total, given a bench rest of 15 min, formed, and proofed at 35°C for 40 min at 80–85% rh. When the temperature of the dough is lowered by freezing at -24°C, activity of the yeast stops almost completely when the fermentable carbohydrates generated by the enzymes have been consumed. The frozen dough pieces may then be stored for as long as one year without losing commercially acceptable baking and organoleptic qualities.

The frozen Danish pastry product is prepared for consumption by being placed in an oven heated to 220°C for 12 min. Action of the enzyme Fungamyl on starch in the dough generates fermentable sugars as the dough thaws through the 27–55°C range, which is also its final proof. At about 55°C, the yeast cells die, and the glucose liberated by the heat-resisting enzyme AMG 300 MG undergoes a Maillard reaction, resulting in a suitably browned crust color and desirable taste profile.

A U.S. patent (Seneau, 1989) assigned to General Foods Corporation, discusses a method of improving the shelf life of a preproofed frozen dough product, such as a croissant. This method involves the addition of a mixture of whey protein and skim milk to the croissant dough, in addition to a small admixture of water.

This addition provides moisture during the freezing and frozen preservation of the dough product, thus extending its storage shelf life without the addition of gluten supplements to the flour. Previous efforts to extend the shelf life of preproofed croissant dough involved the addition of gluten or the use of high-gluten flour to the formula. Both of these additions had a negative impact on the organoleptic qualities and the desired appearance and structure of the croissant, which became more breadlike and less flaky in texture.

In industrial production, the application of the invention would involve the combination of skim milk with whey protein on the basis of 0.06% whey protein to every pound of skim milk. This mixture is added to the dough at about 2.2% by weight of flour, the finished dough having a fat or butter content of about 25–30% by weight. For nonlaminated products, it is necessary to increase the amount of the skim milk-whey protein mixture to between 2 and 5% (flour weight). In use, the compound is diluted with an equal amount of water before being mixed into the dough.

A typical production batch expressed in baker's percent (based on weight of flour) includes 100% flour, being an admixture of 78% patent and 22% clear flour. Yeast ranges from 2 to 4%, while sugar is added in the amount of 8%. About 1.75% salt is also added to the dry ingredients, which are thoroughly mixed in a dry state. About 58% of water by weight of flour is then added, at a temperature so that the mixture is maintained at about 2°C. About 2.2% of the skim milk-whey protein mixture is also added before mixing the dough. The fully mixed dough is cut into blocks of about 5.44 kg and refrigerated for 6 hr before being further processed by lamination of fat with the sheeted dough. After conventional makeup, the croissants are proofed at 70% humidity and 29.5°C for

45–75 min, then flash-frozen at about -34°C until the core temperature of the product is approximately -23.5°C. A standard egg wash is applied, after which the croissants are packaged and stored at -17.1°C until needed.

Use of the above invention in the production of laminated pastry products such as croissants permits the extension of frozen shelf life to 12–14 weeks, as compared with an average frozen shelf life for conventional proofed frozen croissants of 6–8 weeks. The product is prepared for use by being baked for 15–17 min in an oven preheated to 177°C.

Another approach to production of a preproofed laminated pastry dough specifically for croissants, which may also be baked immediately upon removal from the freezer, is described in the French patent developed by Mathieu (1991). This method involves the addition of commercially available baking additives to a sponge prepared by prefermentation of a yeast and flour sponge, mixing the sponge with flour, milk powder, baking powders, dough improver, sugars, and eggs. The resulting dough is then sheeted and laminated conventionally, and made up into finished individual units before being egg-washed and frozen.

Another method of making frozen croissant dough is given in a French patent invented by L. Le Duff (1987b) and assigned to the Société Générale de Pâtisserie Armoricaine. The frozen dough obtained by the method described in this patent has a frozen storage life of at least several months, and the baked product possesses good exterior shine, desirable crispness and mouthfeel, good interior softness, improved keeping qualities, and superior taste due to long fermentation.

A typical dough is prepared on a pilot scale from 1 kg of flour, 20 g of salt, 100 g of sugar, 10 g of inverted sugar, 30 g of sucroglyceride of palm oil, 30–40 g of fresh yeast, 500 g of water, 50 g of lemon juice, and 435 g of butter. The ingredients are mixed conventionally until "clean-up," the salt being added at the end of the mixing procedure. The dough is covered, allowed to rest for 1 hour, then transferred to a suitable container and frozen at -20°C.

The dough is defrosted for use by removing it from frozen storage to a refrigerator maintained at 5°C. After approximately 12 hr, the dough is sheeted and laminated conventionally and proofed at 38°C and 80% rh before baking at 210°C for 10–15 min.

Another French patent developed by Le Duff (1987a) and assigned to the Société Générale de Pâtisserie Armoricaine describes a method of producing frozen brioche dough. This procedure uses the same approach of replacing part of the sugar normally used in the dough by sucroglycerides, preferably also supplemented by inverted sugar. The recommended quantity of sucroglycerides used in this procedure ranges from 20 to 35% by weight of the sugar normally used in a typical brioche formula, sugar generally being between 10 and 20% of flour weight. As in the preceding invention, it is thought that the sucroglycerides protect the yeast cells from the damaging effects of freezing, thus permitting the desired degree of fermentation even after the frozen brioche dough has been in storage for several months.

A U.S. patent (Yamaguchi and Watanabe, 1987), assigned to Riken Vitamine

Co., Ltd., describes an invention to inhibit the deterioration of doughs in frozen storage. Through improvement of the characteristics of the gluten in the frozen dough, the inventors claim to eliminate or reduce damage to the dough due to formation of large ice crystals in the dough and to the presence of reducing agents produced in the course of yeast fermentation.

The additive described in this invention is produced by mixing emulsifiers, polymeric substances, and other functional additives such as cystine, sodium hyposulfite, protease, lactic acid, lactate, or similar components, with wheat gluten. The gluten used in the production of this additive is by preference fresh gluten, although ordinary vital wheat gluten or modified gluten may be used as well.

An emulsifier such as a fatty acid ester of glycerin or polyglycerin, diacetyl or tartaric acid ester of monoglycerides, sucrose fatty acid ester, soybean phospholipids, or calcium or sodium stearoyl lactylate, is kneaded into the fresh gluten at a preferred level of five to 15 parts by weight to 100 parts by weight of gluten, and the resulting mixture is dried and pulverized. Polymeric substances such as alginic acid, sodium alginate, propylene glycol alginate, or xanthan gum are added to the gluten mixture at a preferred rate of two to 15 parts by weight per 100 parts by initial weight of the wheat gluten. Other ingredients such as L-cystine, sodium hyposulfite, protease, or lactic acid may be added to total not more than 30 parts by weight of the wheat gluten. The resulting composite dough improver is said to be equally suitable for frozen and unfrozen dough manufacture, and the synergistic effects of the components of the improver allow the production of soft bakery products of good volume.

Special Processes and Equipment for Frozen Dough Products

A French patent (Faucquenoy and Savoglou, 1984), assigned to the Société Nouvelle Fima, discusses a procedure for par-baking of proofed dough pieces, precooling the par-baked dough pieces under slightly reduced atmospheric pressure, and then freezing conventionally as soon as cell structure of the partially baked dough piece has stabilized.

In conventional production of prebaked or par-baked frozen dough products, a considerable thermal shock is experienced by the dough units. When par-baked units emerge from an oven, they have an interior temperature of about 90°C. After a brief cooling period, they are rapidly conveyed to the interior of a -40°C freezing chamber, which causes the partially baked dough to collapse significantly. This occurs because the interior structure of the loaf has not become sufficiently cool to achieve cell stability.

According to the procedures described in this invention, the use of a cooling tunnel within which the par-baked loaves pass from a temperature of about 90°C to approximately 30°C, while at the same time undergoing a reduction in atmospheric pressure, permits the production of par-baked frozen loaves that maintain volume and texture similar to those of freshly par-baked bread loaves at emergence from the oven. The quality of these par-baked loaves depends on both the time of conveyance through the cooling tunnel and the degree of reduction in atmospheric pressure. If the reduction in pressure is significant, less time must be spent by the par-baked loaves in the tunnel; if the reduction in atmospheric pressure is slight, a longer period in the cooling tunnel will be required. A diagram of the cooling and atmospheric pressure reduction apparatus is included in the patent.

A French patent by Nomura and Ishigami (1985), assigned to the Nisshin Flour Milling Co., Ltd., describes a procedure for the preparation of a variety of yeast-leavened frozen doughs suitable for use in the manufacture of variety rolls (*miches*), butter croissants, sweet buns with red bean paste, or fried cakes (*beignets*).

Modifications of this procedure are useful in producing high-quality frozen dough by both the no-time and sponge-and-dough methods. In the past, frozen bread dough has been made almost universally by the no-time method. The invention is characterized by the high-speed emulsification of part or all of the water required in the formula with a fat or oil, then the mixing of the resulting emulsion with the remaining ingredients to form a dough, which may be further processed before freezing.

In the preparation of frozen bread dough according to this invention, water equal to 60 parts by weight of flour, five parts of fat, and an emulsifier consisting of a fatty acid ester and glycerol are thoroughly homogenized at high speed. The resulting emulsion is mixed with other ingredients for 2 min at low speed and 8 min at high speed in a standard mixer, reaching a dough temperature of 27°C. The resulting dough is fermented for 20 min at 27°C and 78% rh, divided into 450-g units, and allowed a 10-min bench fermentation. The dough units are then degassed, sheeted, and formed before being frozen at -40°C for 30 min and placed into storage at -18°C.

The frozen dough units are prepared for consumption by removing them from frozen storage directly to a proof cabinet maintained at 30°C and 78% rh, thawing and proofing under these conditions, then baking conventionally. Tests carried out at intervals from one to 10 weeks showed that the time necessary to achieve full proof varied between 90 and 94 min.

Preparation of frozen doughs suitable for use in the manufacture of butter croissants, sweet buns with red bean paste, or *beignets* is also described in the patent. Any type of common cooking fat, such as butter, margarine, vegetable oil, or shortening is suitable. Emulsifying agents may include lecithin, fatty acid esters of glycerol, sugar, sorbitan, or propylene glycol, and calcium sterol lactate. Emulsifying agents may be omitted when the doughs contain eggs, soy flour, or other ingredients with a substantial emulsifying effect. Sweeteners suitable for use in this process include monosaccharides or glycerides such as glucose, fructose, saccharose, lactose, rice syrup, and others.

A U.S. patent (Petrofsky, 1987) describes a process for the manufacture of frozen bagel dough. This method entails using a combination of oxidizers and boiling the formed dough before freezing. The resulting product is a frozen bagel dough with a shelf life of one to more than four months in the frozen state.

The authors state that, when baked, this product has characteristics that are essentially those of fresh bagels and a commercial retail shelf life that exceeds 6 hr after baking. By comparison, frozen prebaked bagels have a shelf life of only 2-4 hr after thawing or reheating, while bagels made by other frozen dough methods normally have a blistered exterior and a retail shelf life of less than 6 hr.

The process involves mixing bromated high-gluten bleached barley flour with water, varying amounts of sugar or malt, salt or milk powder, yeast, vegetable oil, a reducing agent blend (Beta) or L-cysteine, calcium or sodium propionate, and a calcium peroxide blend containing also soya flour, diammonium phosphate, and tricalcium phosphate. This blend is available commercially as Drize "P" or Emplex. Ascorbic acid added at the rate of 0.1% based on weight of flour performs a critical function, as without it the frozen dough becomes blistered and shrinks within 24 hr during freezer storage.

Dough is mixed for approximately 10 min with a dough hook to a temperature of 29.5°C. It must then be divided and formed to bagel shapes within 20–25 min of mixing. The formed dough pieces are conveyed on an open conveyor to a traveling proofer, where they remain at 43.4°C and 50% rh for 6 min, then through an overhead zone to a wet proofer, where they remain for 45 sec at 32°C and 90% rh before being cooked in boiling water (100°C) for 25–30 sec. Within 8 min of being removed from the boiling water, the dough pieces are placed into a -26°C freezer for 1 hr. They are then packaged and stored at -26°C and may remain in storage without significant loss of quality for four or more months.

Since the bagels have been preproofed before boiling, they do not require additional proofing but are normally thawed at room temperature for 30–40 min or placed in a proof box at 38°C and 90% rh for 20 min. The dough pieces are then washed with a solution of 50% whole eggs and 50% water, topped as desired, and baked conventionally for 20–25 min. The resulting product has a retail shelf life comparable to that of fresh bagels produced from "scratch" ingredients. Normal shelf life is at least 6 hr, and product typically remains edible for 48 hr at room temperature.

A U.S. patent developed by Brooks et al (1988) and assigned to Oscar Mayer describes a method of producing a food product that is composed of a liquid or semiliquid core enclosed within a laminated dough container. The purpose of this invention is to resolve the problems of moisture migration from the filling to the dough during the storage period and to avoid the loss of organoleptic quality and lack of proper browning of the finished baked product.

The dough used in this application is a laminated puff-pastry type of dough, which, after sheeting, spreading with fat, folding, and resheeting as desired, is brought to a final thickness of about 2 mm. The sheet dough is cut by stamping into a pentagon shape that contains a number of venting holes. Filling material that has been frozen in specially shaped molds is placed on the pentagon-shaped pieces of laminated dough. The dough is wrapped around the composite filling in such a manner that it is not pinched, stretched, or compacted and so that the venting holes are on the top surface. The edges of the dough piece are then crimped to seal, and the food product is egg-washed and seeded with sesame seeds before being frozen. The preferred packaging method is in barrier film, backflushed with an inert gas such as nitrogen or carbon dioxide.

Shelf-life studies of the product prepared according to this invention in comparison with similar product made without the use of laminated dough indicated that the nonlaminated product showed visible deterioration after eight to 12 weeks when stored between -12 and -17°C, whereas the laminated dough product showed no visual deterioration until 14–18 weeks. Subsequent testing has shown that the organoleptic qualities of the filling tend to deteriorate after 20 weeks of storage under freezer conditions but that even at that point the laminated dough envelope will not have been substantially affected by moisture migration or freezer burn.

A U.S. patent (Kageyama and Kobayashi, 1991) assigned to Rheon Automatic Machinery Company, Ltd. describes a method of preparing good quality bread, croissants, or other yeast-raised products. This is an improvement on their earlier U.S. patent 4,946,699, 1990, and on European Patent EP 0,311,240 A2, 1989, which are not included in this survey.

The current process avoids damage to the gluten network of the dough by interposing a rest period before a process of vibration during which the dough undergoes stretching. After being stretched into a dough strip, the dough is cut, shaped, fermented, and frozen for preservation.

According to the process of this invention, ingredients such as flour, water, yeast, sugar, butter, etc., are mixed and kneaded to form a dough mass. Following the mixing step, the dough is given a 5-min resting period within a temperature range of 0–16°C. This resting period allows the dough to regain the extensibility that was lost by tightening of the protein bonds during the mixing step. If the dough is to be used in the preparation of laminated products such as croissants or puff pastry, this resting period also allows for cooling of the dough to prevent mixing of the dough and fat layers during lamination and further processing.

Stretching is accomplished by depositing the dough mass on a conveying path formed by three belt conveyors in series, each of which is driven at a different speed. Vibration is applied to the stretching dough by a series of rollers mounted above the conveyor path. The effect of the actions of the conveyors and the rollers is such that the dough is temporarily thinned under the pressure of the rollers, then released, allowing the elasticity of the dough to cause it to become slightly thicker again. The vibrations imparted to the dough by this rapidly repeated process causes the dough to become permanently thinner, without the imposition of any excessive pressure on the dough. This is termed a *thixotropic effect*. The pressure imparted to the dough is only about 70 g/cm^2. Since this is much less than other methods of obtaining a dough sheet, damage to the gluten cell structure of the dough is minimal.

This process may be used for making bread products of several types, including French bread, croissants, and puff pastry. In the case of bread products, the dough may be cut into rectangles, rolled into a bar, fermented at lower-than-conventional temperatures and for a longer time period, and then frozen.

In the case of croissants and puff pastry, an additional step of lamination of dough sheets with fat layers is interposed before the dough sheets are cut to an appropriate shape and formed. Croissants or puff pastry are proofed for 70 min at 30–32°C and 80% rh. Freezing is done at -30°C, following which the frozen product may be retained in frozen storage.

Frozen bread products processed according to this invention are prepared for consumption by being removed from frozen storage and placed immediately in an oven preheated to between 185 and 200°C. Baking of such dough is completed in 13–20 min, depending on the size of the dough units.

A European patent by Tatsukiyo (1992) describes a process for thawing and proving frozen dough in a special chamber within which negative electrons are used to maintain conditions of proper humidity and to permit gradual thawing without dehydration of the surface of the product at a temperature of -3°C.

This method also avoids the problem of sticky or water-spotted dough surfaces, which may occur when frozen doughs are thawed under proof box conditions and which contribute to poor quality in the finished product. The method described in the invention may also be used in the thawing and holding of frozen solid or semisolid foods other than bread or bakery products.

The equipment described in this patent consists of a thawing and proofing chamber equipped with a high-voltage transformer that functions as a negative electron generator. The chamber is insulated from exterior contact as well as from the ground.

The frozen product, in this case frozen dough, is placed on an electroconductive shelf, preferably a stainless steel plate, within the container. The product may be brought to a semithawed state at -3°C and 85% humidity and held for some time without deterioration of the product due to yeast activity.

Summary

Patent activity in the field of frozen doughs continues to be significant, with interest in North America, Europe, and Japan continuing to be especially strong. Development of frozen dough patents in the United States has generally predated widespread developments in other countries, and many novel procedures for conventional frozen doughs and other frozen bakery products were developed in the United States in the years preceding the present review. There has recently been much innovation and activity focused on the production of frozen doughs for European-style products, both in North America and in Europe.

Literature Cited

AFNOR 1974. Détermination pratique de certaines caractéristiques rhéologiques des pâtes au moyen de l'Alvéographe. Norme V 03710, Nov.

Anonymous 1946. Dinner rolls: Bread in small form. Assoc. Retail Bakers Am. Bull. 146, Nov. 5, p. 1-5.

Anonymous 1951. Frozen rolls prove good business. Restaurant South, Apr., p. 8.

Anonymous 1960. In-store bake-off from frozen raw goods: The word "fresh" gains true meaning. Quick Frozen Foods 23(5):89-90, 101-105.

Anonymous 1961. Extrudes bread dough for home baking. Food Eng. 33(10):89.

Anonymous 1963a. Fast rising frozen bread dough industry challenges prebaked and fresh markets. Quick Frozen Foods 26(2):71.

Anonymous 1963b. Bread dough packers confident items are not a fad. Quick Frozen Foods 26(4):218.

Anonymous 1964. Two ready-to-bake Freihofer breads to bow in Philadelphia. Advert. Age, Sept. 21, p. 108.

Anonymous 1984. Country Home Bakers 25th Anniversary Brochure: 1959–1984. Bridgeport, CT.

Benjamin, E. J., Ke, C. H., Hynson, R. B., Hsu, C. M. L. 1990. Method for producing frozen proofed dough. U.S. patent 4,966,778.

Brooks, A. W., Popenhagen, G. R., and Rentschler, D. J. 1988. Enrobed food products and method of manufacture. U.S. patent 4,741,908.

Faucquenoy, J. D., and Savonglou, G. 1984. Procedure and equipment for the production of parbaked frozen dough pieces. French patent FR 2,546,376 A1.

Goux, J., and Clément, P. 1987. Free-flowing frozen yeast in fluidized particles: Procedure to obtain them and application of said yeast to frozen doughs. European patent 0,237,427 A2.

Grandvoinnet, P., Portier, A., and Bonnet, M. 1986. Procedure for the production of bread. French patent FR 2,577,388 A1.

Howard, K. L. 1960. Frozen raw baked product bake-off programs offer vast distributor possibility. Quick Frozen Foods 23(4):59-62.

Kageyama, M., and Kobayashi, M. 1991. Method for producing bread from preserved dough. U.S. patent 5,030,466.

Larsen, P. A. 1991. A method of preparing a frozen yeast dough product. International patent WO 91/01088.

Larson, R. W., Lou, W. C., DeVito, V. C., and Neidinger, K. A. 1983. Method of producing and baking frozen yeast leavened dough. U.S. patent 4,406,911.

Le Duff, L. 1987a. Frozen brioche dough and method of production. French patent FR 2,589,042 A1.

Le Duff, L. 1987b. Frozen croissant dough and method of production. French patent FR 2,589,041 A1.

Le Duff, L. 1987c. Frozen French style bread and method of production. French patent FR 2,589,043 A1.

Lindstrom, T. R., and Slade, L. N. M. N. 1987. A frozen dough for bakery products. European patent 0,114,451 B1.

Marx, V. E. 1932. Freezing bread . . . Bakers' Helper, June 4, 1932, p. 1074.

Mathieu, G. 1991. Procedure for the production of yeast-leavened frozen puff-pastry dough for use in baking and pastry-making. French patent FR 2,663,197 A1.

McPherson, C. M., and Lamb, M. W. 1948. Improved bread made from frozen dough. Food Ind., Sept. p. 95.

Nakatomi, Y., Saito, H., Nagashima, A., and Umeda, F. 1985. Saccharomyces species FD 612 and the utilization thereof in bread production. U.S. patent 4,547,374.

Nomura, S., and Ishigami, S. 1985. Method of production of a frozen yeast-leavened dough for food products. French patent FR 2,549,698 A1.

Nourigeon, A. 1983. Process for preparing deep-frozen yeast bread dough. U.S. patent 4,414,228.

Petrofsky, D., and Petrofsky, R. 1987. Method of manufacturing frozen bagel dough products. U.S. patent 4,657,769.

Seneau, B. 1989. Method for producing a pre-proofed, frozen and unbaked dough having an improved shelf life. U.S. patent 4,839,178.

Tanako, H., Hino, A., Endo, H., Nakagawa, N., and Sato, A. 1990. Novel bakers' yeast. European patent 0,388,262 A1.

Tatsukiyo, O. 1992. Process for thawing, maturing and fermenting frozen dough for preparing bread and apparatus therefor. European patent EP 0,492,765 A1.

Teiser, R., and Harroun, C. 1963. Frozen unbaked bread: New convenience market. Baking Ind.,

120(1513):40.

Uno, K., Oda, Y., and Shigenori, O. 1986. Freeze resistant dough and novel microorganism for use therein. European patent 0,196,233 A2.

Wheeler, F. 1961. Tips on freezing . . . Baker's Rev. 123(1):41.

Williams, E. W. 1963. Frozen foods forum: The bread business. Quick Frozen Foods 26(5):29.

Yamaguchi, T., and Watanabe, A. 1987. Quality improver for frozen doughs. U.S. patent 4,664,932.

Index

Absorption level, for frozen doughs, 137, 185
Acidification, in sourdough, 53, 54, 55, 58, 60
Additives, to doughs, 41, 141–142, 186
  patents for
    amylase and amyloglucosidase, 263
    ascorbic acid, 264
    gluten, 262, 267
    gum-surfactant-protein combination,
      261–262
    invert sugar, 266
    melting-point depressant, 260–261
Air, in cake and muffin batters, 168–169
Airflow
  in freezers, 231, 232–234
  and heat transfer, 202–203
Alcohol dehydrogenase, 45
α-Amylase, 112
Ascorbic acid, 97, 100–102, 106–107, 110, 137,
  138
  in mixtures, 102–103, 107–108, 137
Aspergillus sp., 123, 126
Azodicarbonamide, 97, 103–106, 110
  with ascorbic acid, 107–108
  encapsulated, 105–106
  and sodium stearoyl lactylate, 106

Bacillus sp., 123
  licheniformis, 126
Bacteria, in bakery products, 55, 56, 57, 58, 60,
  120–122, 125
  psychrotrophic, 125
Bagels, 6, 7, 268–269
Baked goods, frozen
  costs of production, 11, 13–14
  types, 1–2
Bakeries, in-store, 2, 3
  growth, 6–15
  operations, 149–151
  profitability, 7–8, 10–15
Bakery products
  microbes in, 126–131
  spoilage of, 123
  thermal diffusivity values for, 199
Baking, 95–97, 164–165
  of cakes and muffins from frozen batters,
    174–175
  of confectionery products, 189–190
  equipment, 164, 190
  in the home, 151
  in in-store bakeries, 151
  with yeast, customized practices, 37–43
Batters, cake and muffin, freezing of, 171–173,
  175

advantages, 167
  baking, 174–175
  formulation, 168–170
  history, 167–168
  thawing, 174–175
Benzoyl peroxide, 103–105
Biot number, 206
Blast freezers, 42
Bread
  from frozen dough. See also Rolls
    ingredients, 136–142
    preparation, 63–65
    quality, factors affecting, 137, 140
    rheological studies, 67–75
    sales, 6, 7
  from retarded doughs, 86–87
  thermal properties, values of, 194–200
Brioche, 266
Bromate. *See also* Potassium bromate
  and mechanism of action, 110–112
  and proof time, 114

Cakes, from frozen batter, 7, 167–175
Candida sp., 55
Carbon dioxide
  in cake batters, 169
  for freezing, 161,181, 182, 222, 234–236
  for packaging, 251, 252
  in yeasted confectionery dough, 189, 252
Cells
  damage by freezing, 21–23
  membrane during freezing, 20, 23
  yeast
    cooling rate, effect, 20
    effect of freezing and thawing, 20–25
Condensation, 163–164, 174, 180, 183
Conductive heat transfer, 200–201
Confectionery doughs, frozen, in Germany
  unyeasted, 177–178
  yeasted
    fermentation interruption, 178–180
    prefermented, 186–191
    unfermented, 180–186
Continuous-mix process, 142
Convective heat transfer, 201–203
Cookies
  from dough, refrigerated, 253
  sales, 6, 7
Cooling
  of yeast cells, rate, 20, 21
  of dough, 56–57, 178
  tunnel for, patent, 267–268
Copper compounds, as oxidants, 109

Corn syrup, 140, 141
Croissants, from retarded doughs, 87, 265–266
Crust-freezing, 226
Cryogenic freezing
　advantages, 226–229
　combined with mechanical freezing, 226, 234
　costs of, 227
　equipment, 222–226
　history, 219–222
　stored-energy carbon dioxide system, 234–236
Cryogenic gases, 161, 222
Cryoprotectants, 33, 36, 46
L-Cysteine, 138

Danish pastry
　patent, 264, 265
　proofing, 83
　retardation of, 86
　sales, 7
Debaryomyces hansenii, 27
Defrosting of doughs. See Thawing
Dehydration
　of frozen dough, principles of, 81–82
　of sourdoughs, 55
Density, of bread, 195
Direct product profitability, 8–10, 11, 12, 14, 15, 16
Distribution, of frozen doughs, 148–149
　centralization, 1, 2, 3
　consolidation, 4, 17
　foodservice, 15–16
　in-store bakeries, 3, 5, 6–15
　outlets, retail, 2
　sales, size and growth, 3–5
Disulfide bonds, and freezing damage, 23
Dough
　conditioners, 138, 157
　thermal properties, values of, 194, 198, 199
Dough, for freezing
　consistency, and quality, 185
　development, 180
　filled, patent, 269–270
　freezing process
　　ice formation, 79–80
　　preparation for, 75–76
　　thermal changes during, 77–79
　gluten in, 65–67
　make-up process, 146, 159
　packaging. See Packaging
　proofing. See Proofing
　rest time, 180, 186–188
　stretching, 270
　sweet. See Confectionery doughs, Sweet doughs
　yeasted dough system, 63–65
Dough, frozen
　gas-retention properties, 23–25
　measurement of properties, 67
　rheological studies, 67–75

strengthening, 71, 73
　weakening of, factors affecting, 67–75, 100
Doughnuts, 6, 7, 150

Egg, microbes in, 122
Emulsifiers, in cake and muffin batters, 169, 170
　patent, 268
Enzymes. See individual enzymes
Escherichia coli
　in bakery products, 128, 130, 131
　cooling rate, 22
　membrane fractions, 131
Ethanol
　and cryoresistance, 37, 39
　as melting-point depressant, 260–261
　yeast tolerant to, 28
Europe
　frozen dough process in, 156
　interest in frozen dough technology, 256
Eutectic point, of frozen dough, 77, 81

Fat, 157, 185–186. See also Shortening
Fermentation
　changes during, 145–146
　equipment, 183–185
　interruption, 178–180
　metabolites, effects on dough, 68–69
　retardation, 178
Fermentation before freezing. See Prefermentation
Film, for packaging
　gas transmission rates, 246–247
　performance testing, 13–4
　properties, mechanical and physical, 247–248
Fingerprinting, of flour quality, 65
Flavor, sourdough for, 54, 58
Flour, in bakery products, microbes in, 120
Flour, for frozen doughs
　protein, 93, 131,185
　rye, 54, 58
　specifications, 40–41, 76, 136, 157, 185
　starch, effects of freezing on, 74–75
　strength, 64
Foodservice industry, 15–16
Formulation. See also Ingredients
　of cake and muffin batters for freezing, 168–170
　of doughs for frozen storage, 40–43, 131
　in Europe, 157–159
　for lean dough, 95
Fourier number, 206
Fourier's law, 201
Freezer stability, 98–100
Freezers and freezing equipment, 147, 157
　blast, 42, 161
　cryogenic. See Cryogenic freezing
　energy requirements, 78, 227, 232, 234
　for in-store bakery storage, 149
　mechanical, 222, 230–234
　　advantages, 231–232

with subcooled carbon dioxide, 234
stored-energy carbon dioxide system, 234–236
Freeze-thaws cycles
effects on dough strength, 71, 72–73
effects on yeast, 42
Freeze-tolerant yeasts, production of, 29–32
Freezing
of cake and muffin batters, 171–173
comparison of systems, 237
of confectionery dough pieces, 178–182
curves, 77
equipment. *See* Freezers and freezing equipment
heat transfer during, 206–207
history, 219–222, 255–256
individually quick-frozen method, 220–222
microbes, effects on, 125–126
process, 20–21, 160–161
principles of, 75–82
rates, 41–42, 76–80, 125, 147, 160–161, 181, 222
temperatures, 147, 156–157, 160, 161, 182, 222, 225, 229, 232
of sourdough, 60
French bread
loaf volume, factors affecting, 40
patents for, 262, 263
sourdough, 56
Frozen dough industry, 130
centralized manufacturing and distribution, 2, 17
in Europe, 156
growth, 6–7, 17
manufacturers, 3–6
patents, for new technology, 255–271
profitability, analysis
accounting techniques, 8–10
of in-store bakeries, 7–15
sales, size and growth, 4–6
success of, 1, 14

Gas flushing, in packages, 252
Gas retention, by dough cells
freezing, effects of, 23–25
and reducing compounds, 68
Gas transmission rates, 246–247
Genetic engineering, of yeast, 43–46
Glass transition temperature, 83–86
Gliadin, 65
Glucoamylase, 112–113
Glutamic acid, 142
Glutathione, effects on dough, 24, 39, 68, 140
Gluten
complex, 65
formation and stability, 65–67
freezing, effects of, 24, 76
function and structure in dough, 63, 64, 65
weakening during frozen storage, 67–75
Glutenin, 65

high molecular weight subunits, 65, 66
Glycerol, 36, 142
Glycogen, 32
Grashoff number, 203

Hansenula anomala, 27
Heat transfer
conductive, 200–201
convective, 201–203
during freezing of foods, 206–207
radiative, 204
and specific heat, 196–198
in steady state, 193–194, 200–204
and thermal conductivity, 193, 194–196
and thermal diffusivity, 198–200
in unsteady state, 193, 205–206
High-fructose corn syrup, 140, 141
High-protein yeasts, 36
Hybrid yeast strains, 29–30
Hydrogenated vegetable oil, 170

Ice
crystals, damage from, 22–23, 24, 39, 75
formation
effect of, on dough structure, 23, 66, 69–74, 80–81
in food systems, 77
process, 79–80
recrystallization, 21
thermal conductivity of, 195–196
Ingredients. See also Formulation
effects of, on frozen dough quality, 136–142
microbes in, 120–122, 125
microingredients in frozen doughs, 91–116
Instant active dry yeast, and trehalose levels, 34–35
Iodate salts, 101

Japan, interest in frozen dough technology, 256

Kluyveromyces thermotolerans, 27, 28, 34

Labor, and profitability, 12–15
Lactobacillus spp., 55, 57, 60, 121, 127, 130
brevis, 55, 56, 60
Leavening, chemical, for frozen batters, 168–169, 175
Leuconostoc sp., 121
mesenteroides, 126, 127
Lipids, during frozen storage, 163
Liquid nitrogen, 222
Liquid sourdough, 55
Listeria sp., 123, 130
monocytogenes, 125

Maleate, 60
Manufacturers, of frozen dough, 3–6
Makeup of dough, 146, 159
Market
for frozen doughs, 255–256

segments, 2
labor, 12–15
Microorganisms (Microbes)
   contamination, control of, 123
   freezing, effects on, 125–126
   inactivation, 121
   levels in bakery products, 126–131
   origins in bakery products, 120–122
   refrigeration, effects on, 123–125
Milk
   in doughs, 141
   microbes in, 121–122
Mixing
   delayed salt addition method, 143–144, 159
   function, 64, 66
   temperature, 91–93, 98, 99, 144–145, 159
   time, 145
Modified-atmosphere packaging, 251–252
Moisture
   content
      and mold growth, 120
      and thermal properties, 194, 195
   migration, in frozen dough, 81–82
Molds, in bakery products, 120, 122, 123
Muffins
   from frozen batters, 167–175
   sales, 6, 7
Mutant yeast strains, 31–32

Nitrogen, for packaging, 251, 252
Nucleation, of ice, during freezing, 79

Osmotolerance, in yeasts, 27–29. See also
   Freeze-tolerant yeasts
Oxidants, in frozen doughs, 41, 157. See
      also individual oxidants
   bromate replacers, 100–109
   and enzymes, 112–113
   level of, 97, 137
   loss of, 110
   mechanism, 109–112
   types used, 97–100, 137
   and yeast, 113–115
Oxygen absorbers, in packages, 251

Packaging
   of bakery products, 126
   of batters (cake and muffin) for freezing,
      170–171
   of confectionery dough units, 182
   costs of, 249
   of doughs for freezing, 148, 162, 249–250
      equipment, 250
      material for, 246–249
      package requirements, 246
      product requirements, 245–246
   modified-atmosphere, 251–252
   of refrigerated dough products, 250–253
   of sourdough, 55. 56
Pasteurization of milk, 121

Pastry doughs, 177–178
Patents
   for additive use, 260–267
   for special processes and equipment, 267–271
   for yeast technology, 256–260
Peanut oil, 157
Penicillium sp., 122, 123, 126
   roqueforti, 127
Pie crust, frozen, 250
Pie dough, refrigerated, 253
Pizza
   dough, retardation of, 87
   refrigerated, 130, 253
Planck's equation, 207
Polymer science concepts, application to
   freezing, 83–86
Polypropylene films, 247–249
   multilayered, 249
   regulation of, by FDA, 248
Potassium bromate, 41, 73, 95, 97–98, 137, 138
Potassium iodate, 97
Prandtl number, 203
Prefermentation. See also Preproofing
   of confectionery products, 186–191
   fermentation state at freezing, 188–189
   stability of dough, effect on, 37, 145–146
Preproofing. See also Prefermentation
   and baking time, 160
   patents for methods, 260–263
   and proofing time, 164
   and type of yeast, 159
Proof times
   and dough ingredients, 113–115
   in doughs with active dry yeast, 39, 140
   and mixing conditions, 92–93, 144
   and oxidation levels, 138
   for rolls, 160
   and storage period, 137–138
   of thawed doughs, 83
Proofing
   before freezing. See Preproofing
   in the home, 151
   in in-store bakeries, 150–151
Protein
   cryoprotectant, 46
   level in flour, 64, 93, 136, 157
   level in yeast, 36
Proteolytic enzymes, and dough weakening, 68
Protoplast fusion, yeast, 31
Pseudomonas spp., 125
Puff pastry, 177

Quality of frozen dough
   and freezing system, 222, 227
   and industry growth, 17
   parameters, for confectionery products, 185
   practices to maximize, 37–43, 135
      during preparation stage, 91–95

Radiative heat transfer, 204

Rapid freezing, 42, 76, 80,126, 147
Recombinant DNA technology, for yeast improvement, 43–46
Recrystallization, of ice in cells, 21
Reducing compounds, effects on frozen doughs, 68, 138
Refrigerated dough products, 125, 250–253
in cans, 252
Refrigeration
effects on microbes, 123–125
equipment, 230–231
Relative humidity, during proofing, 150
Rest time, during dough preparation, 93, 116, 186–188, 191
Retardation
for in-store baking, 149-150
principles of, 76, 86-87
Reynolds number, 203
Rheology, of frozen dough, 67-75
Rhizopus spp., 123
Rolls, from frozen dough
quality, 155
sales, 6, 7
Rye bread, sourdough in, 53, 54

Saccharomyces sp., 27, 33, 43, 259
cerevisiae, 27, 28, 29, 30, 31, 32, 34, 43, 258–260, 263
Sales
by employees, 14
of frozen doughs. *See* Distribution, of frozen doughs
Salmonella sp., 122, 123
aureus, 130
enteritidis, 122
typhimurium, 130
Salt, in doughs, 141
Shelf life
of bakery products, extension of, 126, 265–266
of frozen doughs, 135
factors affecting, 23, 140
Shortening. *See also* Fat
in frozen batters, 169–170
in frozen doughs, 41, 93, 141
Slow freezing, 161
Soda crackers, 130
Sodium-aluminum phosphate, 168
Solution effects, during cooling of cells, 21, 23
Sourdough, 159
acidity in, 53, 54
cooling, 56–57
definition, 53–54
drying, 56, 58
evaluation of, 57–59
freeze-drying, 57
functions, 54
quality, extension of, 54–57
starters, 59
Specific heat, 196–198

Spices
microbes in, 120–121
in sourdough, 56
Sponge and dough system, 40, 143
Staphylococcus sp., 122, 123
aureus, 128, 130
Starch, in flour
damage, 136
effects of freezing , 74–75
Steady-state heat transfer, 193–194, 200–204
Stefan-Boltzmann law of radiation, 204
Storage, frozen
of batters, 171–173
changes in dough during, 161–163
conditions, 161–162
and dough strength, 68–75
equipment/facilities, 149, 161–162
inventory of product, 149, 175
time
and amount of freezing, 147
and amylose-amylopectin ratios, 74
and bread quality, 137
and gas production by yeast, 138
and mixing methods, 144
and proof times, 39, 138
Straight-dough procedure, 40, 144
Streptococcus sp., 60, 121, 122, 127
Sucrose, 140, 141
Sugars
and freezing, 81
levels in frozen doughs, 41, 140, 185
and proof times, 84, 140–141
Sulfhydryl content, in dough, 25
compounds, effects, 71
Supercooling, of dough, 20, 79
Surfactants, in doughs, 93–95, 141–142
Sweet doughs, 268
retardation of, 87
Sweeteners, in dough, 140–141

Tartrate, 168
Temperature
of bacterial growth, 57
of baking, 164, 175
of batter freezing, 171, 172
of dough, and dough quality, 40, 187, 189, 190, 191
during dough make up, 146
during mixing, 91–93, 99, 145, 159
of dough cooling, 178
of dough freezing, 147–148, 156–157, 160, 161, 180
of freezing systems, 222–225
glass transition, 83–86
gradients, in dough, 82
starch gelatinization, 75
during storage
of batter, 171, 172
of dough, 162
thawing, 163, 174

Thawing. *See also* Retardation
  of batters, 174–175
  chamber for, patent, 271
  equipment, 149–150, 183
  in the home, 151
  principles, 82–83
  rates, 41–42, 126, 150, 163–164
  and relative humidity, 184
  and surface wetness, 163
Thermal conductivity, 78, 82–83, 193, 194–196
Thermal diffusivity, 198–200
Tortillas, refrigerated, 253
Torulaspora delbrueckii, 27, 28, 31, 33
Torulopsis sp., 57
Transportation of frozen doughs. *See*
  Distribution of frozen doughs
Trehalose, 159
  as a cryoprotectant, 33–35
  levels in yeast, 36
  metabolism of, modifications, 43–36
  as a stress-protectant for yeast, 33
  yeast strains enriched in, 32–35

Underoxidation, 99
Unsteady-state heat transfer, 193, 205–206

Waffles, 6
Warehouse (wholesale) clubs, 2, 6, 14
Water. *See also* Ice
  on dough or batter surface. *See* Condensation
  free, amount in dough, 137, 160
  and frozen storage, 163
  microbes in, 122
  replacement, in yeast cells, 33
  and thermal properties of foods, 194, 196–197, 200

Xanthan gum, 142

Yeast
  addition to dough, timing, 39
  baking practices, customized, 37–43
  bulk liquid, 37
  changes during storage, 19, 139, 163

coculture, 28
compressed, 37, 39, 140
in confectionery dough, 178–191
deep-freezing of, 257
diploid, 28
and DNA technology, 43–46
dry, 37, 39, 140, 158
ethanol-tolerant strains, 28
fermentation, and mixing temperature, 93
fermentation metabolites, effects of, 68–69
food for, 137
freeze-dried, 257, 258
freezing in a dough system, 139
gassing power of, 131, 139
hybrids, 29–30, 259–260
improvements, future, 43–47
instant, 39, 140
level in frozen doughs, 40, 138–139
maltose-inducible, 34
mutants, 31–32, 43
newly developed, 258–260
nontraditional strains, 27–29
performance, improvement of, 25–43
production of, modifications, 14–21
  aeration, 35–36
  heat shock, 35
  nutrient starvation, 35
  protectants, added, 36
  protein content, 36
and protoplast fusion, 31
rapid-gas-production, 158
in sourdough, 58
and spoilage of bakery products, 120, 122, 125
strains, customized, 7–13
time of addition, 159
and trehalose, 32–35, 43–46
in "vermicelli" form, 257–258
viability, 20, 23, 130, 139, 161
  patents for, 257
Yersinia enterocolitica, 125

Zygosaccharomyces rouxii, 27, 33